LotsOfLots

LotsOfLots

Jason Fulford

2025

Mack

London NewYork Berlin

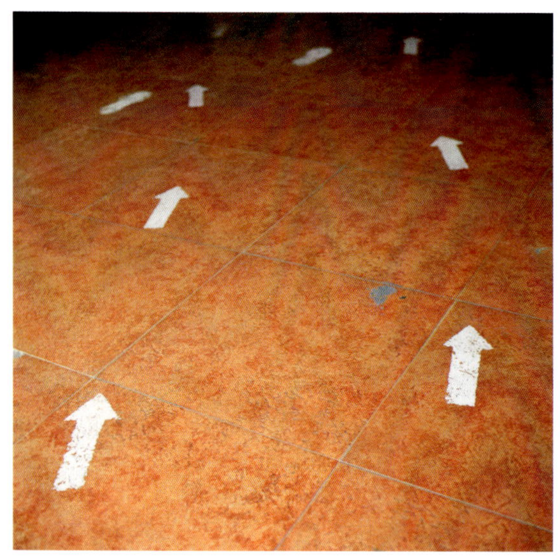

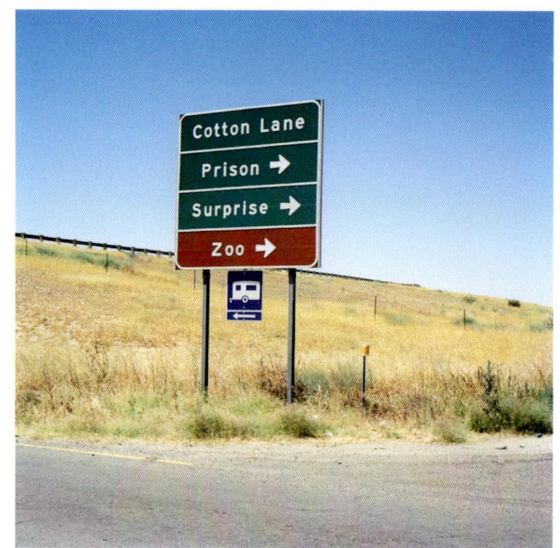
Cotton Lane
Prison
Surprise
Zoo

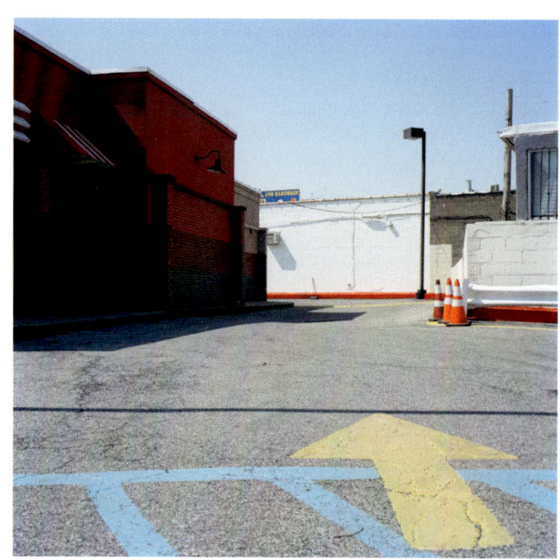

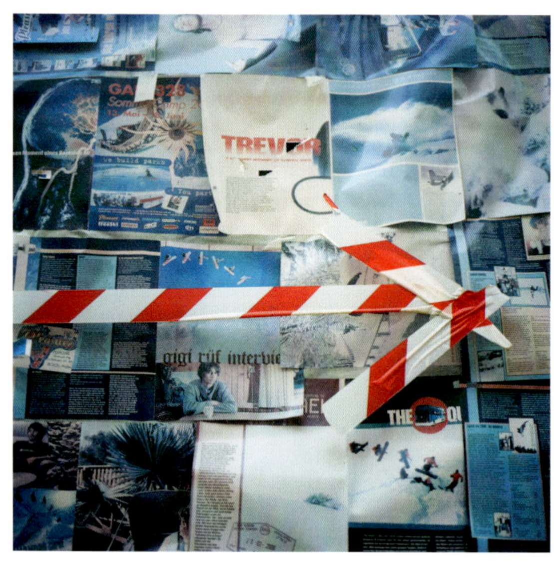

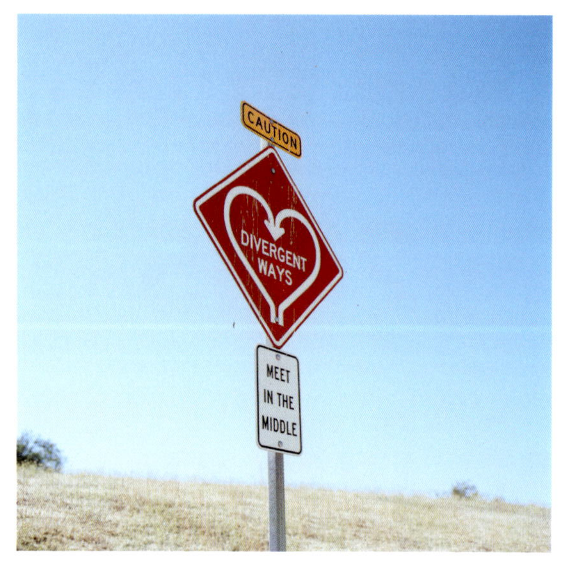
CAUTION
DIVERGENT WAYS
MEET IN THE MIDDLE

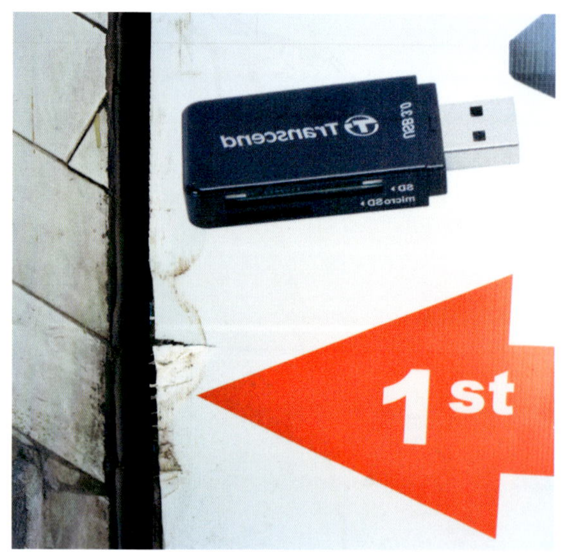
1st

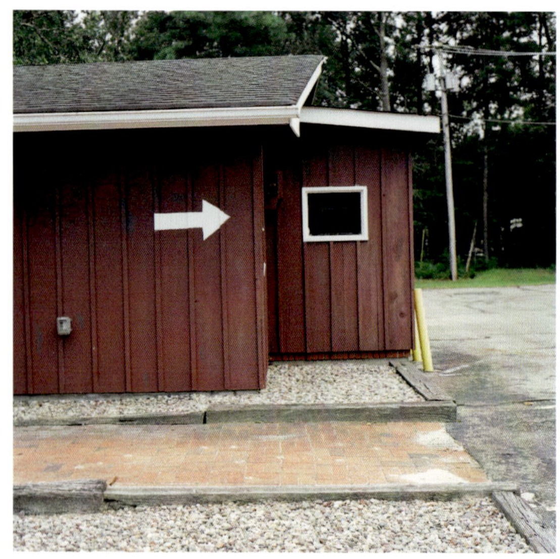

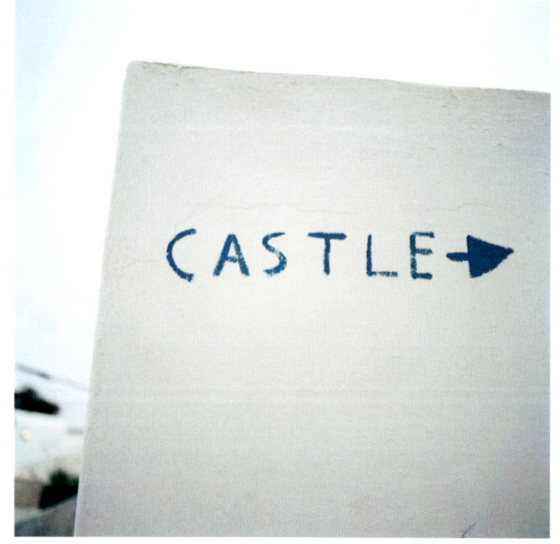
CASTLE

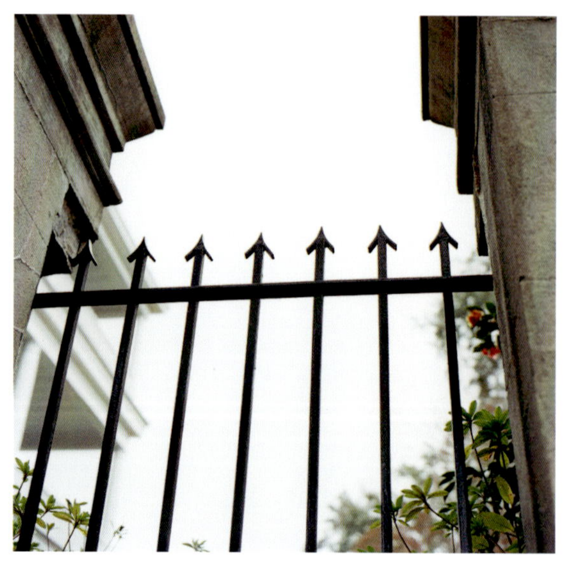

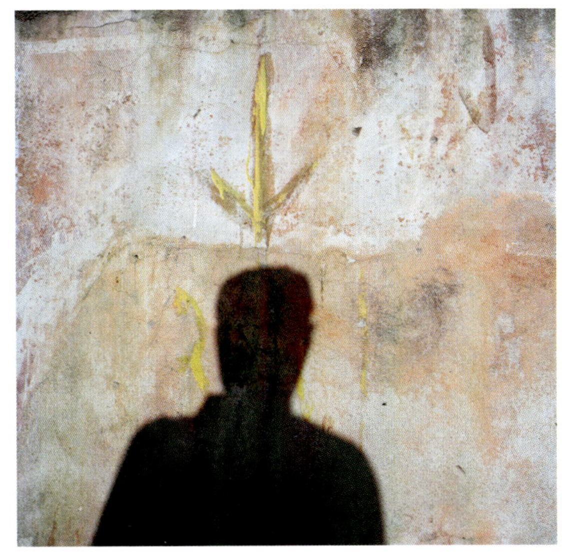

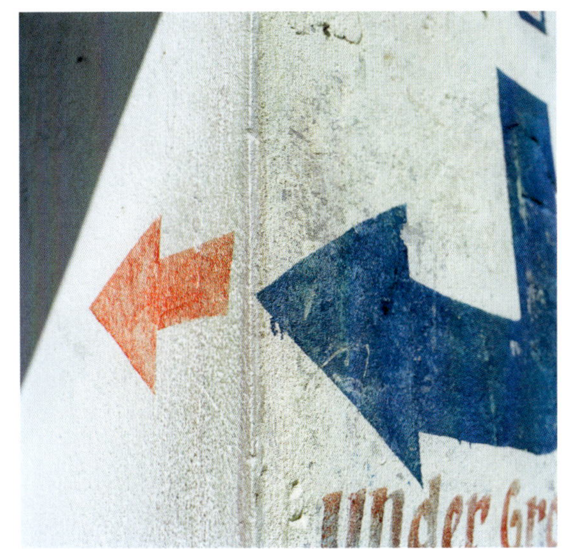
under

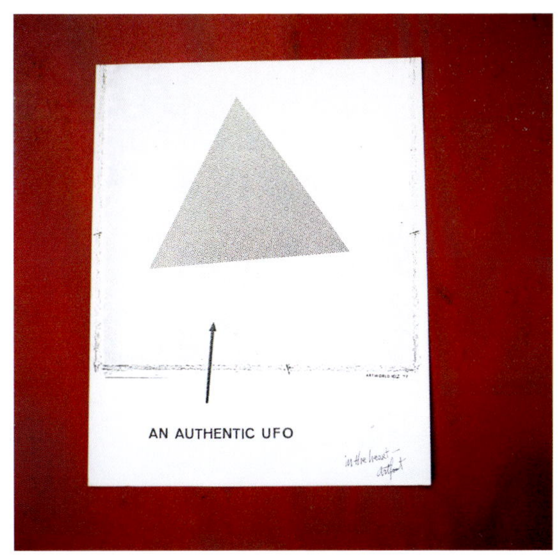
AN AUTHENTIC UFO

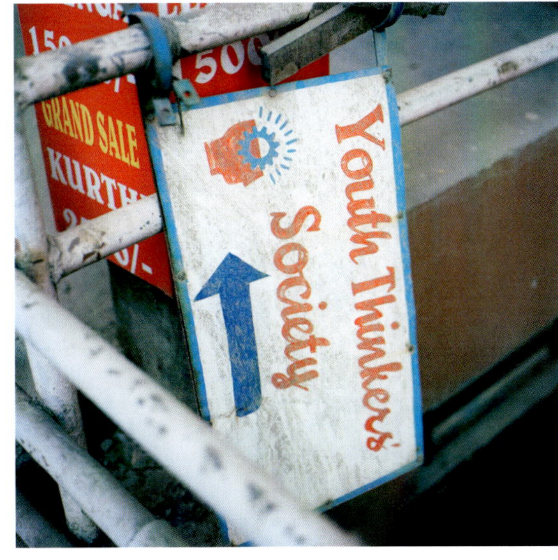
GRAND SALE
Youth Thinkers' Society

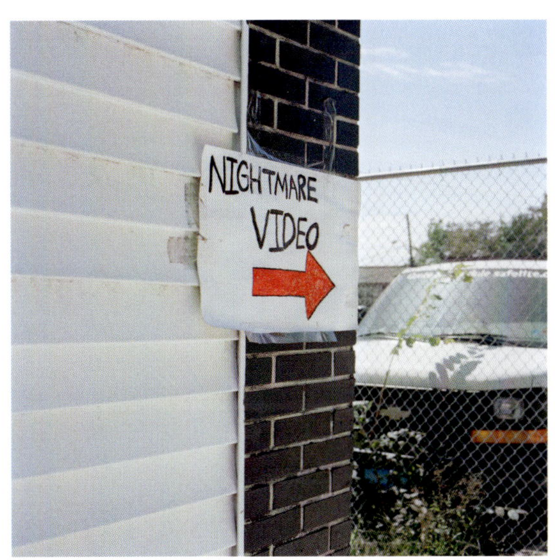
NIGHTMARE
VIDEO

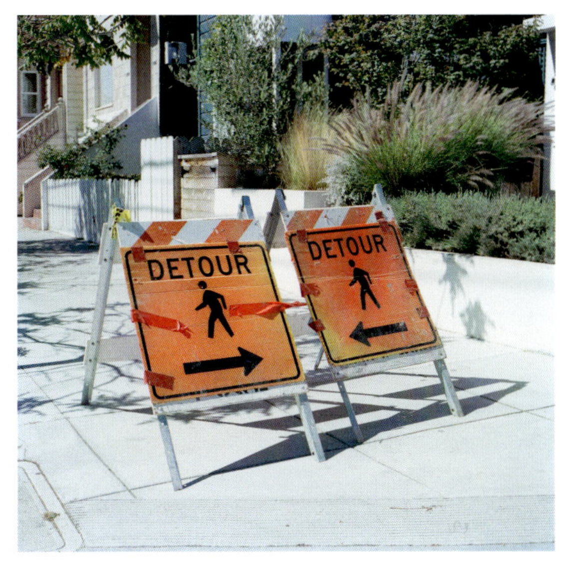
DETOUR
DETOUR

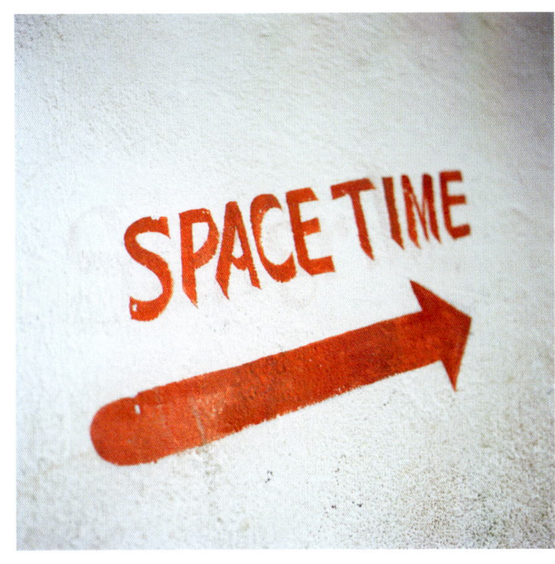
SPACE TIME

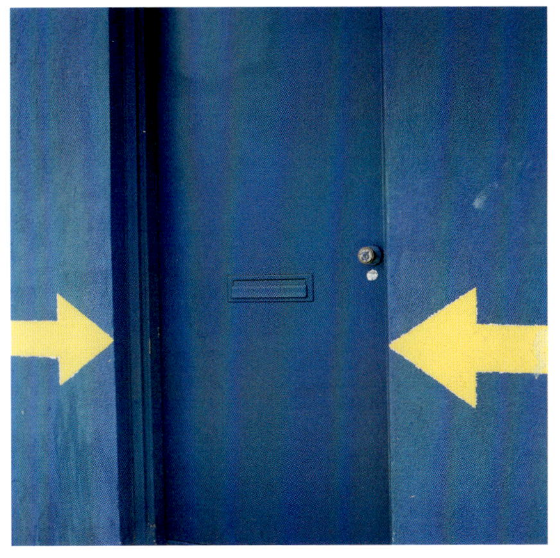

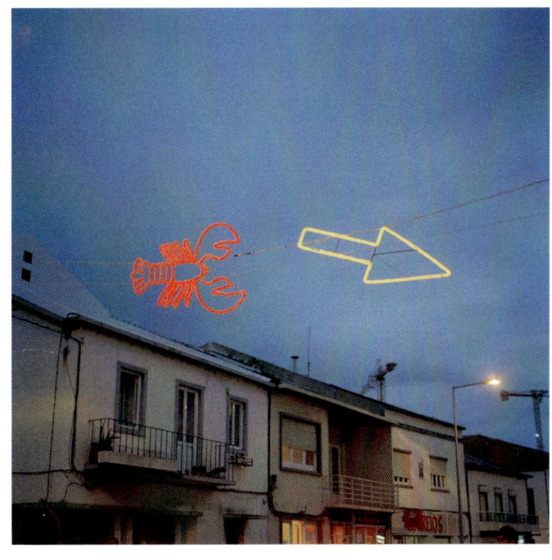

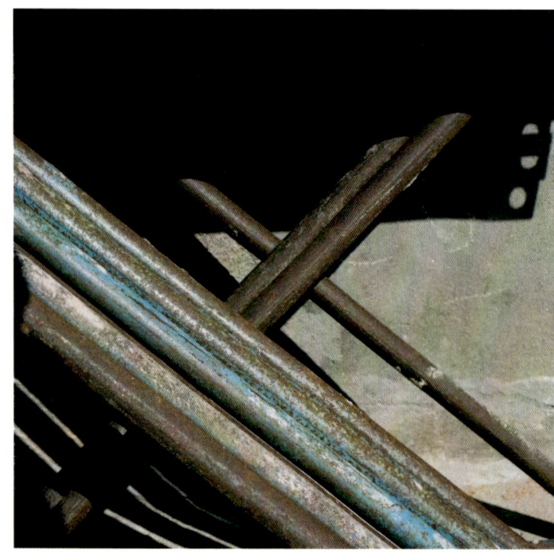
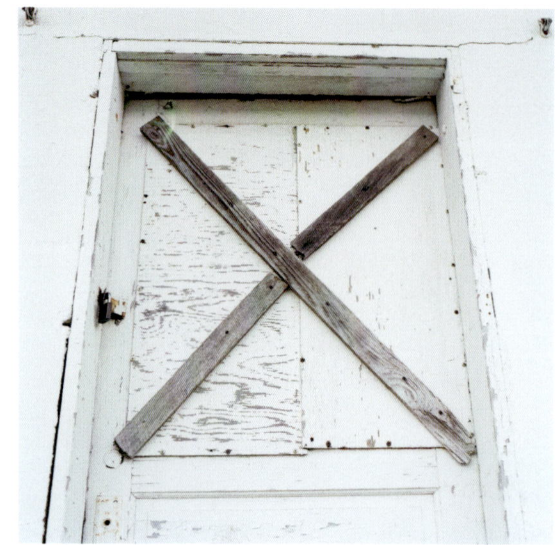
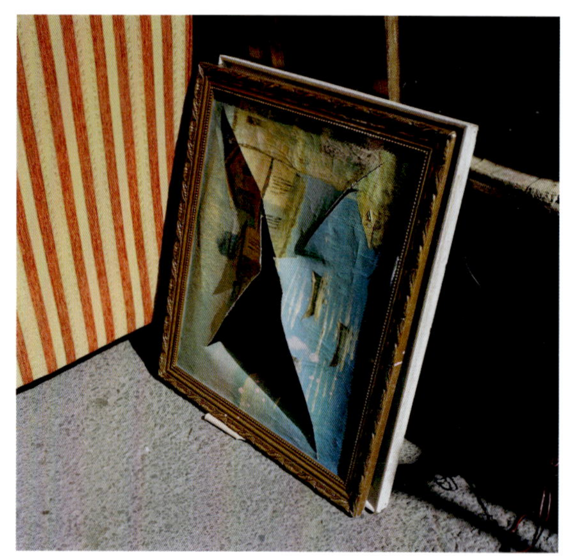
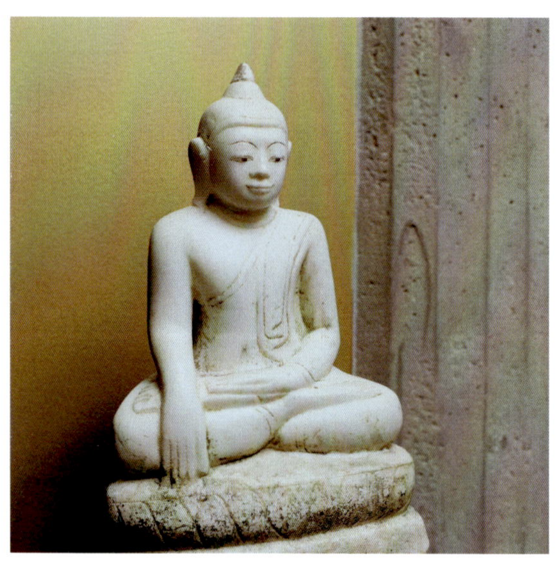
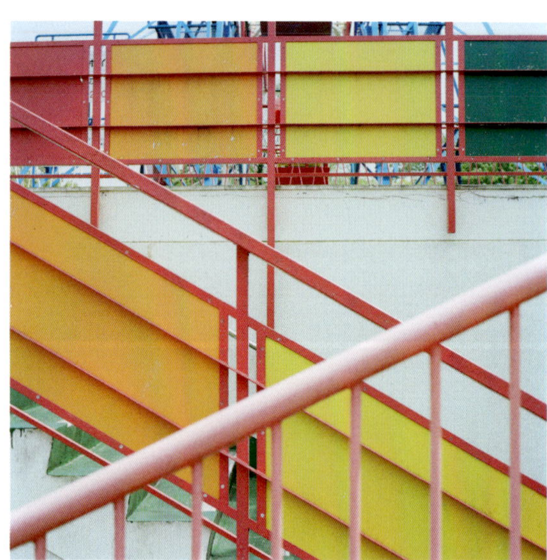
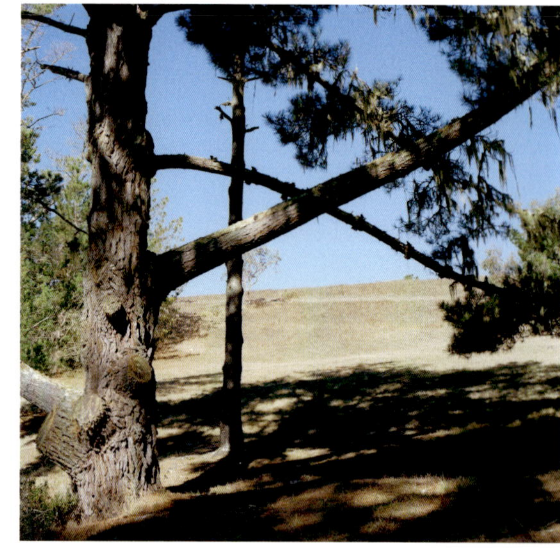
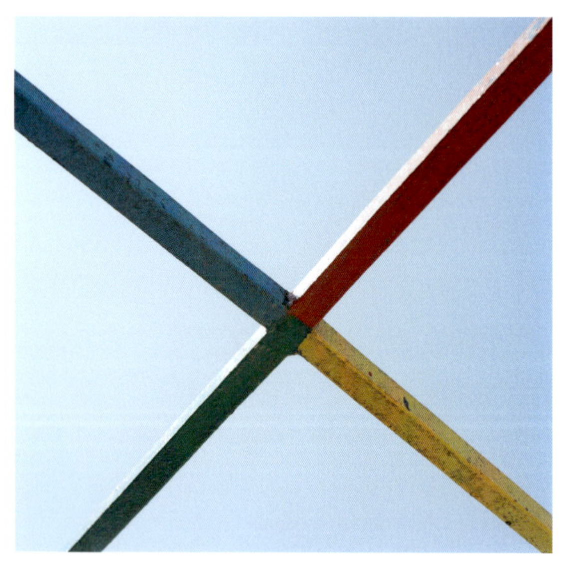
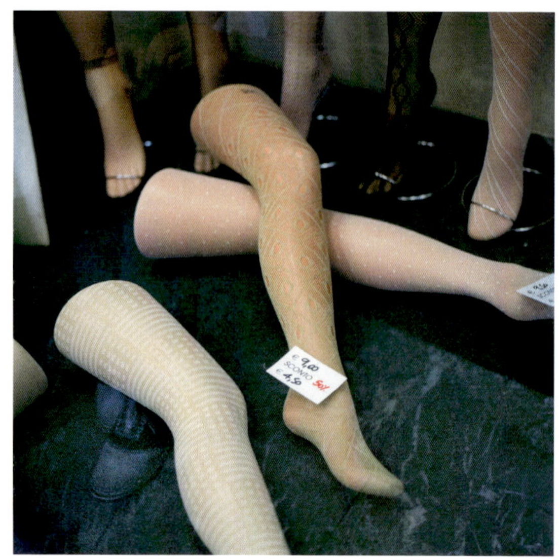
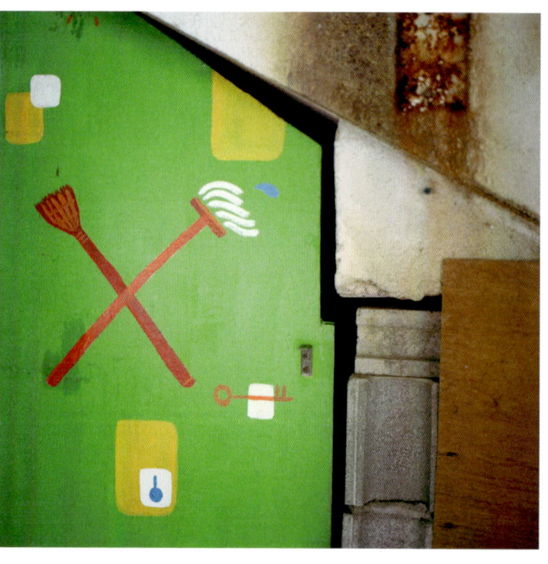

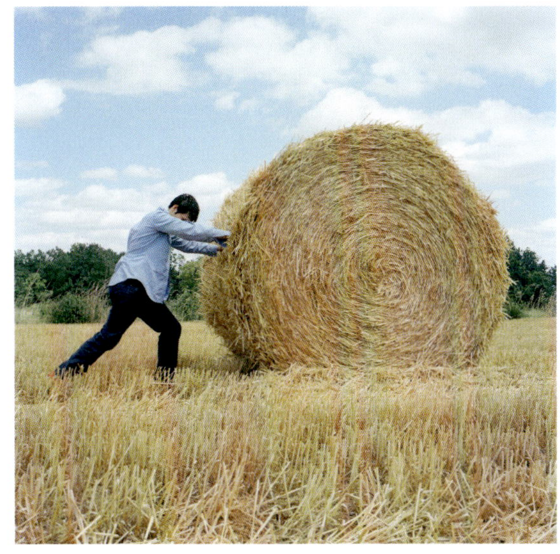

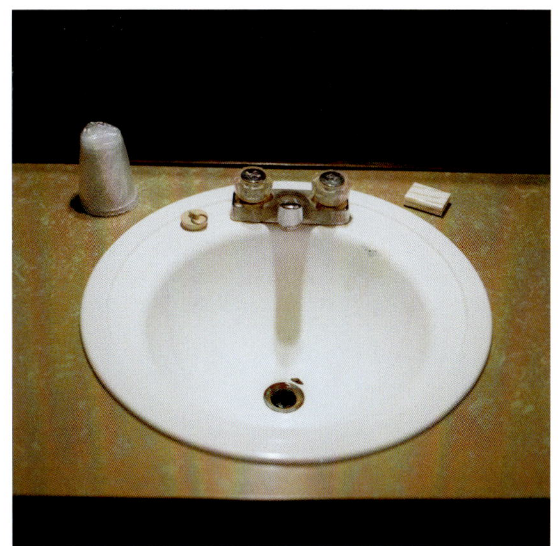

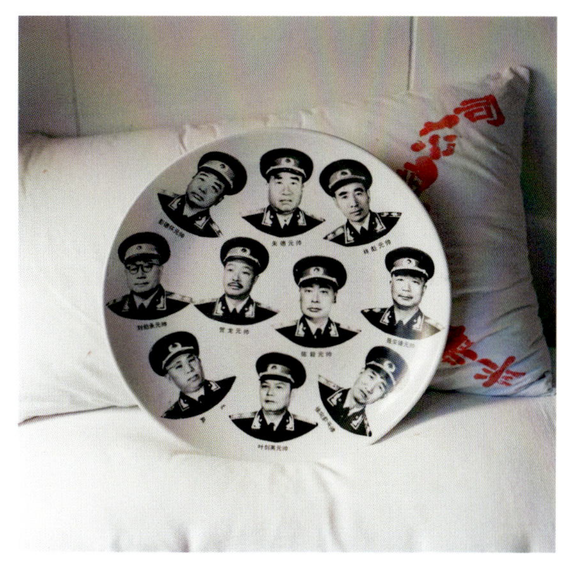

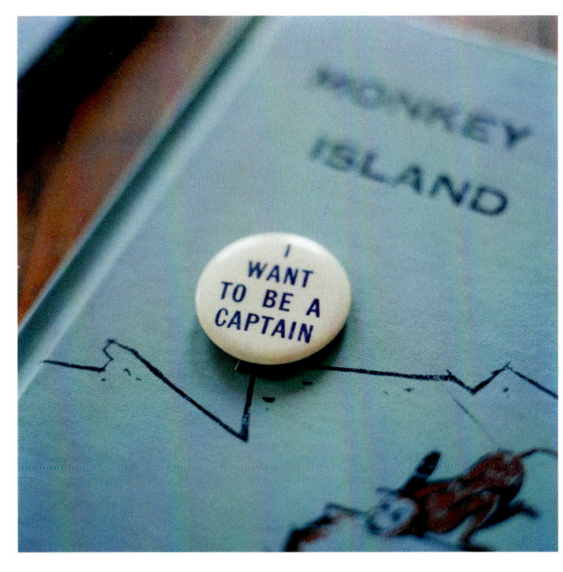
MONKEY
ISLAND
I WANT TO BE A CAPTAIN

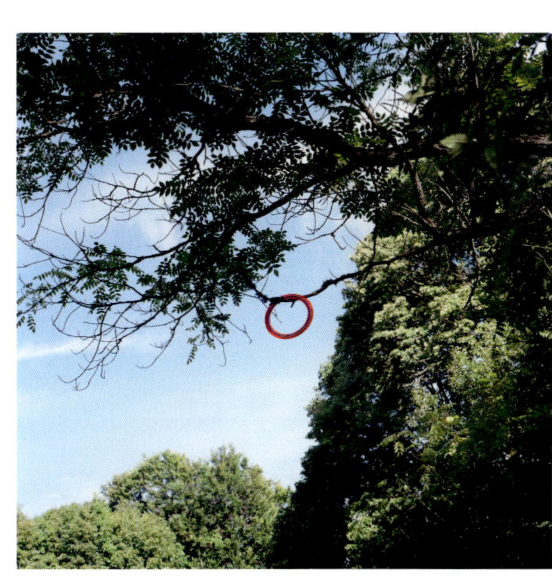

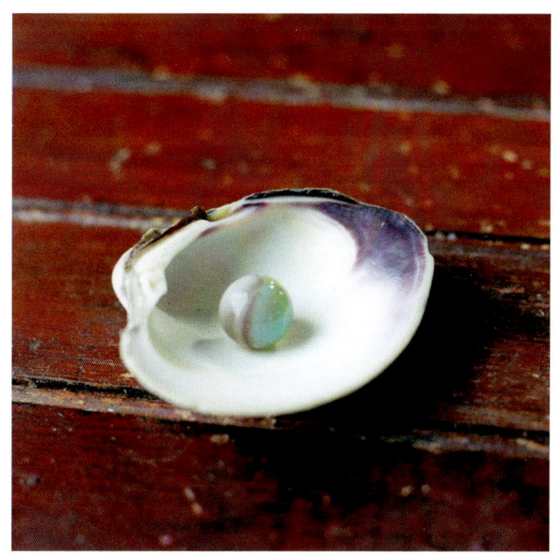

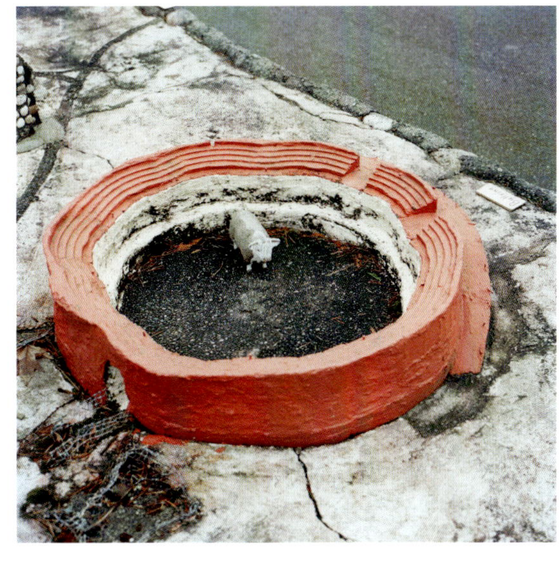

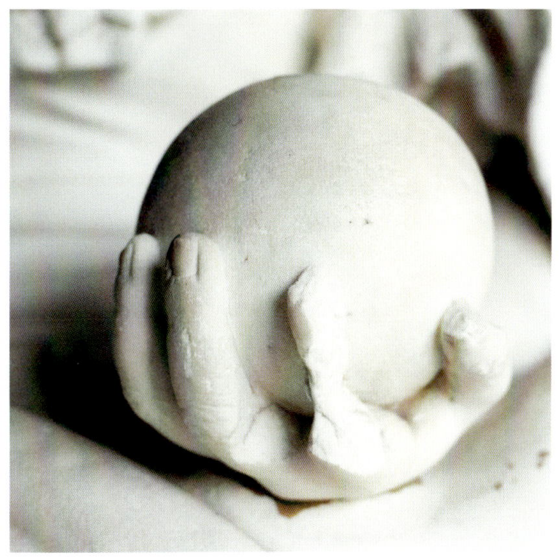

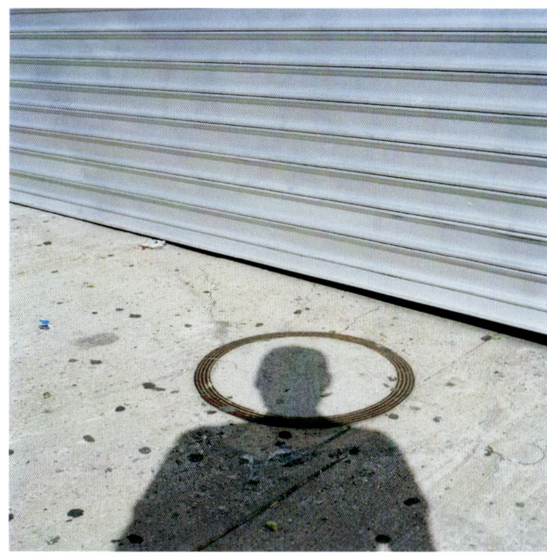

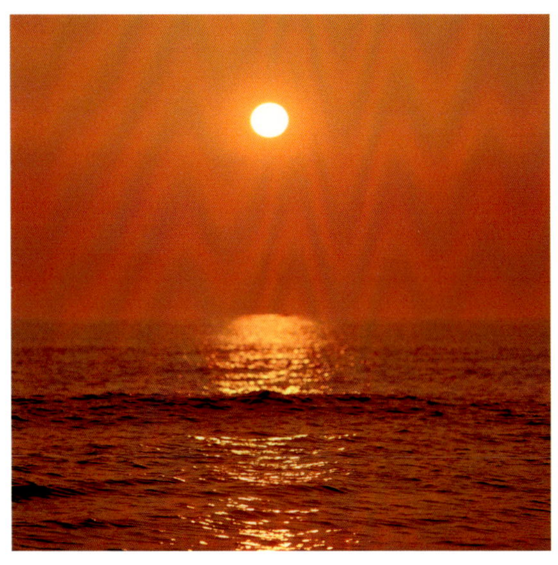
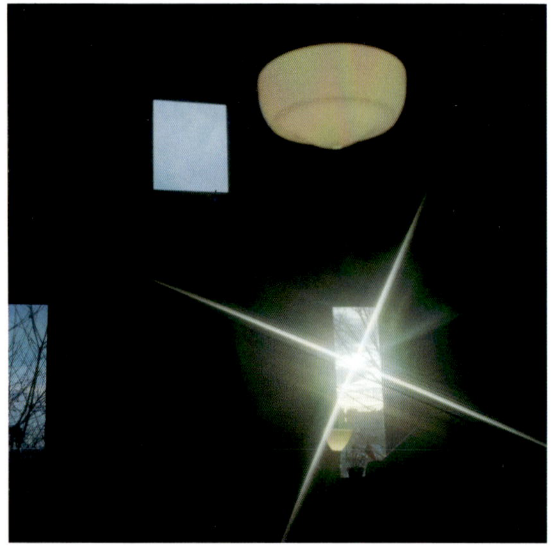
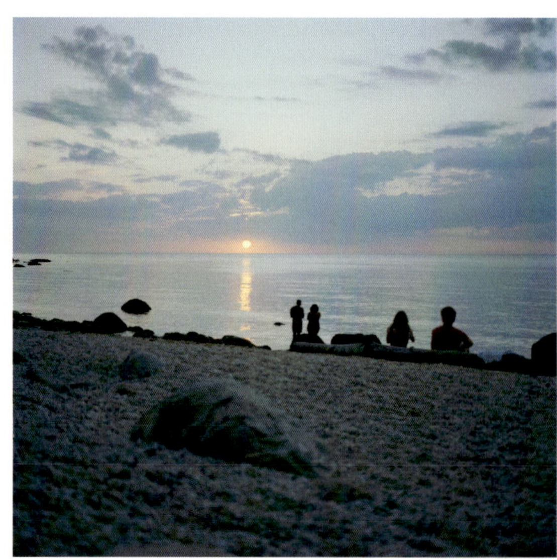
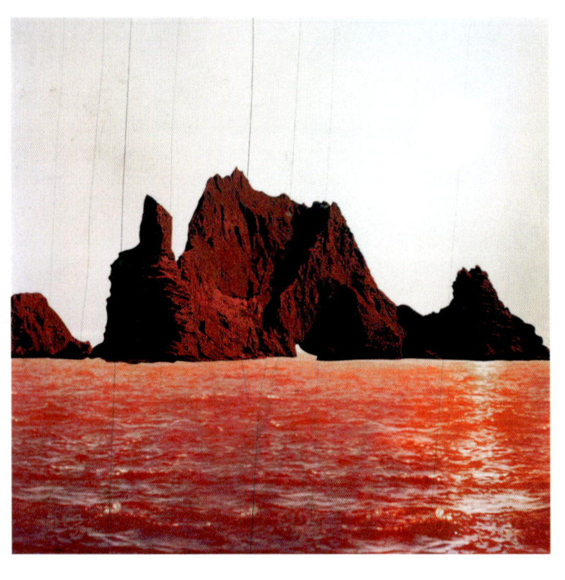
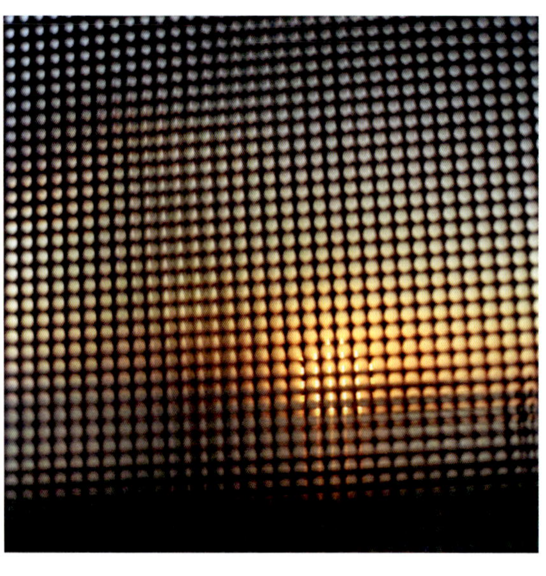
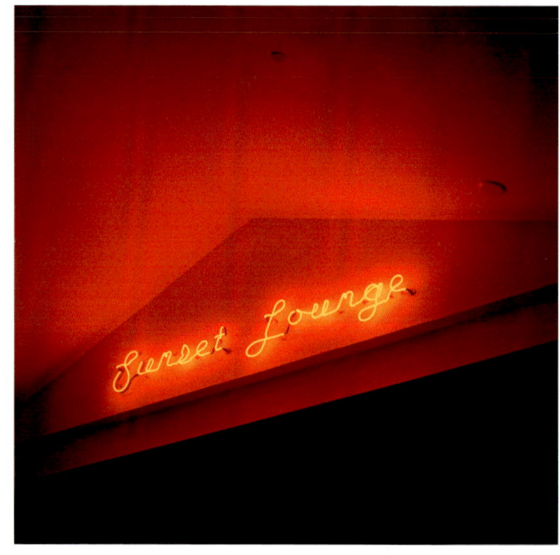
Sunset Lounge
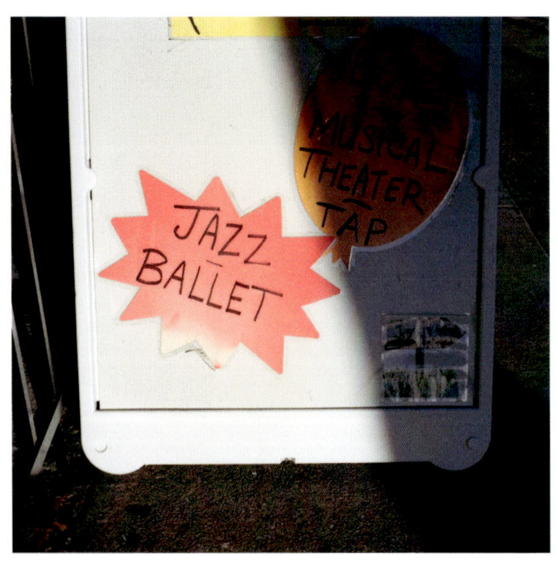
JAZZ
BALLET
MUSICAL
THEATER
TAP
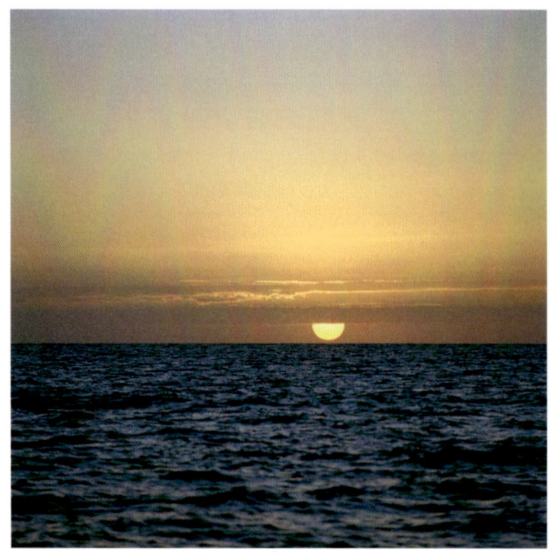
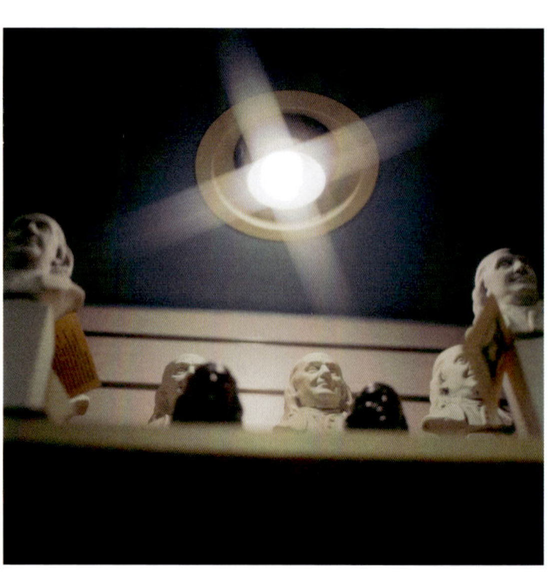

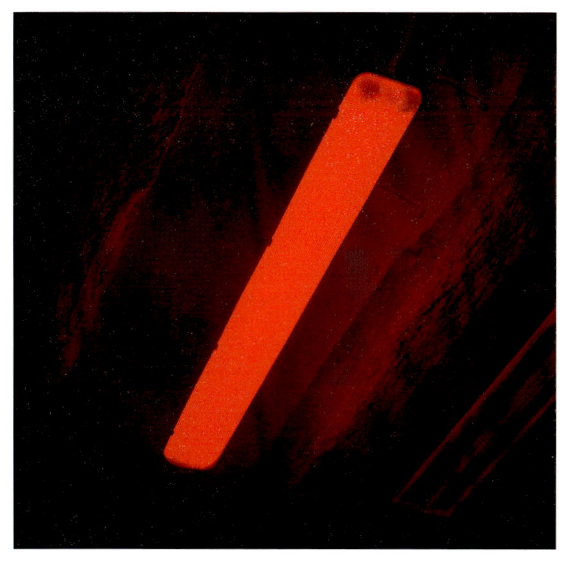
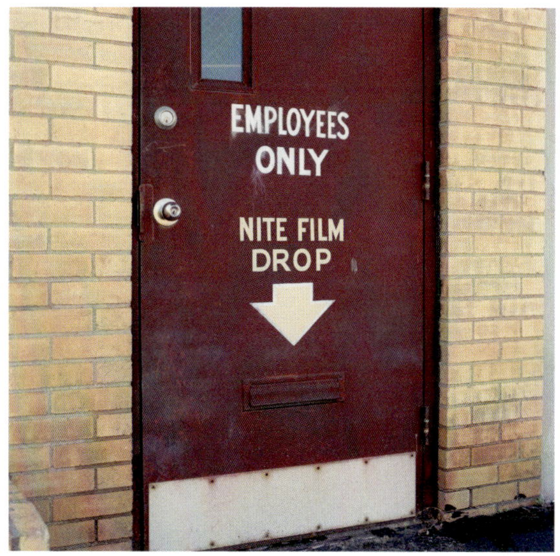
EMPLOYEES
ONLY
NITE FILM
DROP
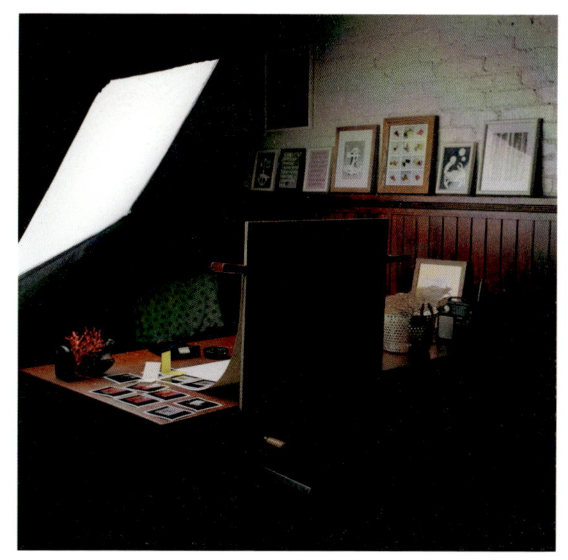
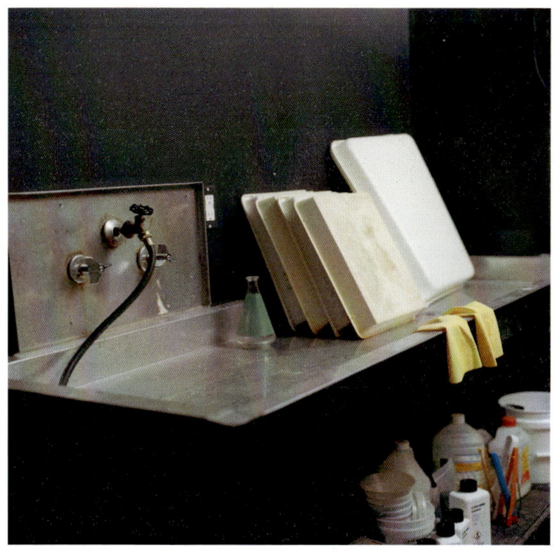
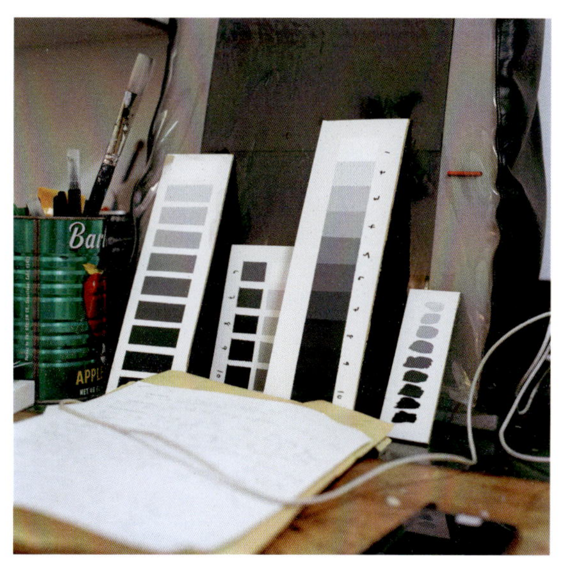
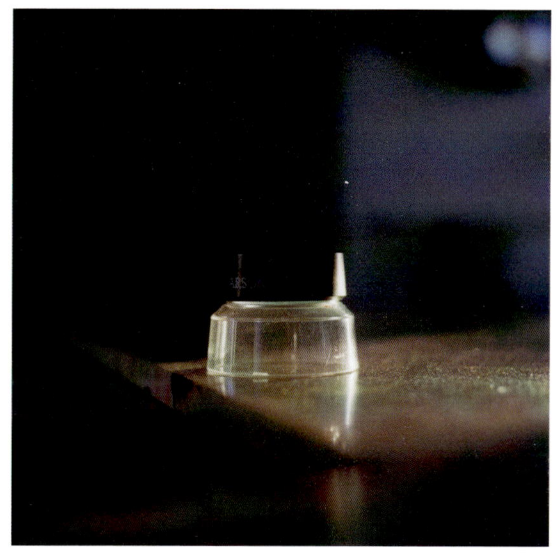
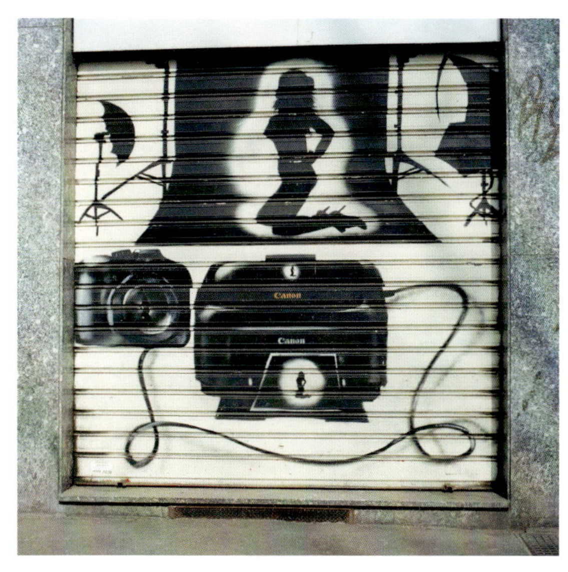
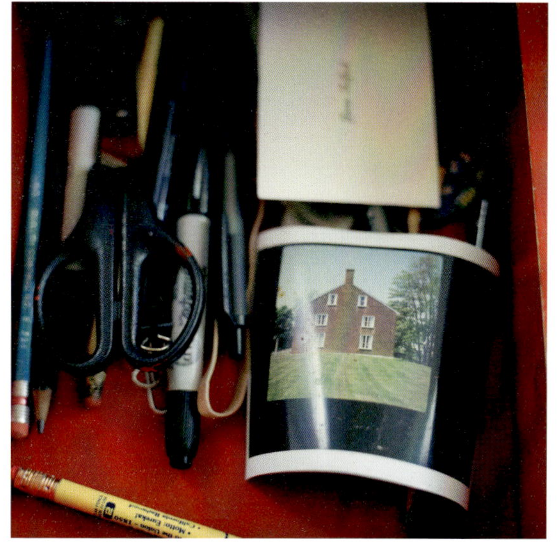
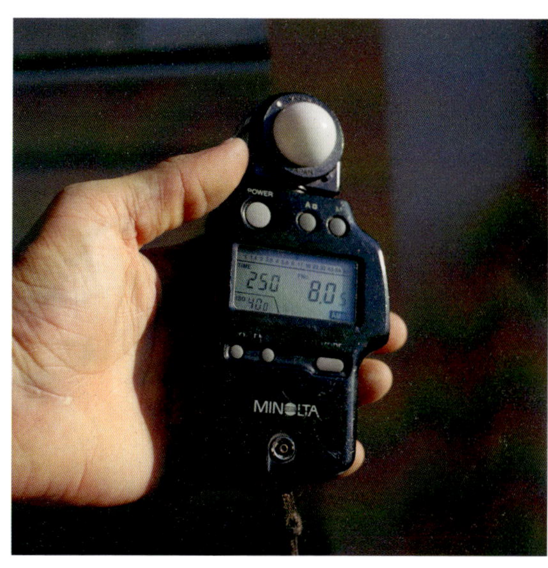
MINOLTA

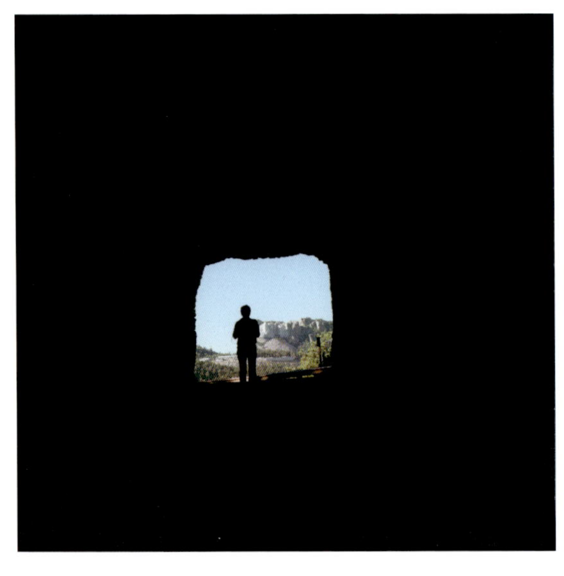

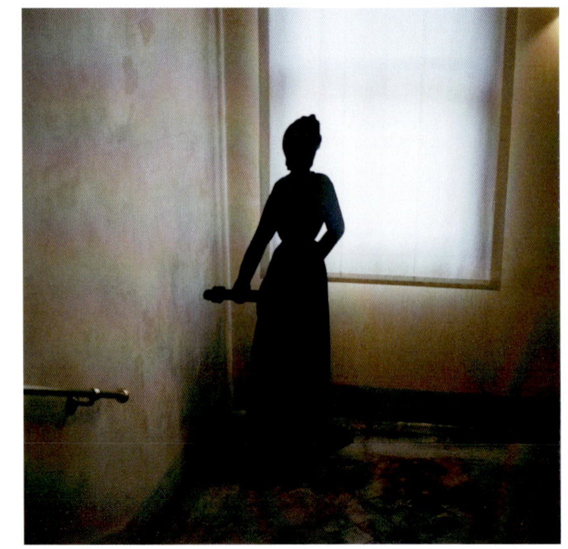

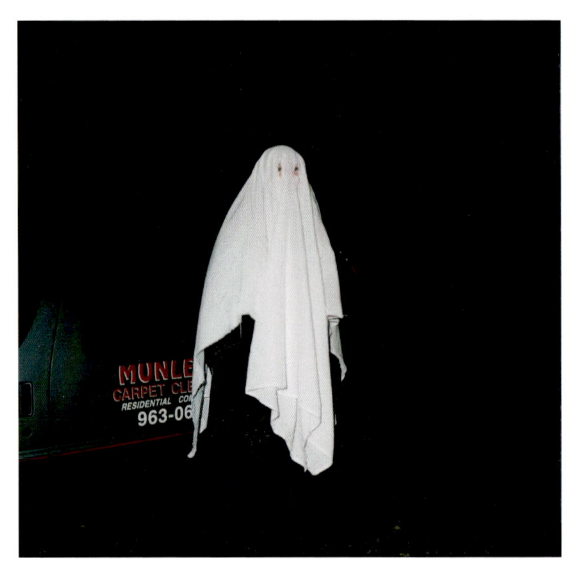
MUNLE
CARPET CLE
RESIDENTIAL
963-06

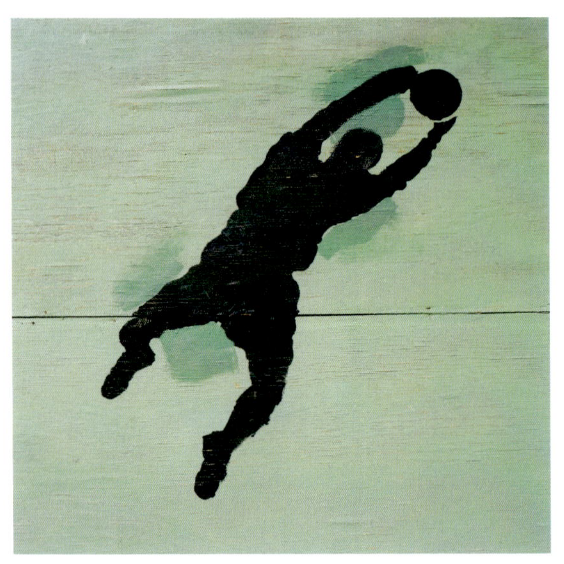

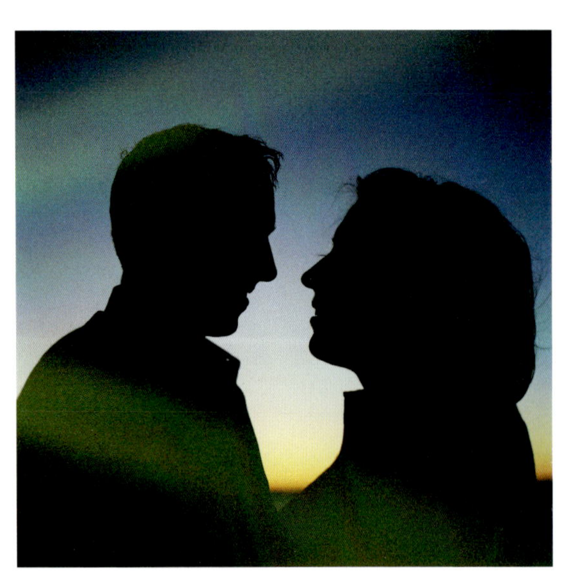

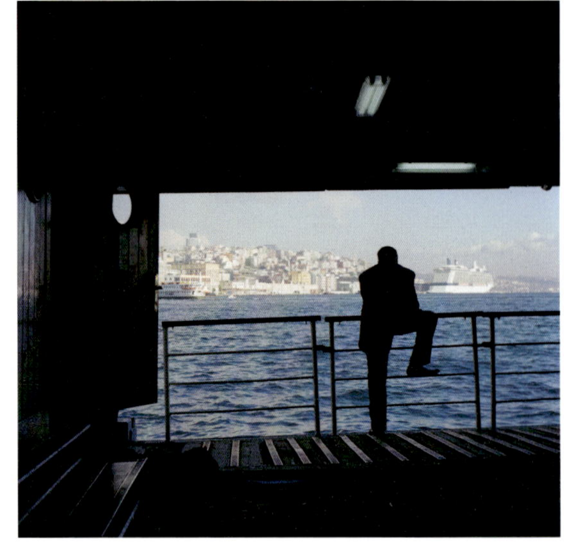

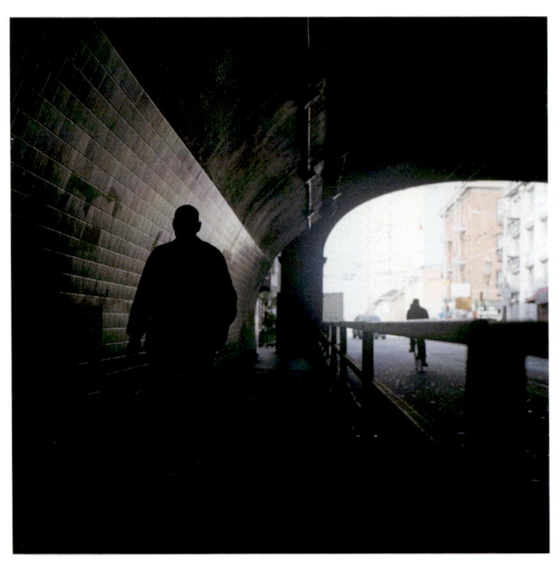

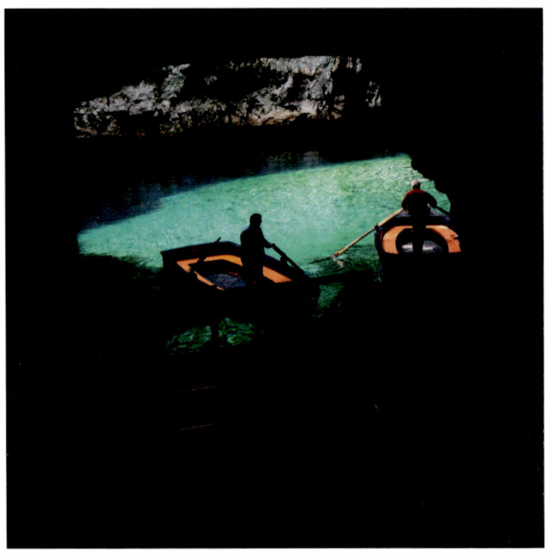

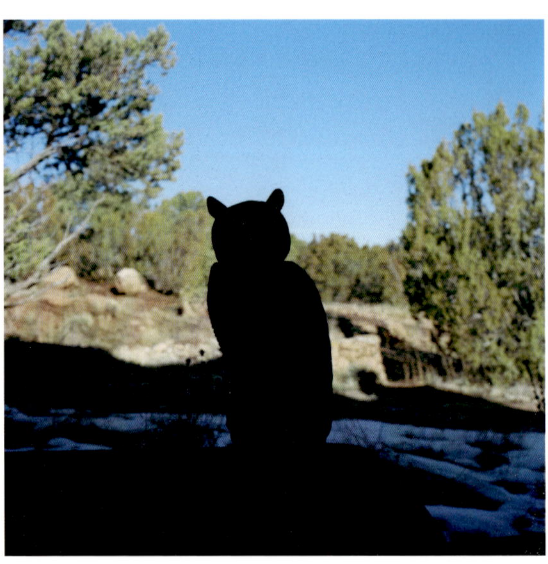

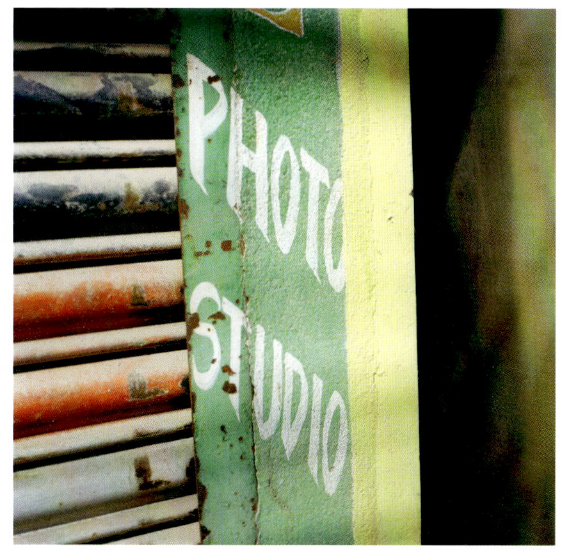
PHOTO
STUDIO

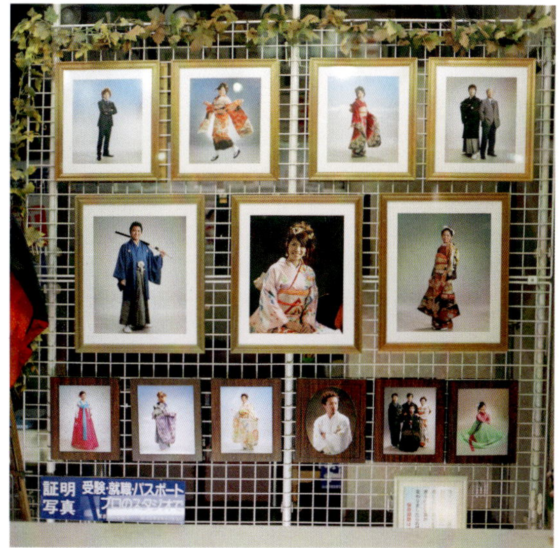
証明 受験・就職パスポート
写真

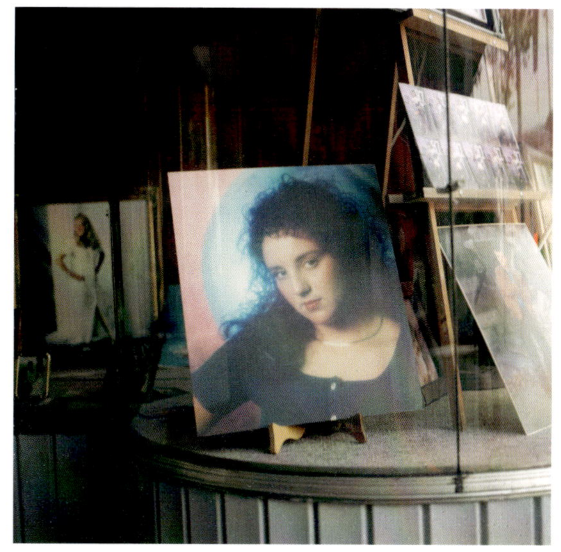

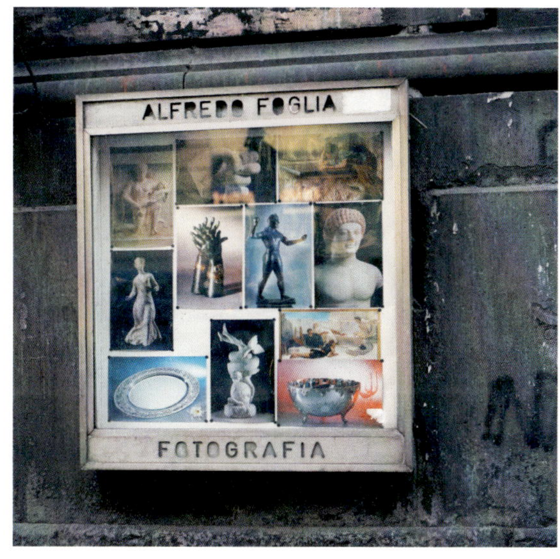
ALFREDO FOGLIA
FOTOGRAFIA

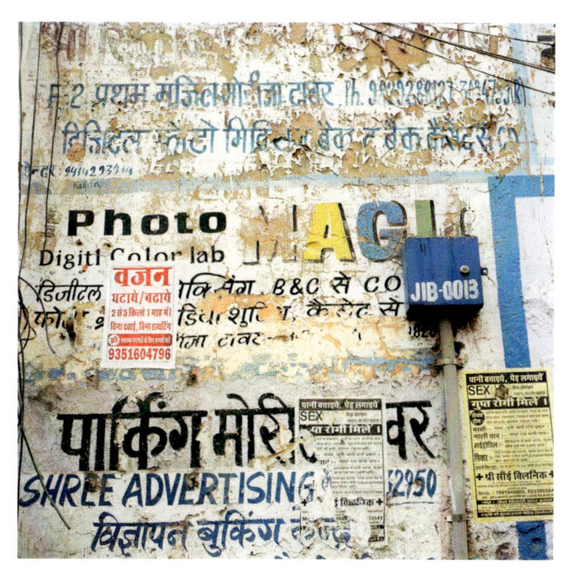
Photo
Digitl Color lab
वजन
घटाये/बढाये
2 से 5 किलो 1 माह में।
बिना दवाई, बिना डायटिंग
9351604796
B&C से CO
JIB-0013
पानी बढाइये, पेड़ लगाइये
SEX
गुप्त रोगी मिलें।
+ श्री सॉंई क्लिनिक +
SHREE ADVERTISING

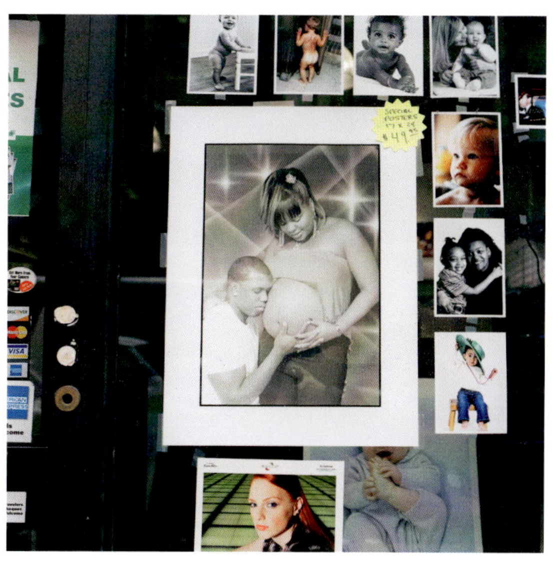

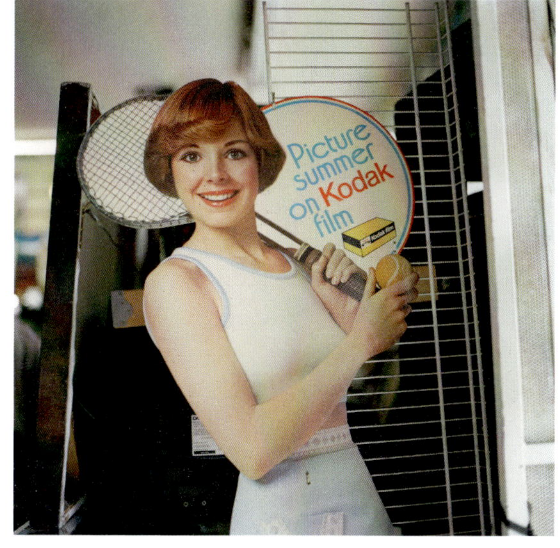
Picture summer on Kodak film

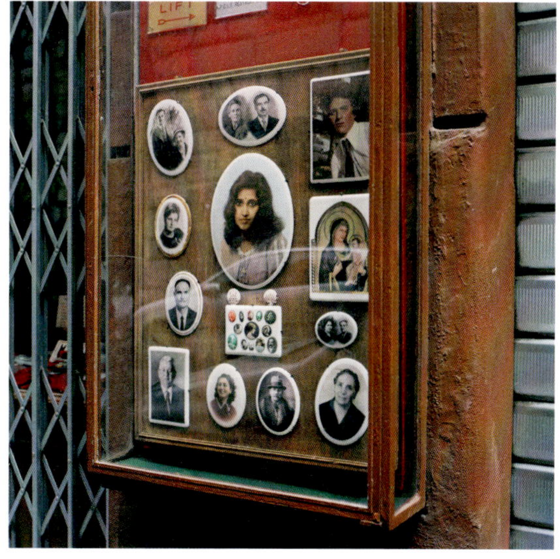

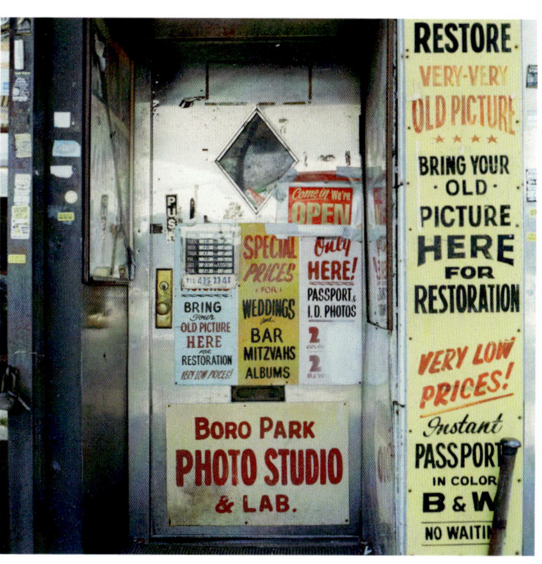
RESTORE
VERY-VERY
OLD PICTURE
BRING YOUR
OLD
PICTURE
HERE
FOR
RESTORATION
VERY LOW PRICES!
Instant
IN COLOR
Come in We're OPEN
PUSH
BRING your OLD PICTURE HERE for RESTORATION
VERY LOW PRICES!
SPECIAL PRICES FOR WEDDINGS and BAR MITZVAHS ALBUMS
Only HERE!
PASSPORT & I.D. PHOTOS
2
2
BORO PARK
PHOTO STUDIO
& LAB.

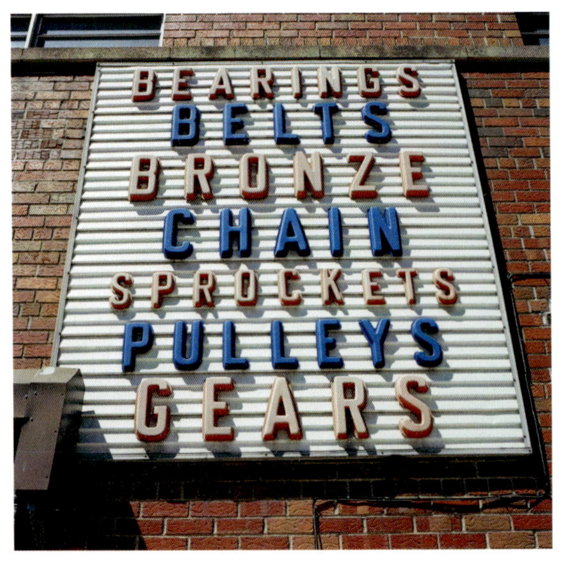
BEARINGS
BELTS
BRONZE
CHAIN
SPROCKETS
PULLEYS
GEARS

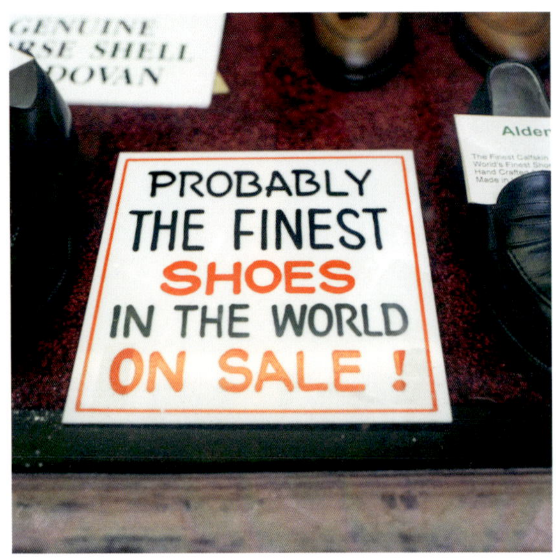
PROBABLY THE FINEST SHOES IN THE WORLD ON SALE !

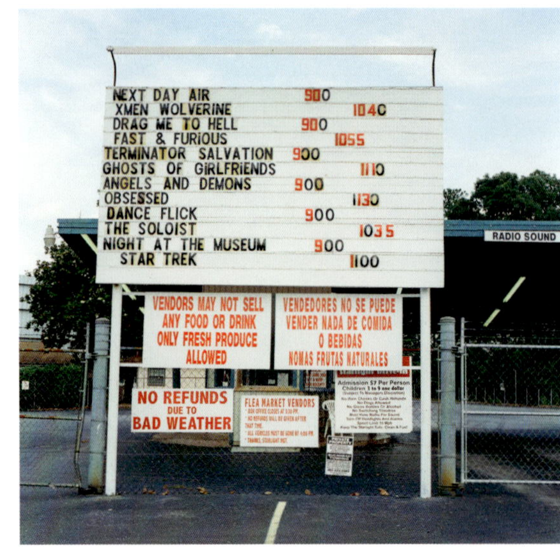
NEXT DAY AIR 900
XMEN WOLVERINE 1040
DRAG ME TO HELL 900
FAST & FURIOUS 1055
TERMINATOR SALVATION 900
GHOSTS OF GIRLFRIENDS 1110
ANGELS AND DEMONS 900
OBSESSED 1130
DANCE FLICK 900
THE SOLOIST 1035
NIGHT AT THE MUSEUM 900
STAR TREK 1100
RADIO SOUND
VENDORS MAY NOT SELL ANY FOOD OR DRINK ONLY FRESH PRODUCE ALLOWED
VENDEDORES NO SE PUEDE VENDER NADA DE COMIDA O BEBIDAS NOMAS FRUTAS NATURALES
NO REFUNDS DUE TO BAD WEATHER
FLEA MARKET VENDORS

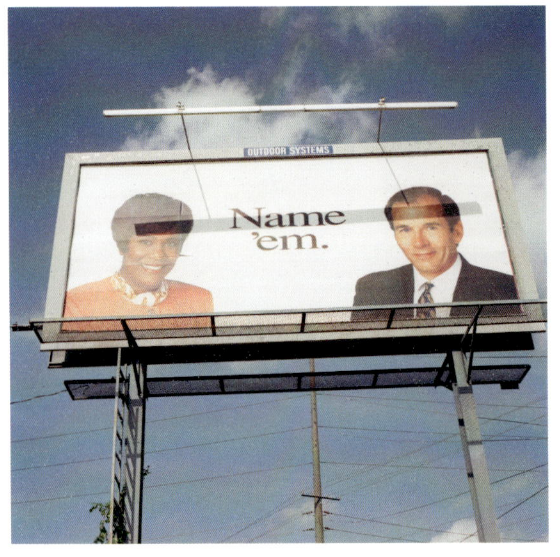
OUTDOOR SYSTEMS
Name 'em.

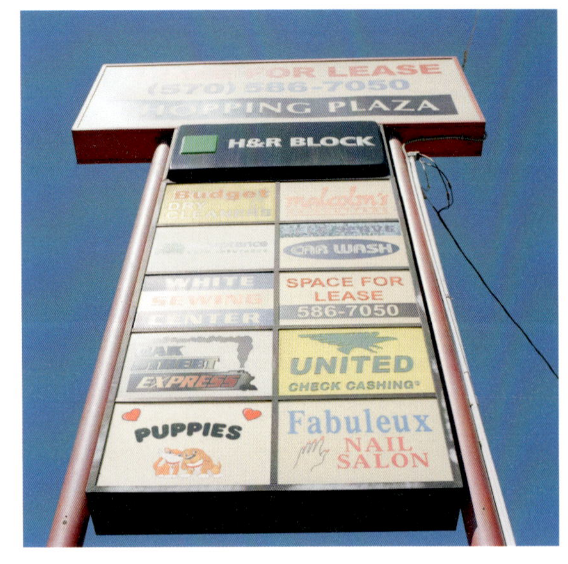
FOR LEASE
(570) 586-7050
H&R BLOCK
Budget
CAR WASH
WHITE SEWING CENTER
SPACE FOR LEASE 586-7050
EXPRESS
UNITED CHECK CASHING
PUPPIES
Fabuleux NAIL SALON

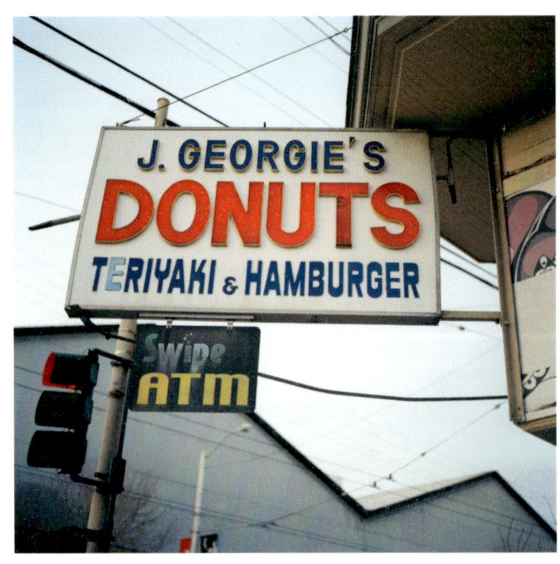
J. GEORGIE'S
DONUTS
TERIYAKI & HAMBURGER
Swipe ATM

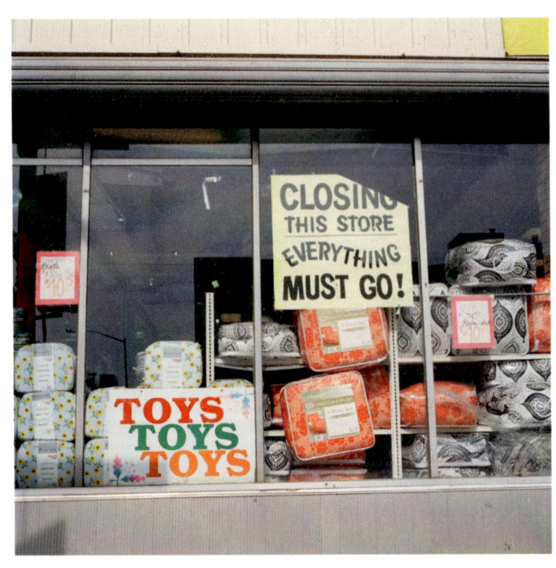
CLOSING THIS STORE EVERYTHING MUST GO!
TOYS TOYS TOYS

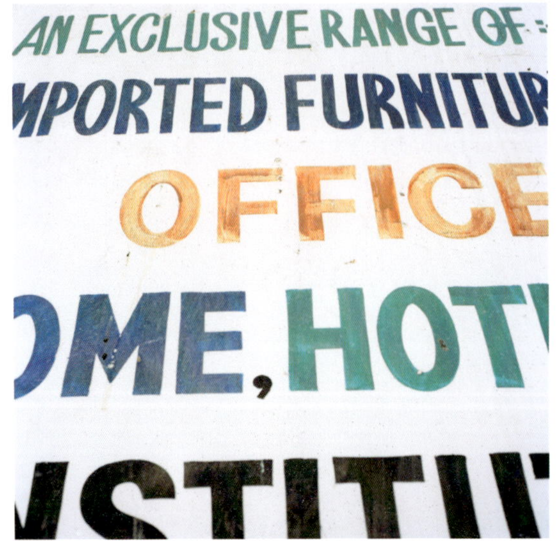
AN EXCLUSIVE RANGE OF
MPORTED FURNITUR
OFFICE
OME, HOT
NSTITU

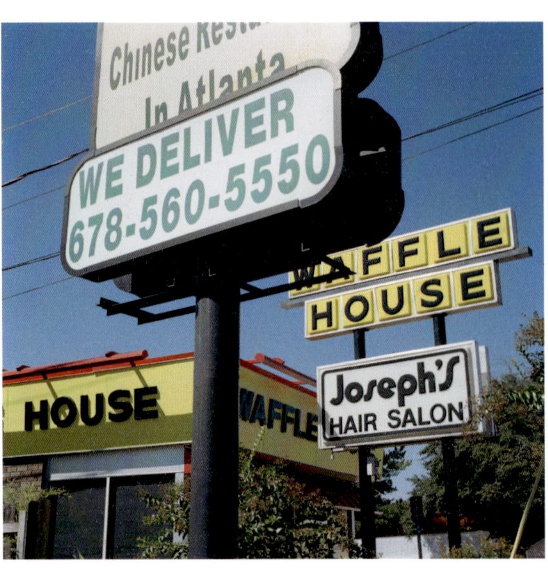
In Atlanta
WE DELIVER 678-560-5550
WAFFLE HOUSE
Joseph's HAIR SALON
HOUSE
WAFFLE

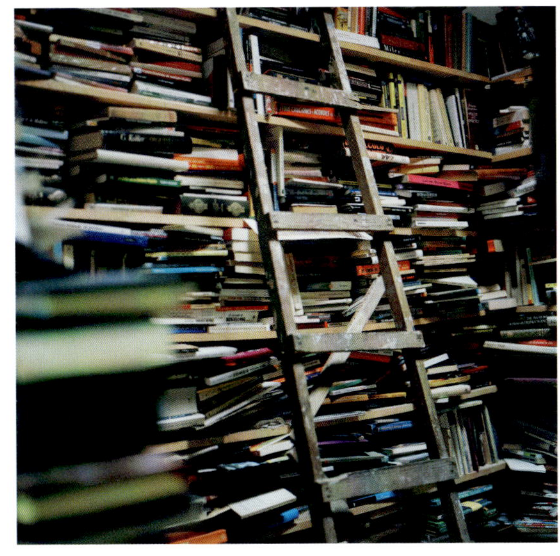

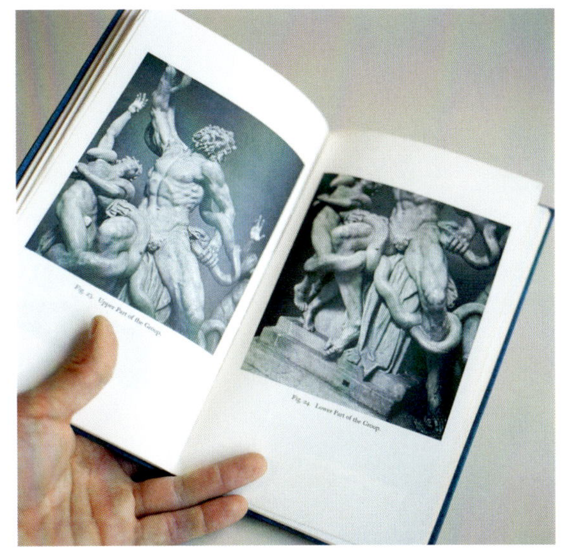

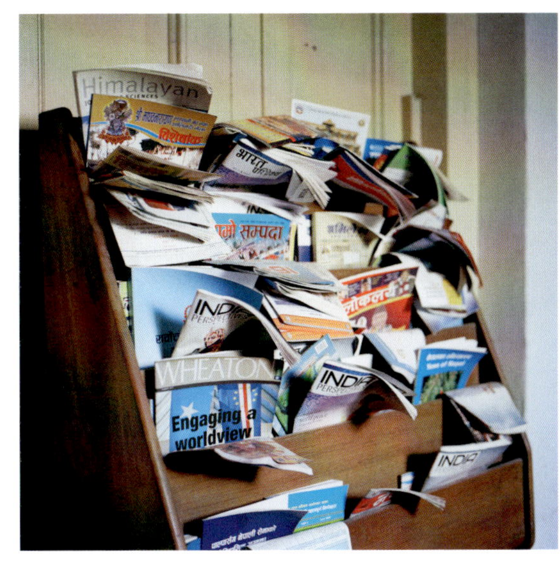
Himalayan
WHEATON
Engaging a worldview

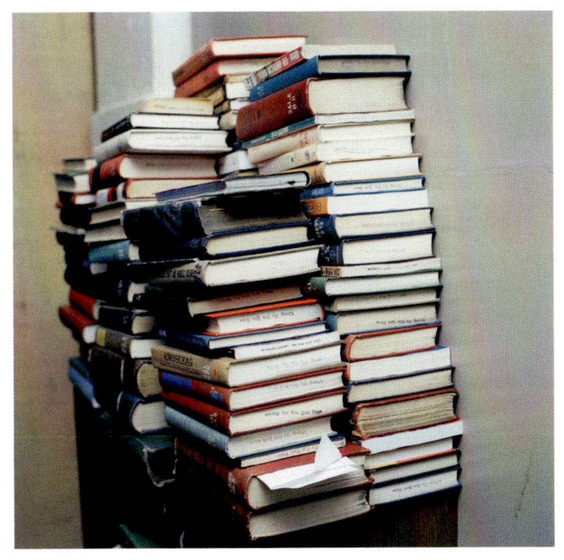

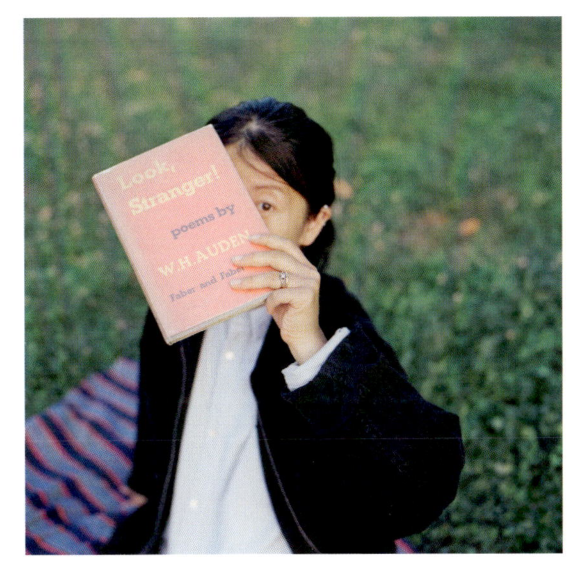
Look, Stranger!
poems by
W.H.AUDEN

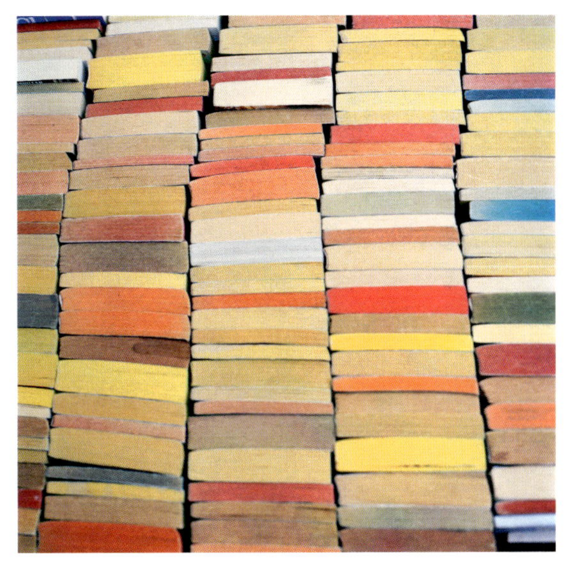

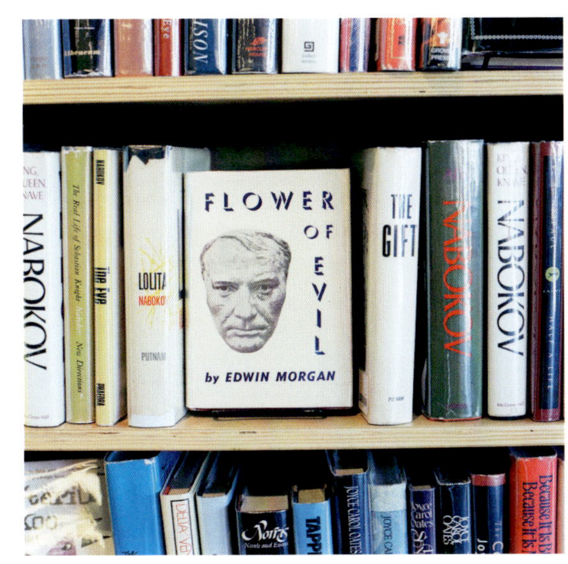
NABOKOV
LOLITA
FLOWER OF EVIL
by EDWIN MORGAN
THE GIFT
NABOKOV
NABOKOV

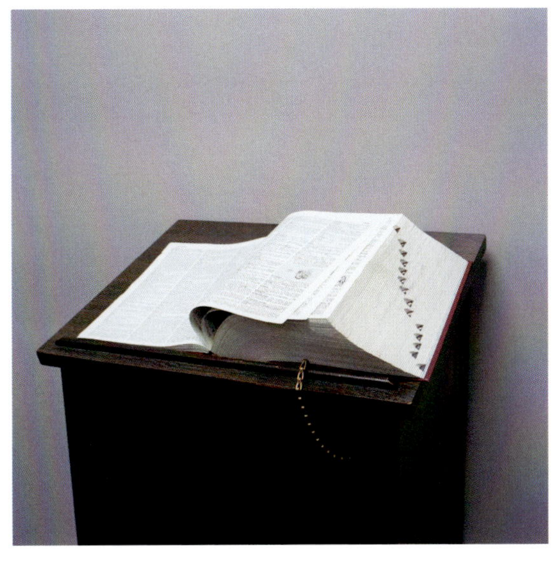

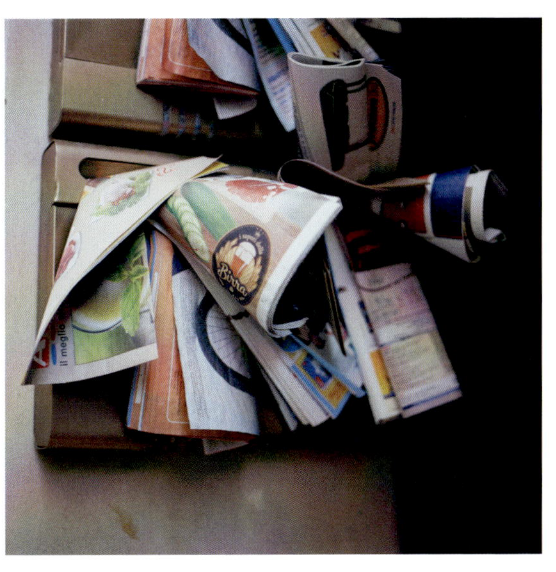

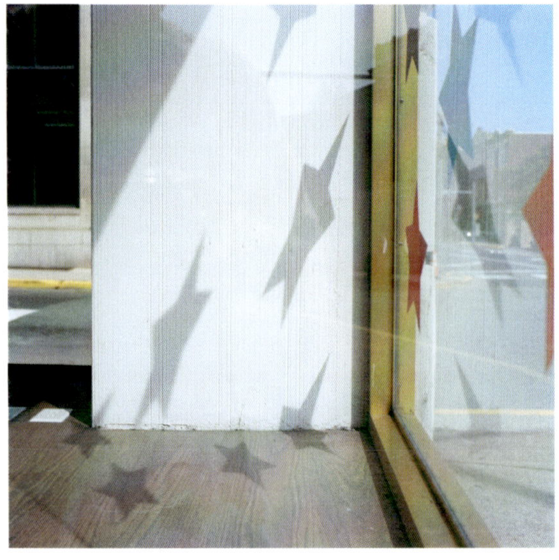
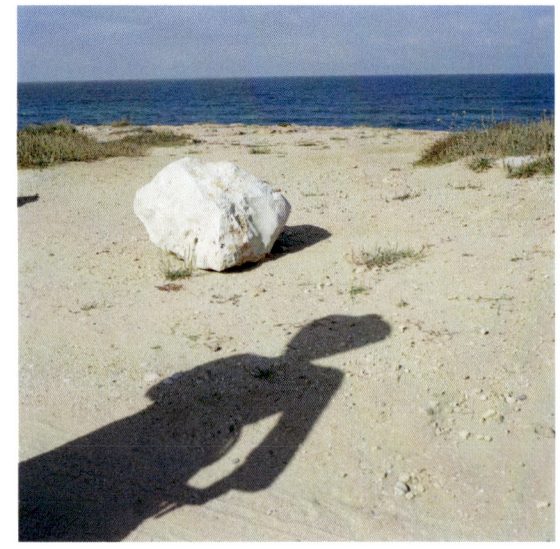
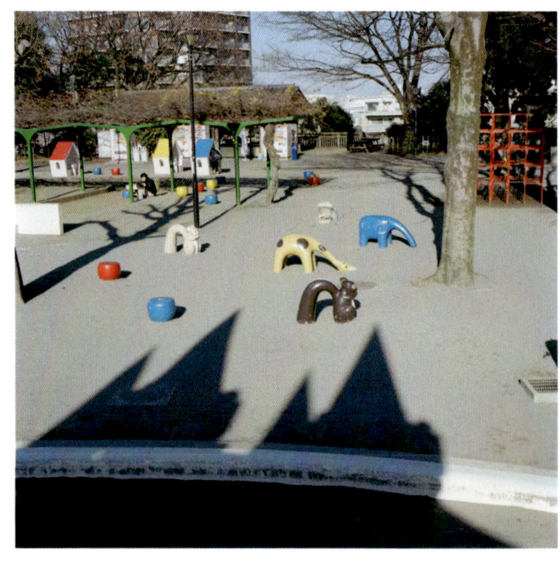
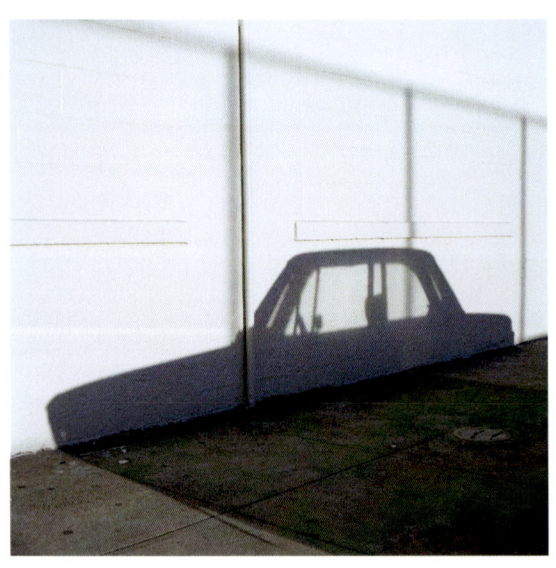
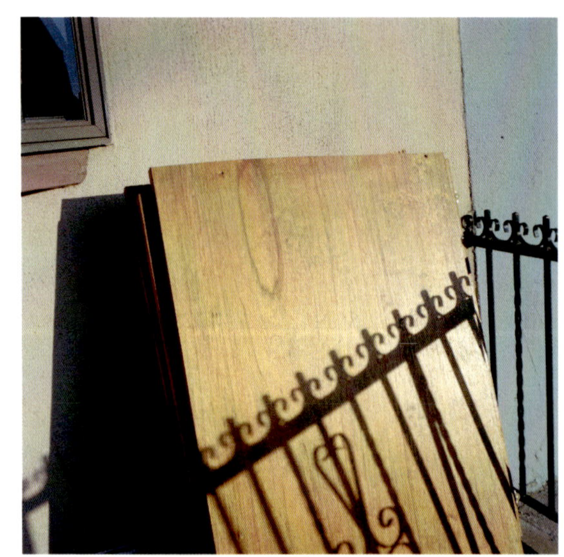
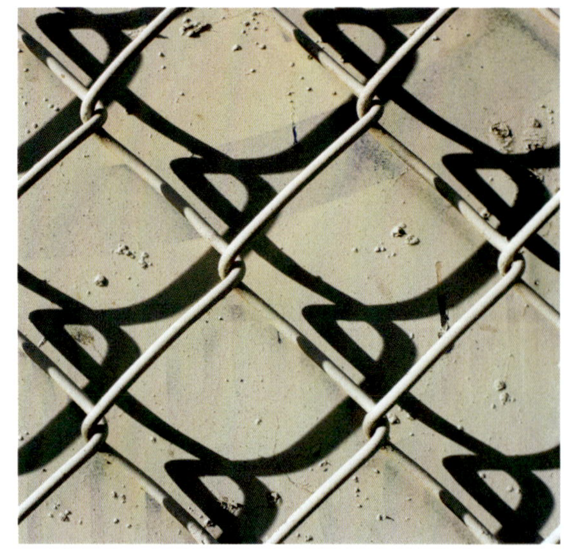
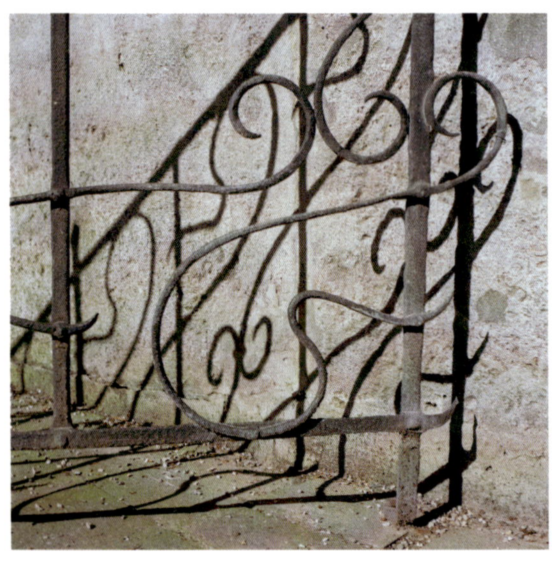
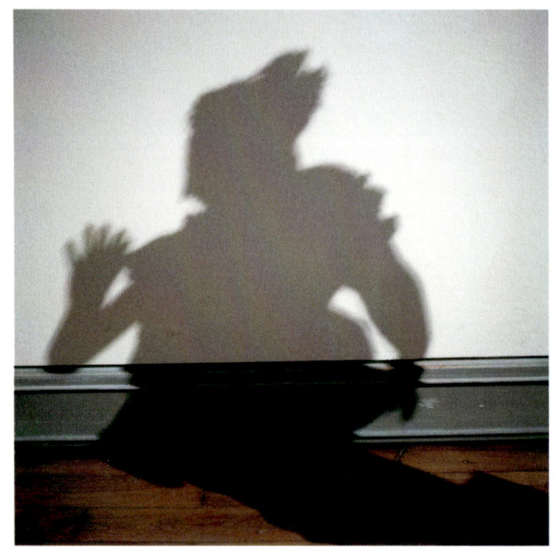
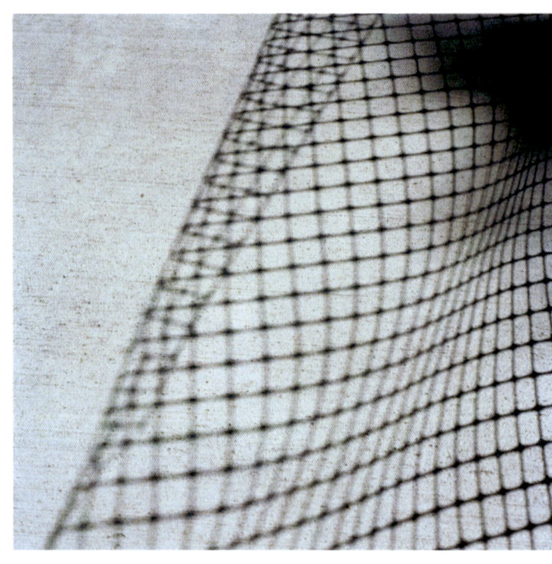

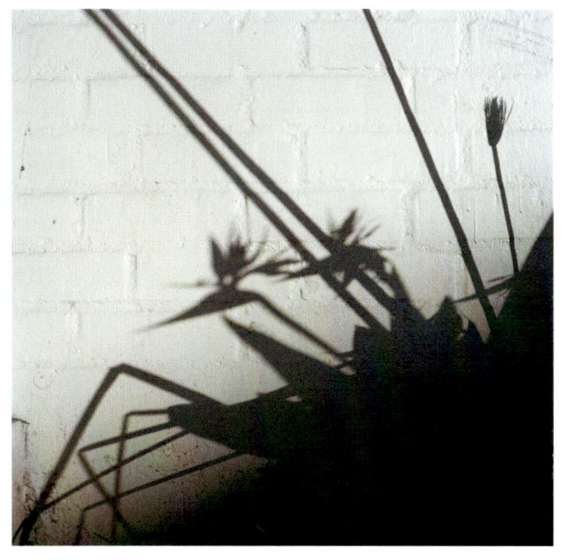
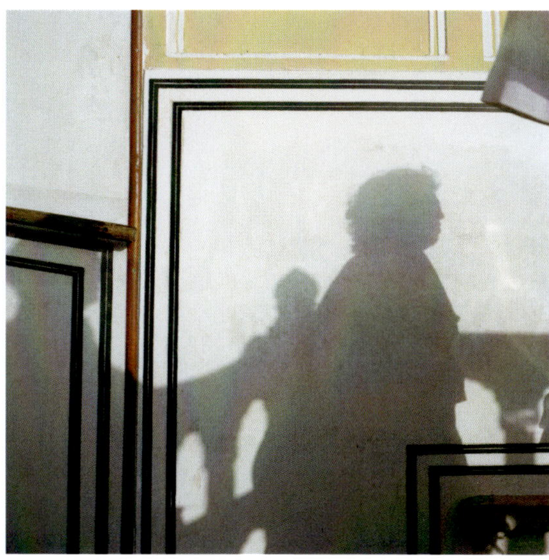
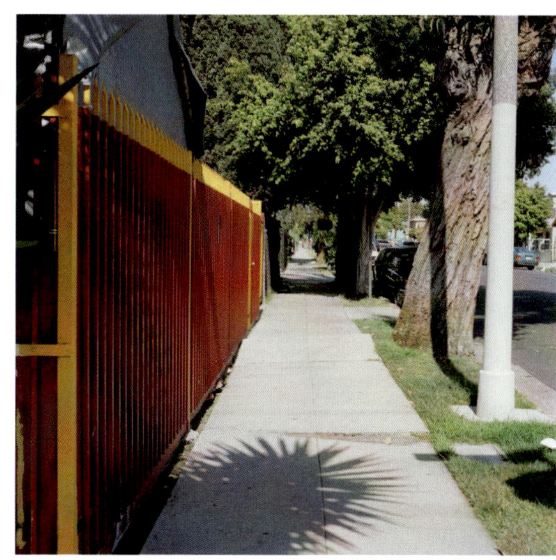
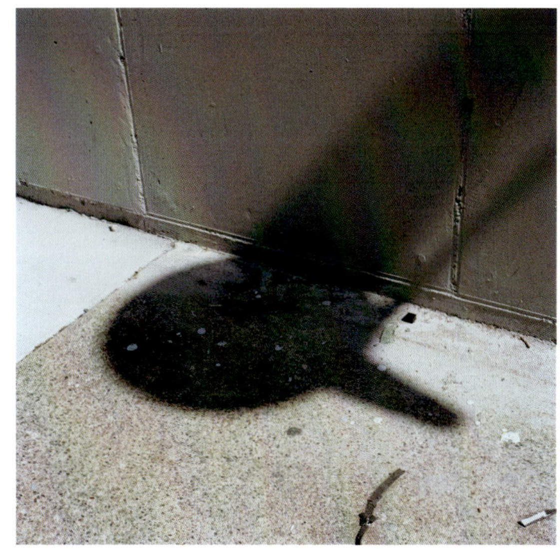
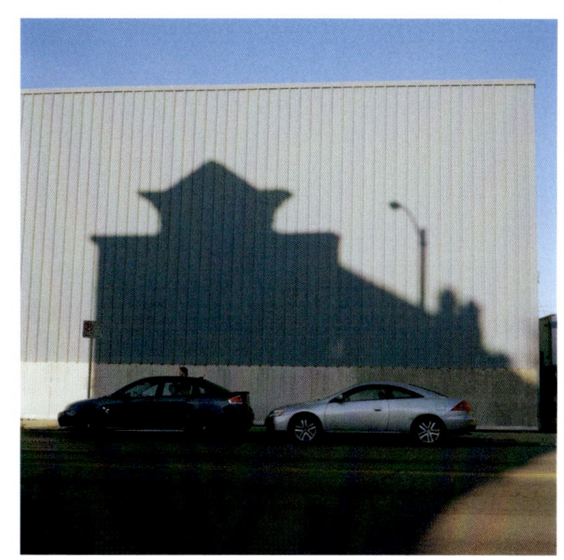
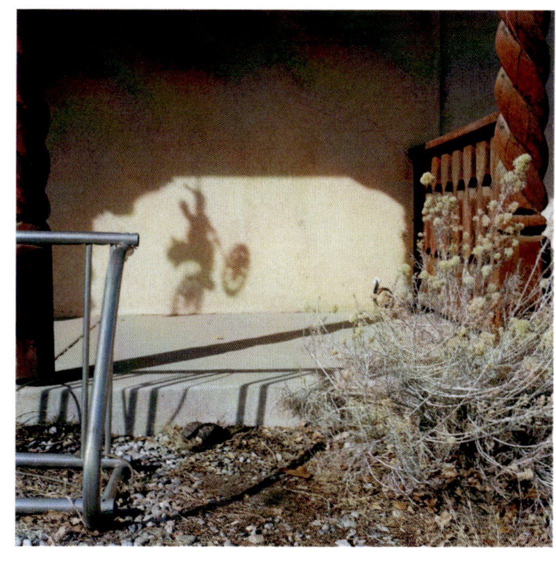
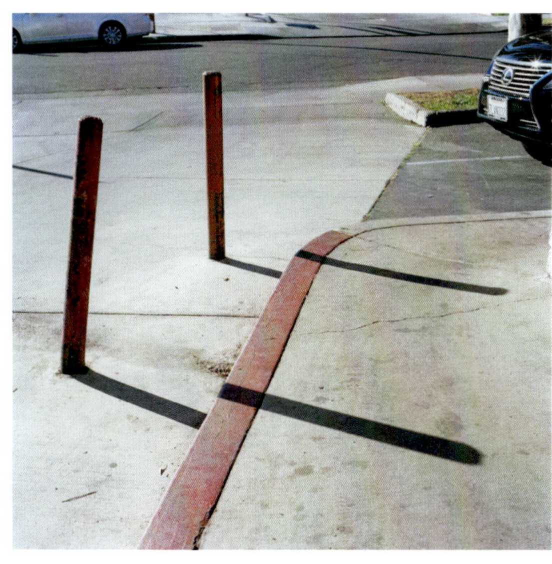
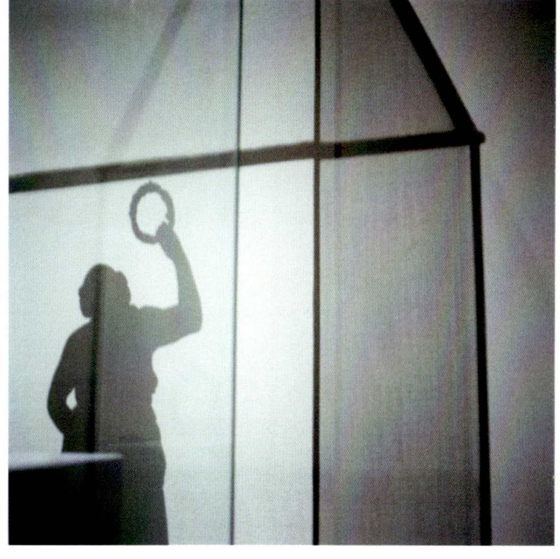
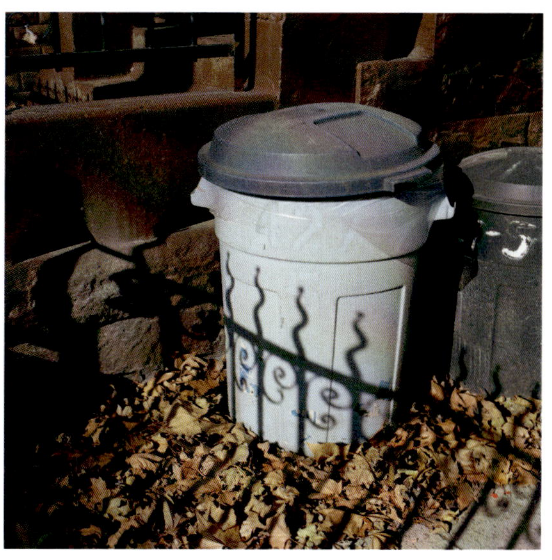

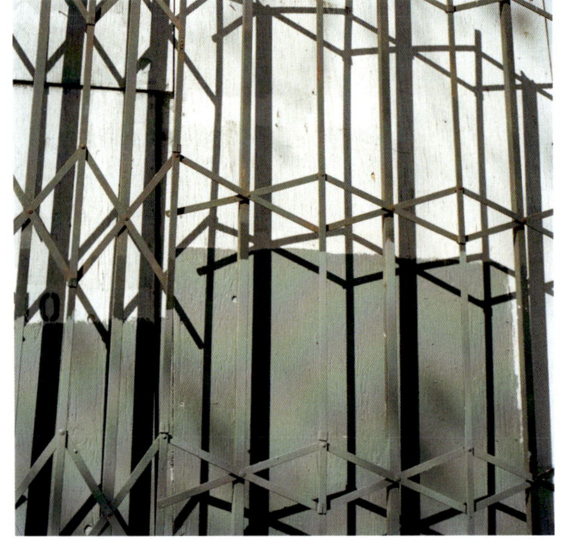

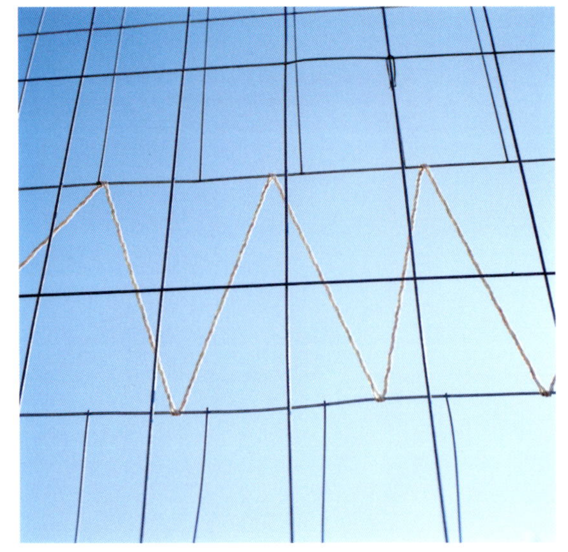

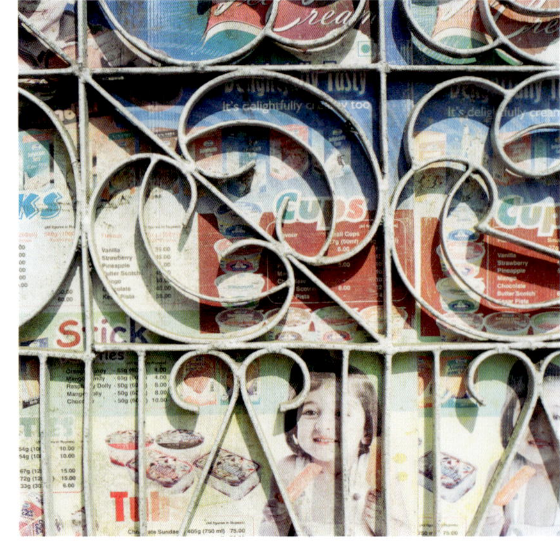
Cups
Vanilla
Strawberry
Pineapple
Mango
Chocolate
Butter Scotch

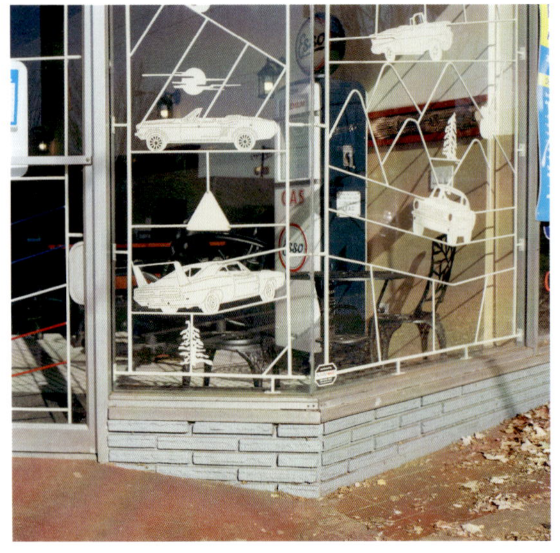

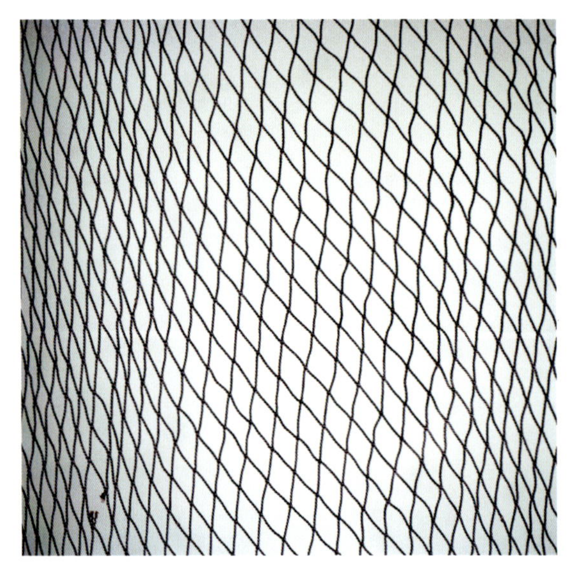

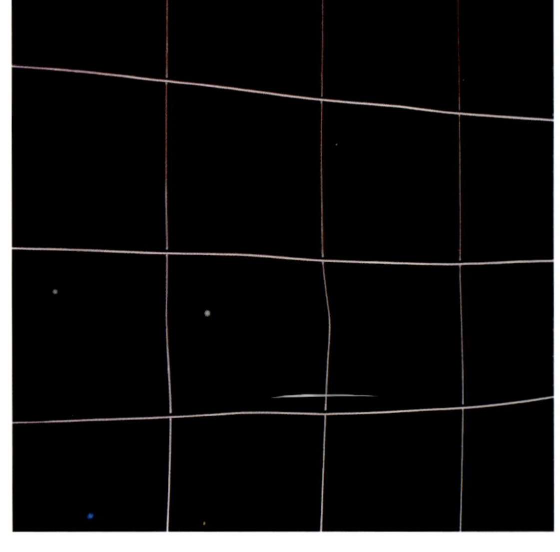

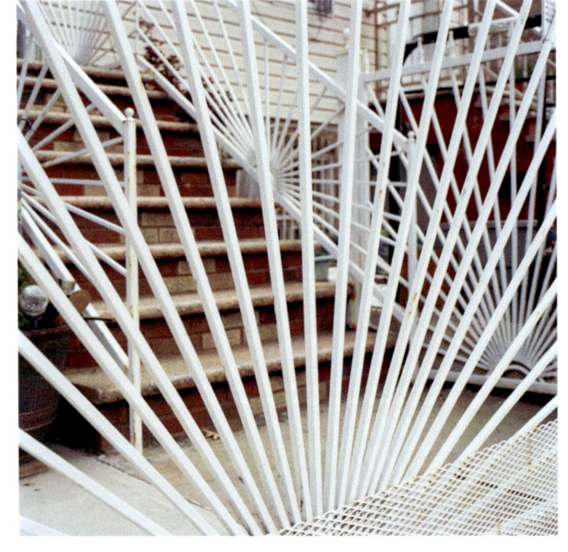

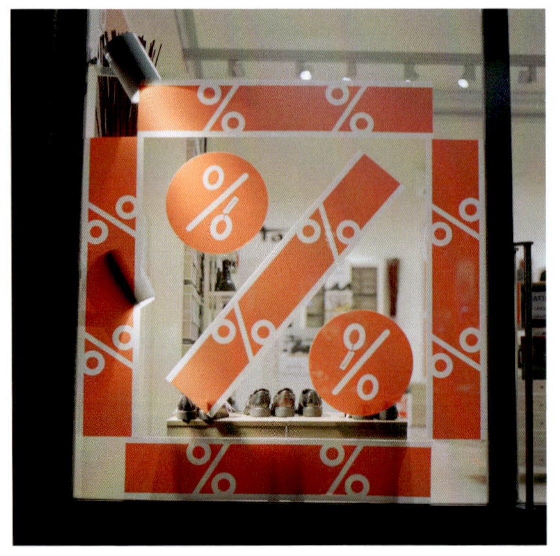

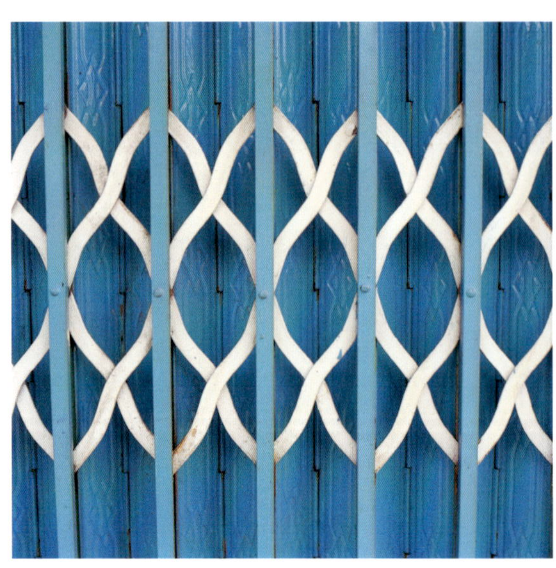

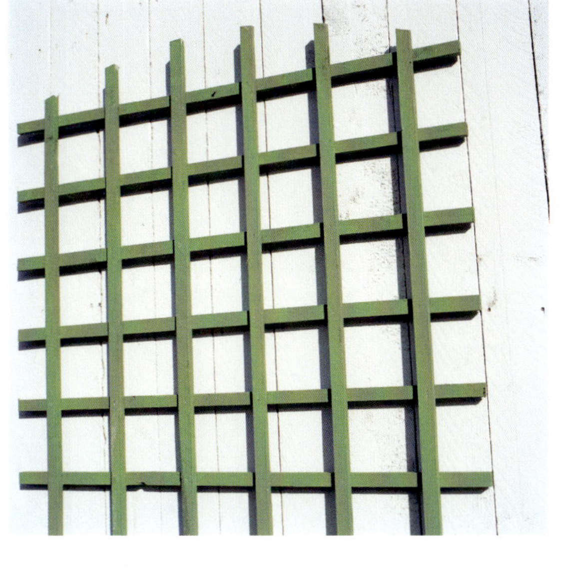
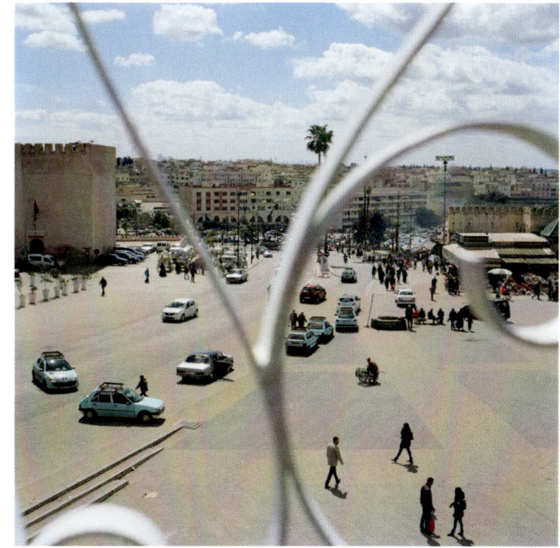
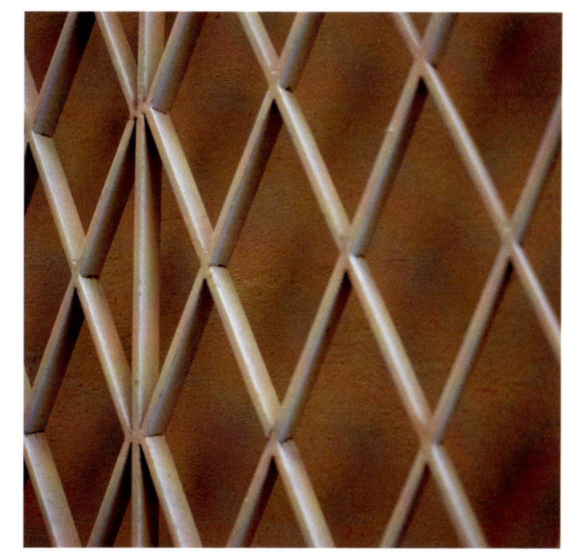
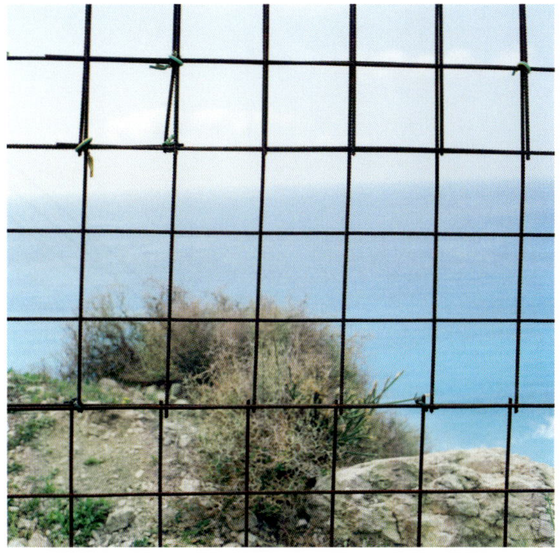
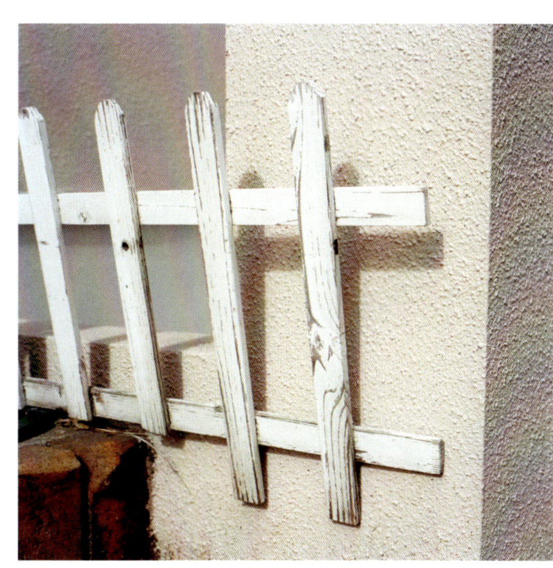
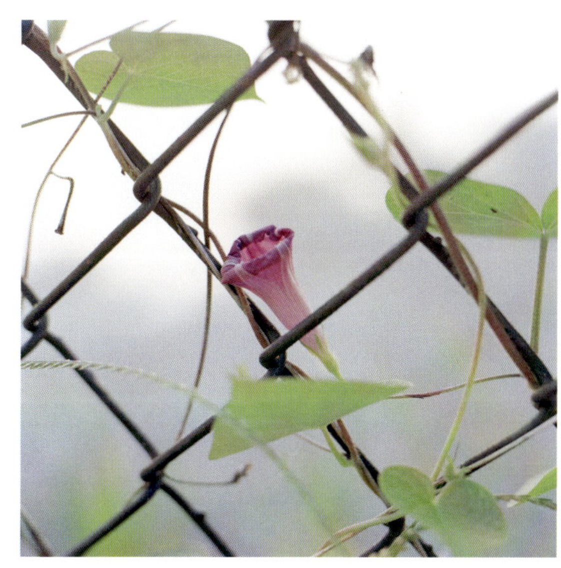
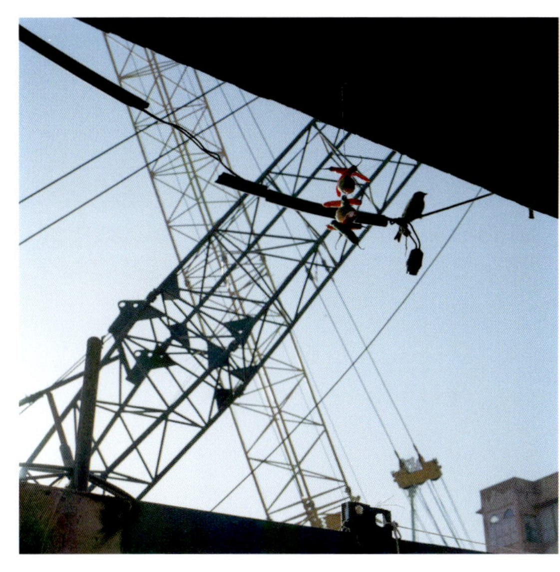
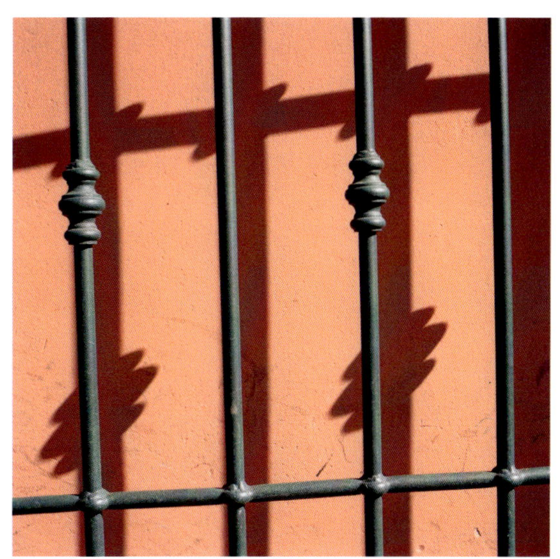
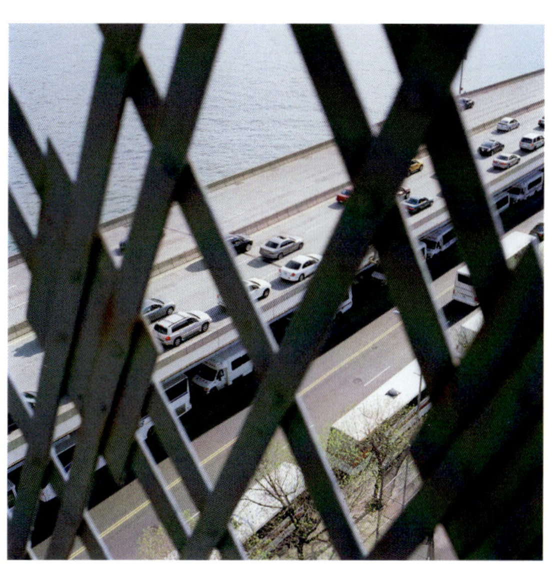

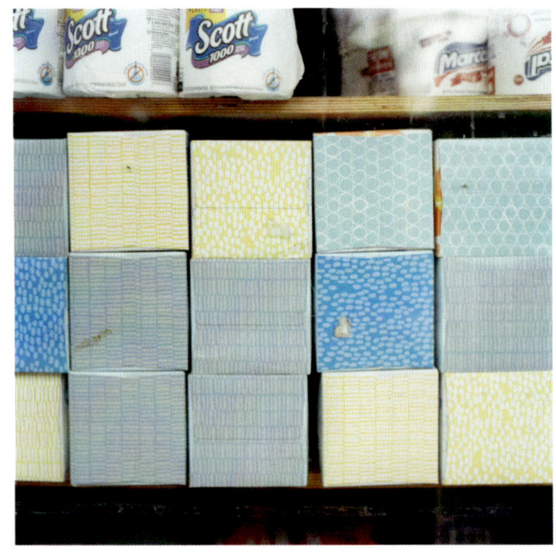
Scott
1000
Scott
1000
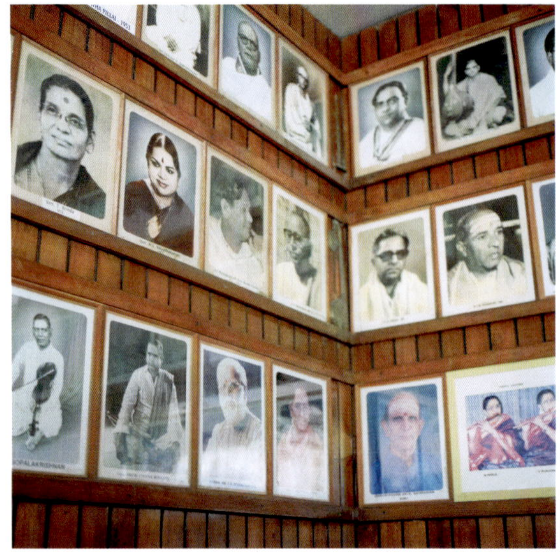
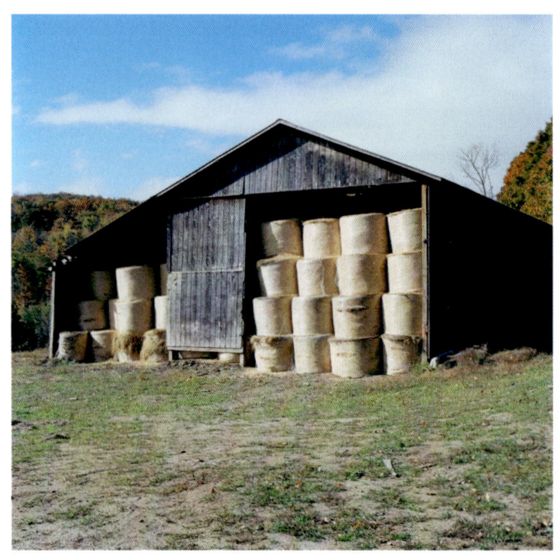
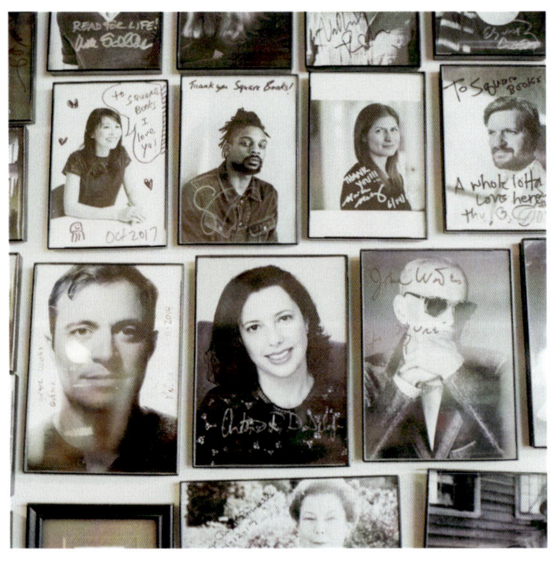
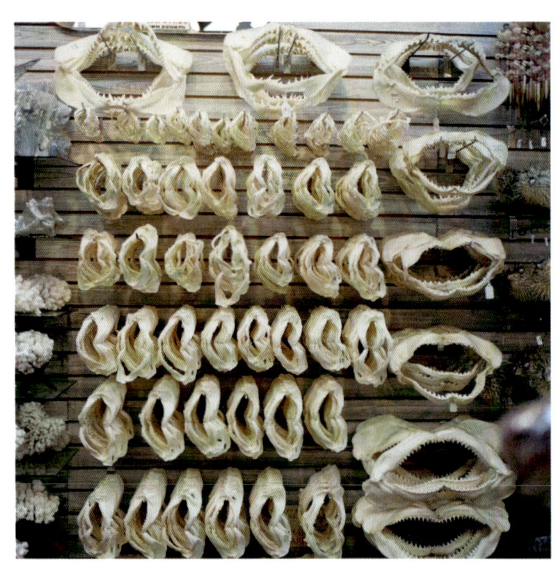
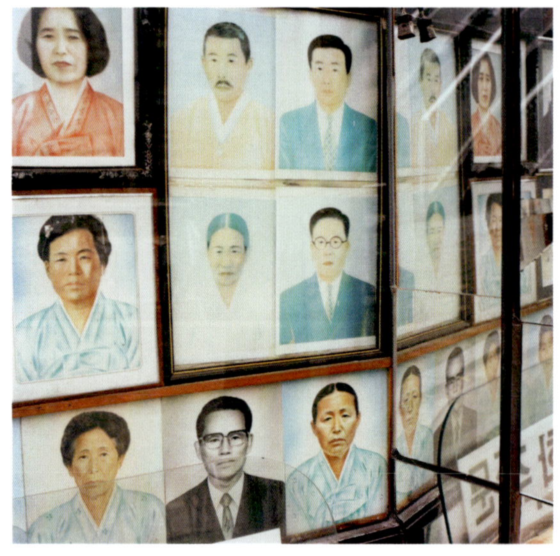
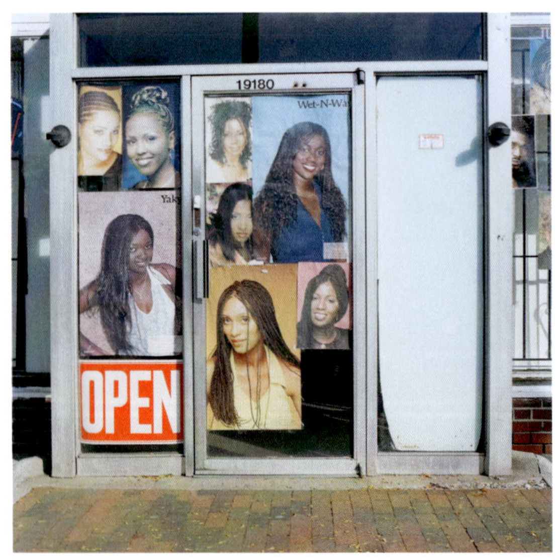
19180
OPEN
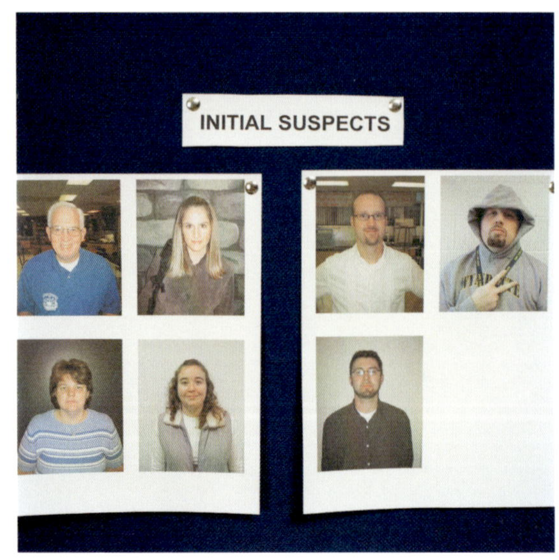
INITIAL SUSPECTS
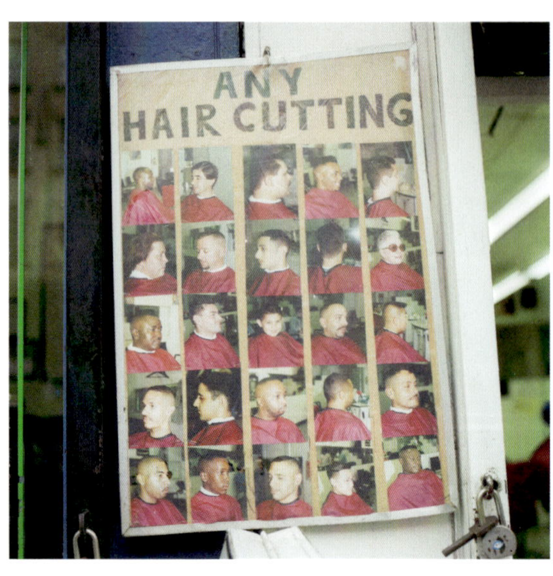
ANY
HAIR CUTTING

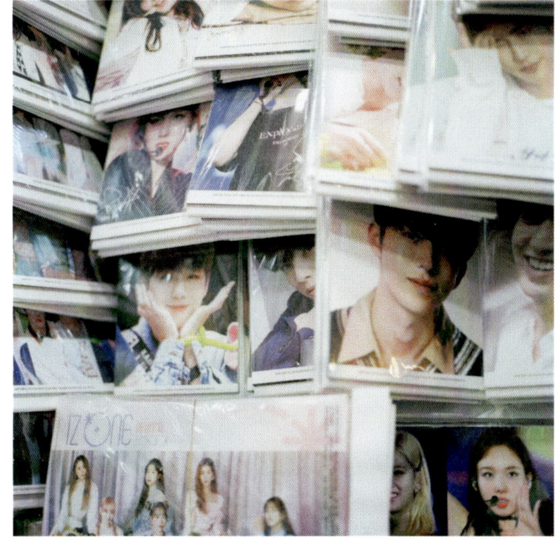

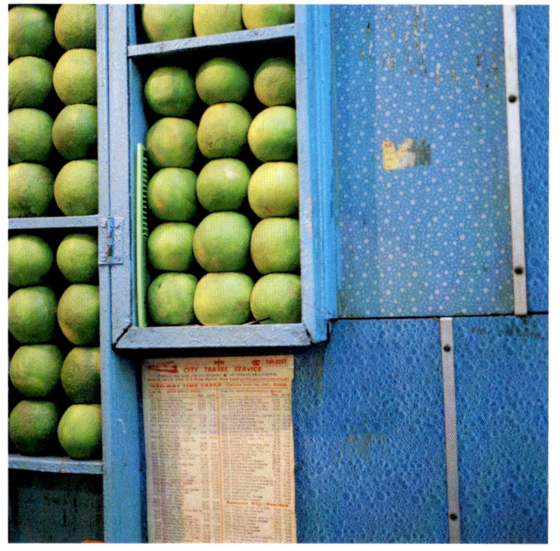

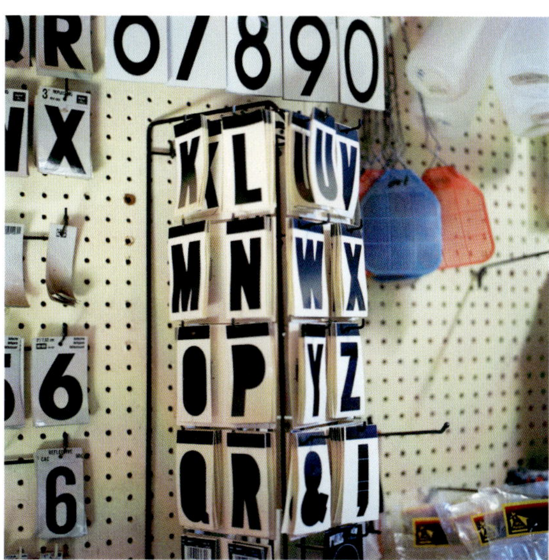

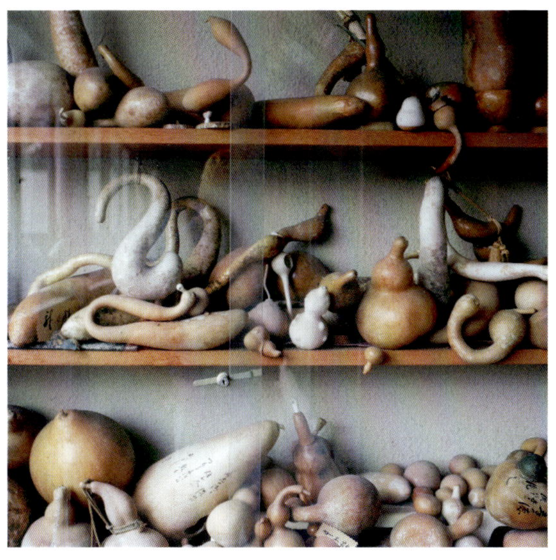

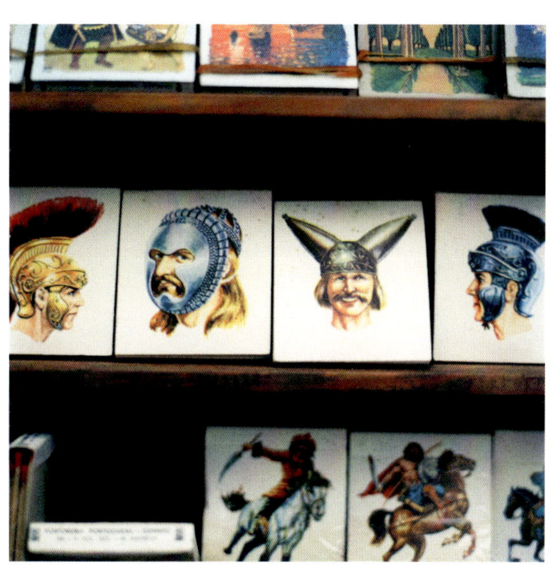

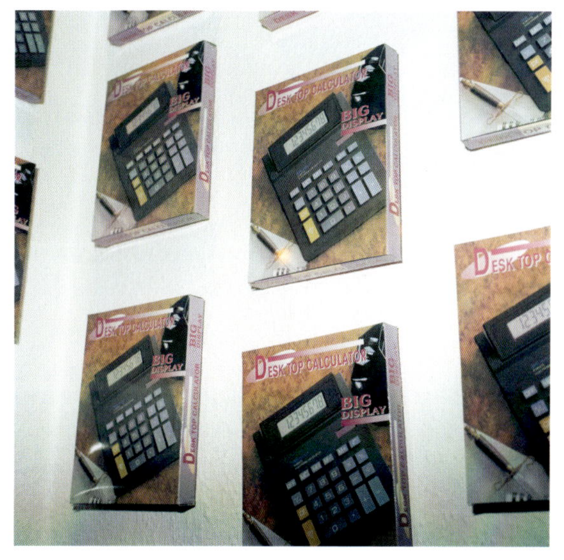
DESK TOP CALCULATOR
BIG DISPLAY

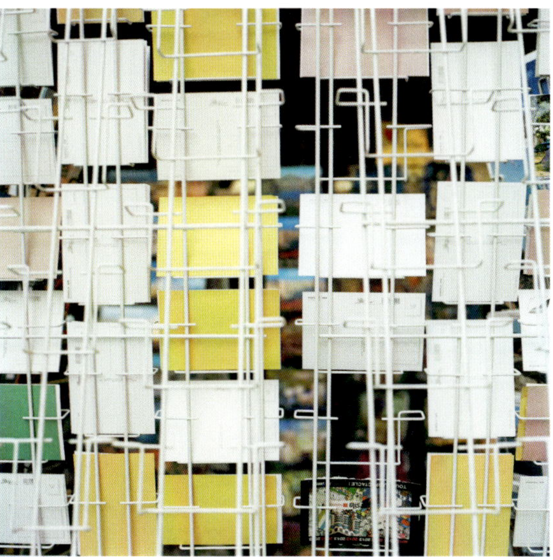

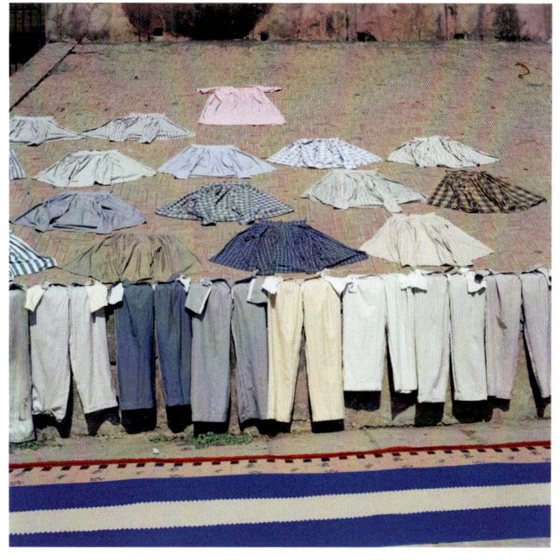

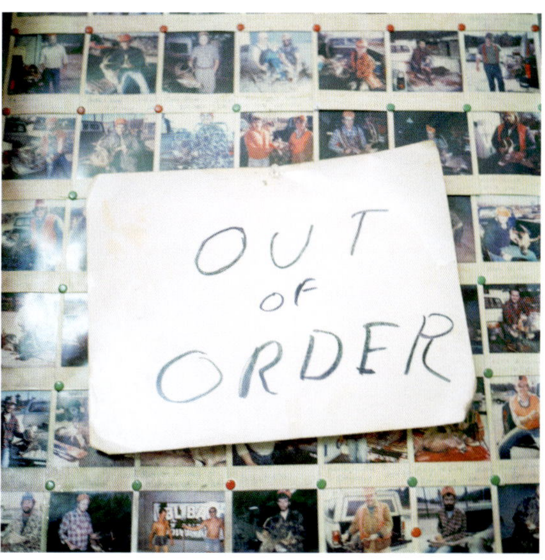
OUT
OF
ORDER

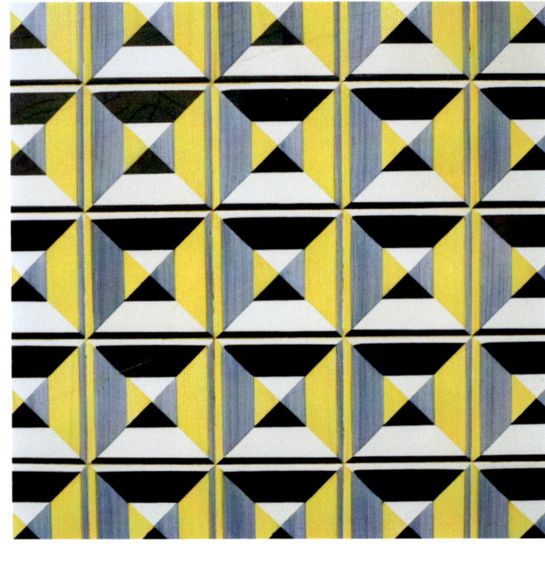
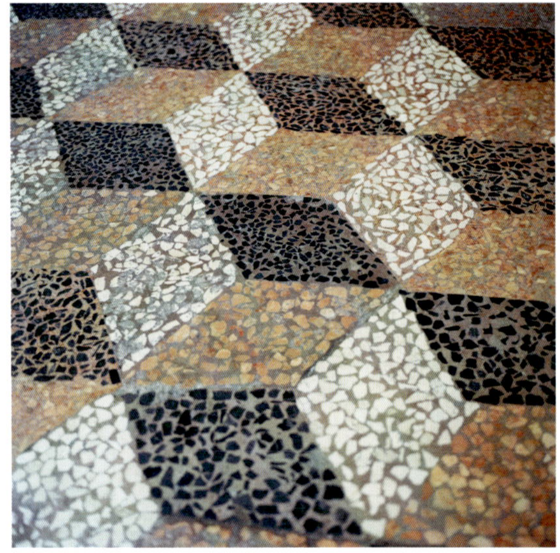
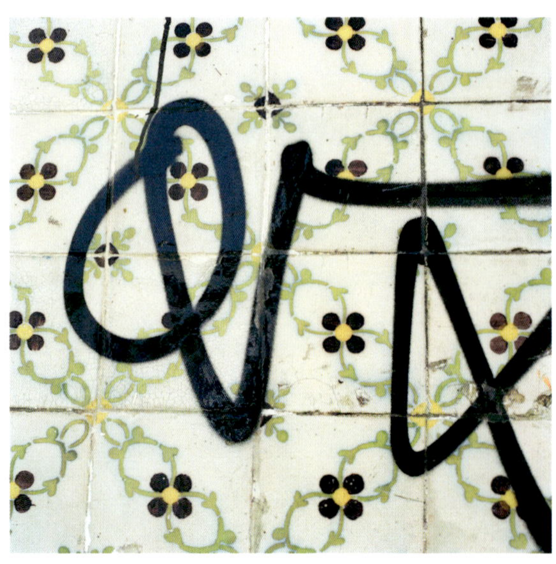
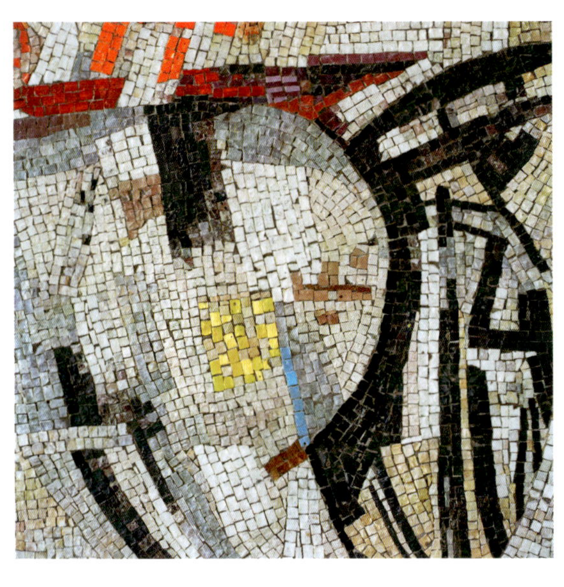
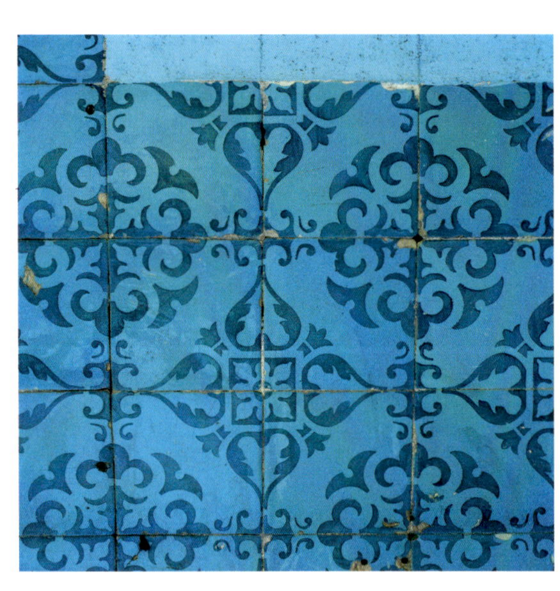
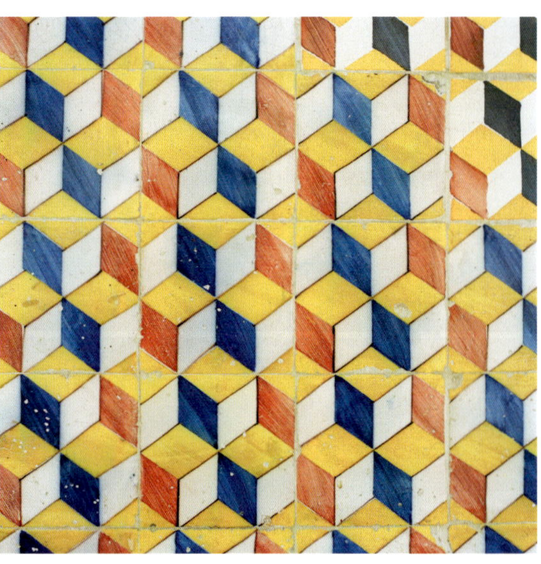
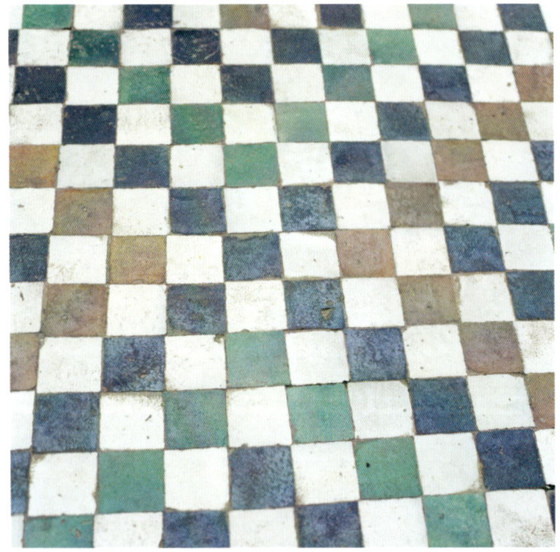
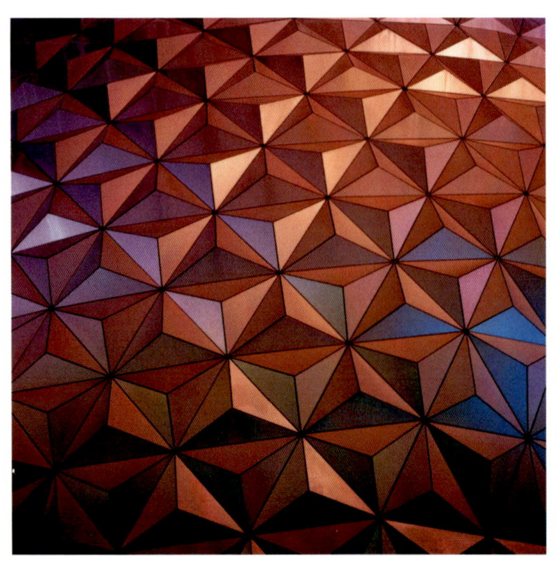
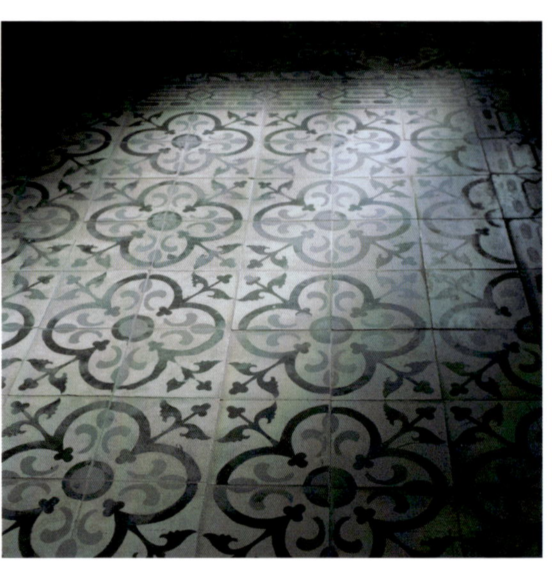

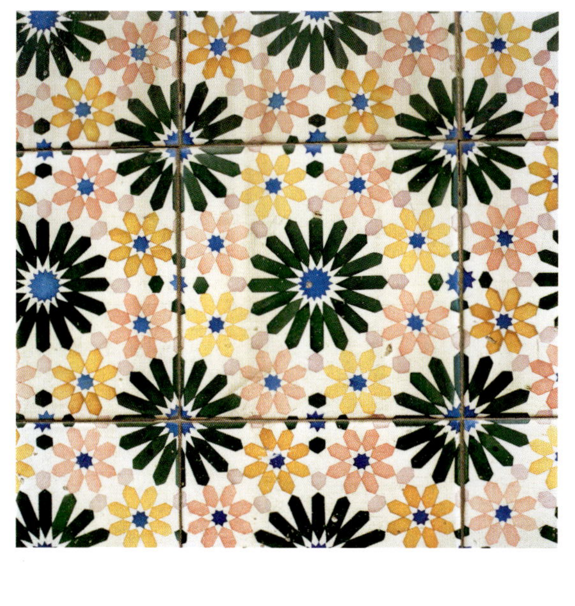
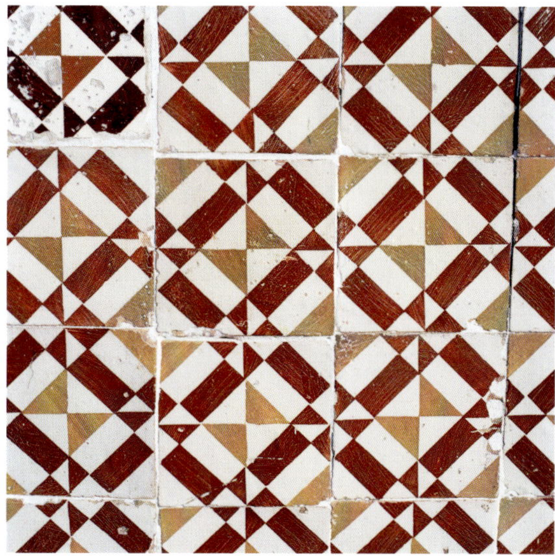
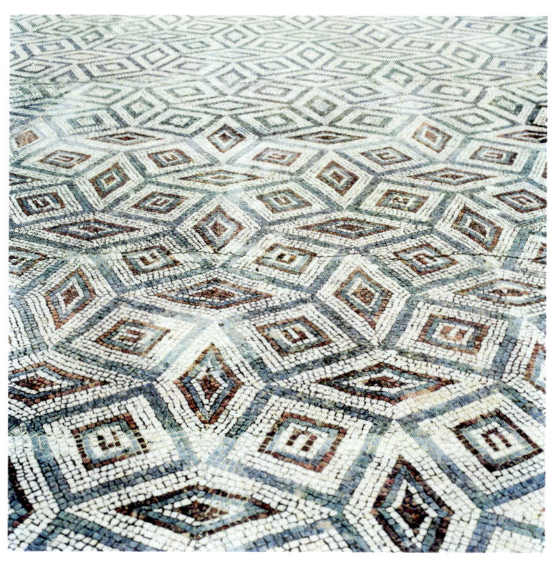
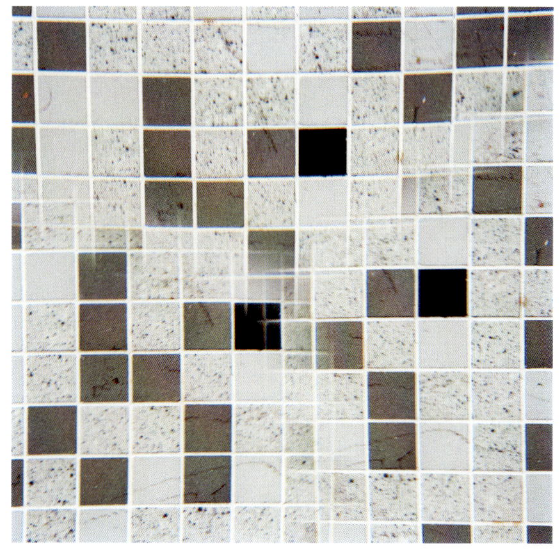
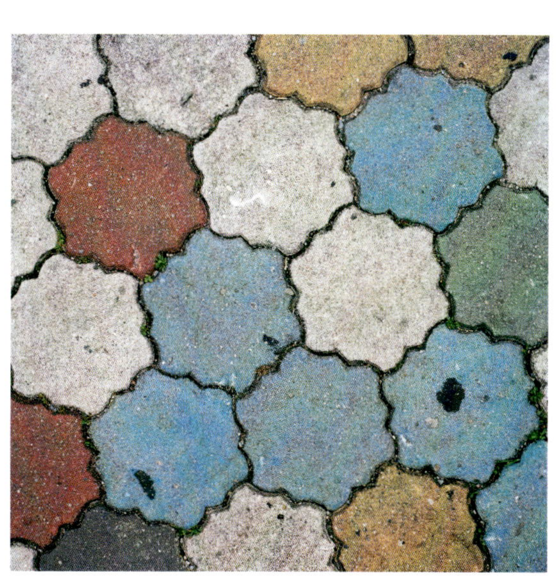
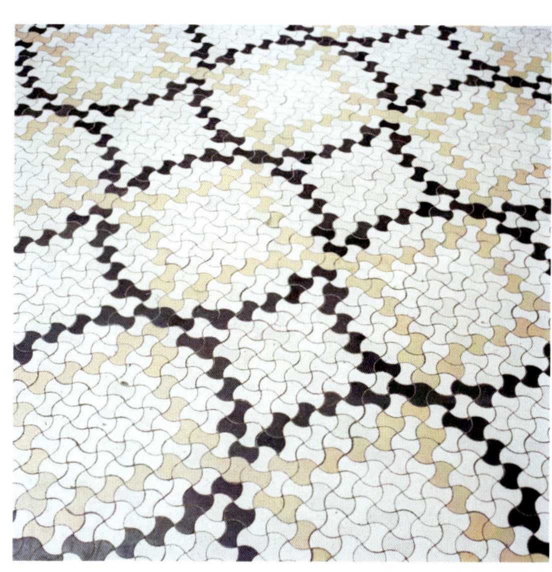
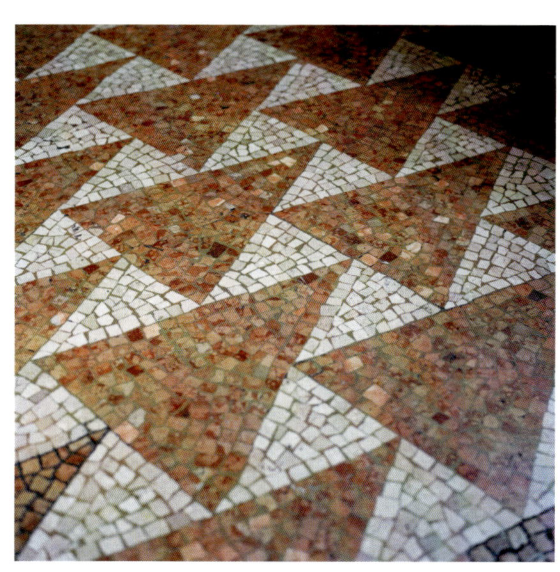
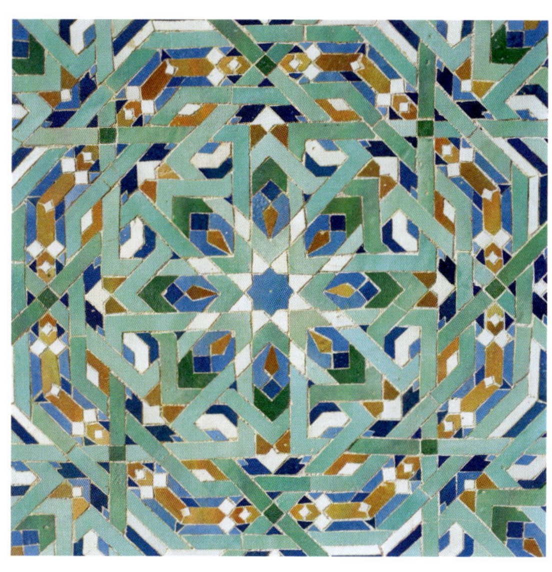
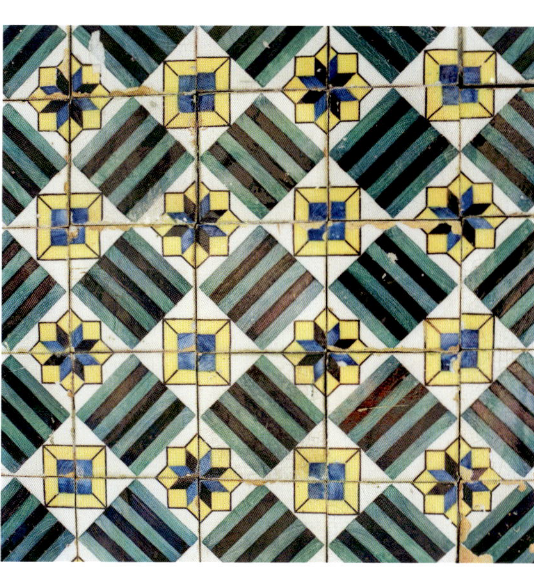

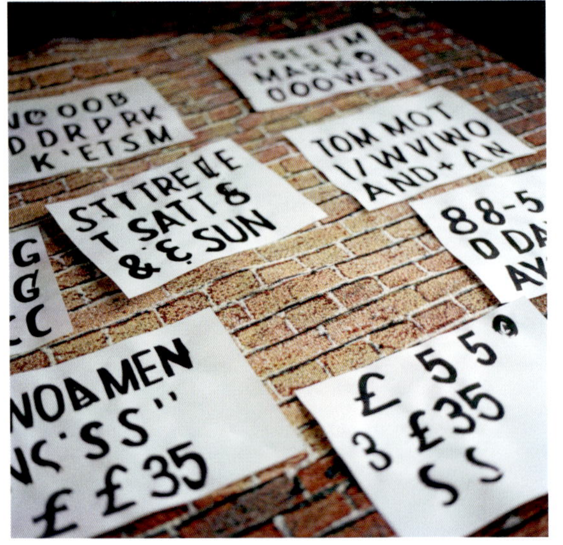
TOM MOT
£ £35
3 £35
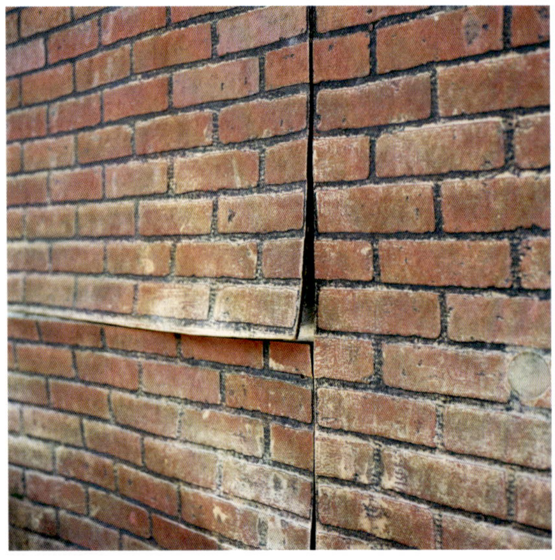
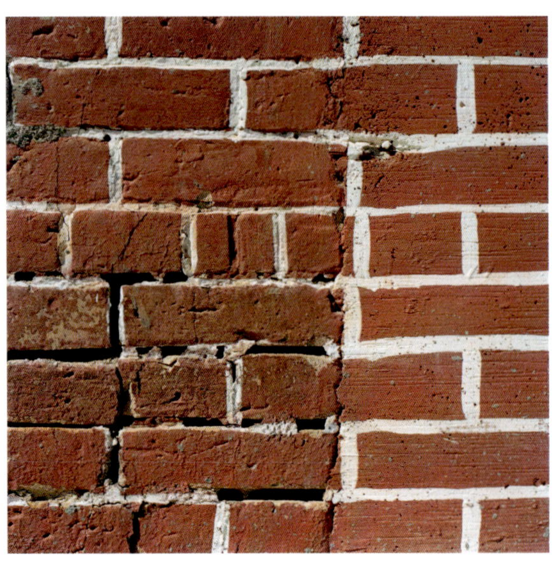
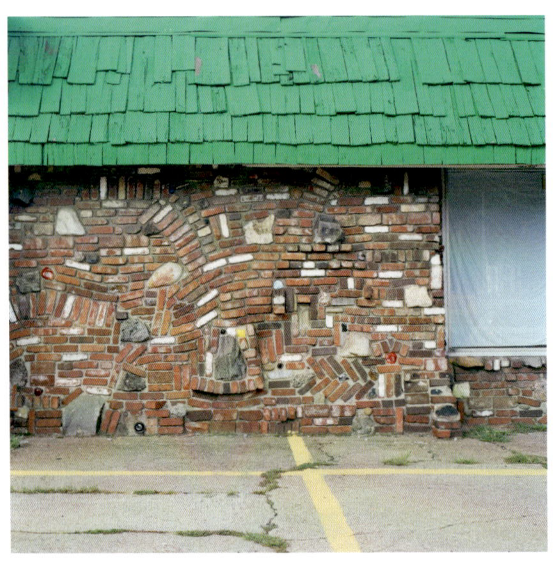
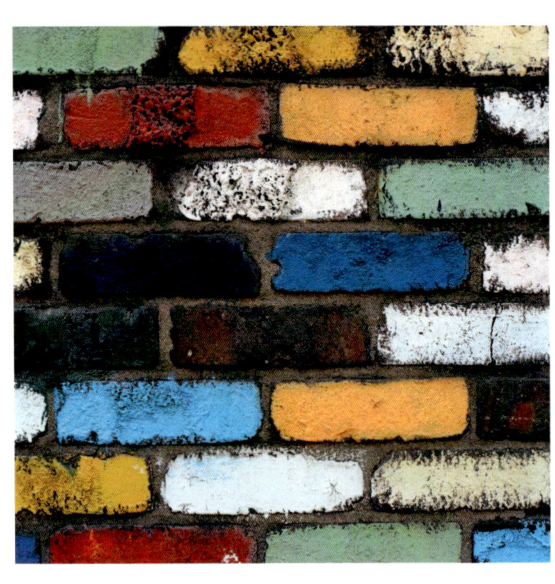
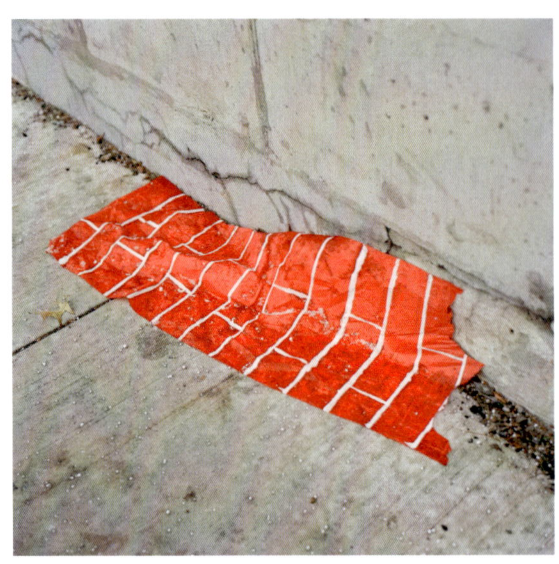
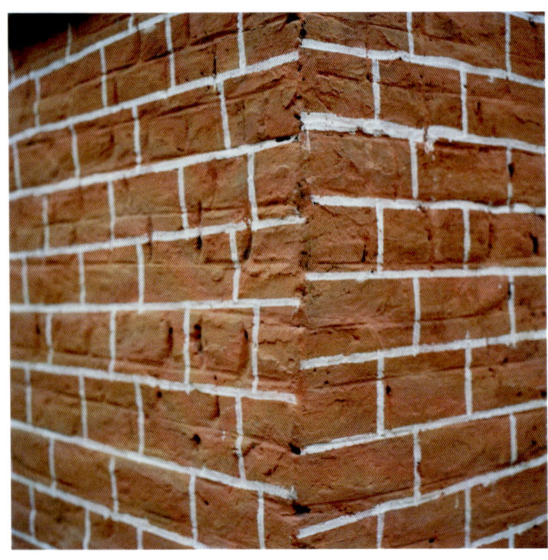
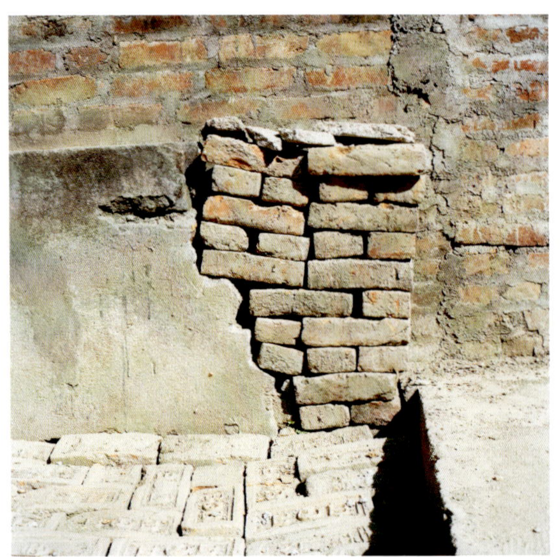
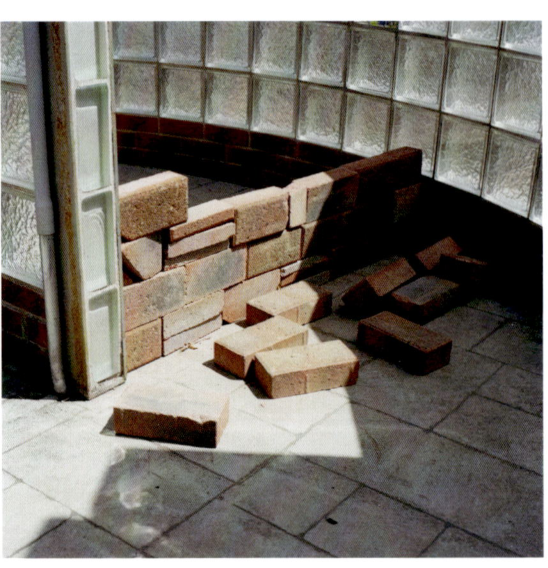

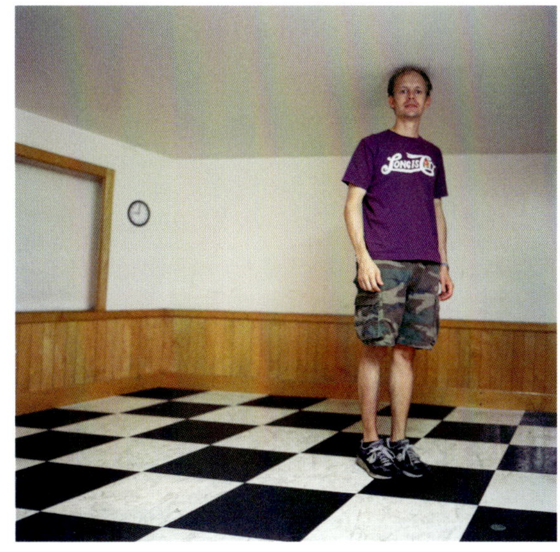

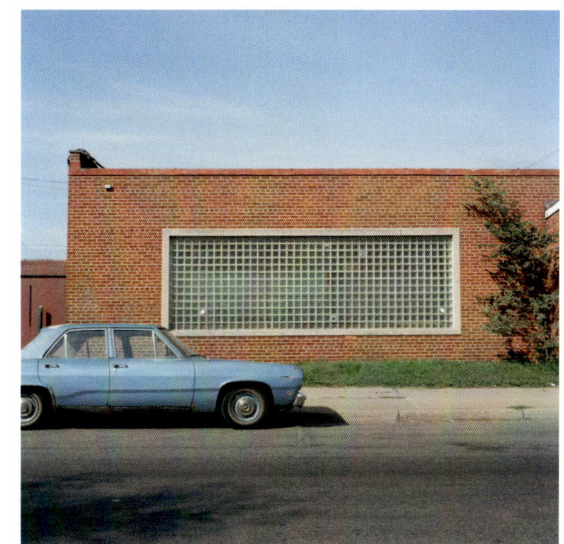

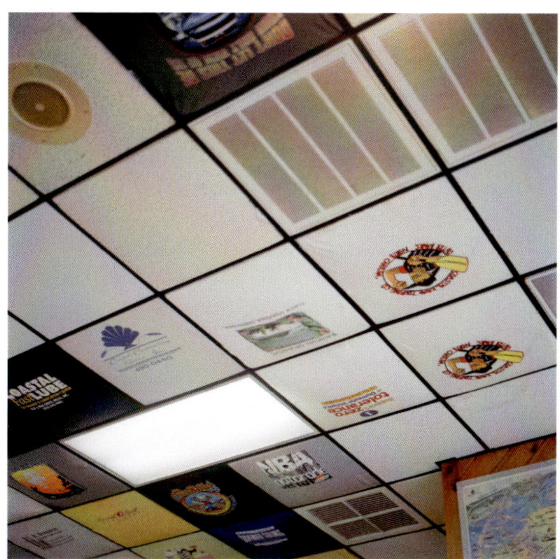

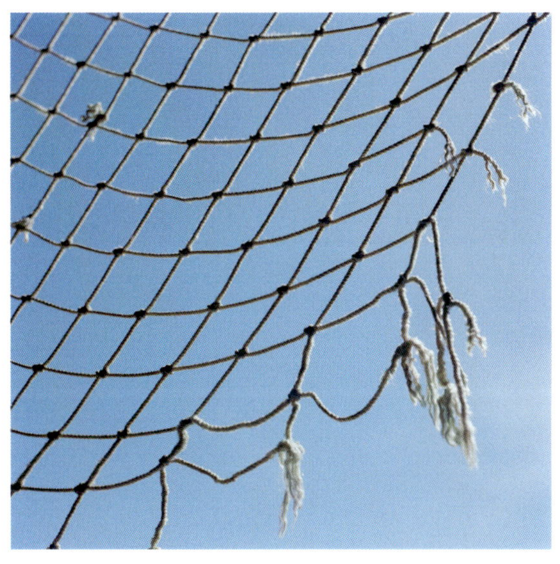

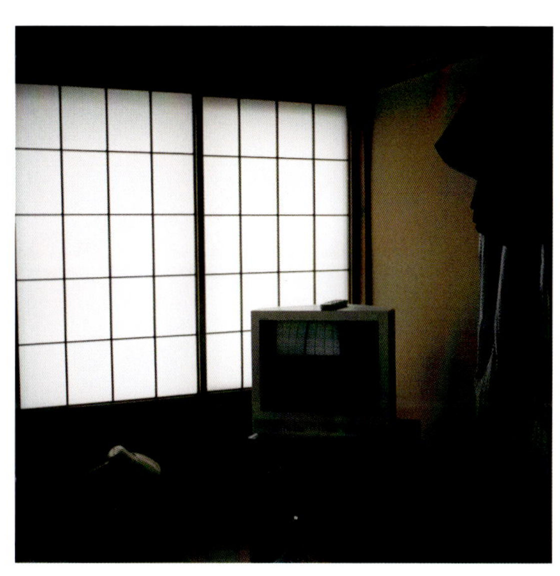

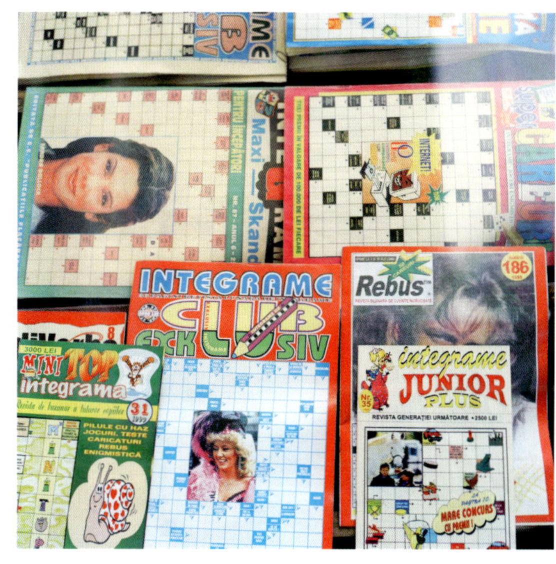
INTEGRAME
Rebus
186
integrame
JUNIOR
PLUS
MINI TOP
integrama

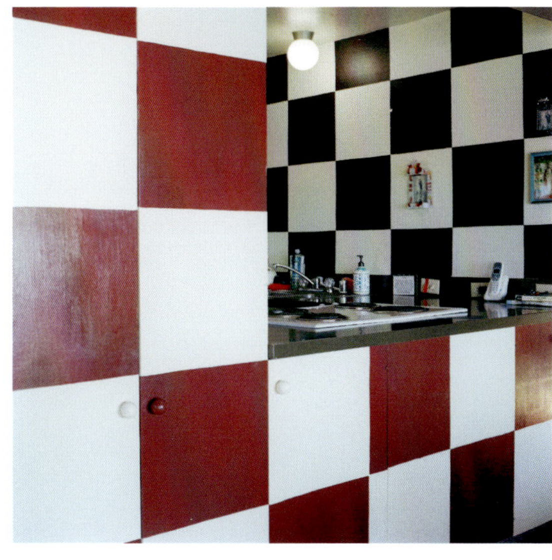

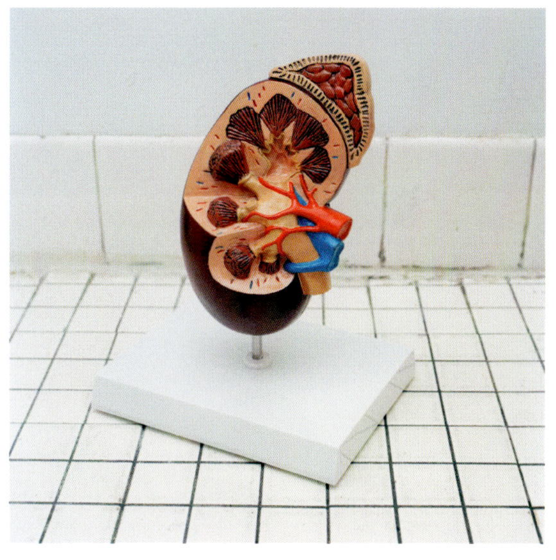

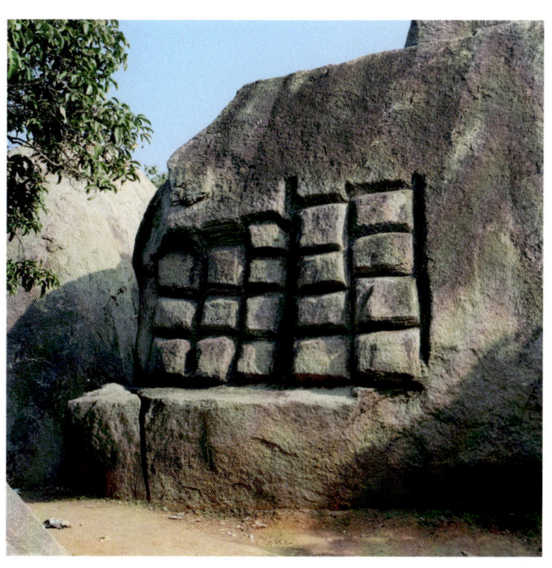

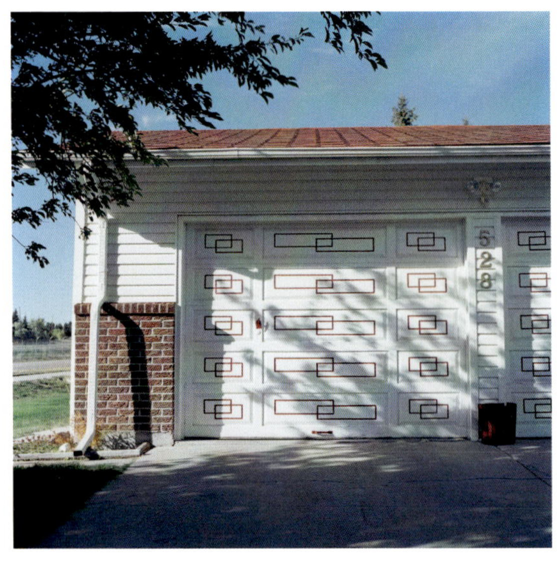
528

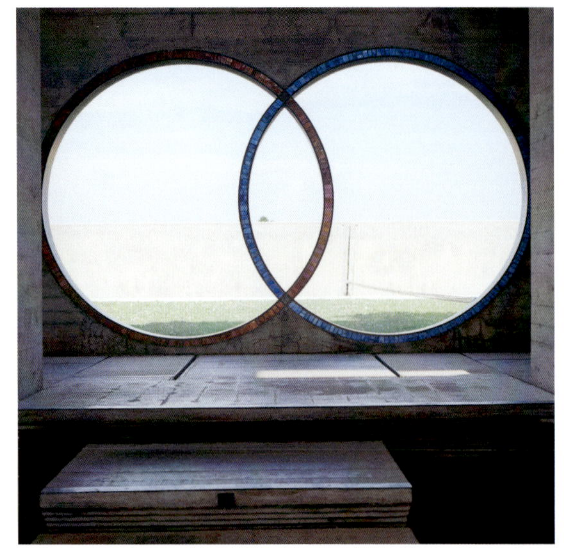

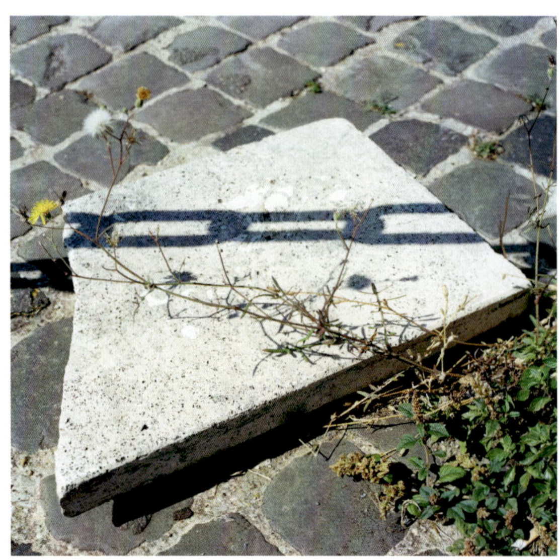

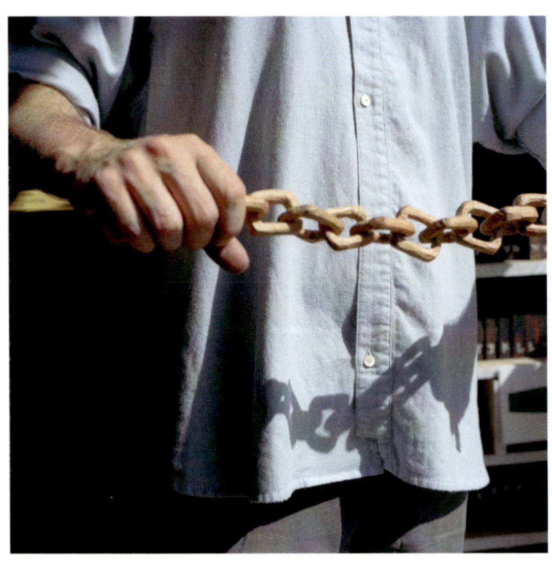

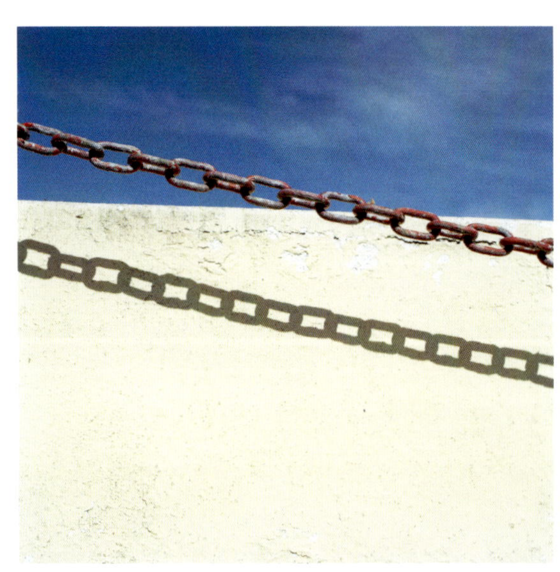

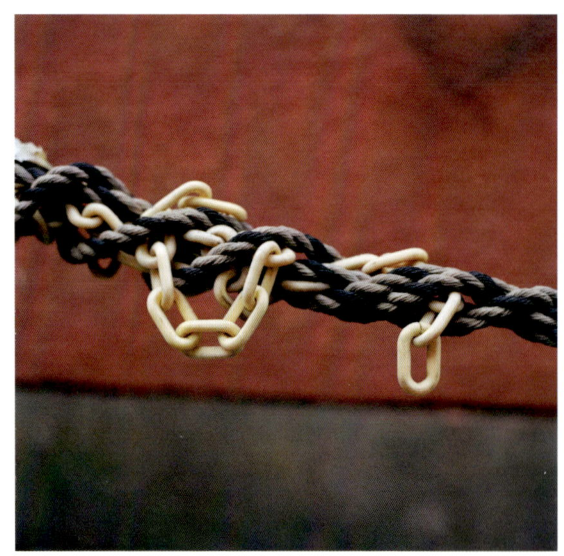

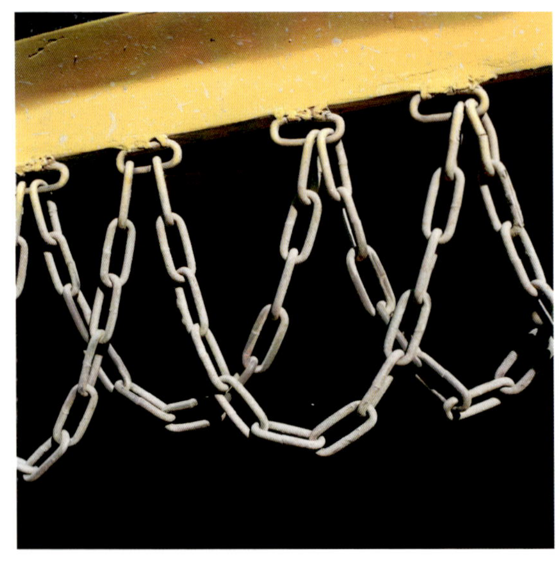

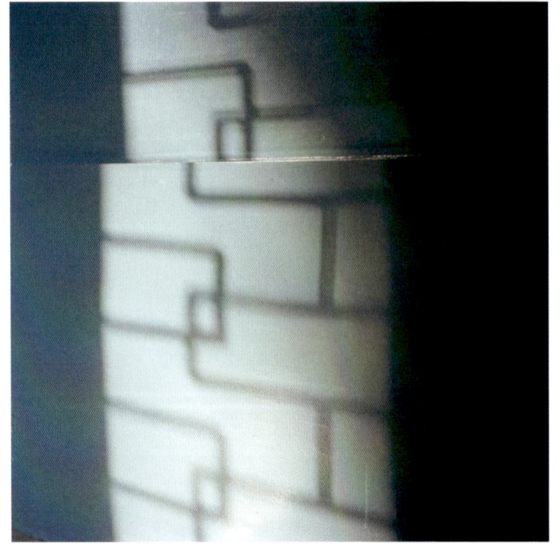

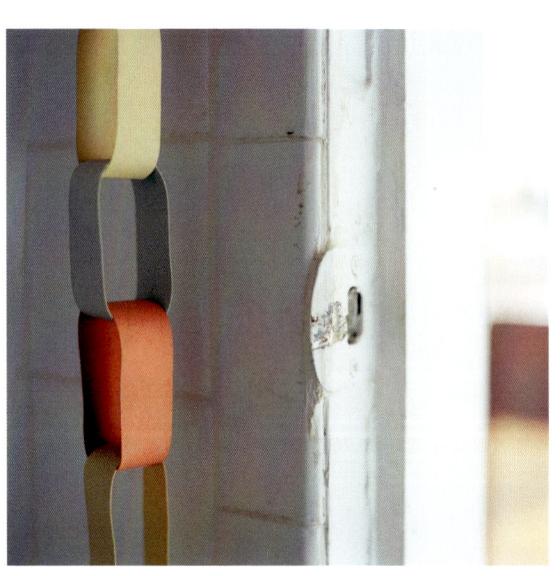

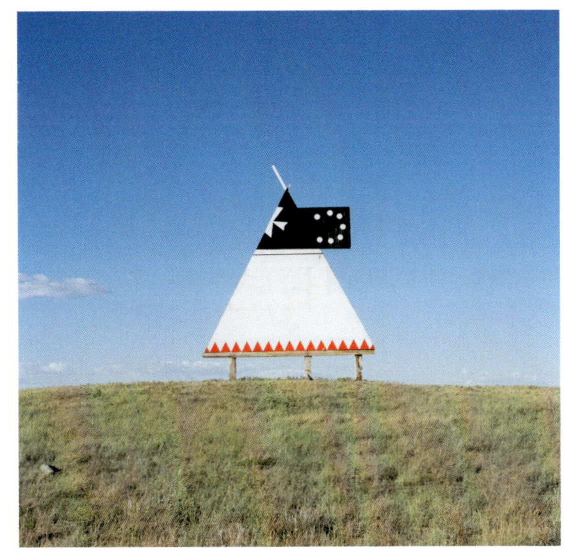
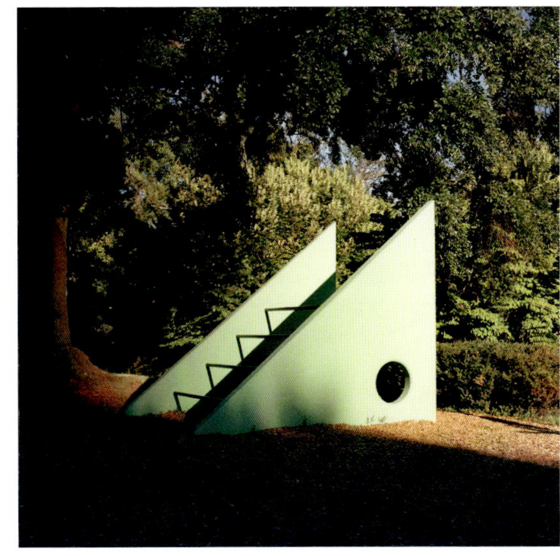
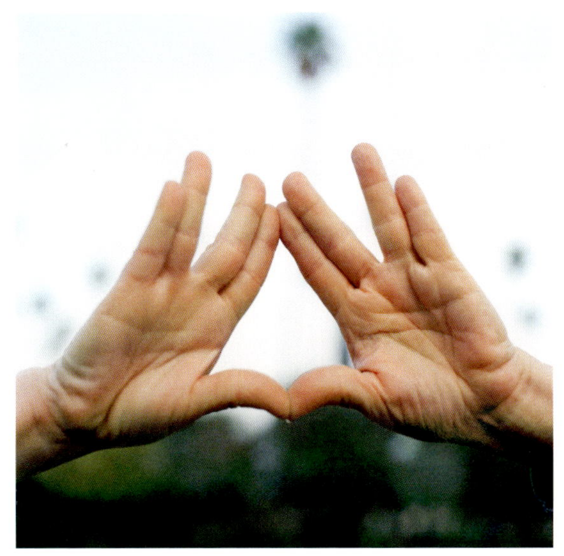
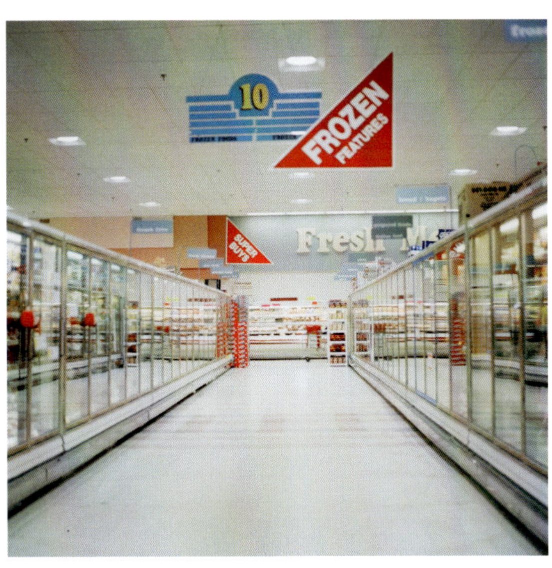
10
FROZEN FEATURES
SUPER BUYS
Fresh
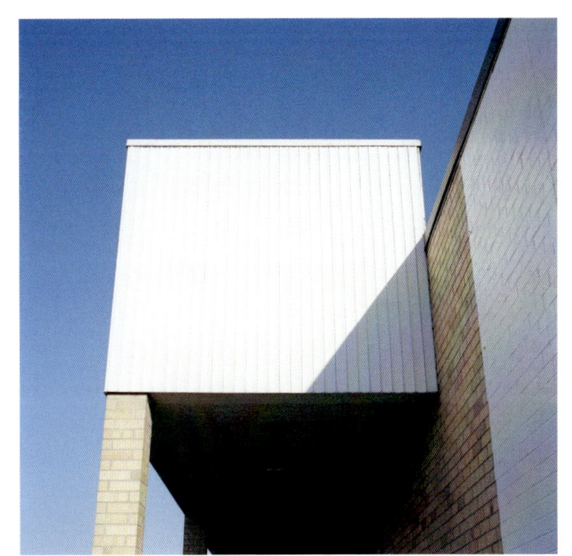
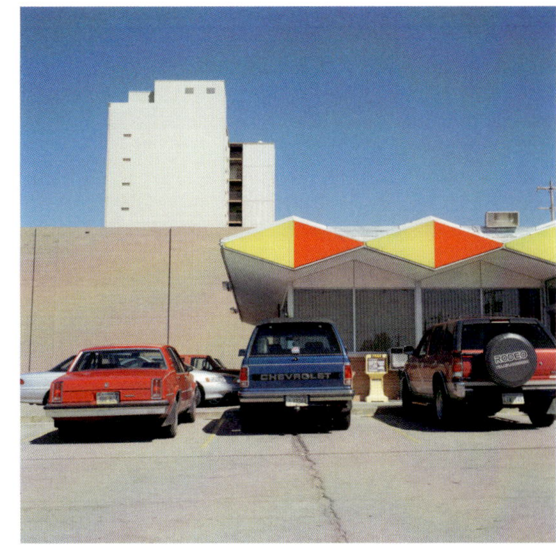
CHEVROLET
RODEO
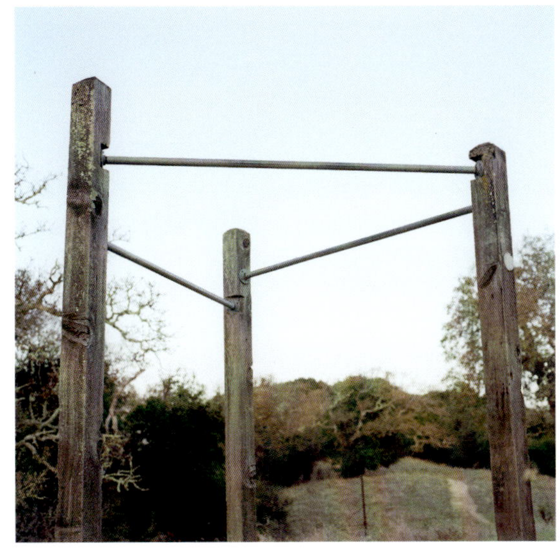
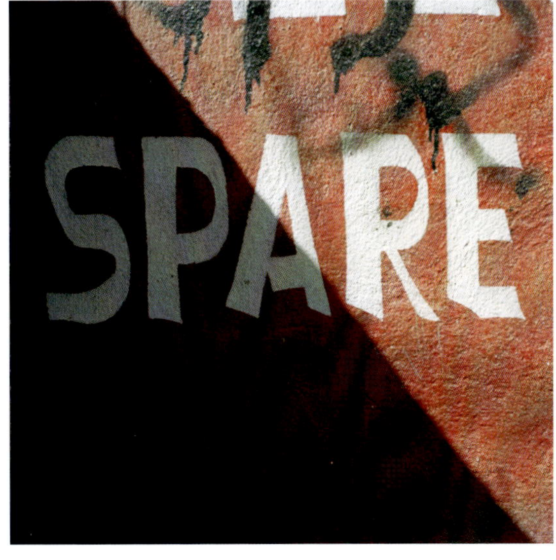
SPARE
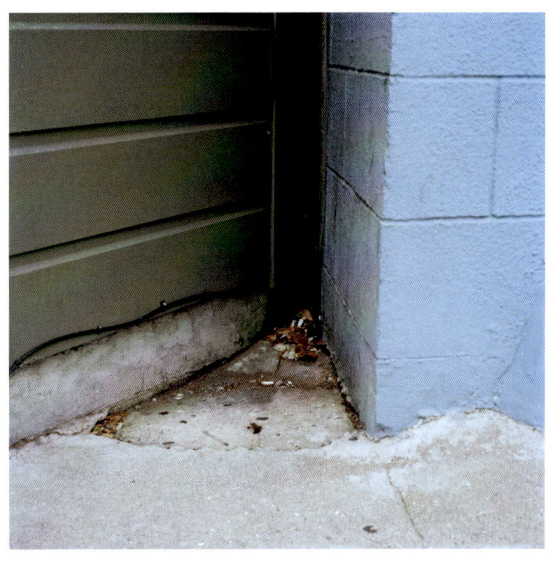

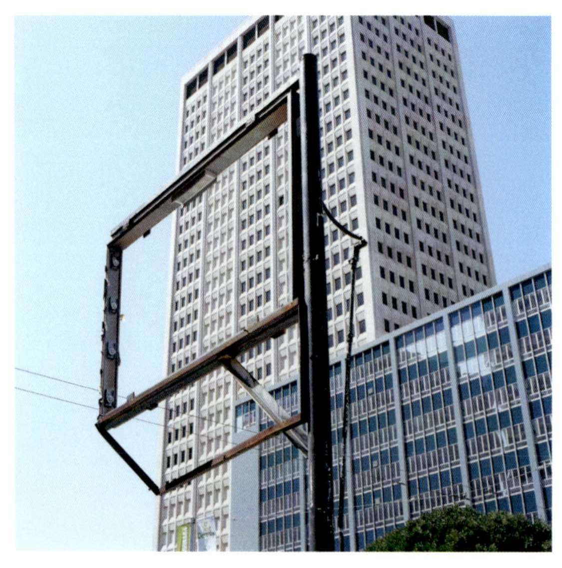
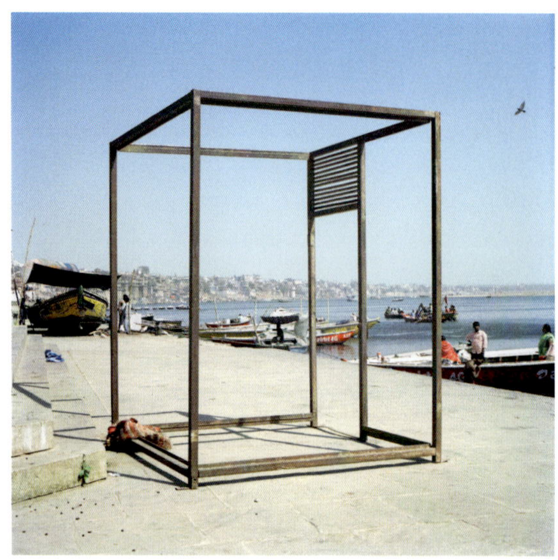
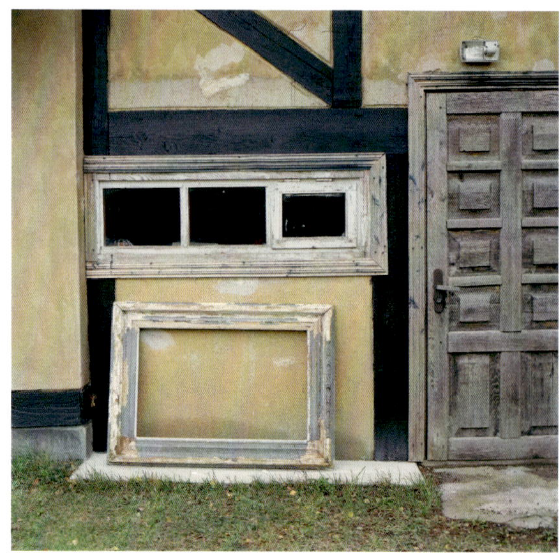
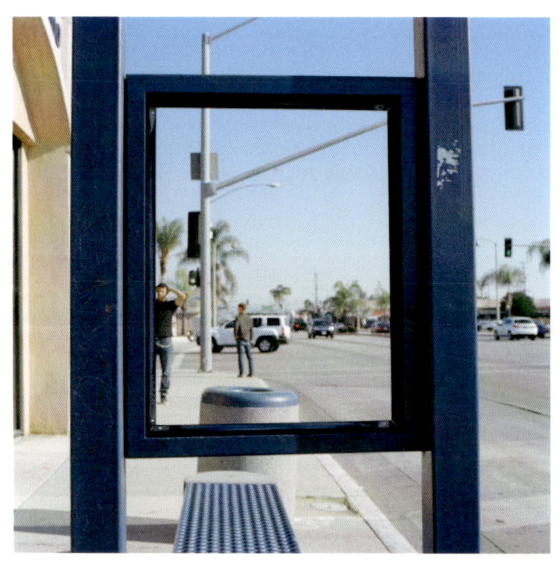
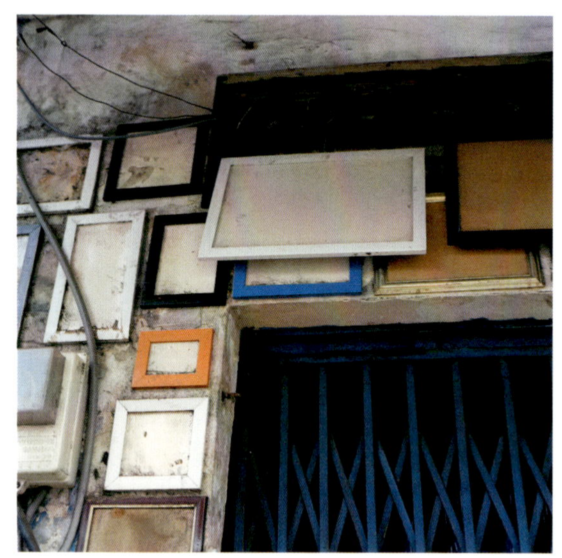
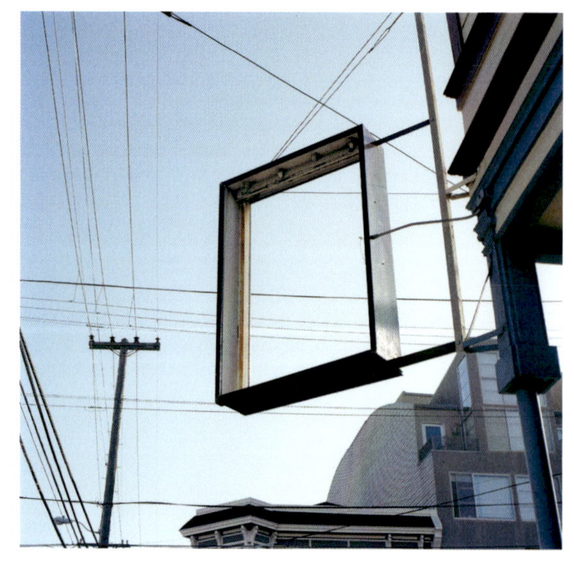
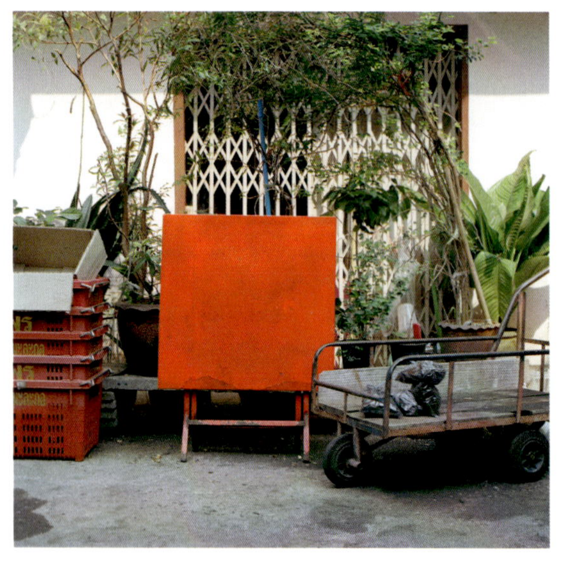
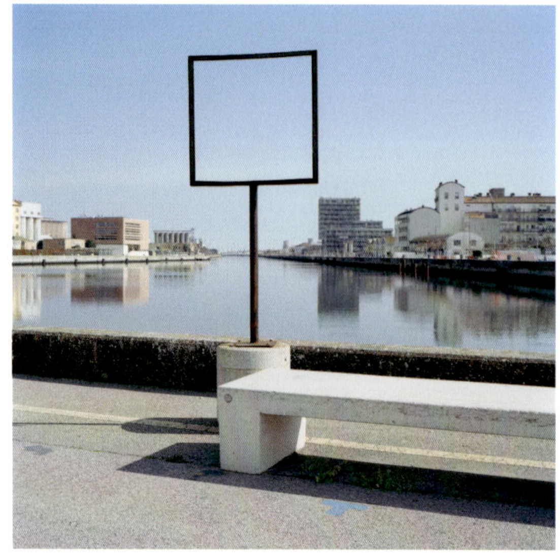
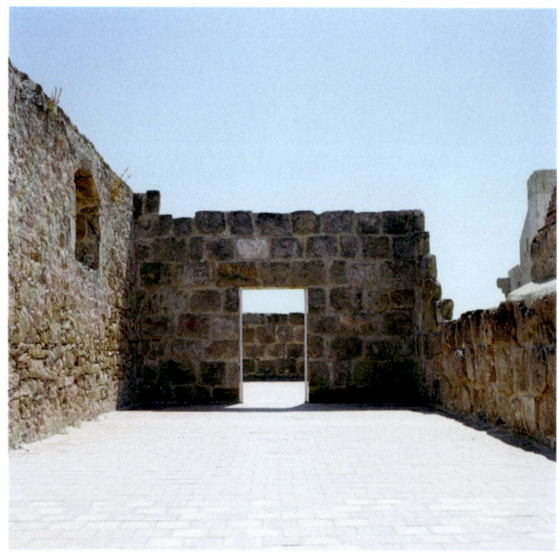

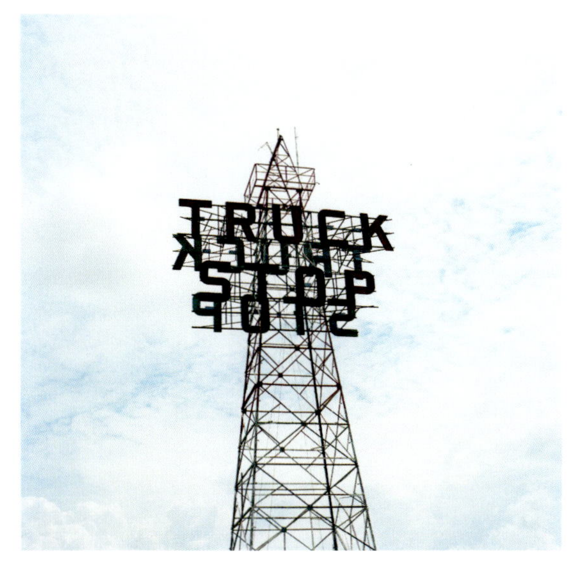
TRUCK

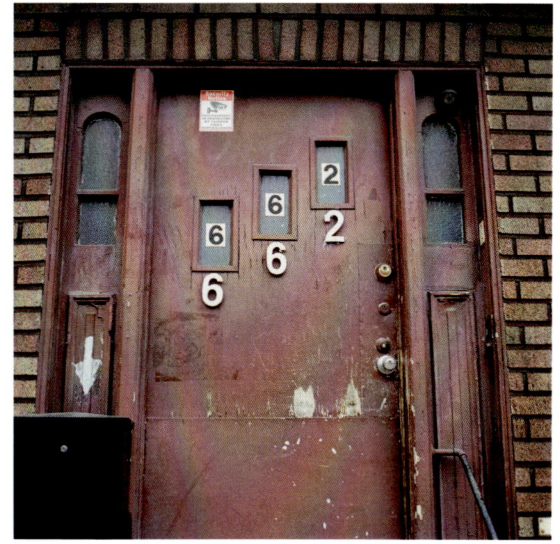
662
662

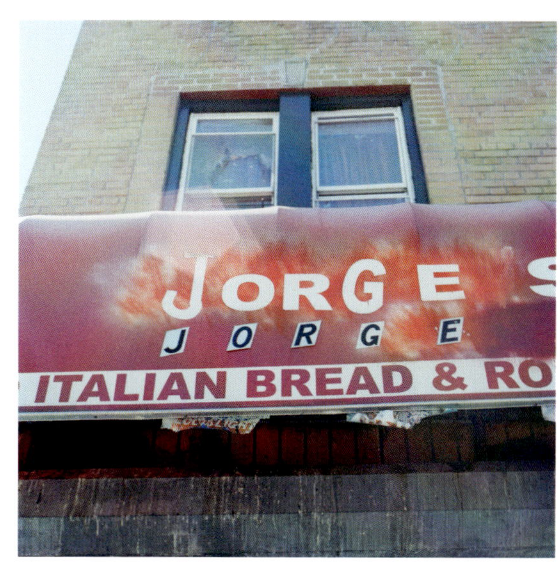
JORGE S
JORGE
ITALIAN BREAD & RO

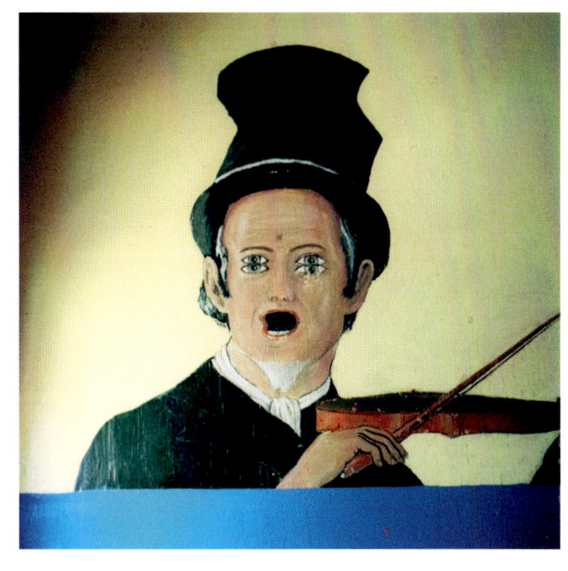

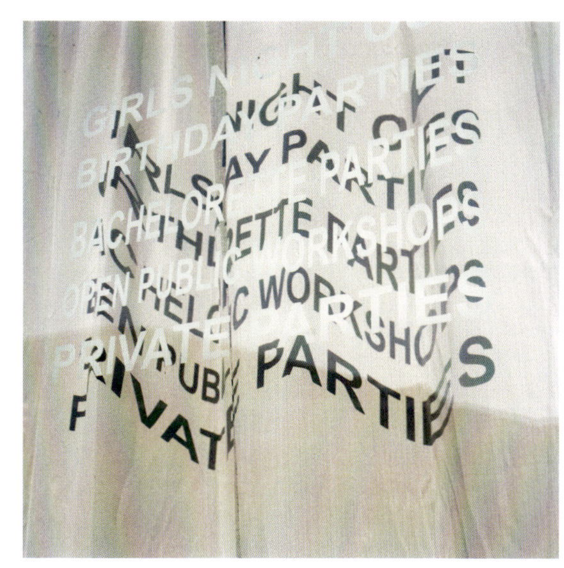
GIRLS NIGHT
PARTIES

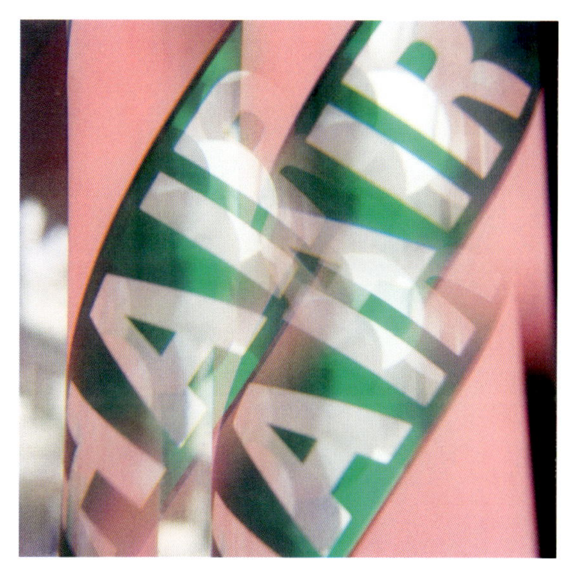

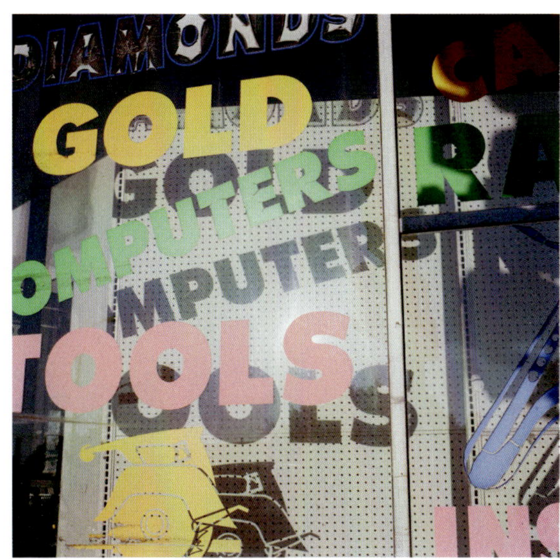
DIAMONDS
GOLD
COMPUTERS
TOOLS

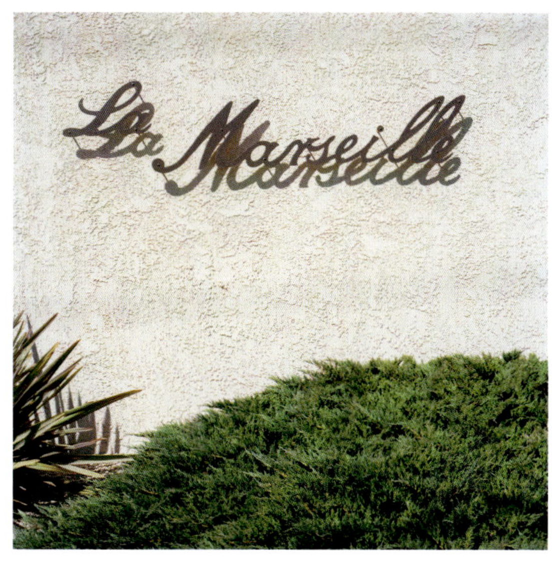
La Marseille

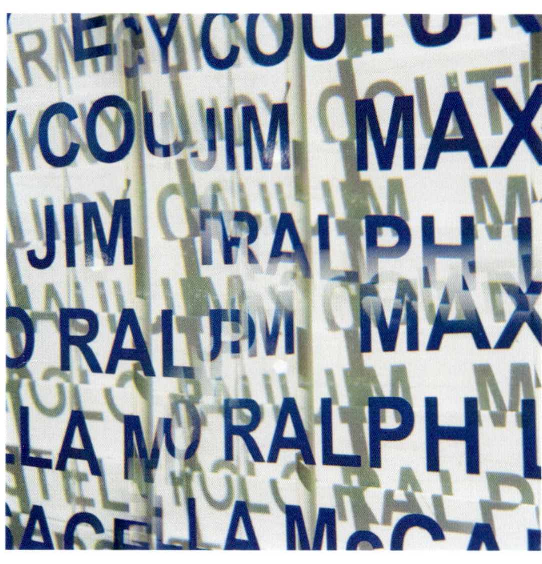
JIM
MAX
RALPH

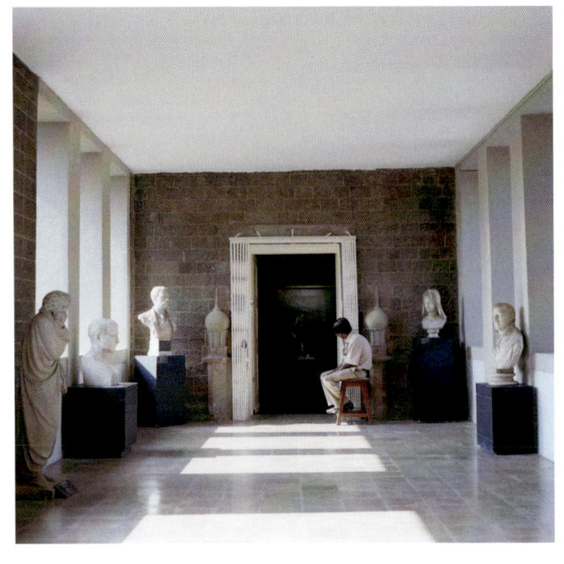
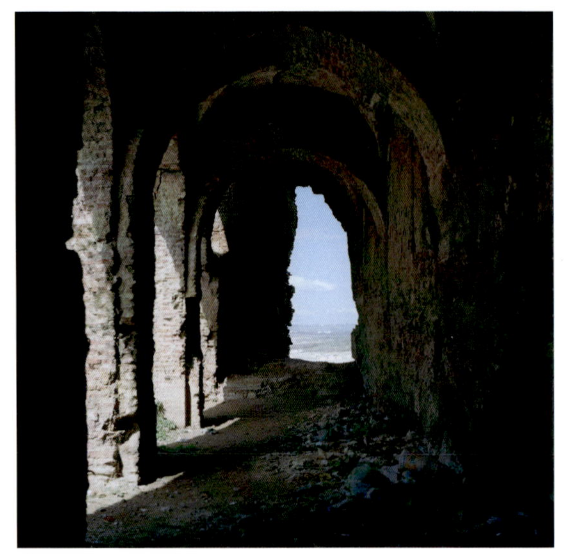
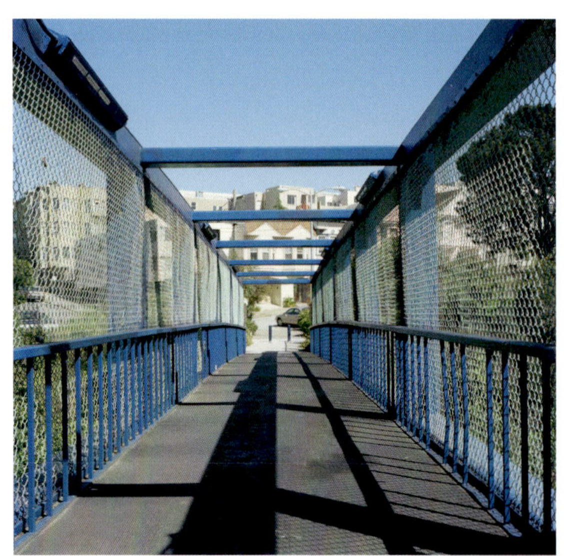
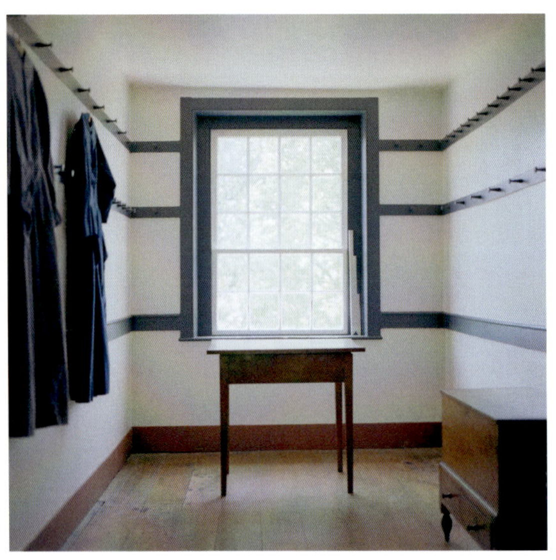
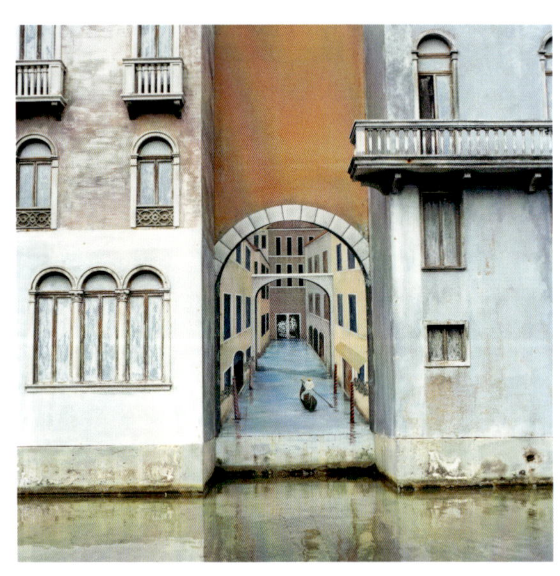
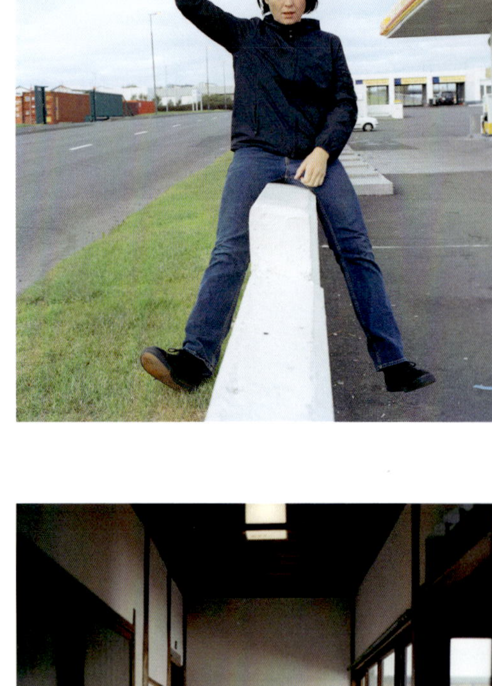
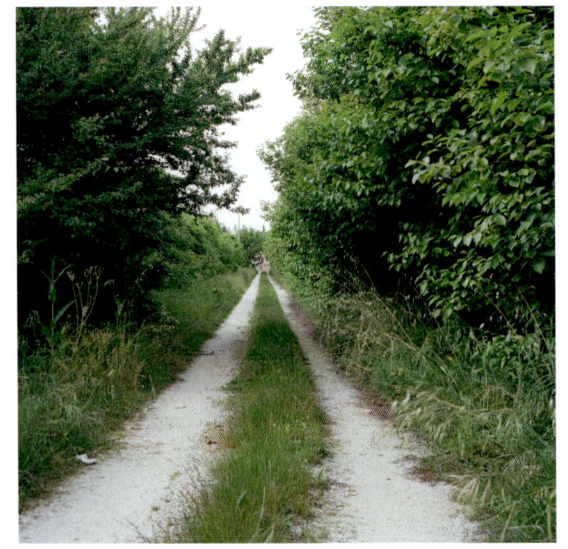
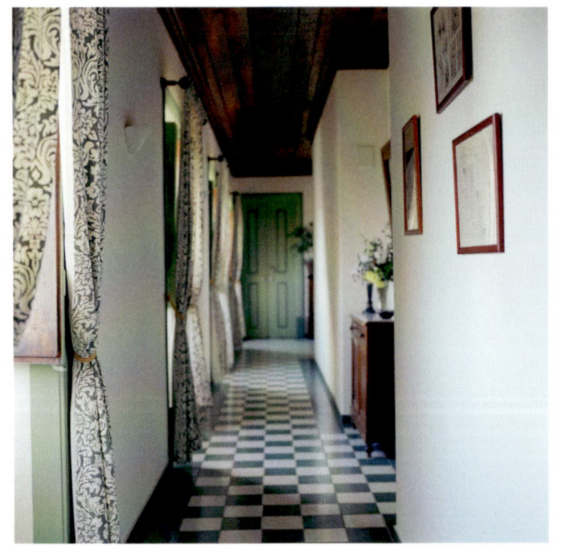
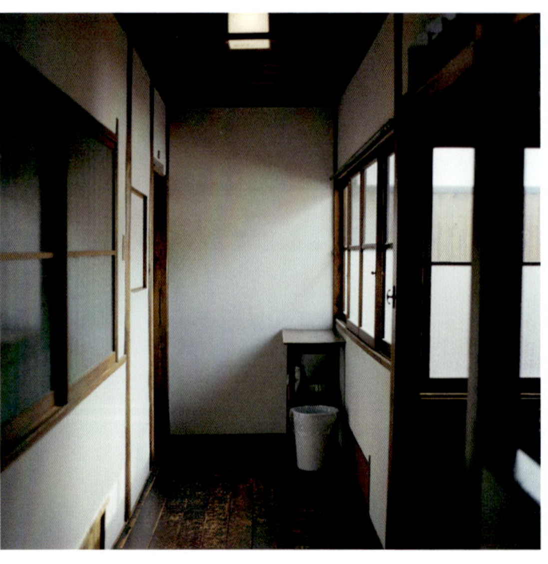

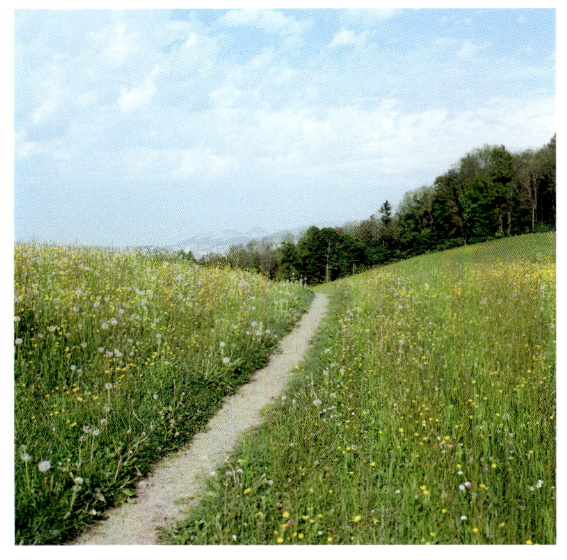
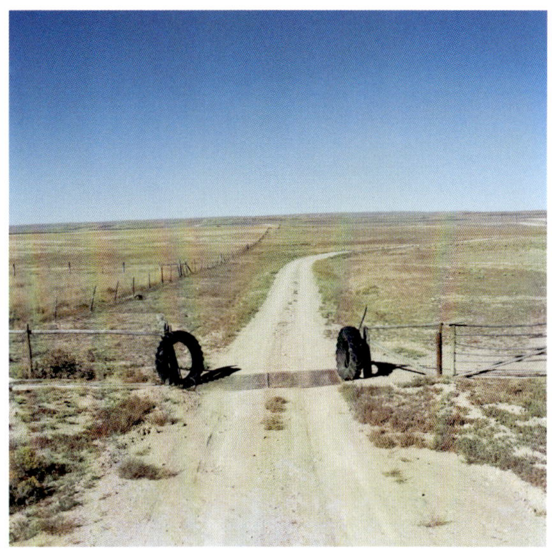
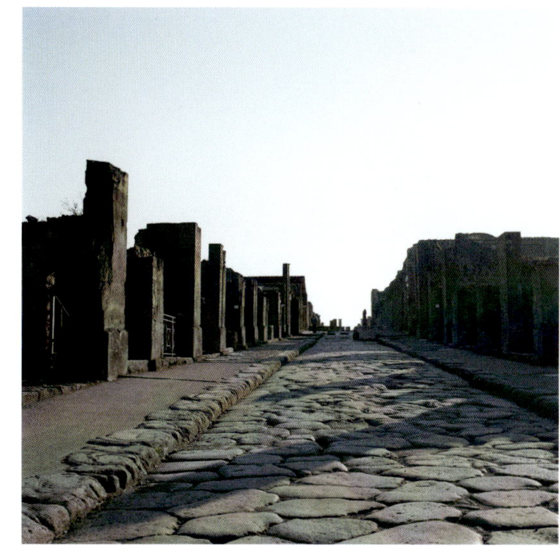
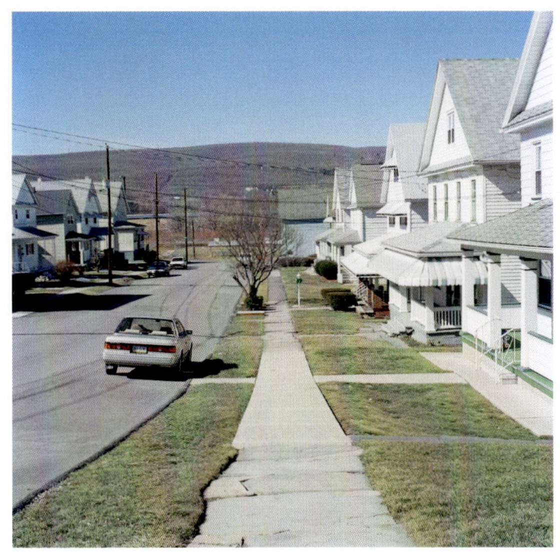
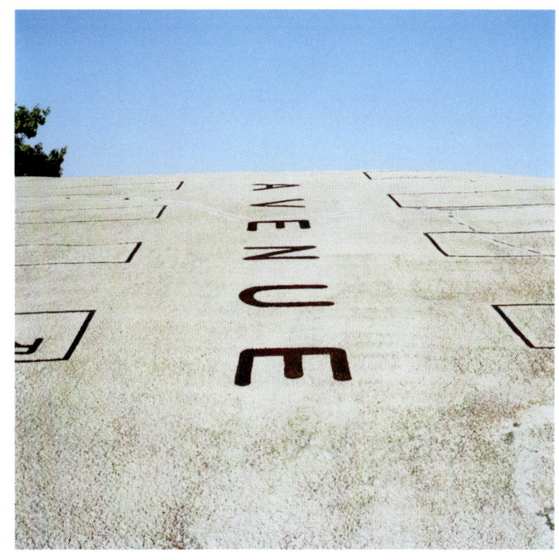
AVENUE
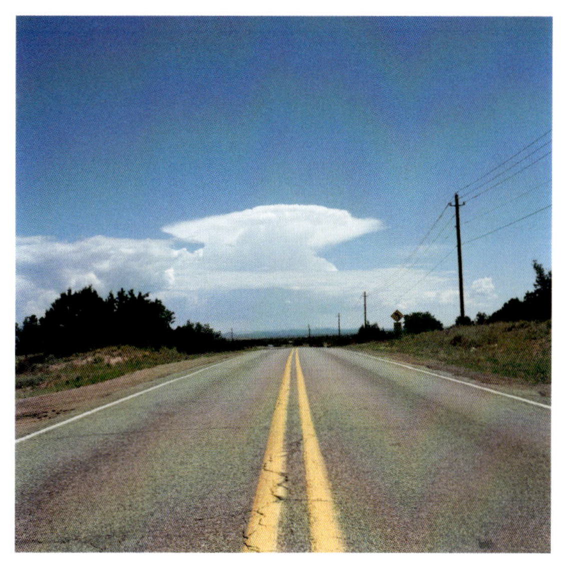
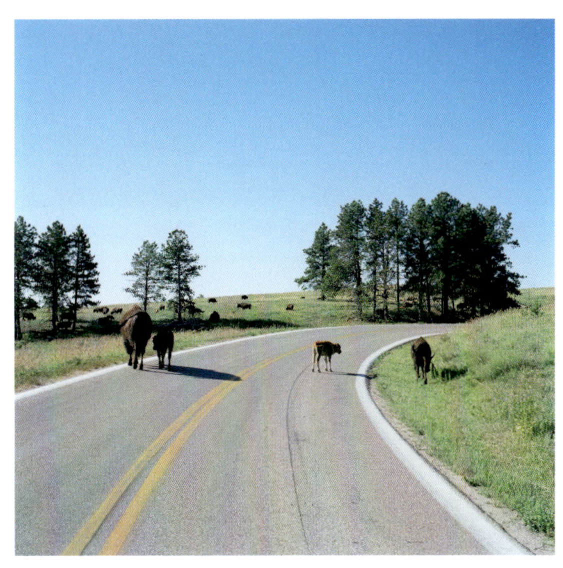
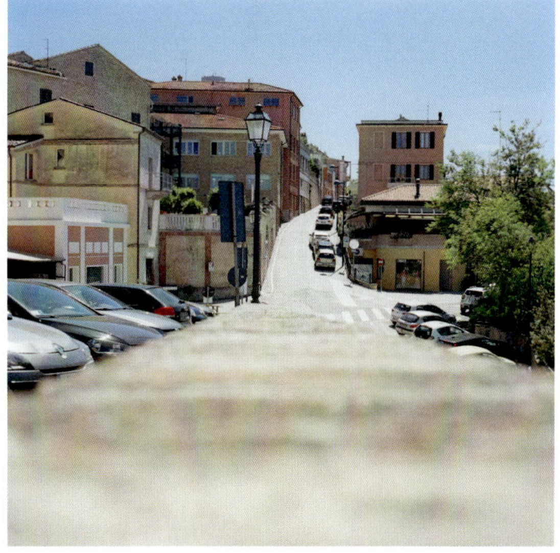
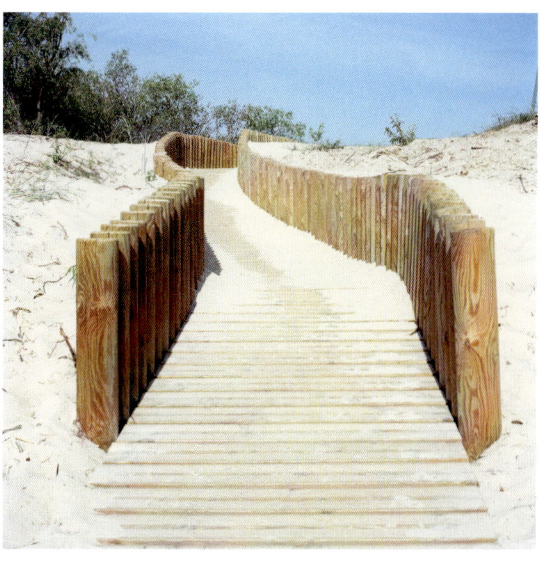

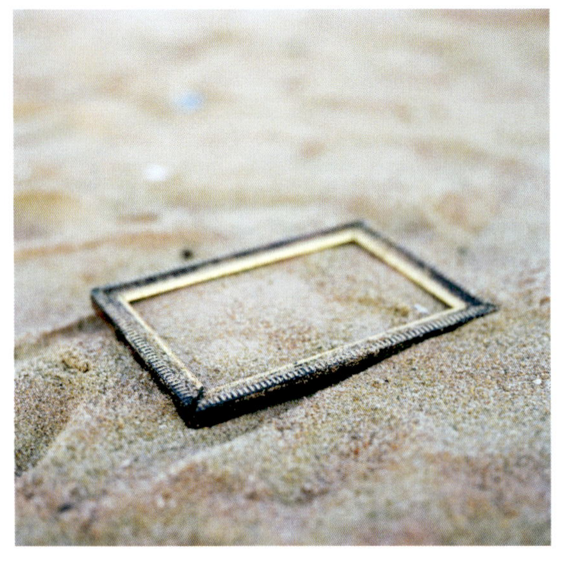
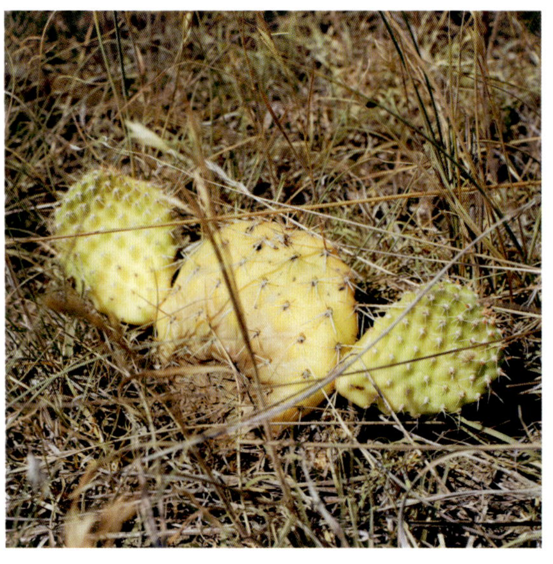
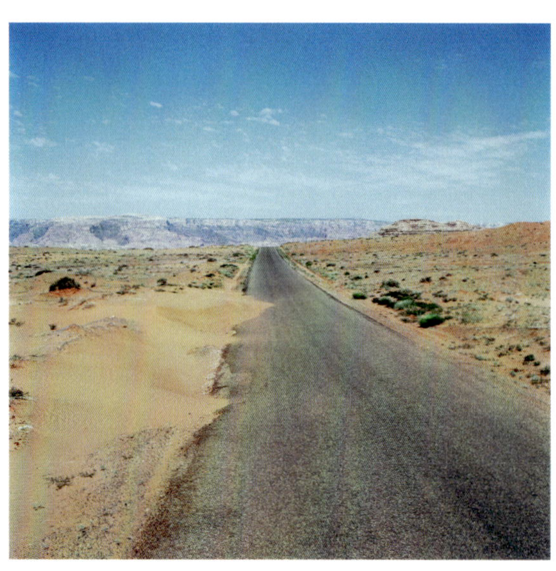
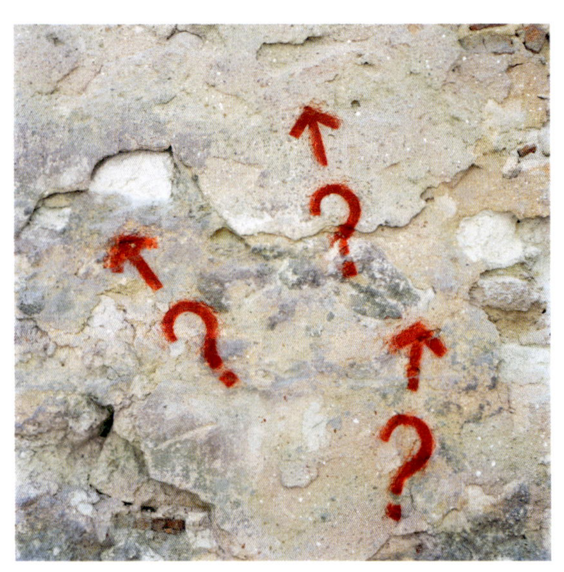
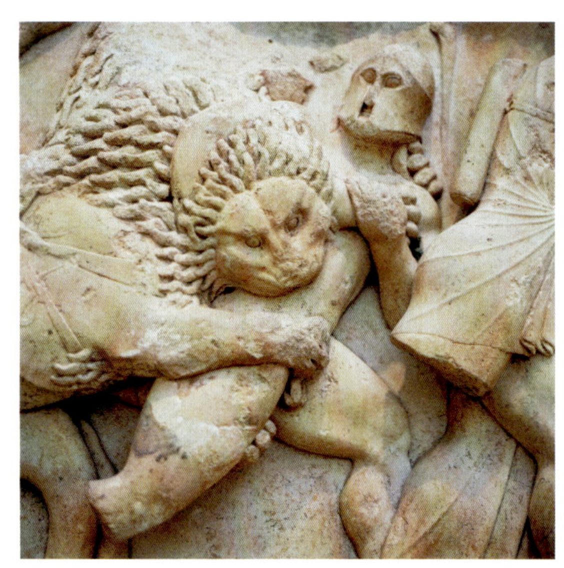
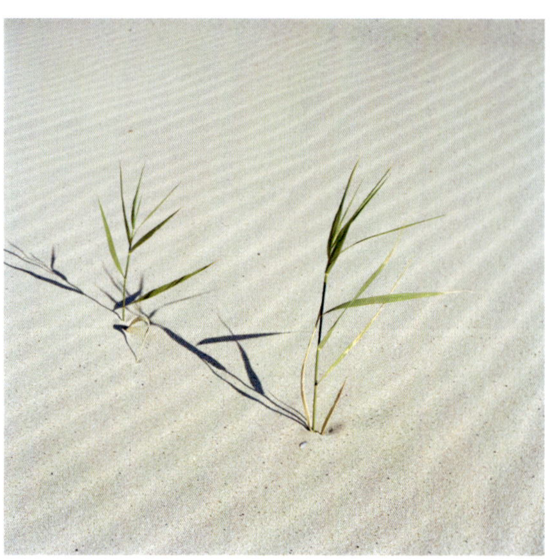
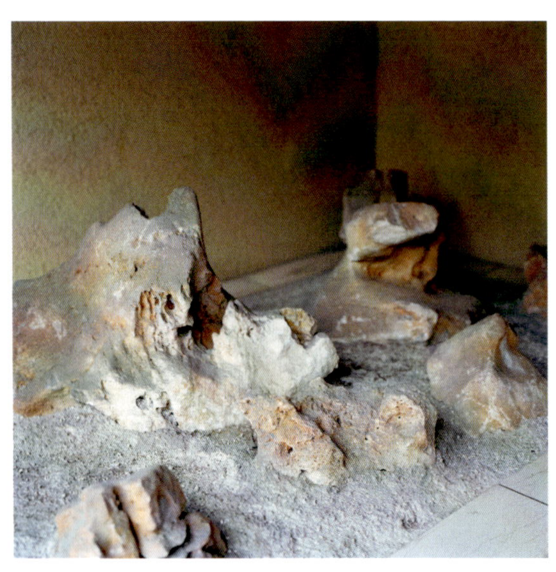
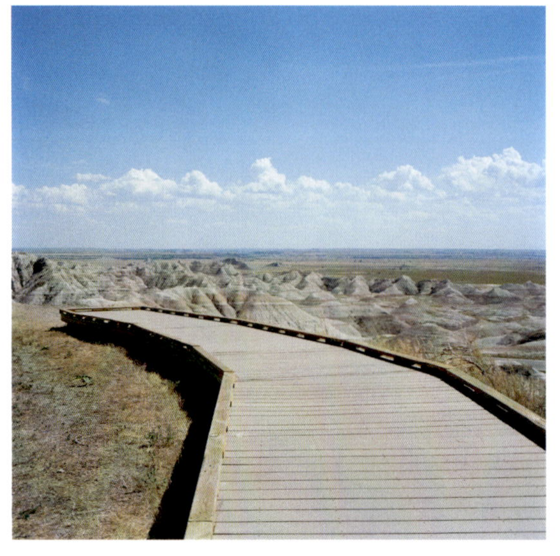
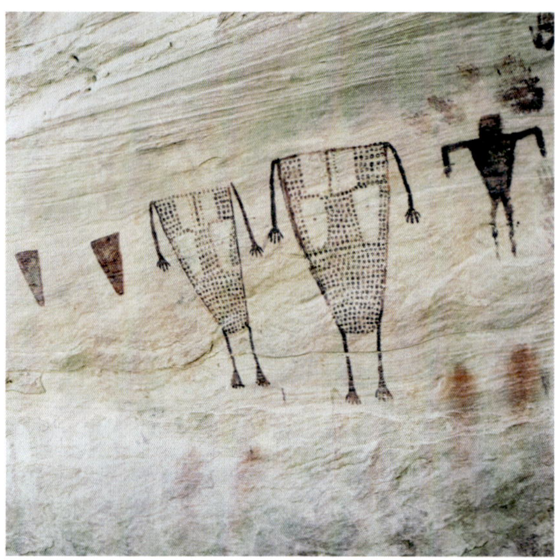

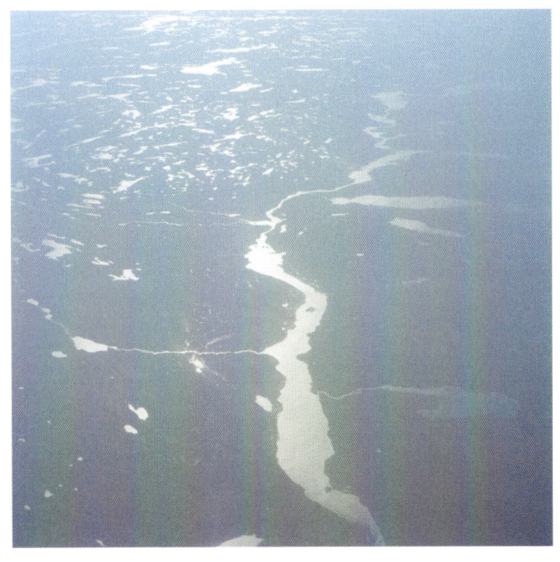
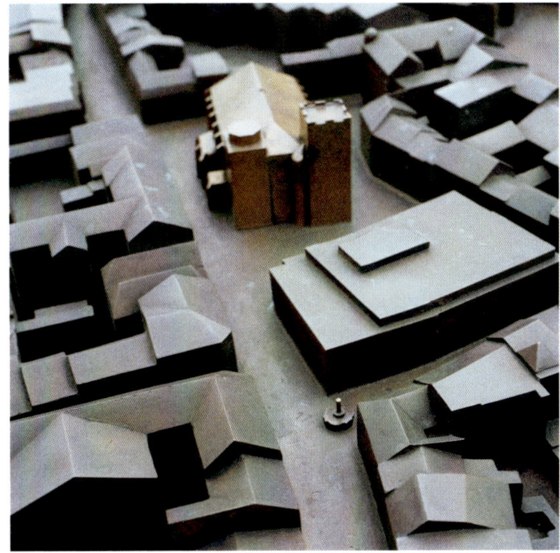
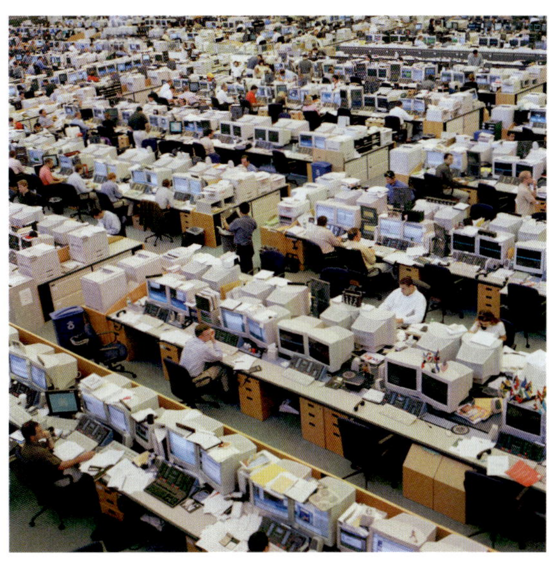
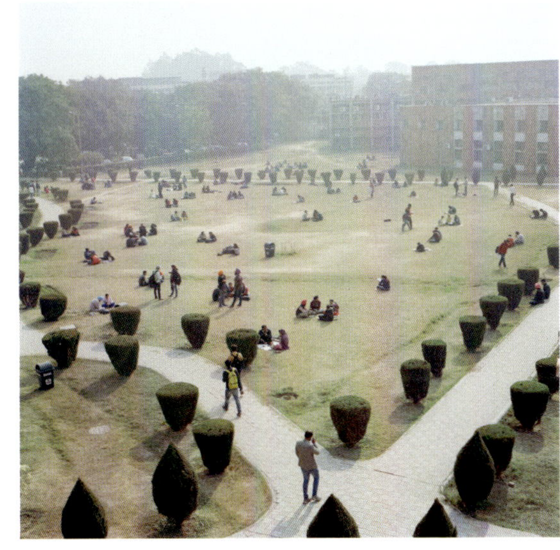
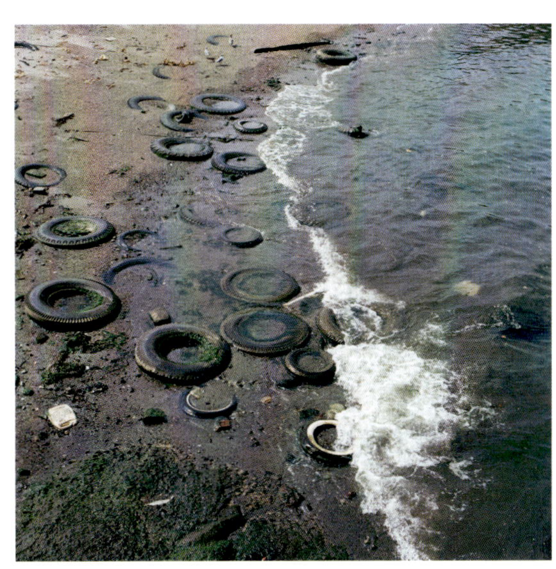
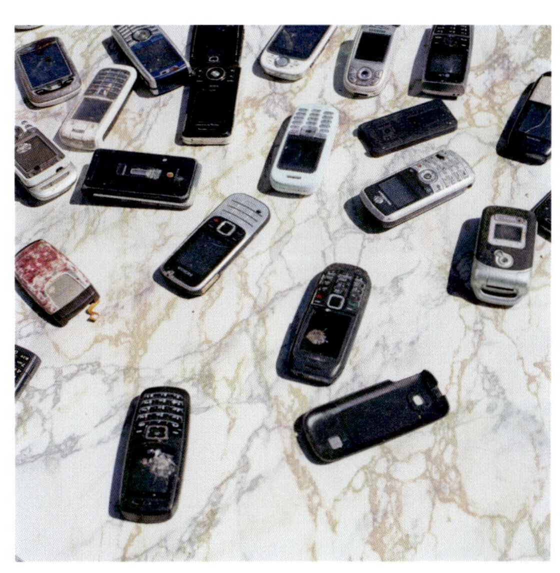
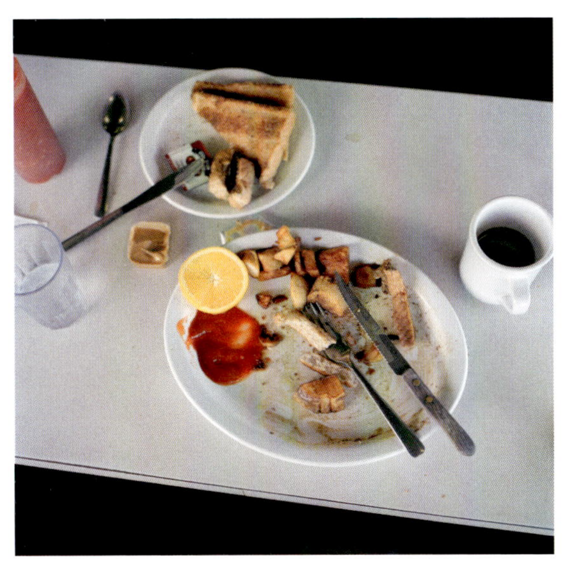
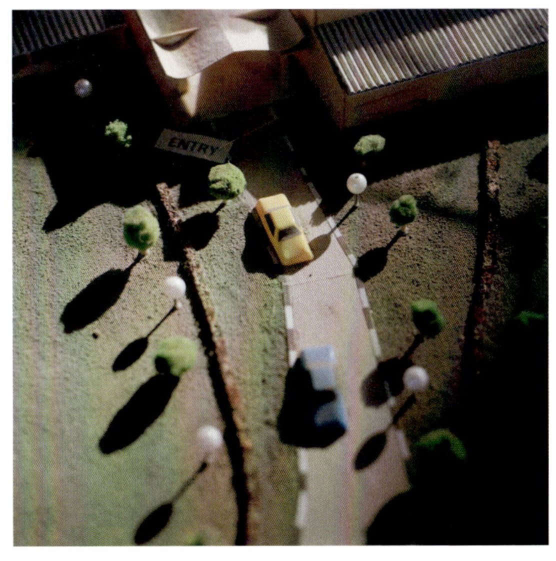
ENTRY
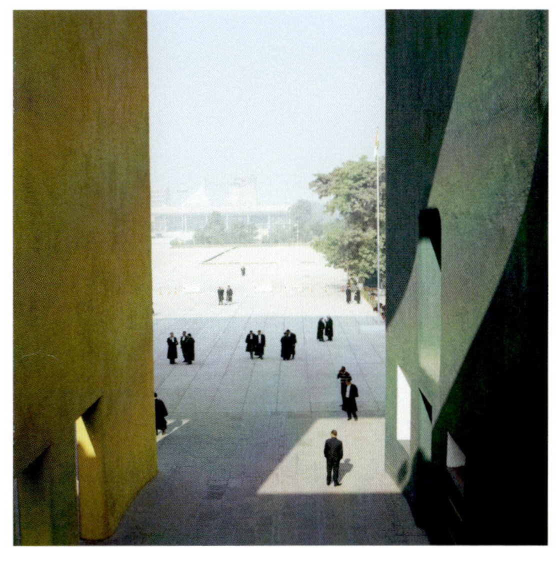

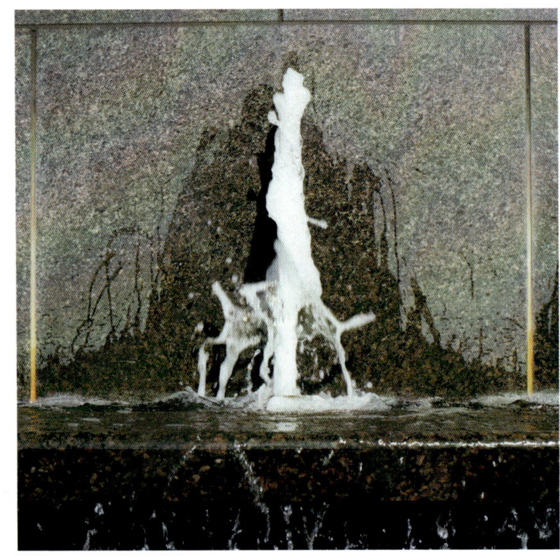

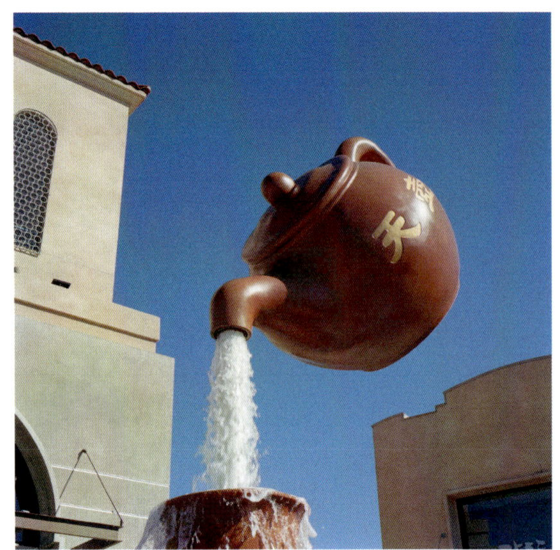

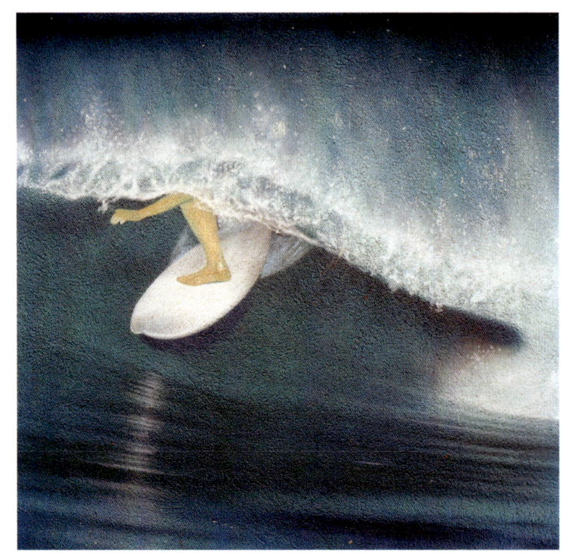

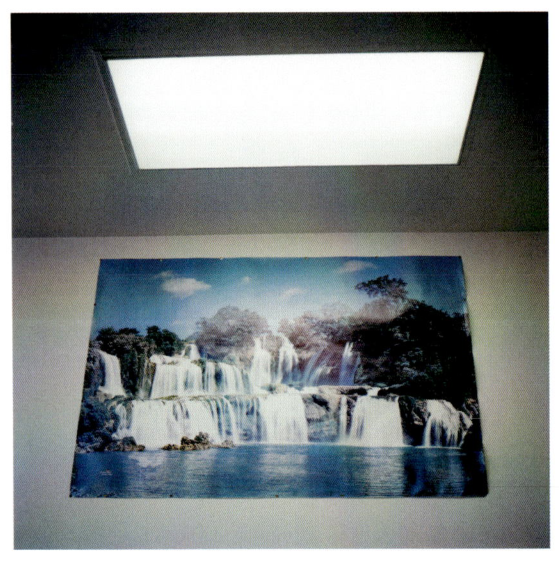

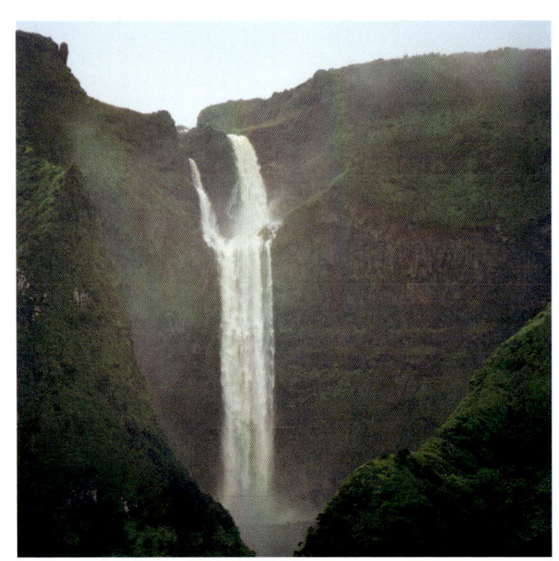

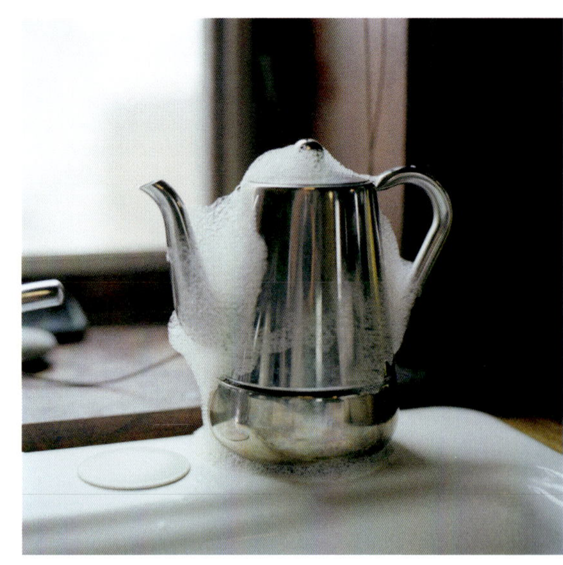

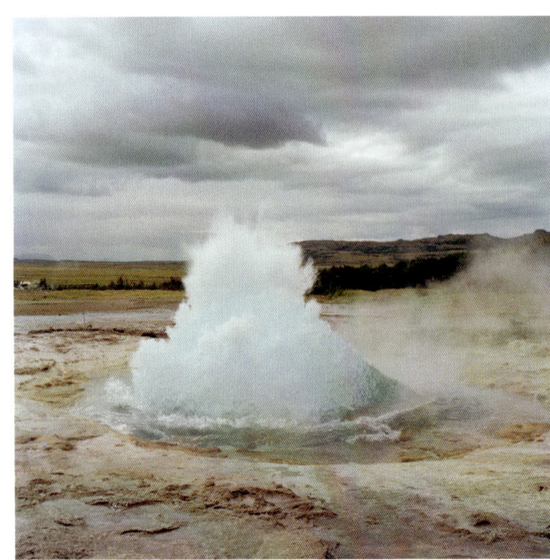

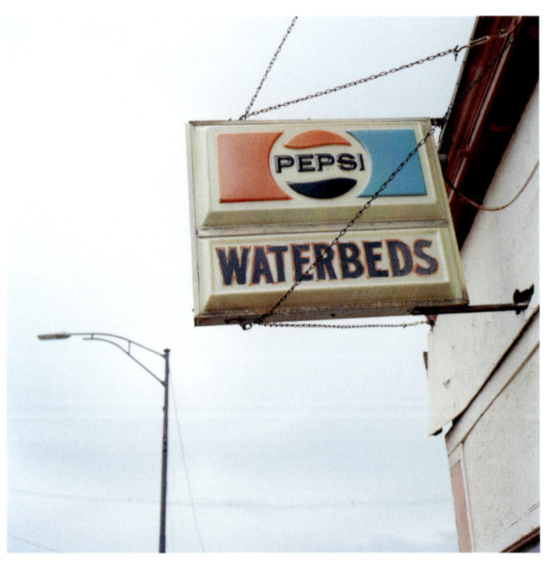
PEPSI
WATERBEDS

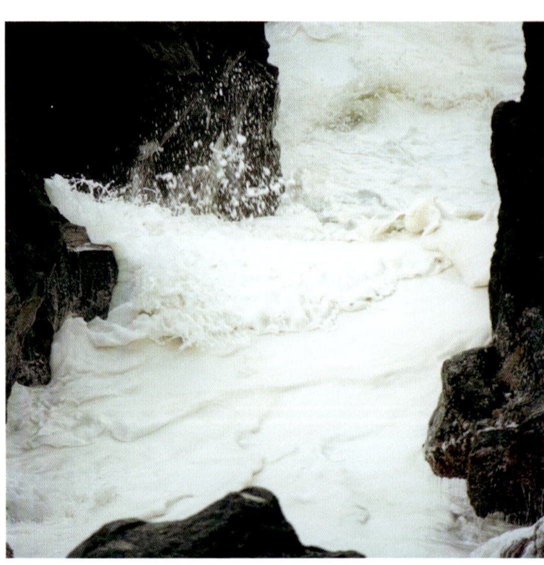

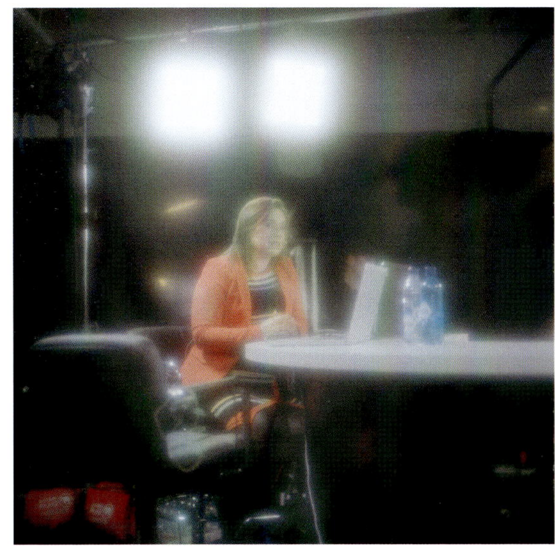
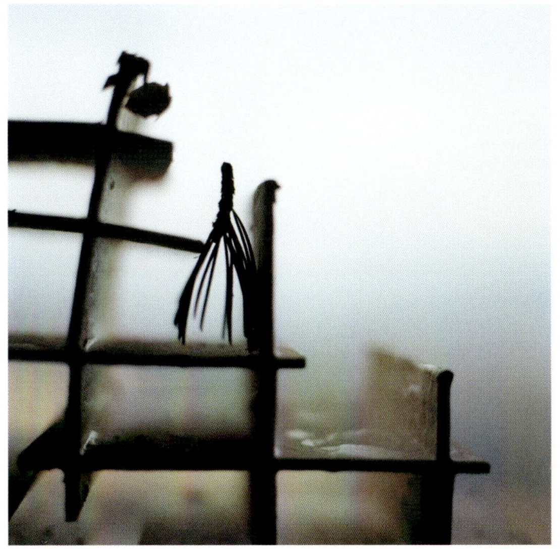
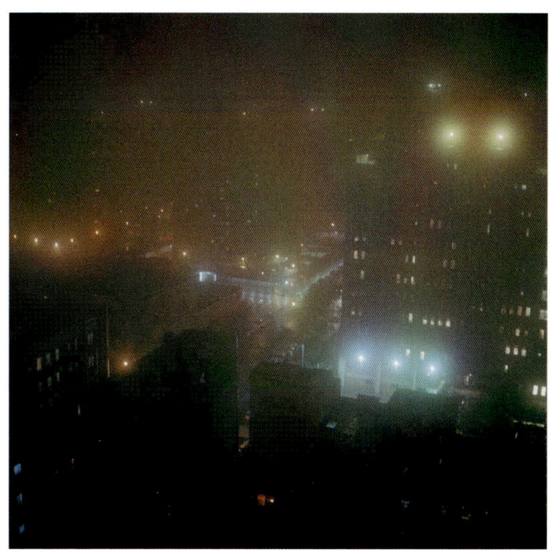
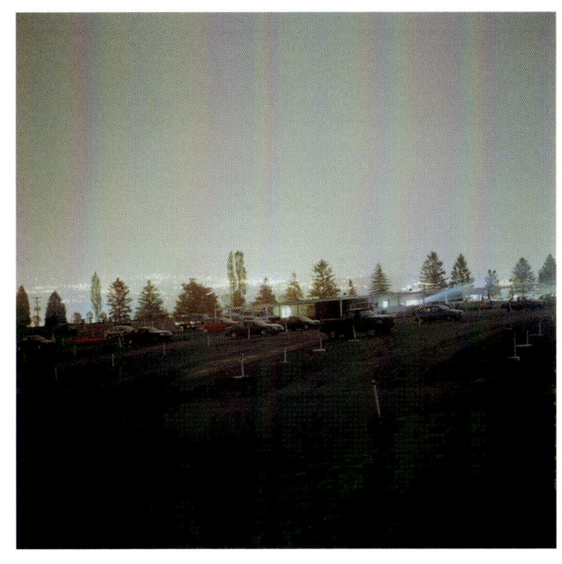
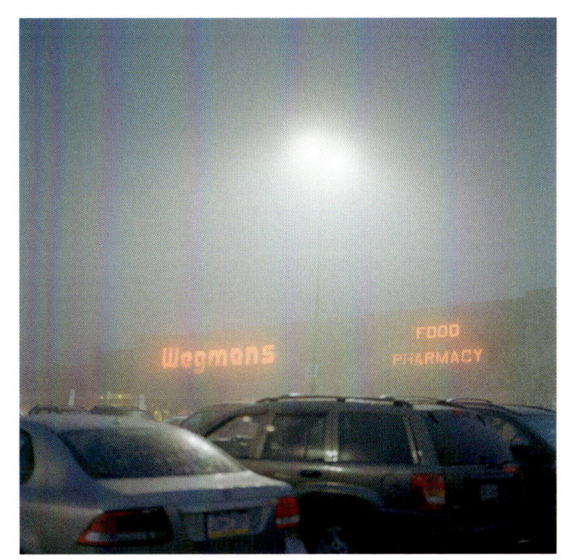
Wegmans
FOOD
PHARMACY
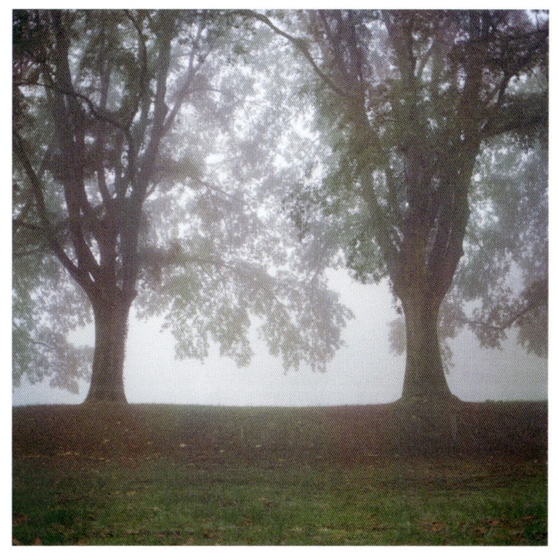

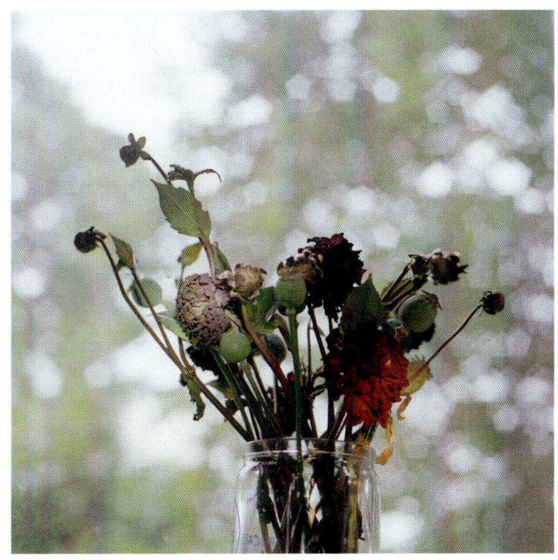
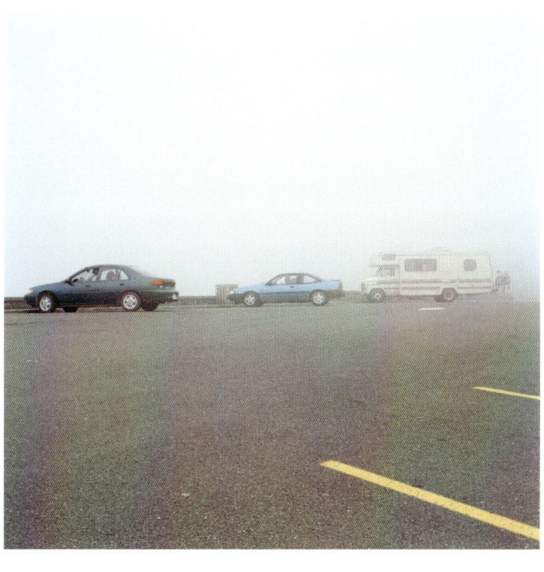

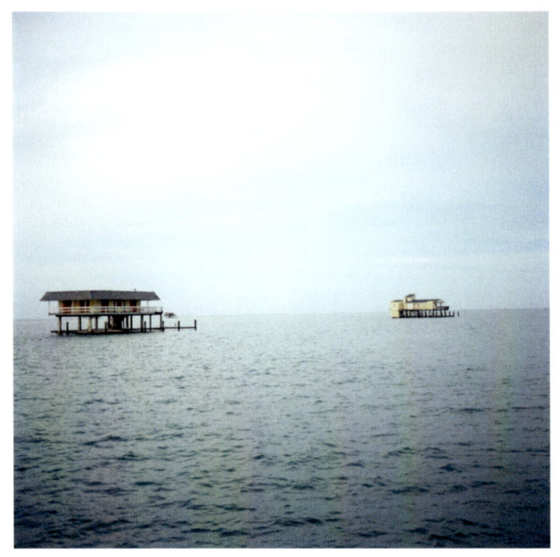
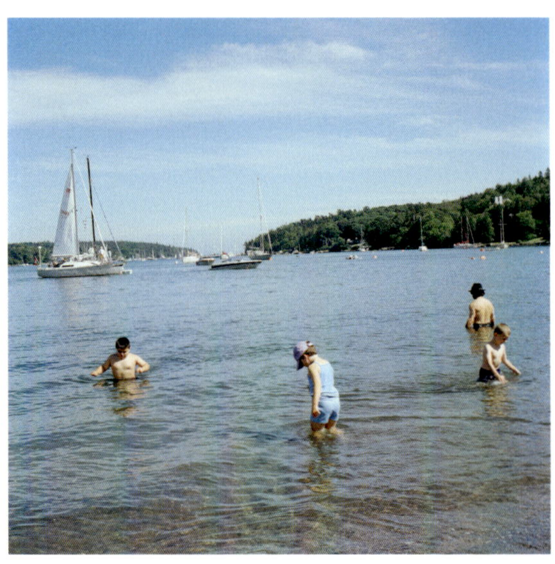
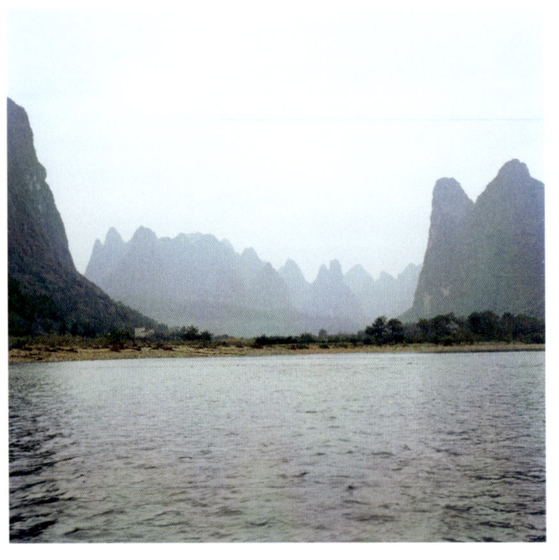
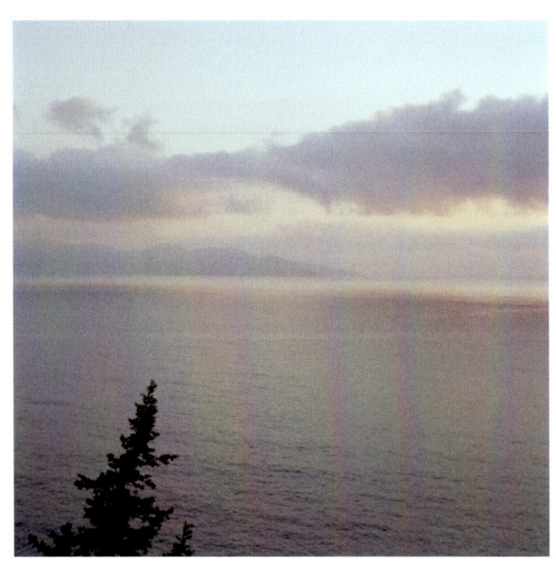

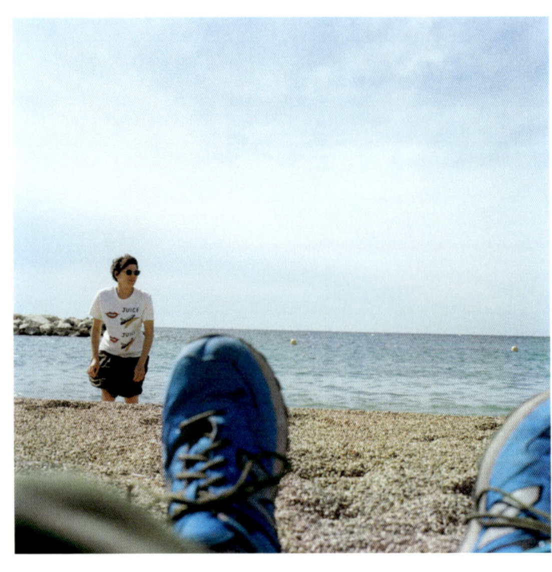

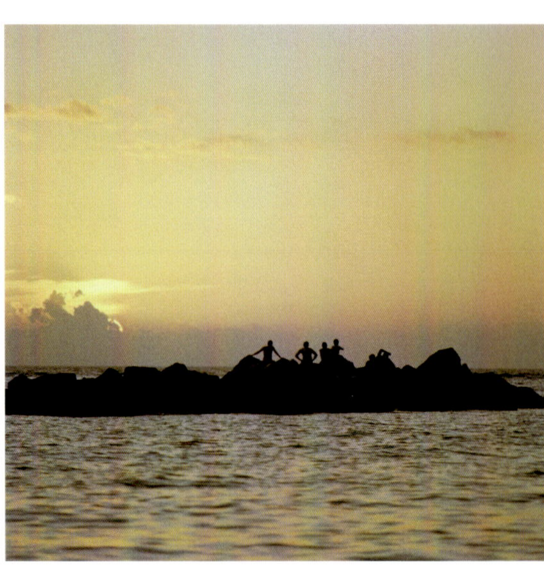

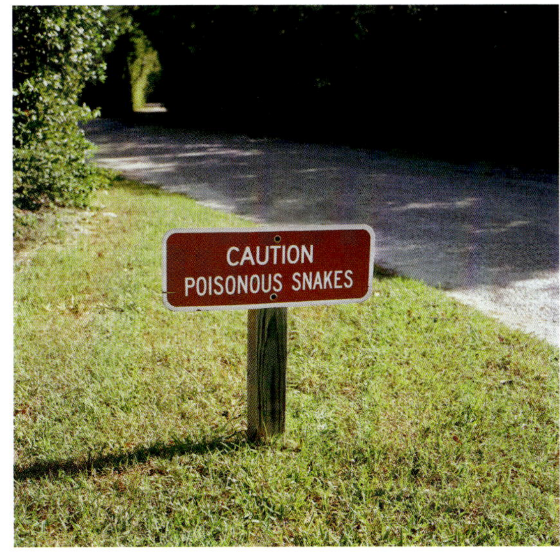
CAUTION
POISONOUS SNAKES

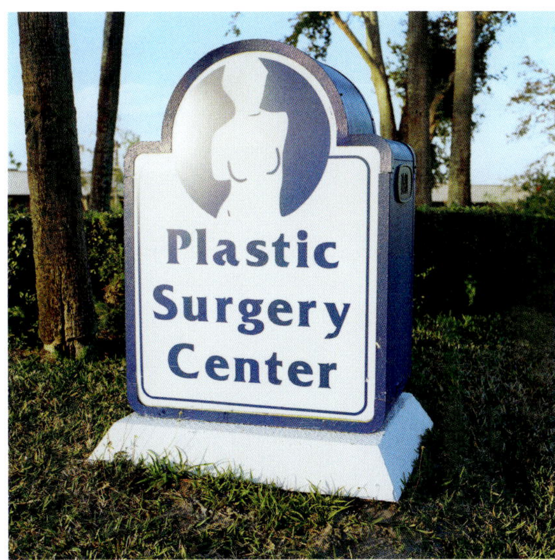
Plastic
Surgery
Center

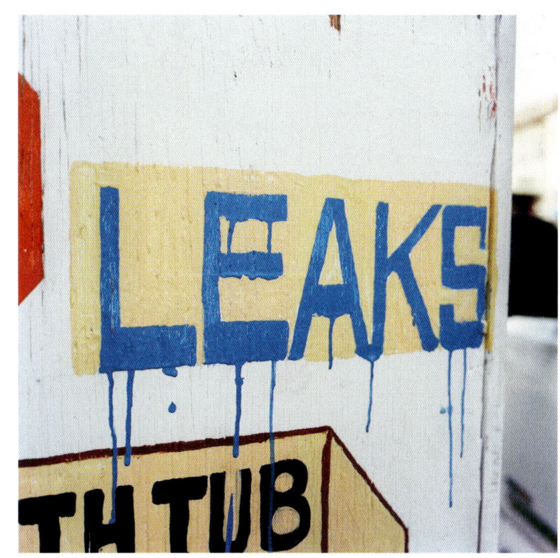
LEAKS

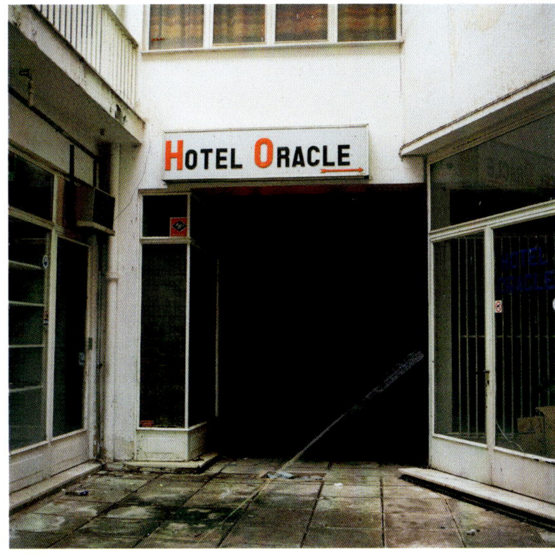
HOTEL ORACLE

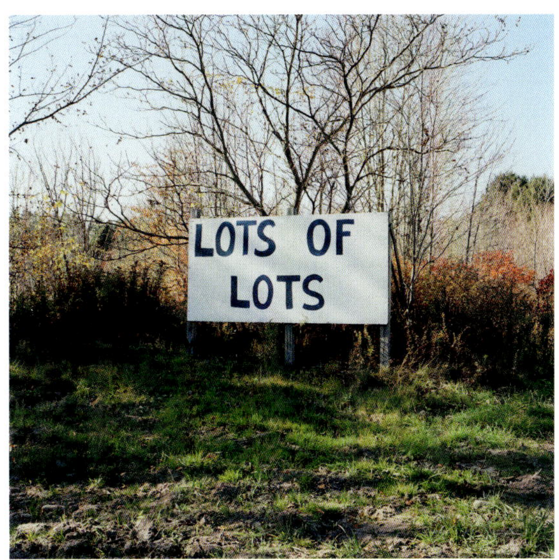
LOTS OF
LOTS

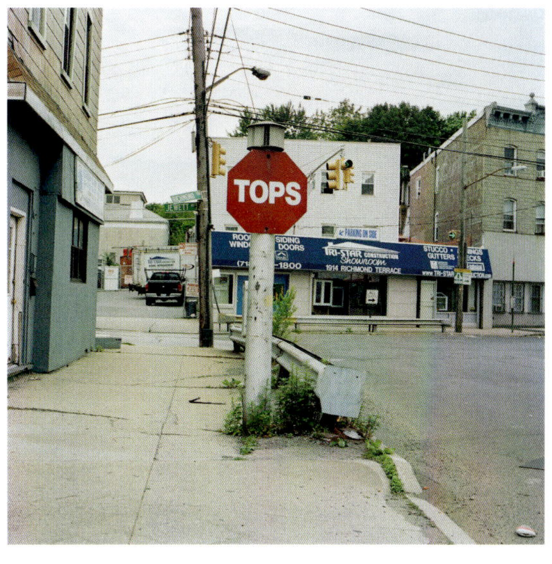
TOPS

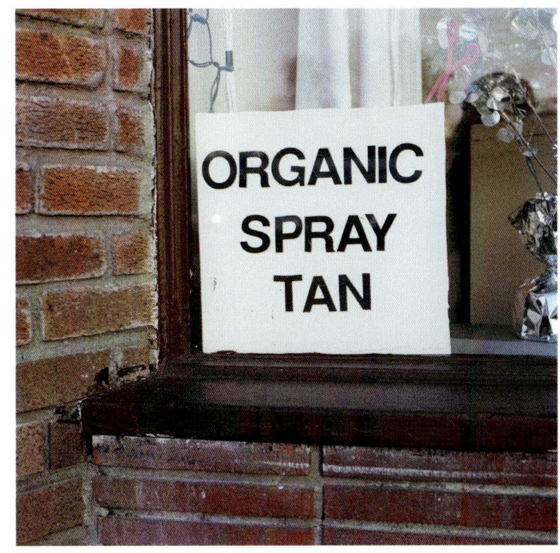
ORGANIC
SPRAY
TAN

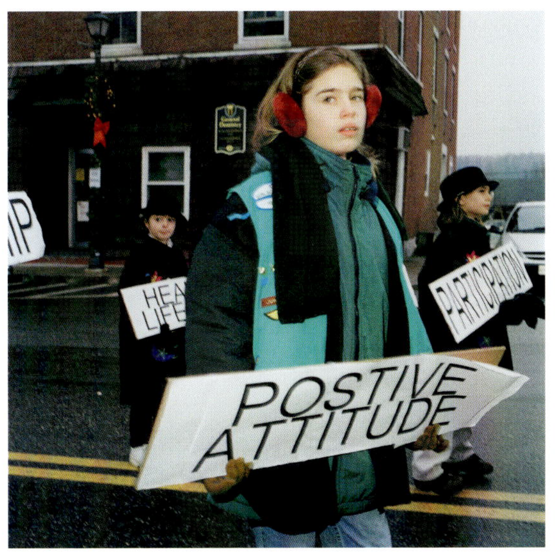
POSTIVE
ATTITUDE

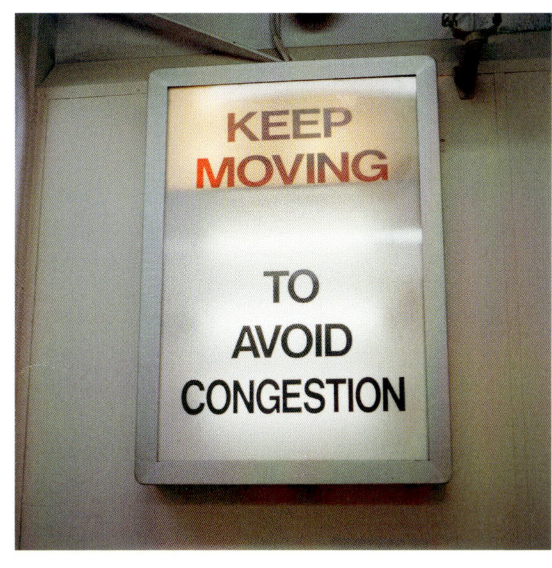
KEEP
MOVING
TO
AVOID
CONGESTION

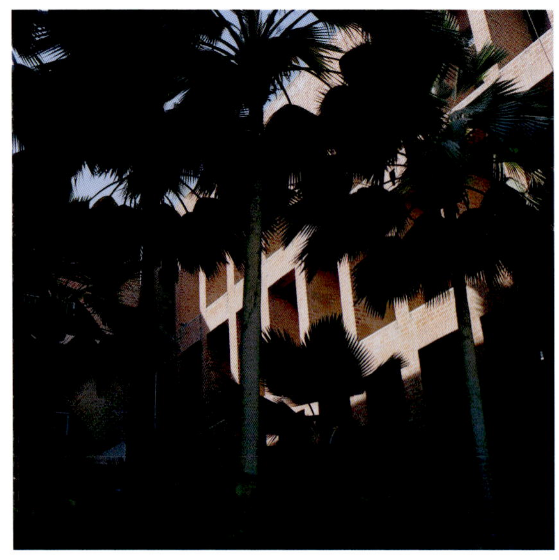
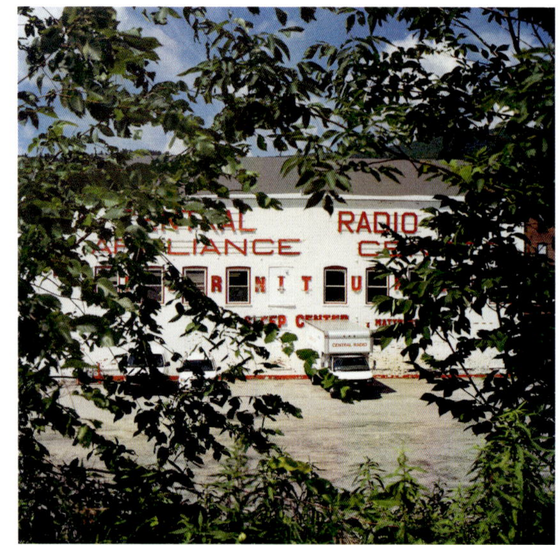
RADIO
CENTRAL RADIO
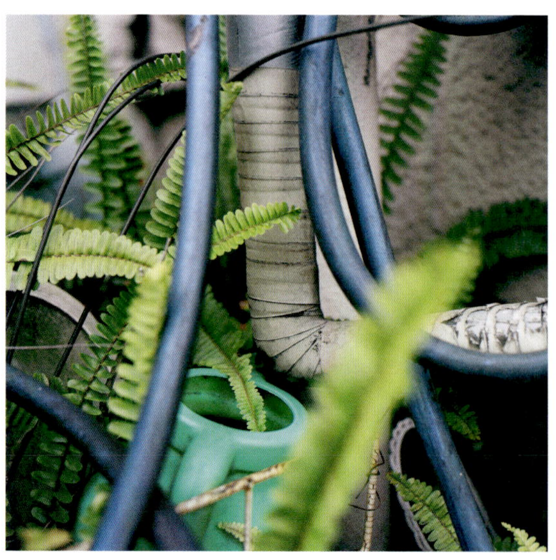
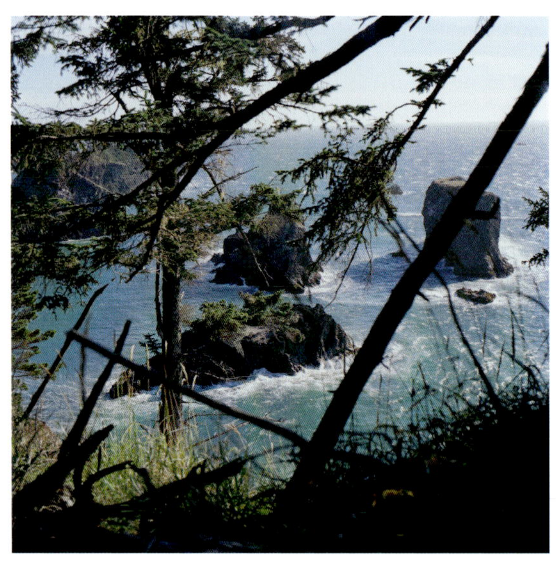
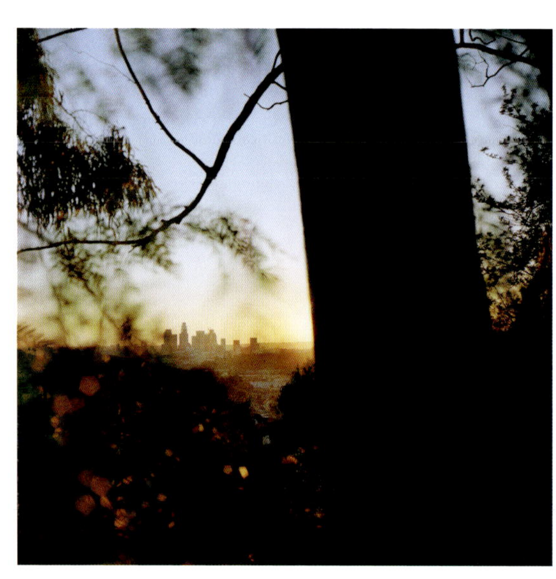
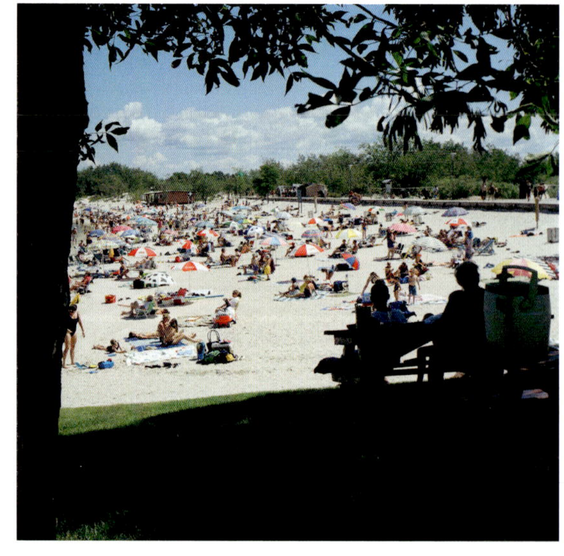
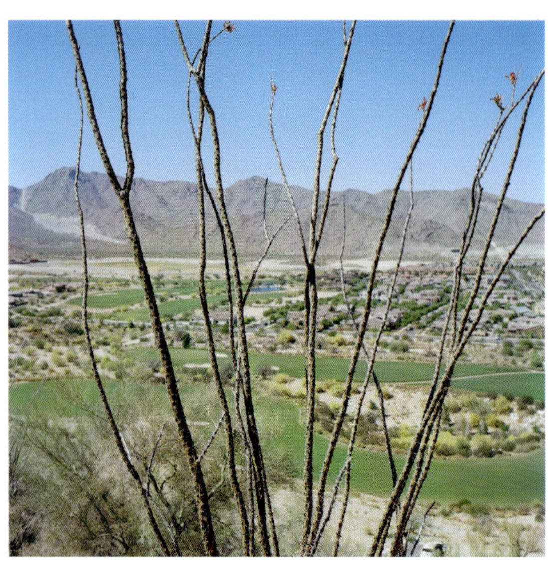
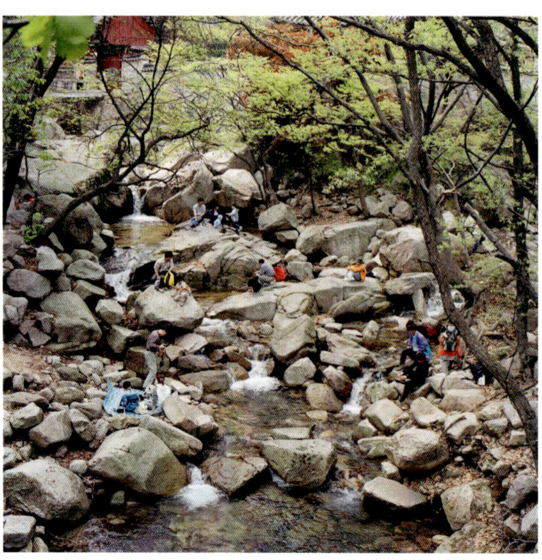
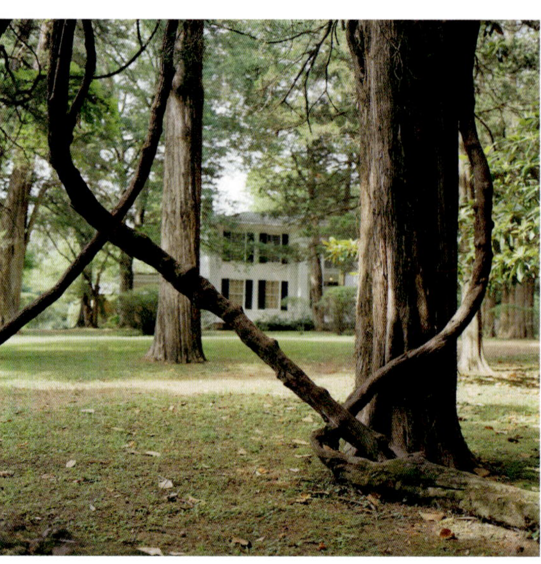

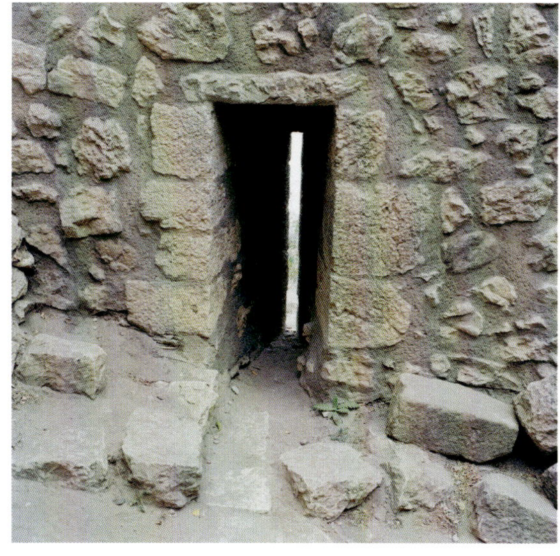
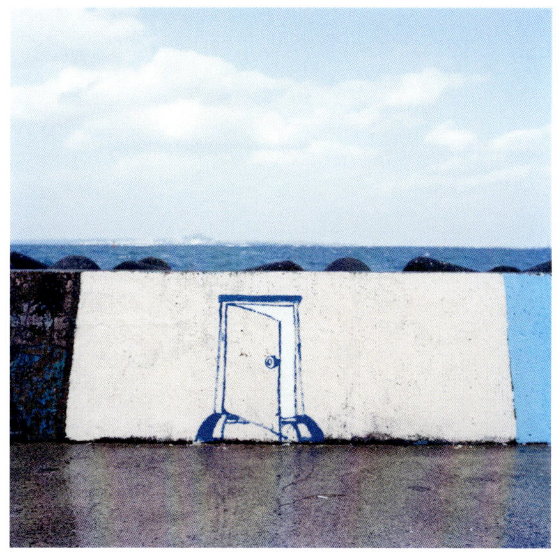
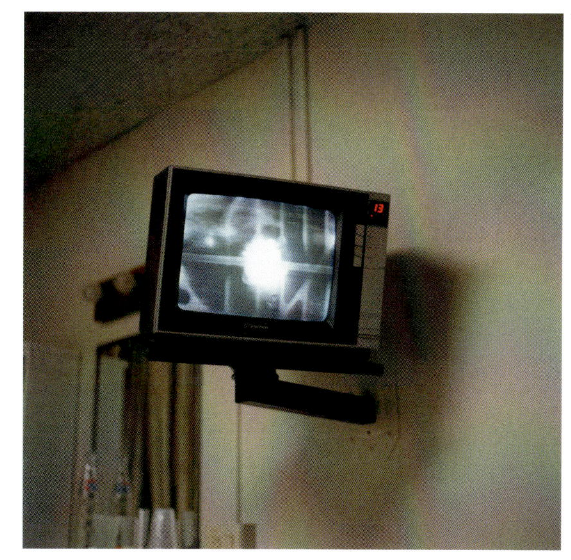
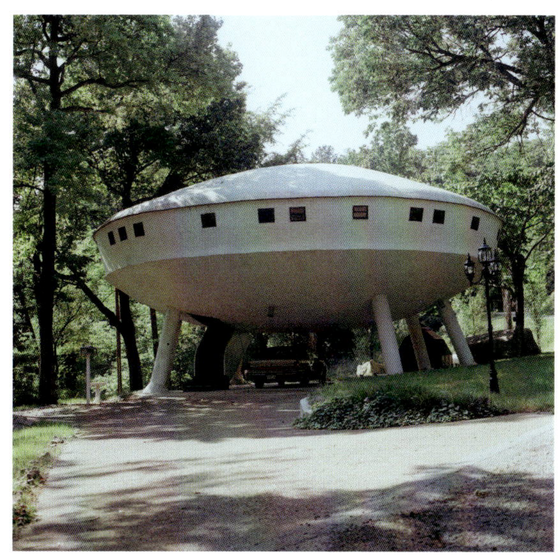
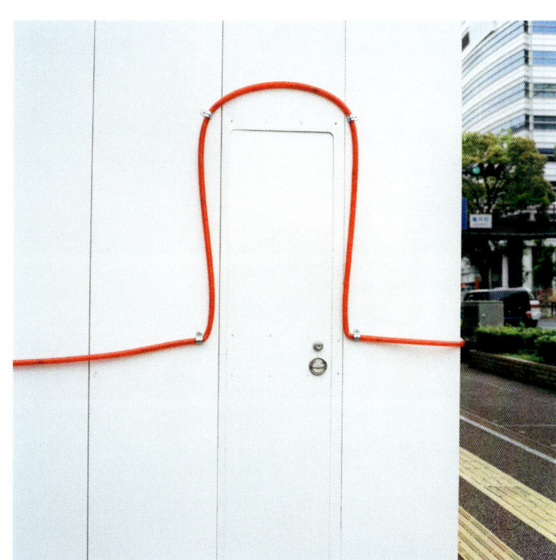
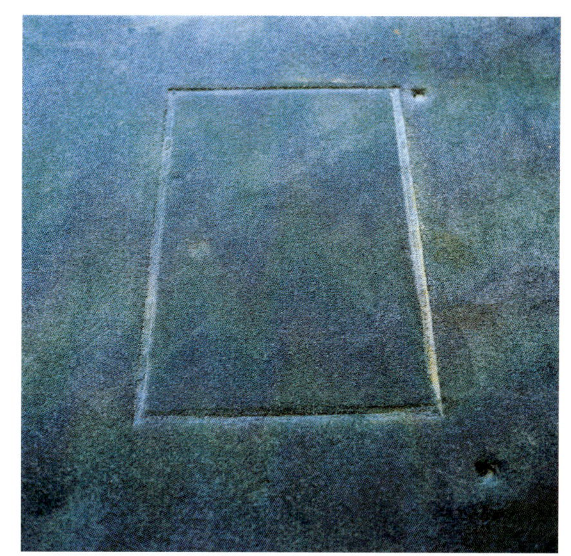
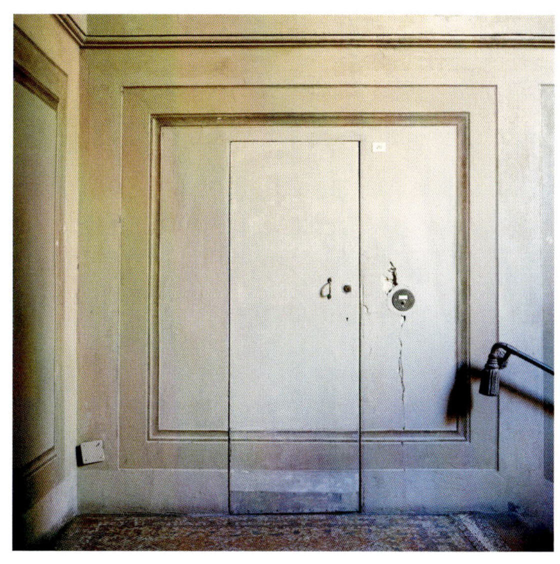
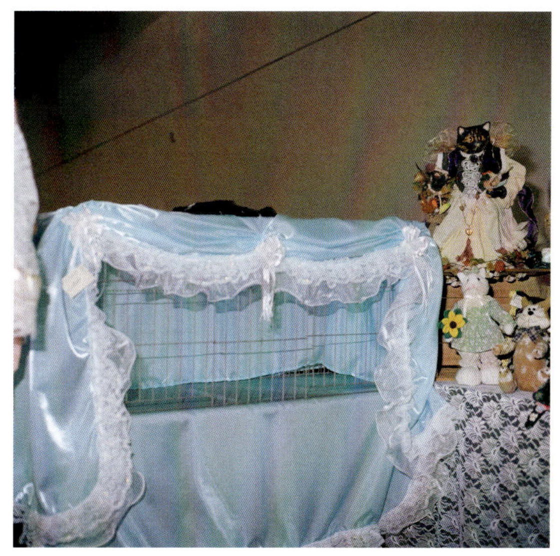

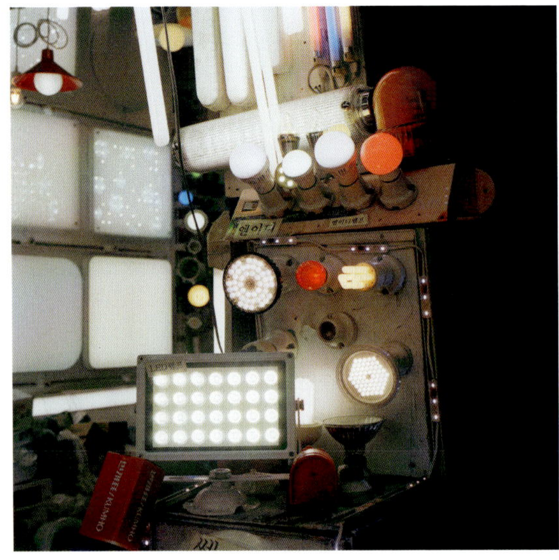

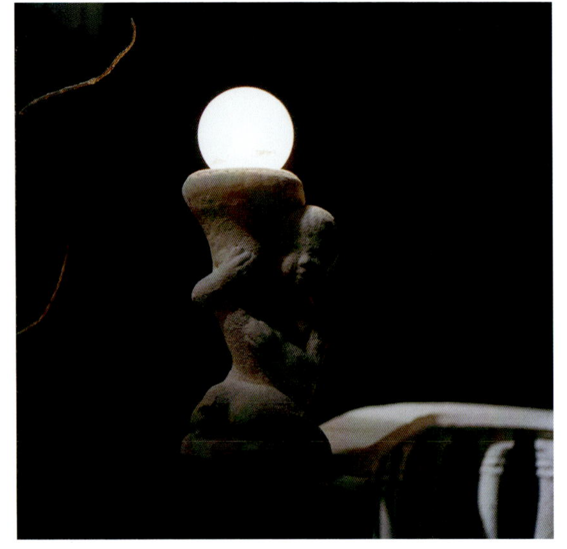

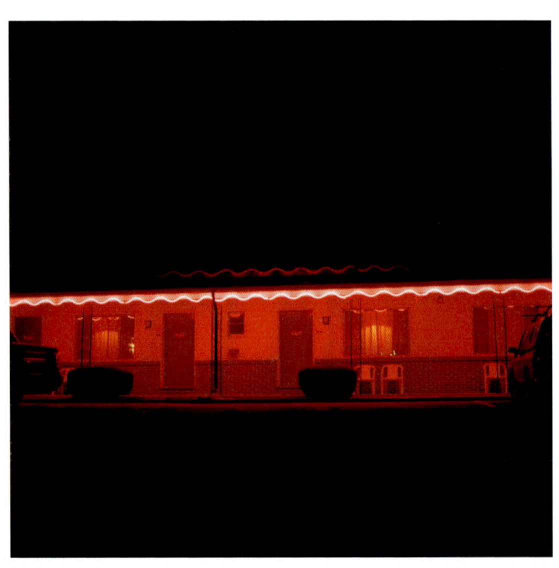

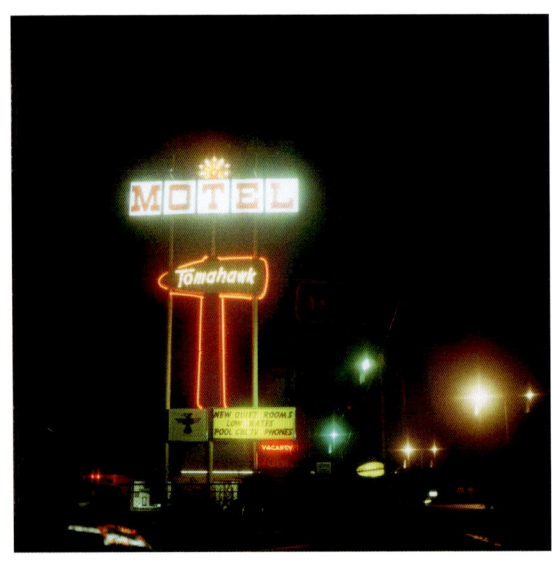
MOTEL
Tomahawk
NEW QUIET ROOMS
LOW RATES

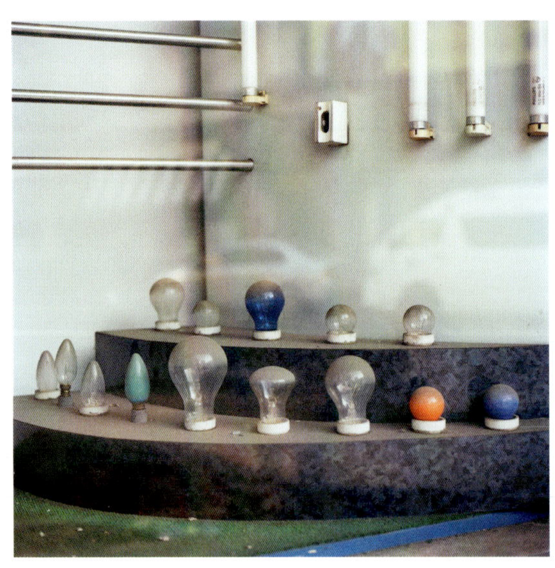

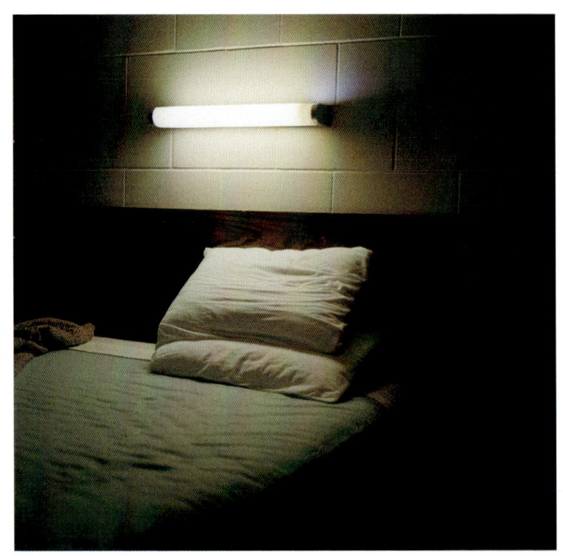

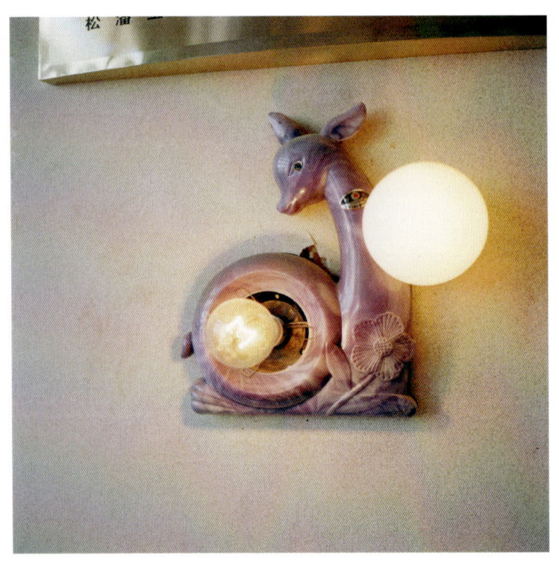

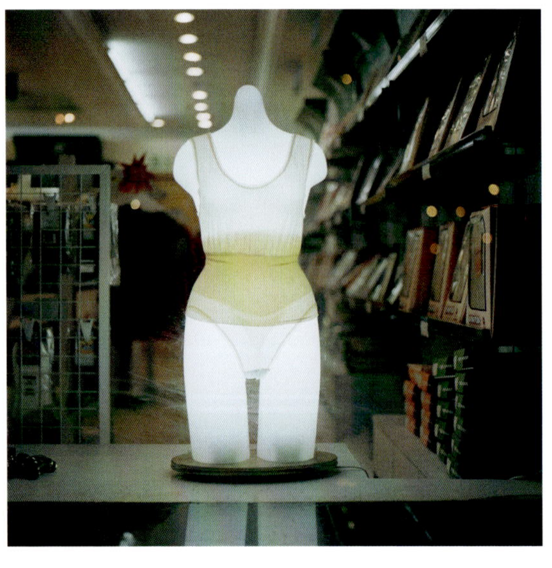

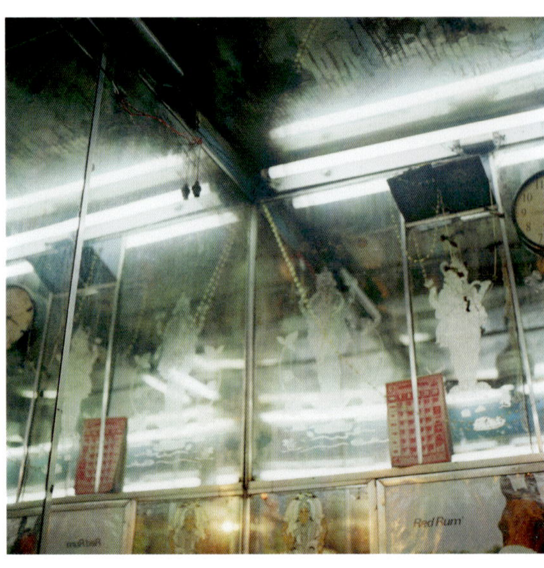

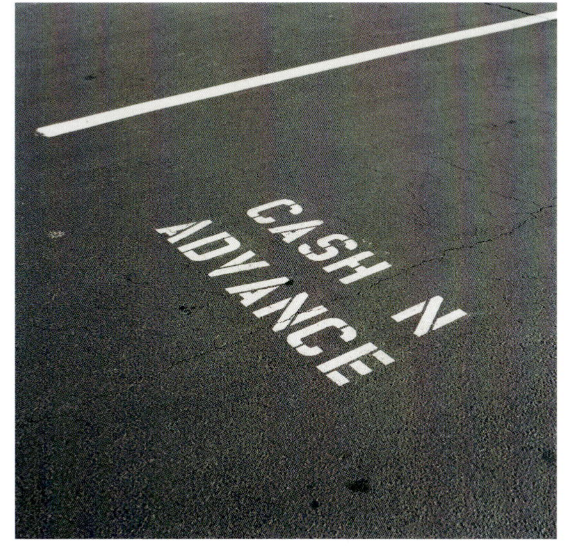
CASH N
ADVANCE
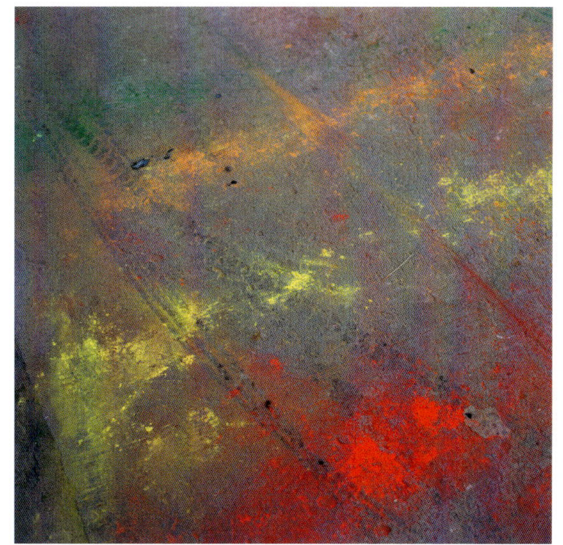
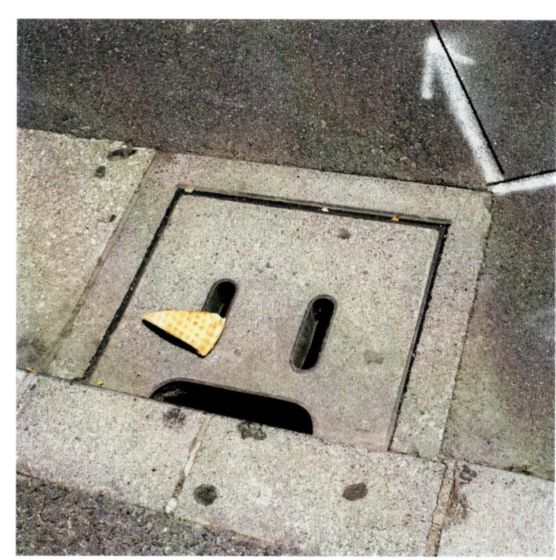
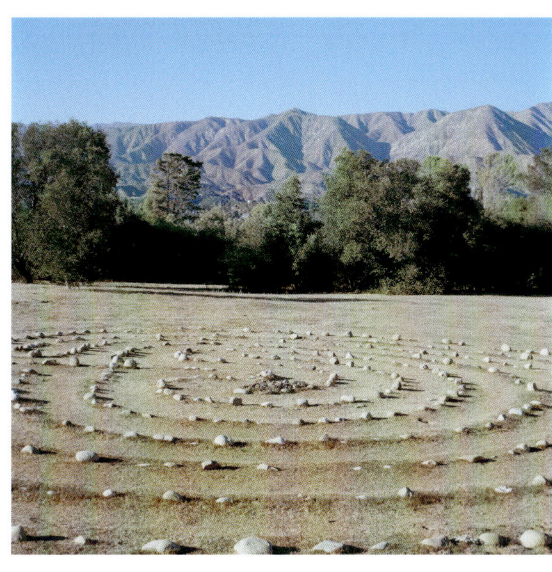
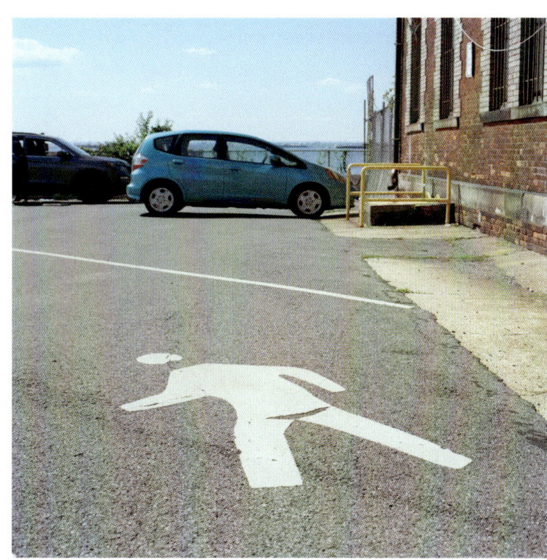
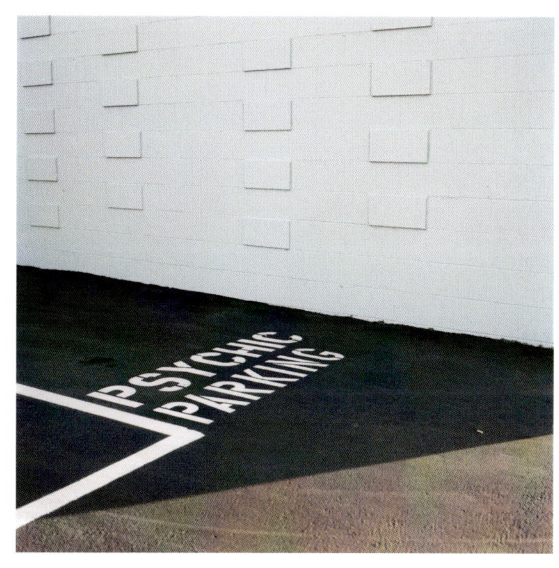
PSYCHIC
PARKING
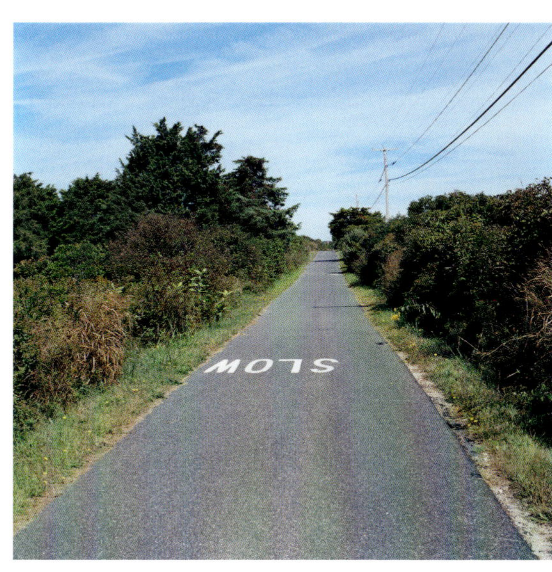
SLOW
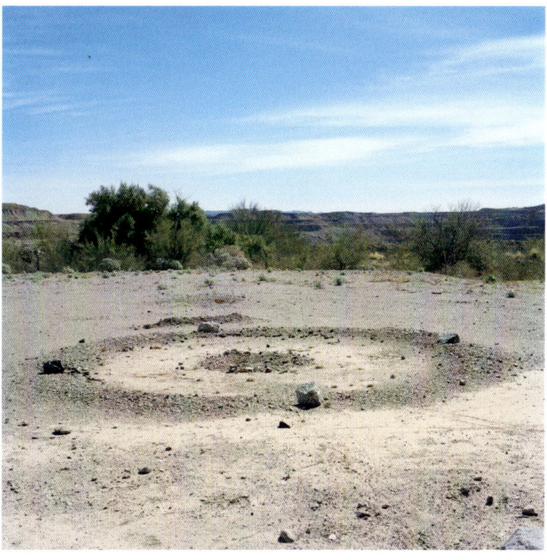
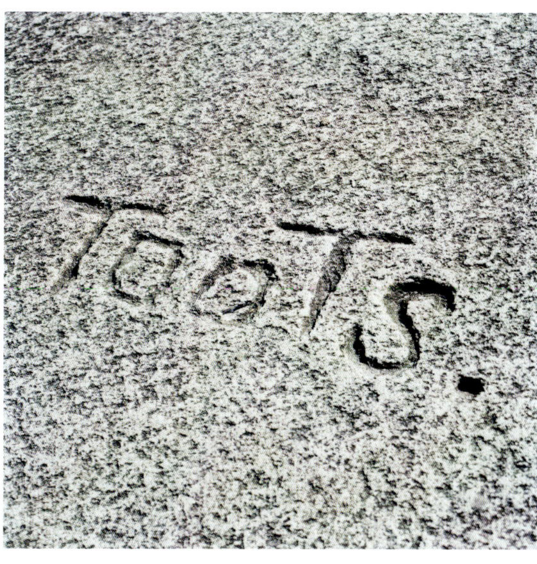
Toots.

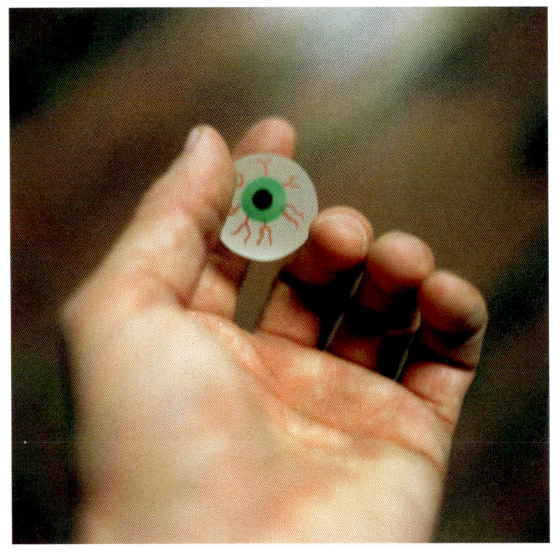
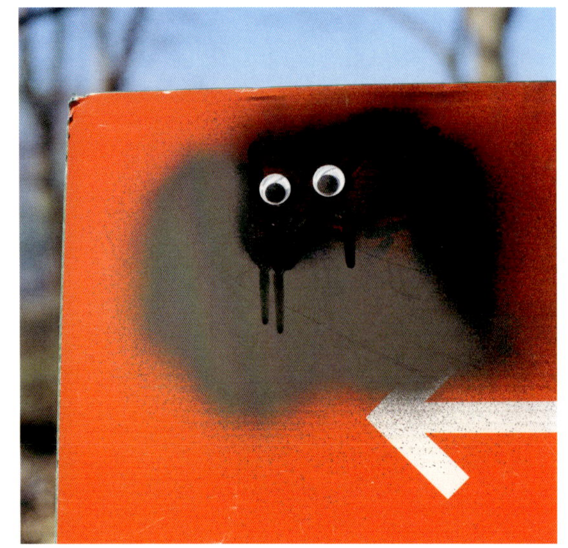
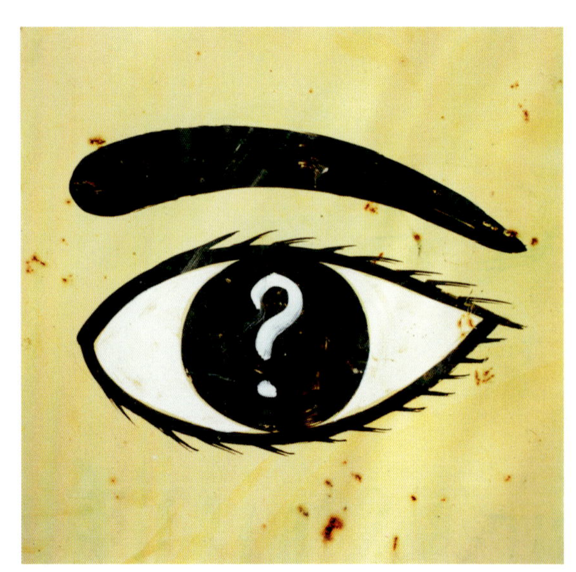
?
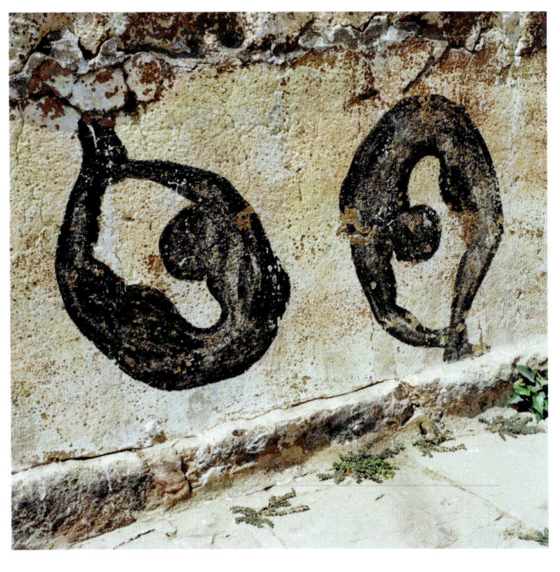
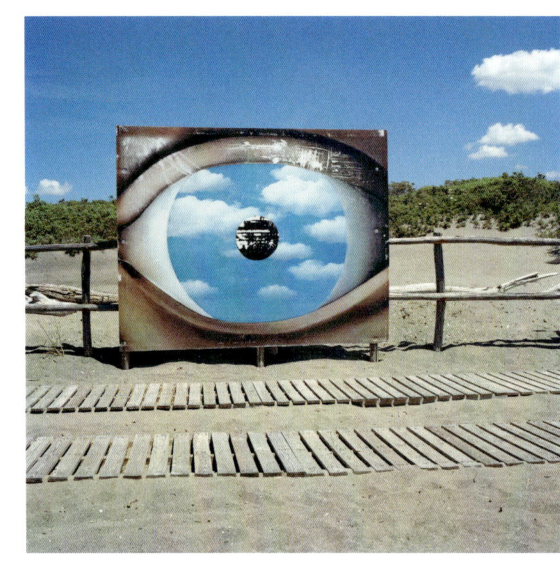
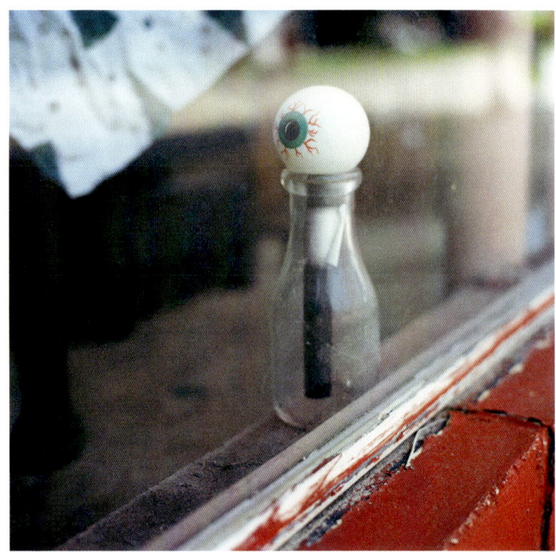
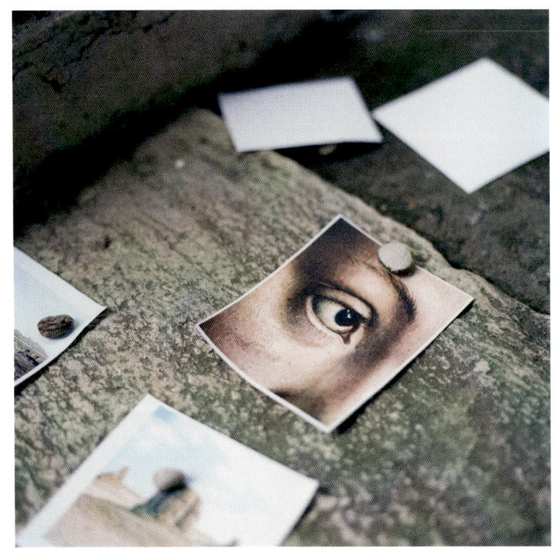
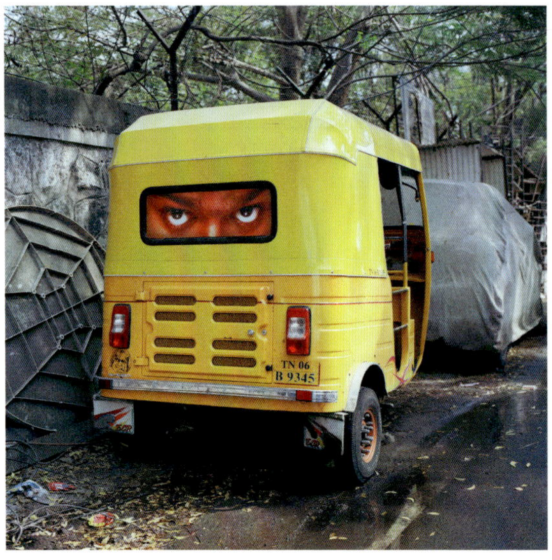
TN 06
B 9345
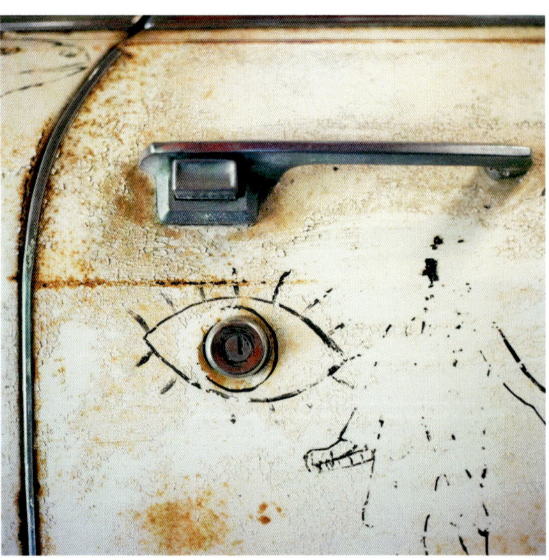

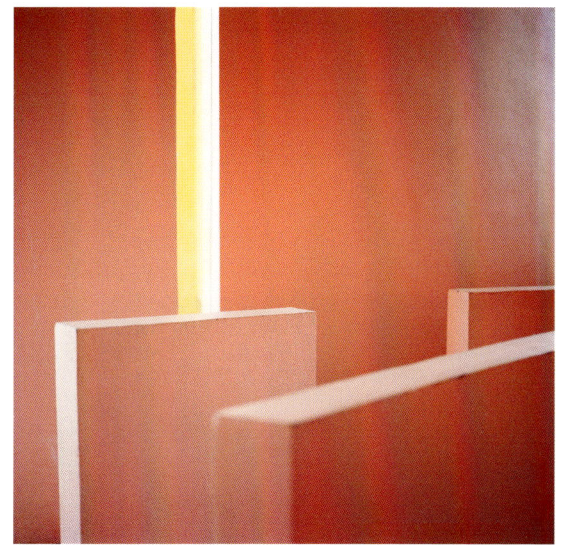

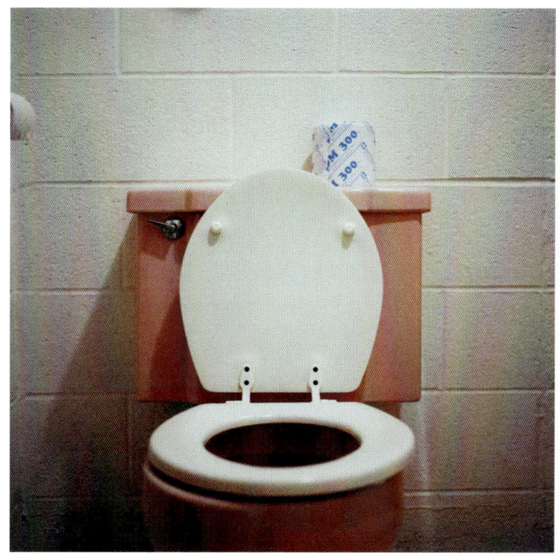

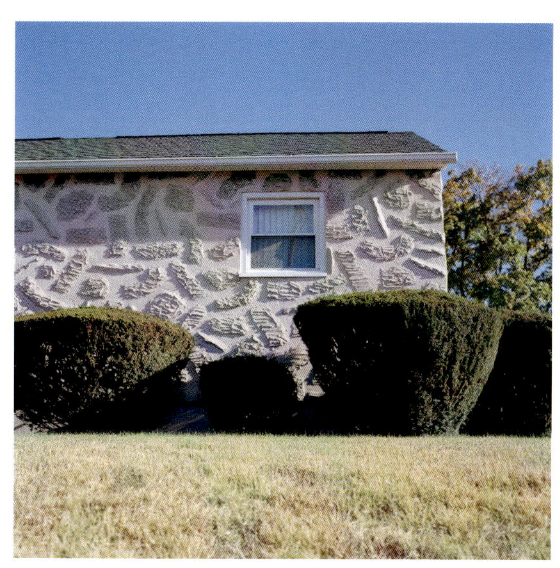

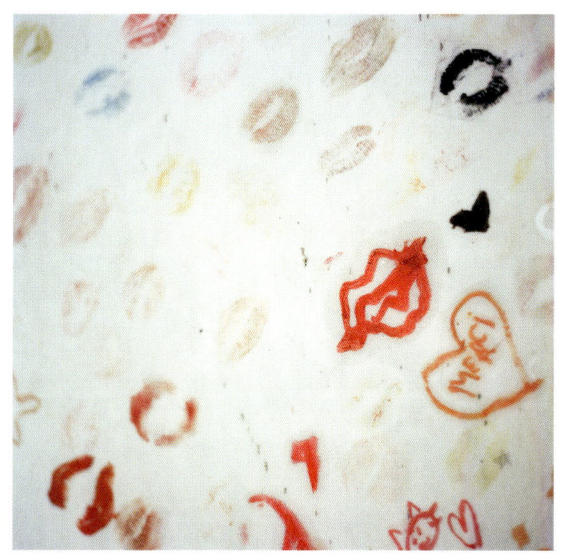

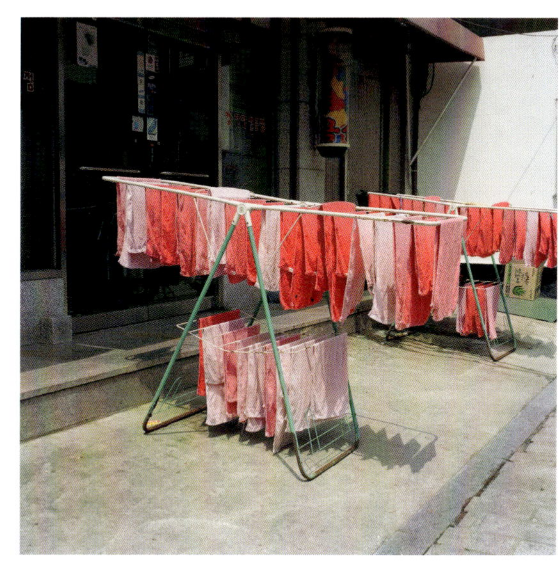

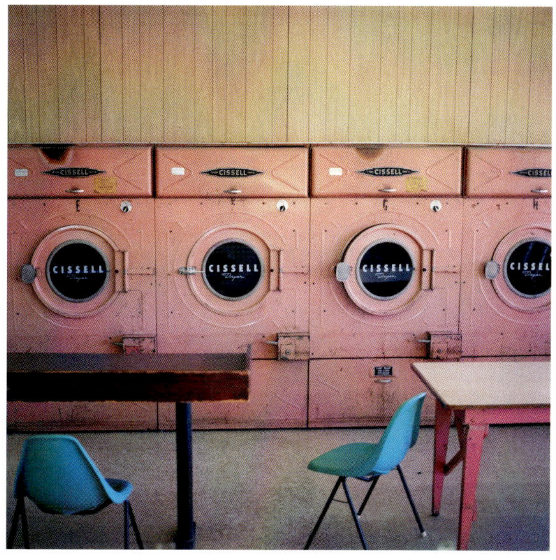
CISSELL
CISSELL
CISSELL
CISSELL

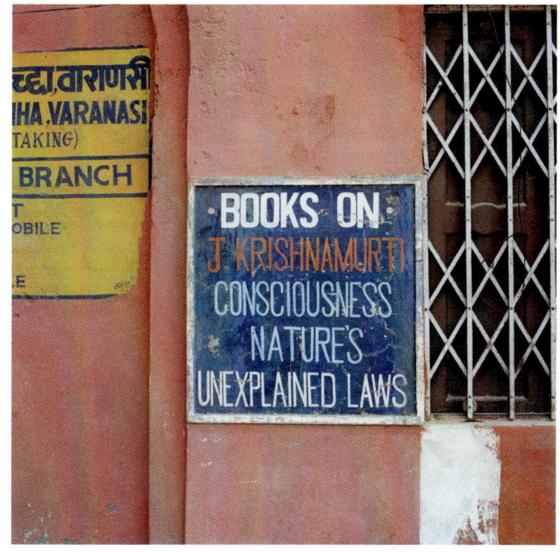
BRANCH
BOOKS ON
J. KRISHNAMURTI
CONSCIOUSNESS
NATURE'S
UNEXPLAINED LAWS

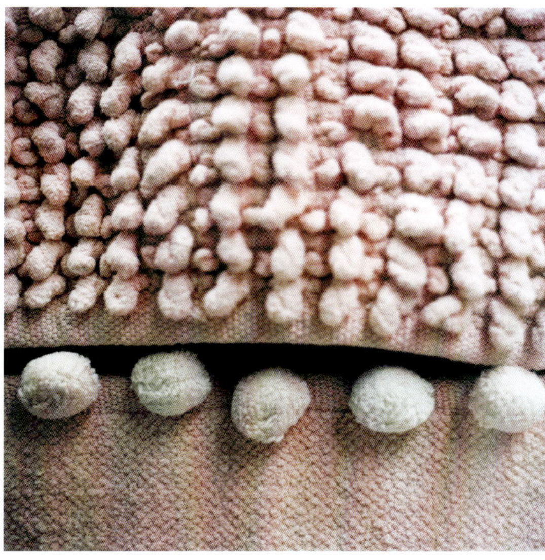

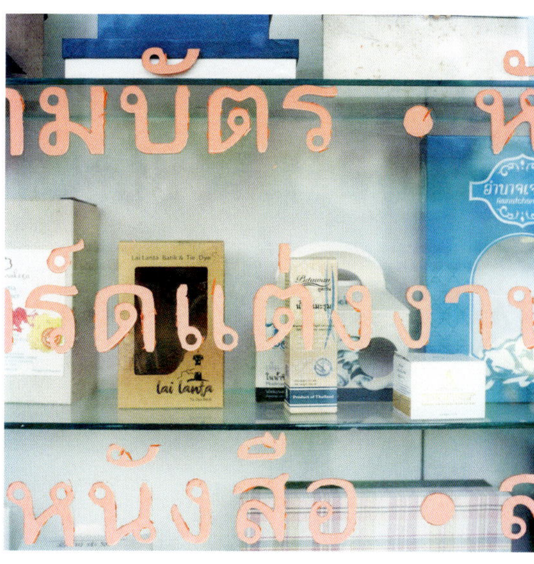
หนังสือ

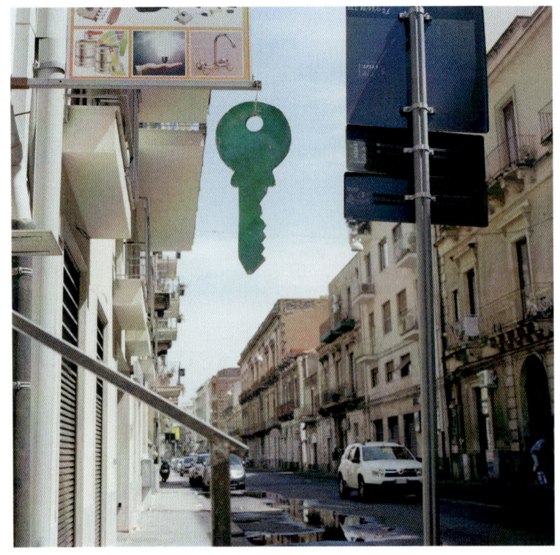
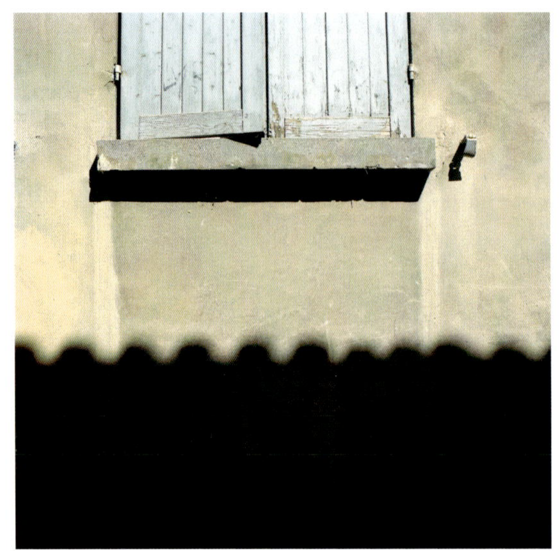
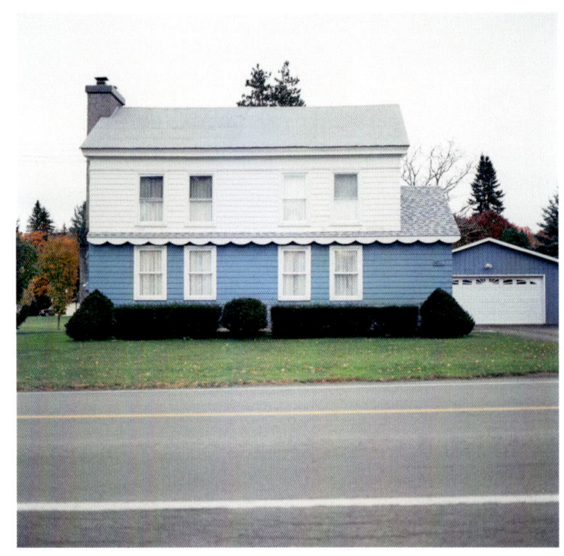
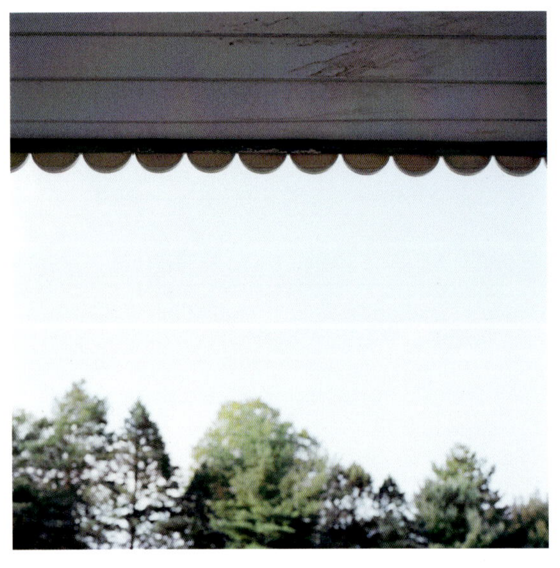
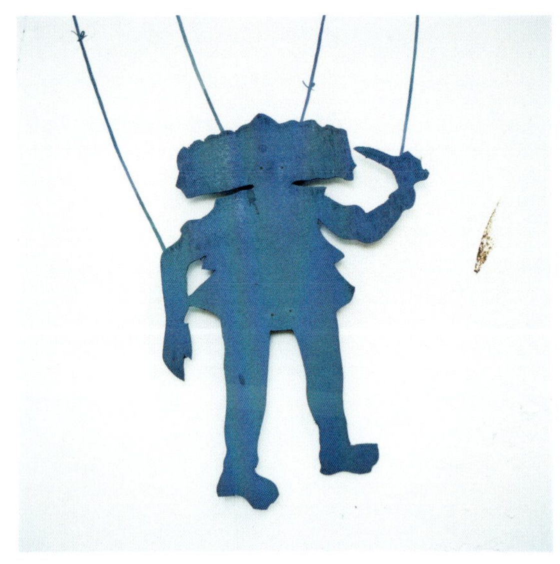
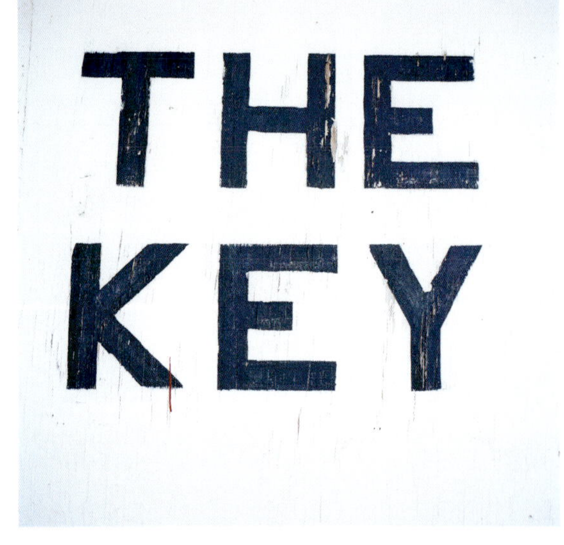
THE
KEY
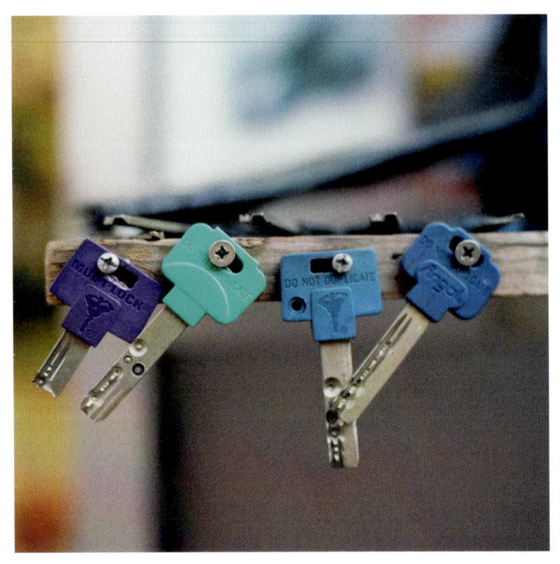
DO NOT DUPLICATE
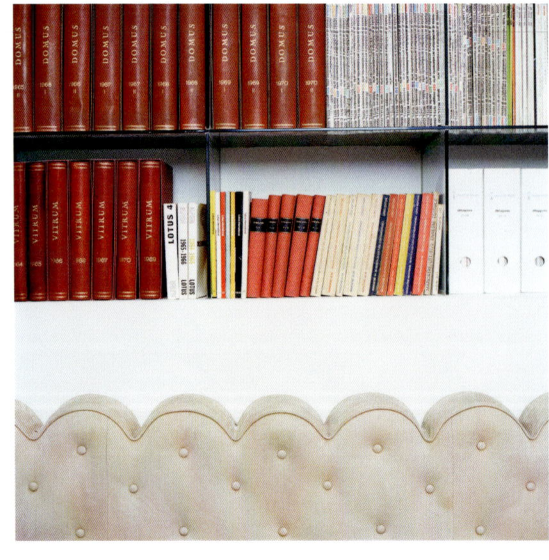
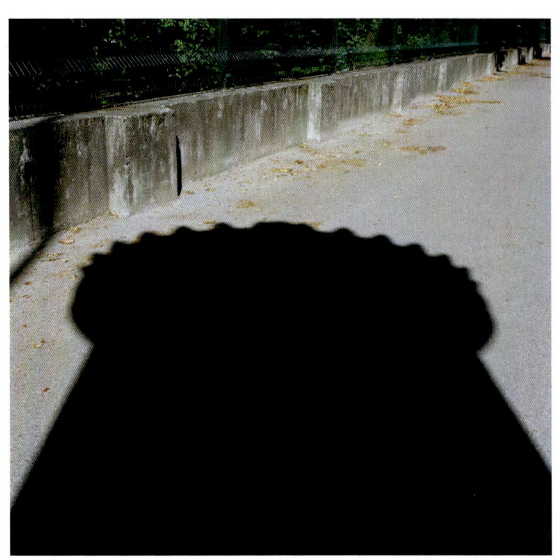

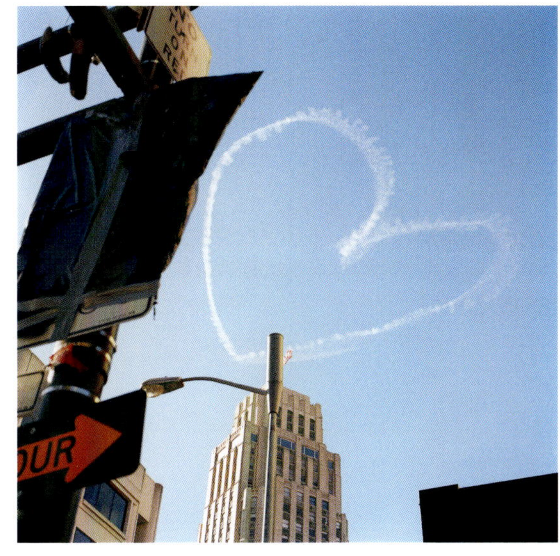
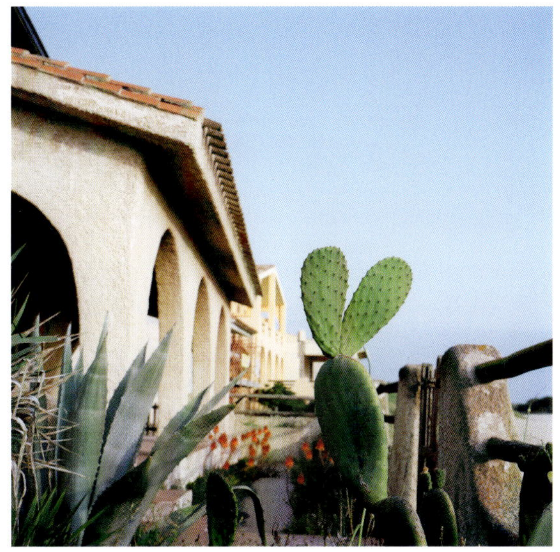
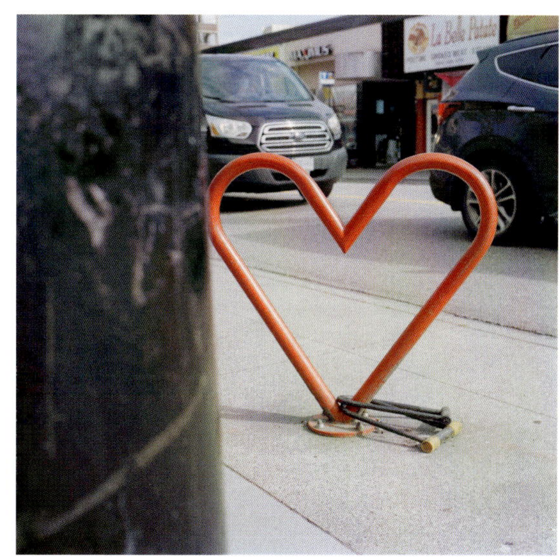
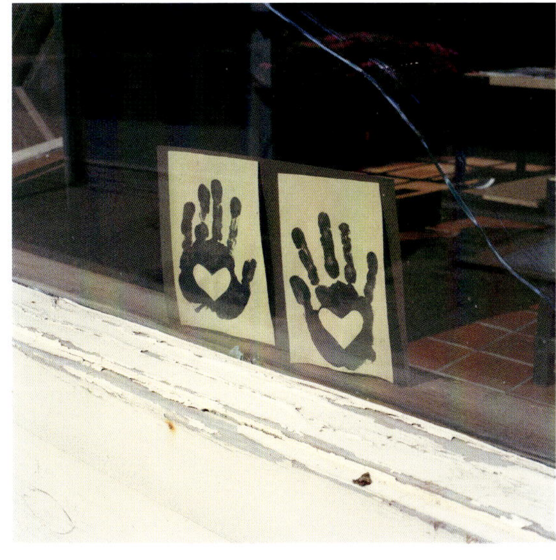
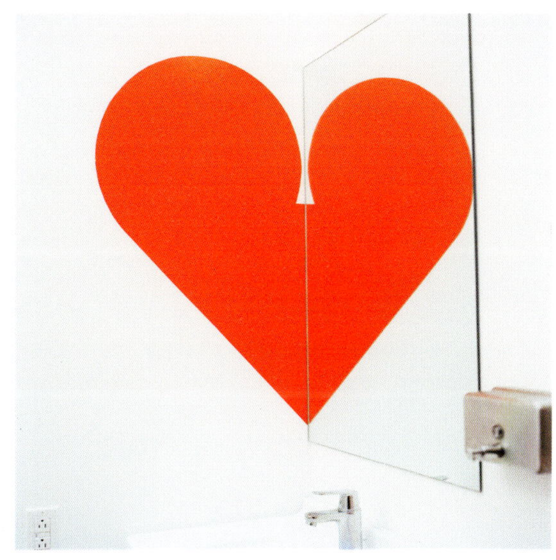
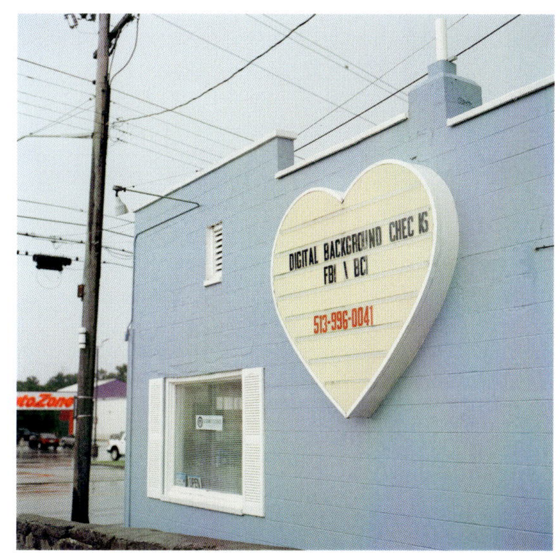
DIGITAL BACKGROUND CHEC KS
FBI \ BCI
513-996-0041
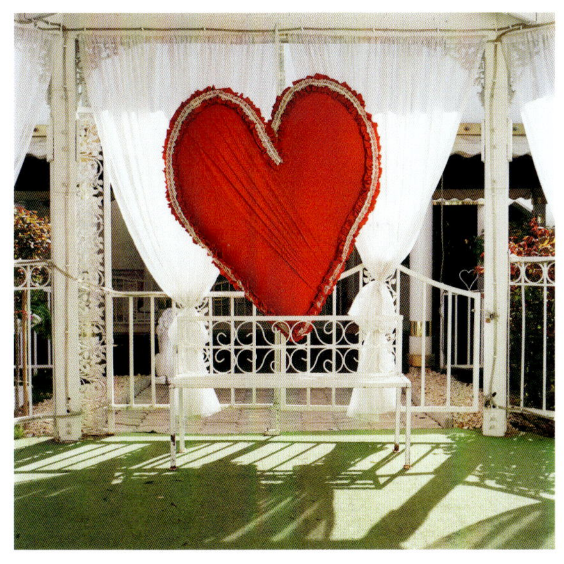
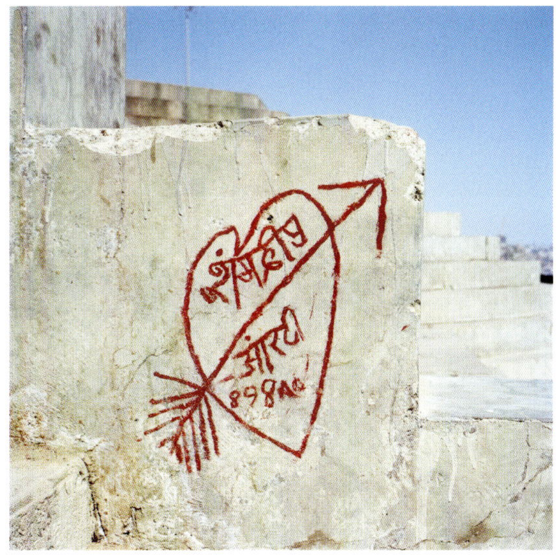
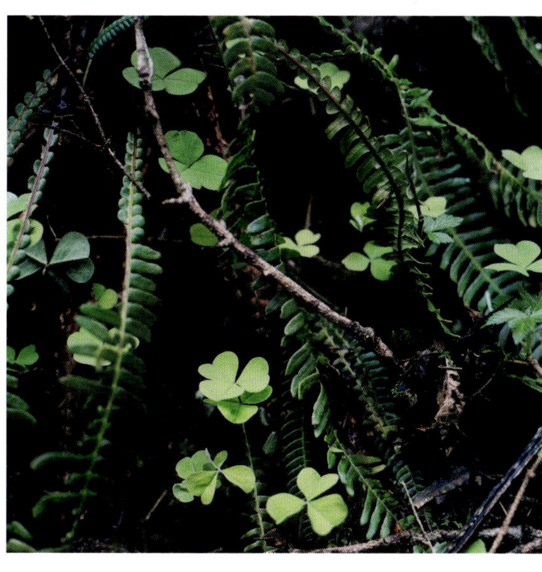

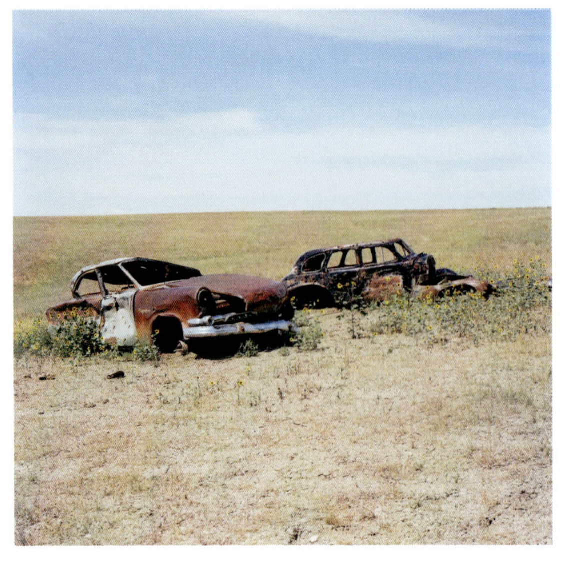

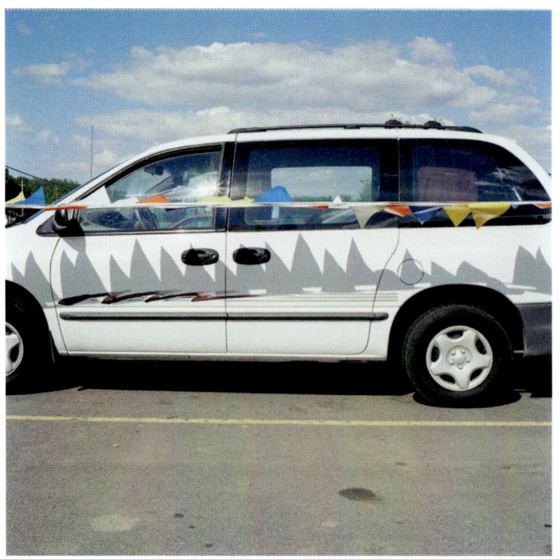

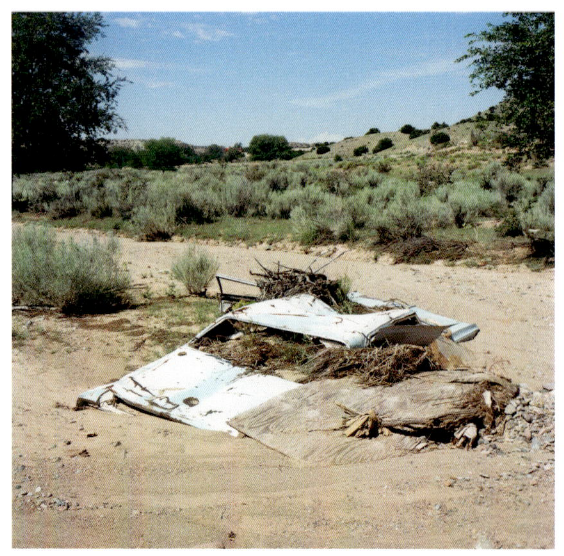

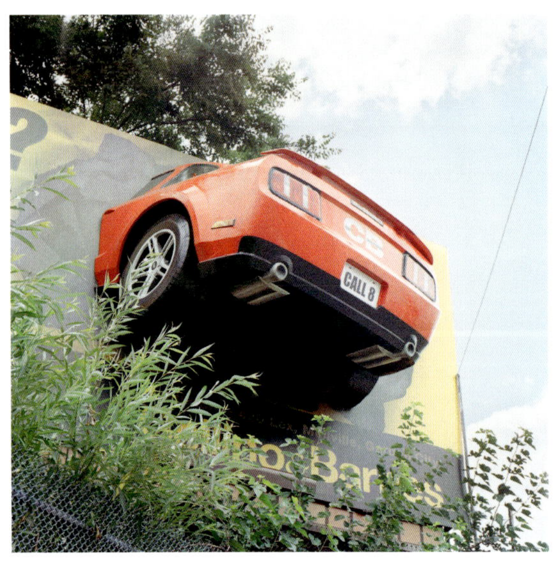
CALL 8

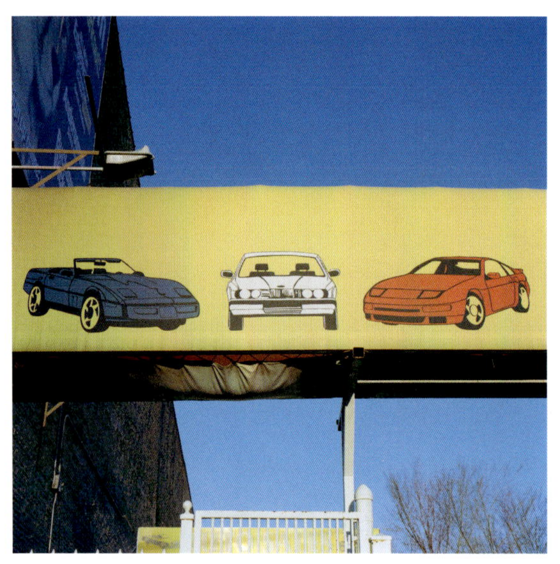

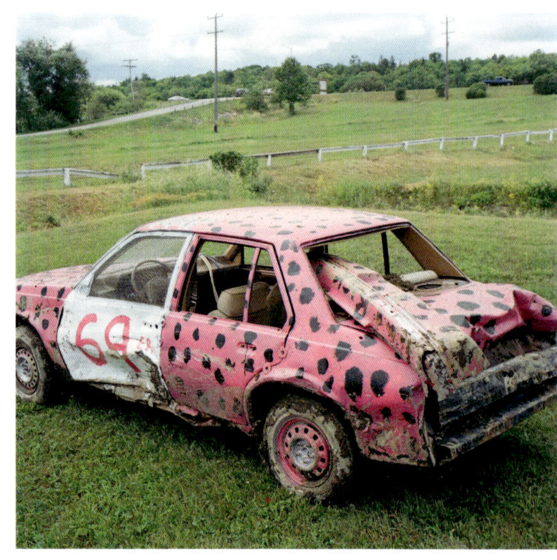
69

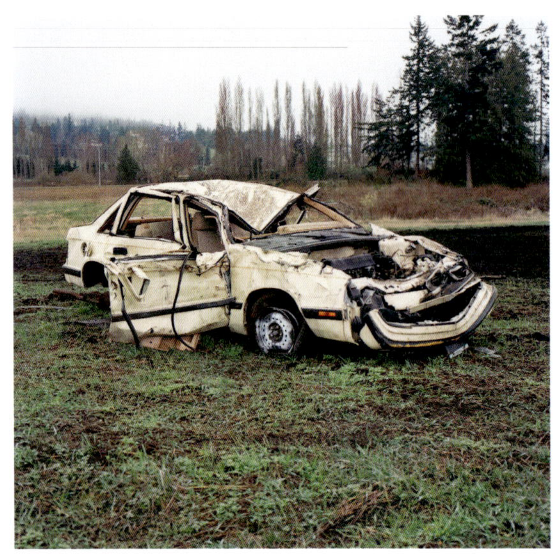

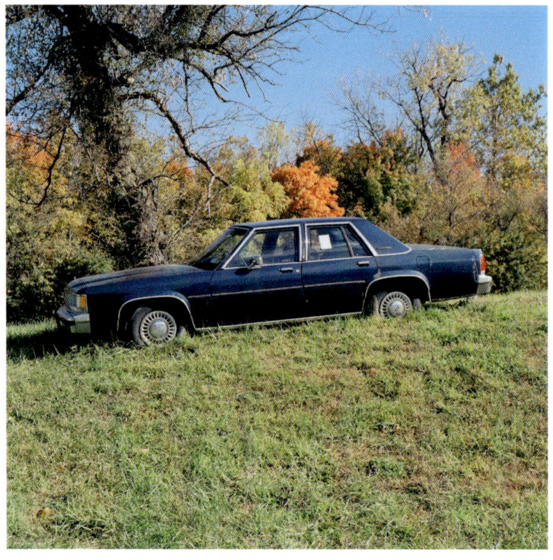

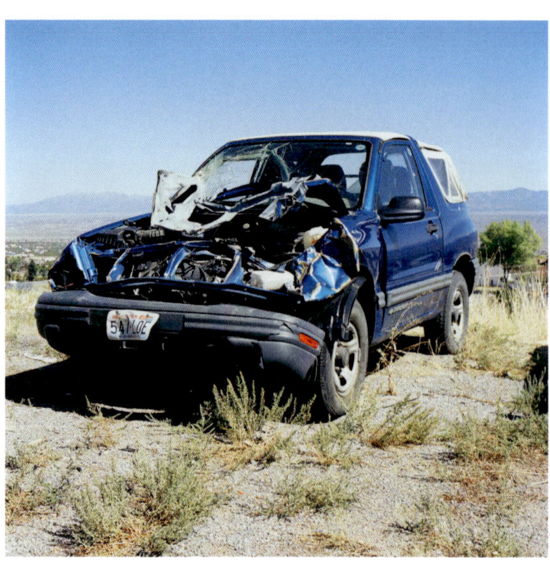

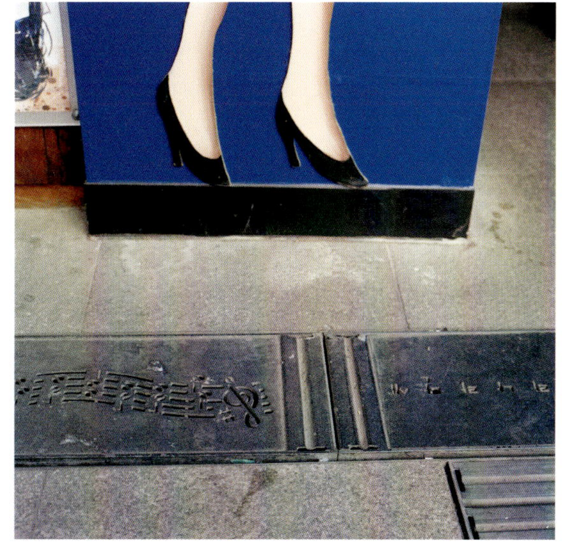
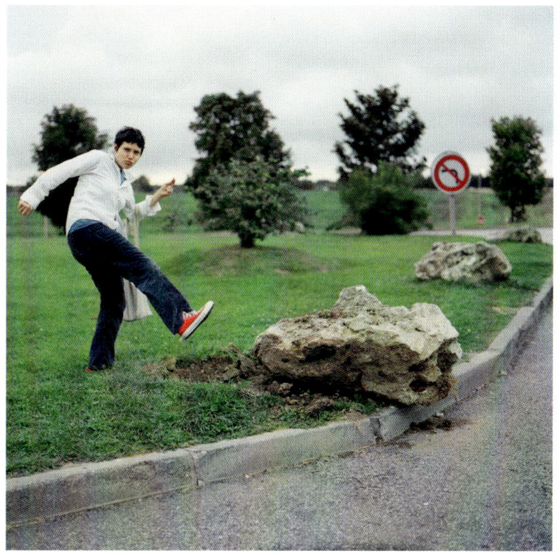
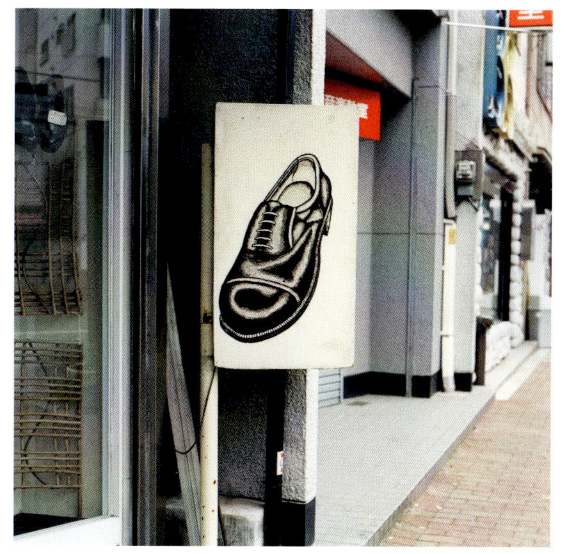
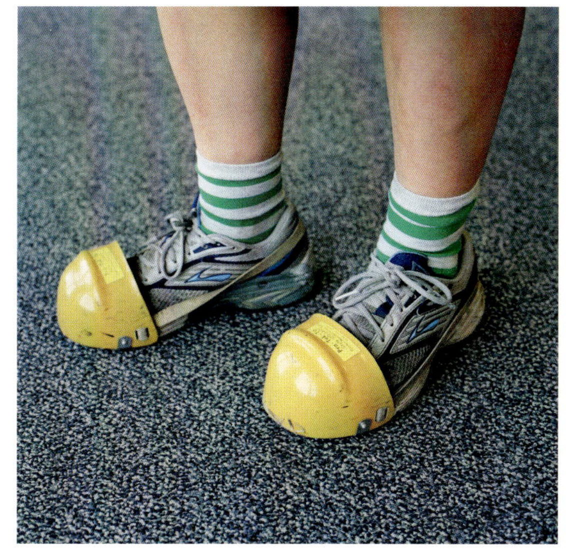
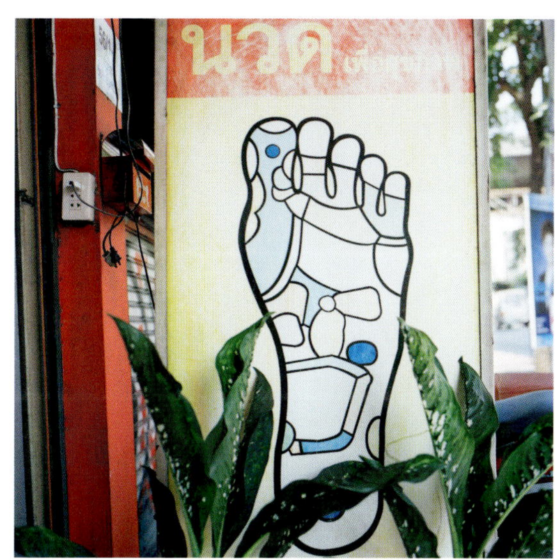
นวด
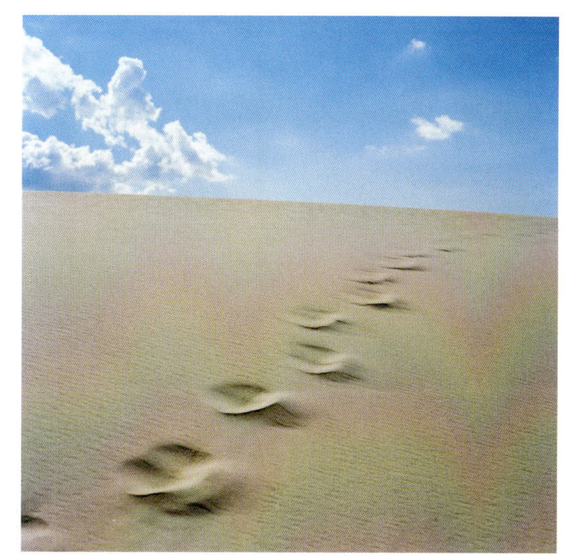
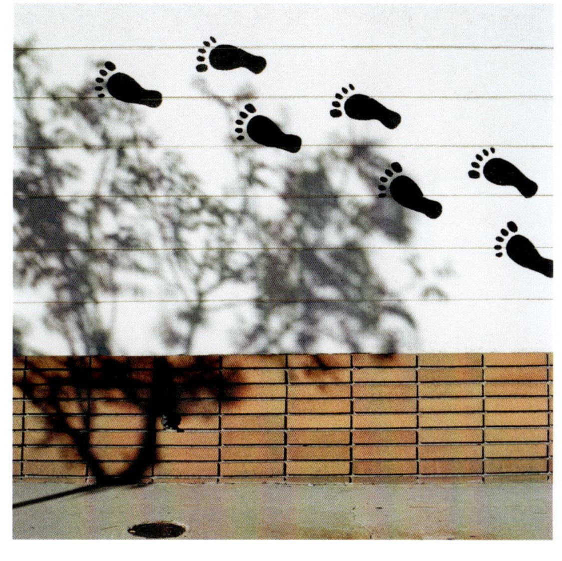
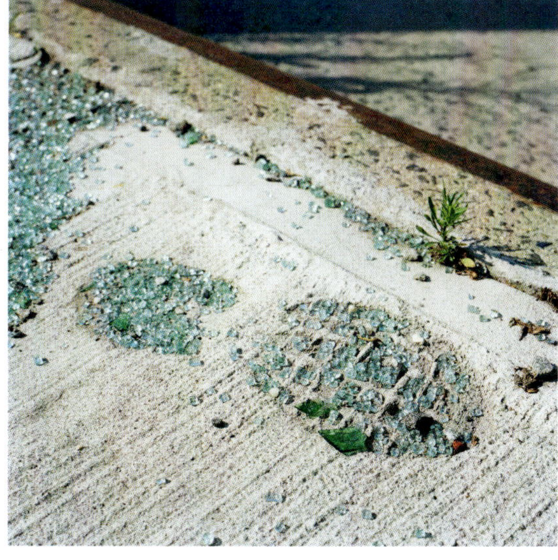
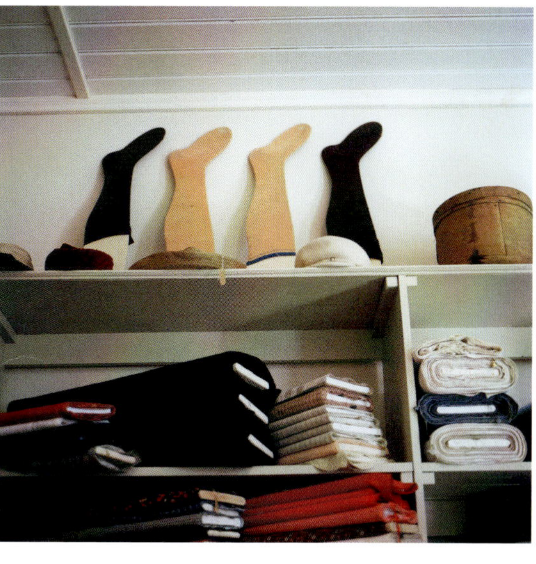

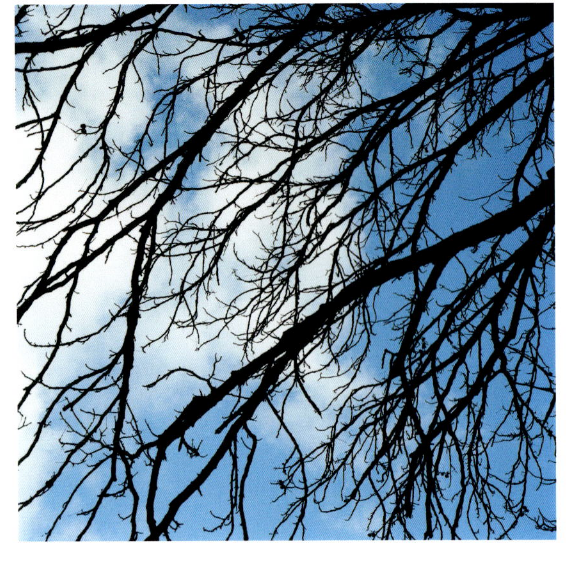
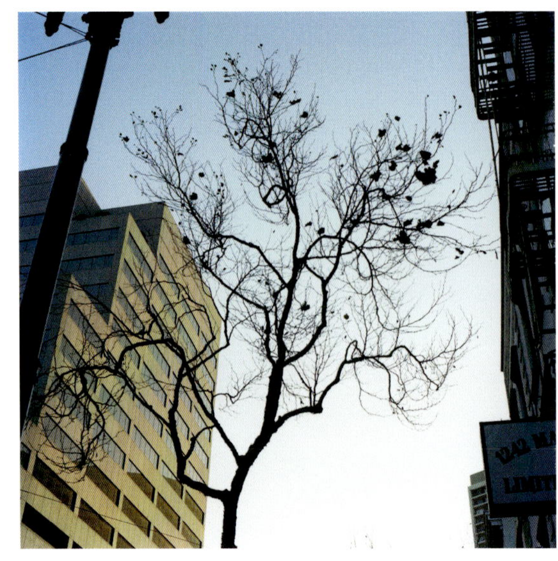
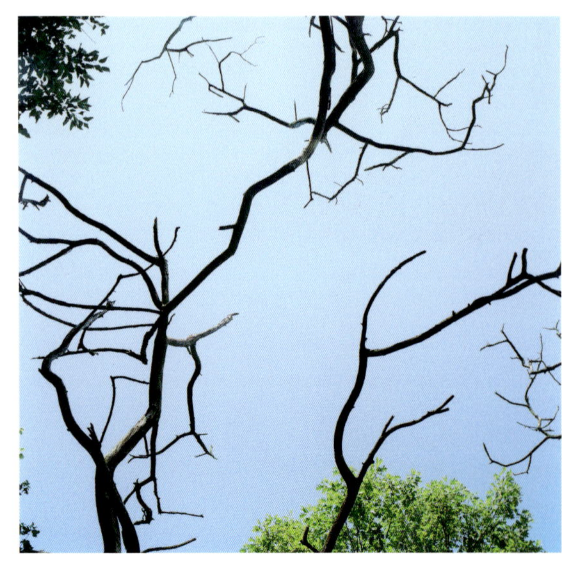
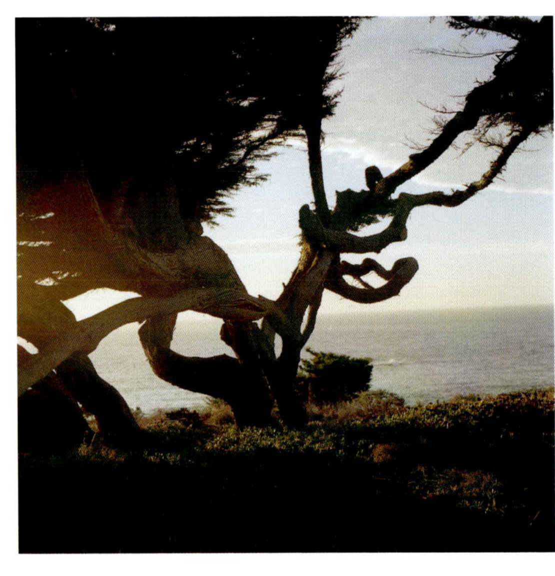
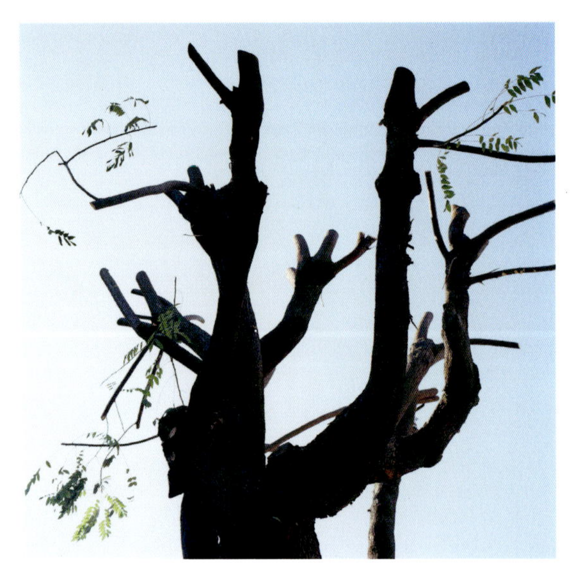
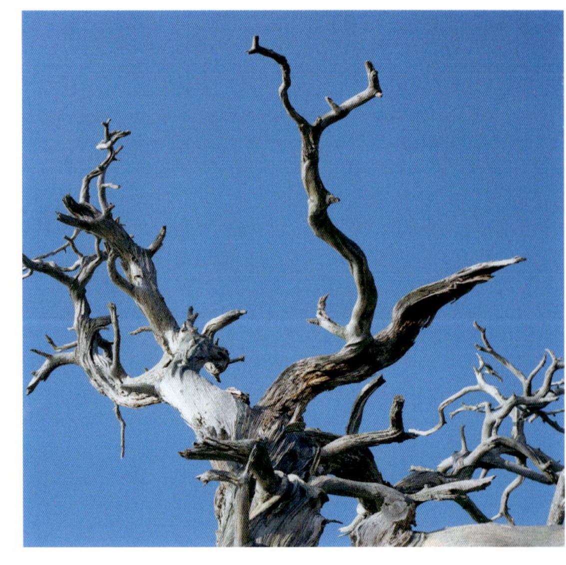
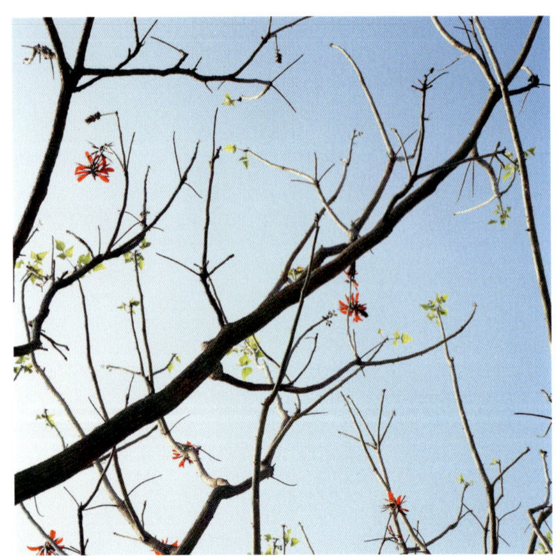
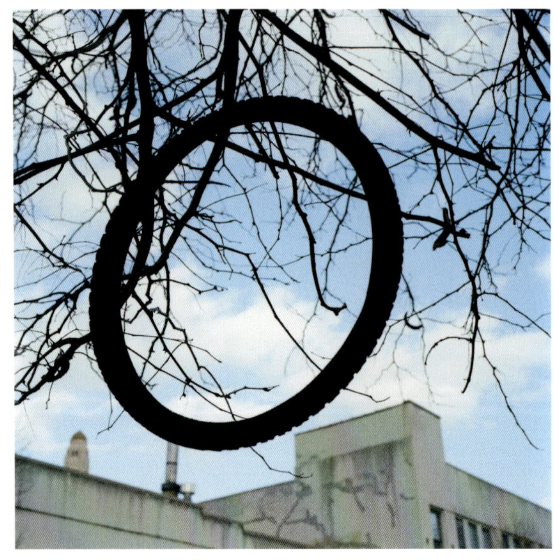
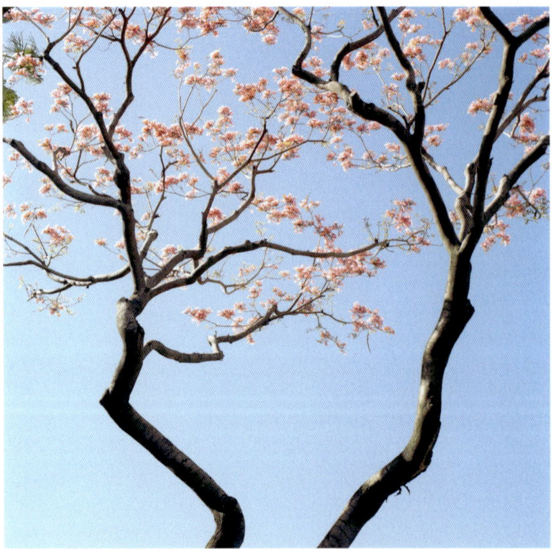

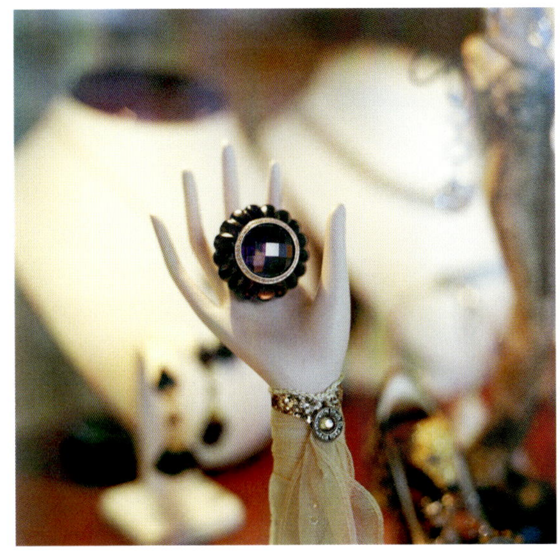

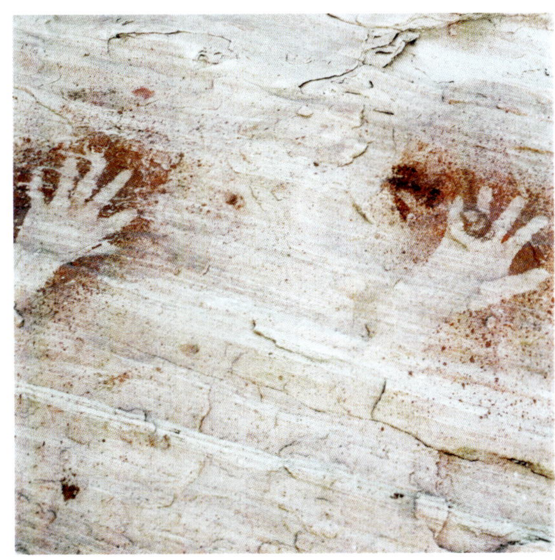

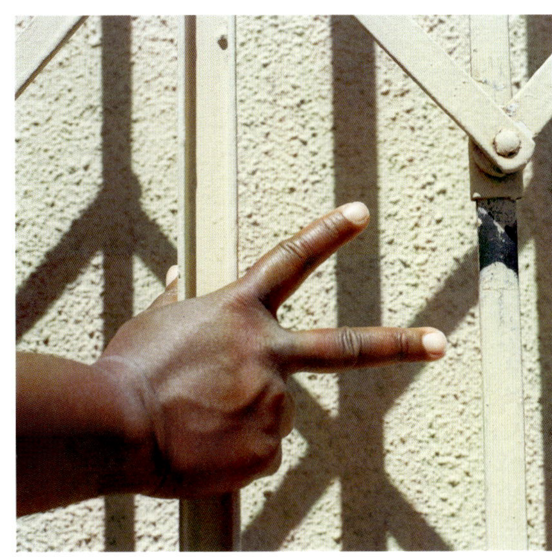

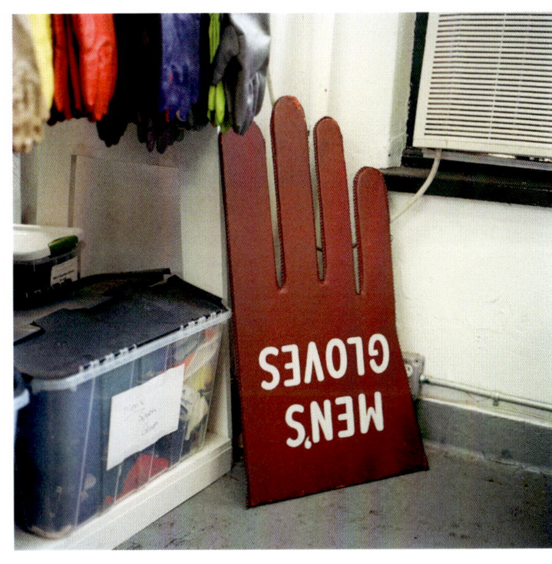
MEN'S
GLOVES

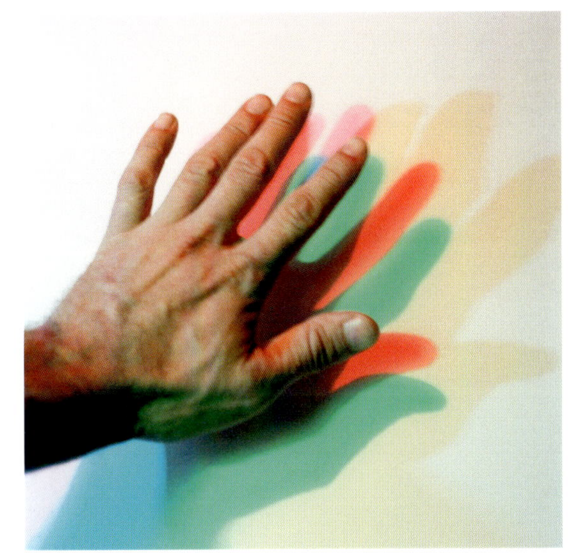

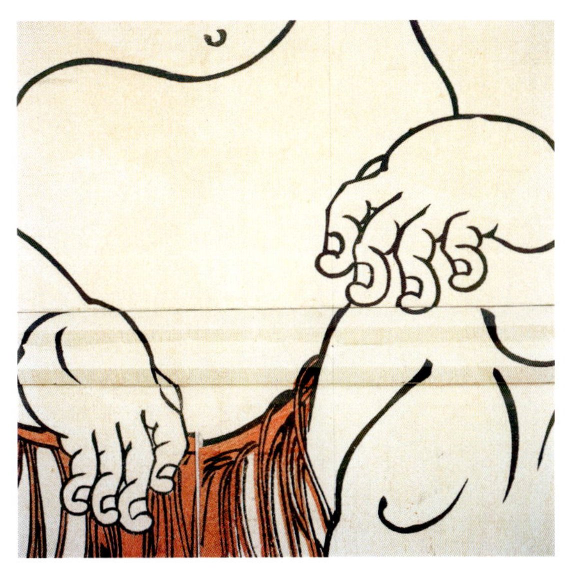

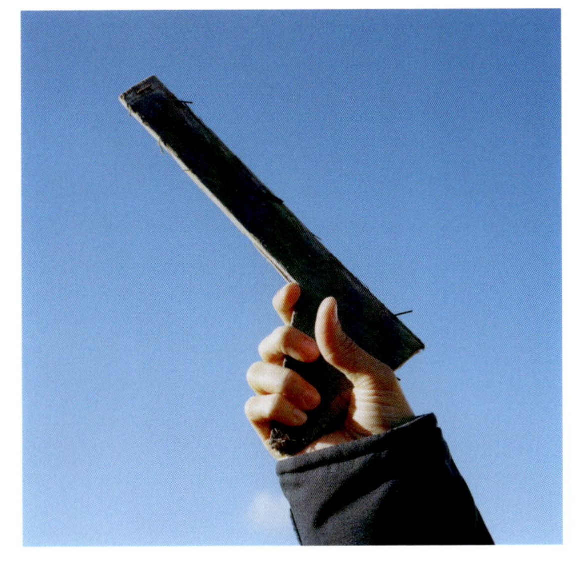

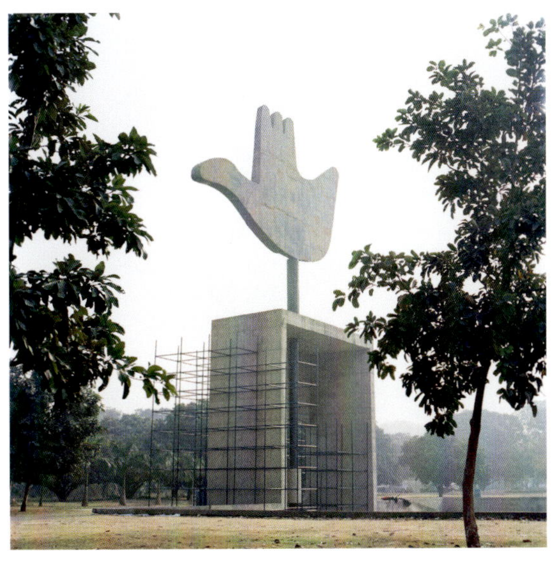

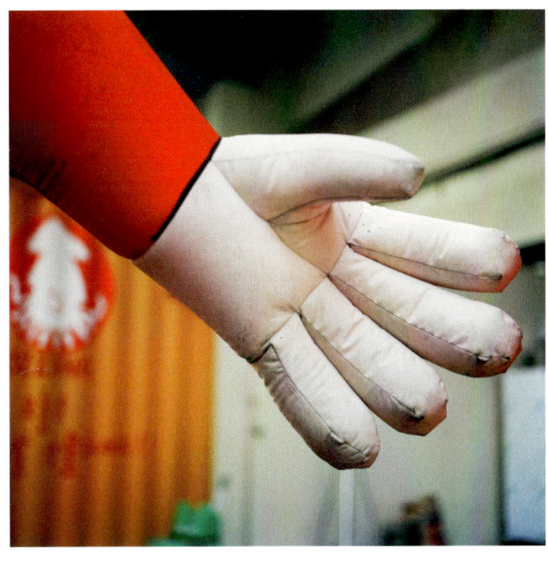

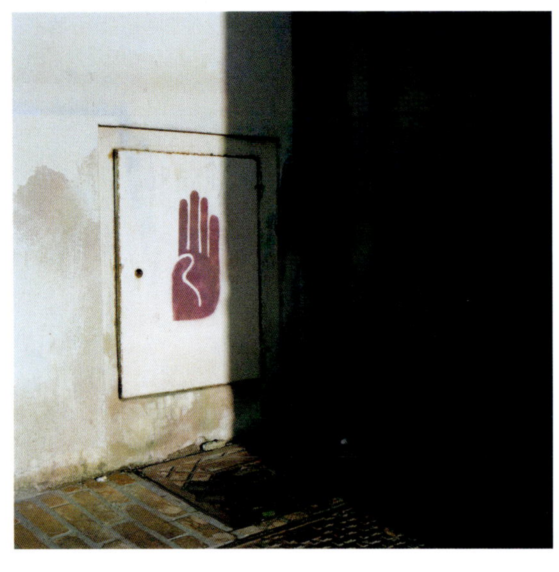
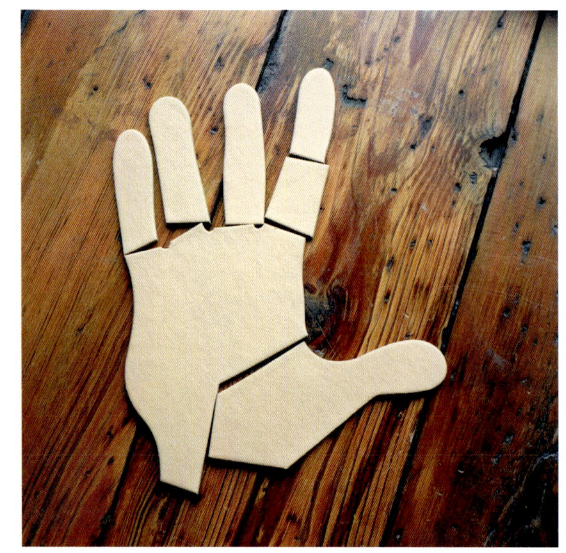
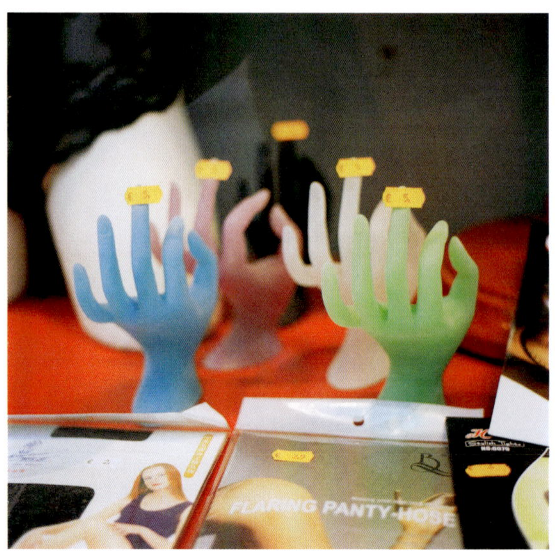
FLARING PANTY-HOSE
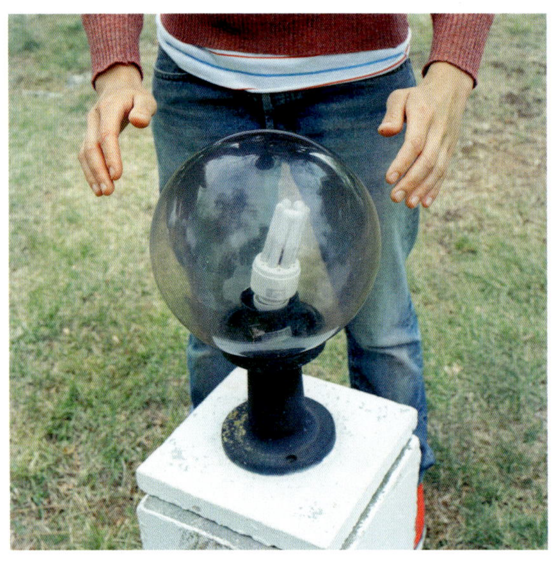
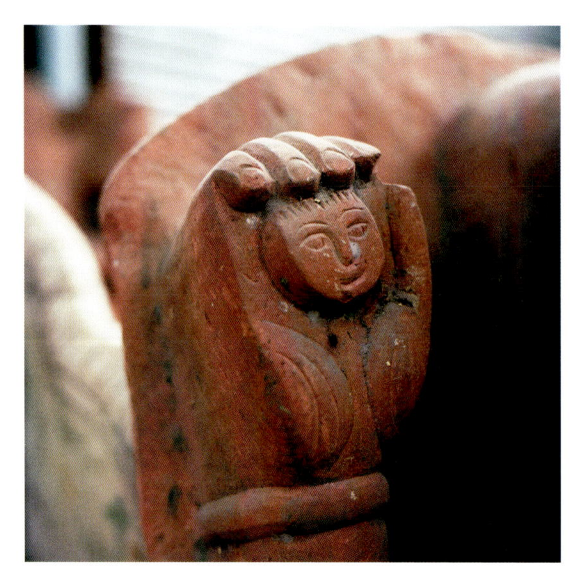
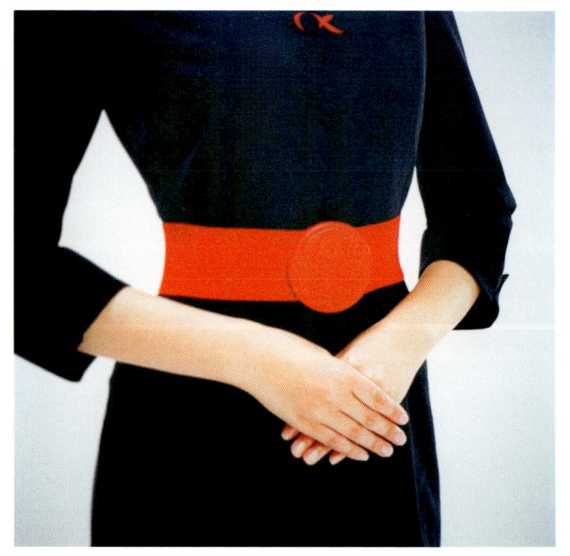
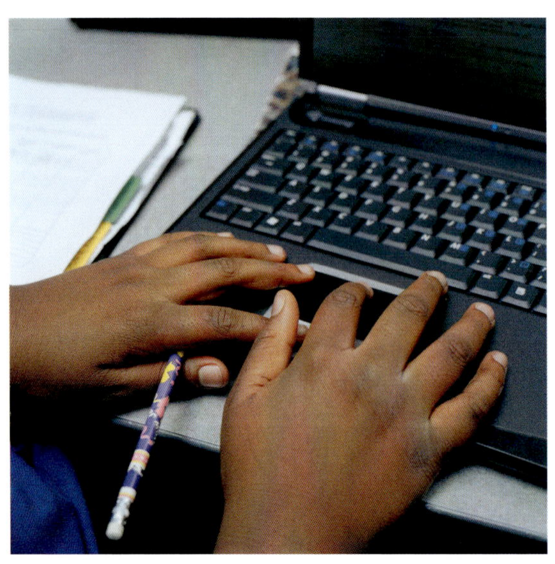
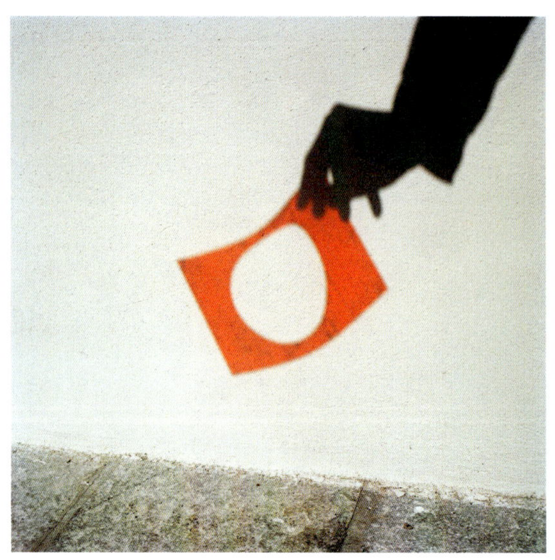
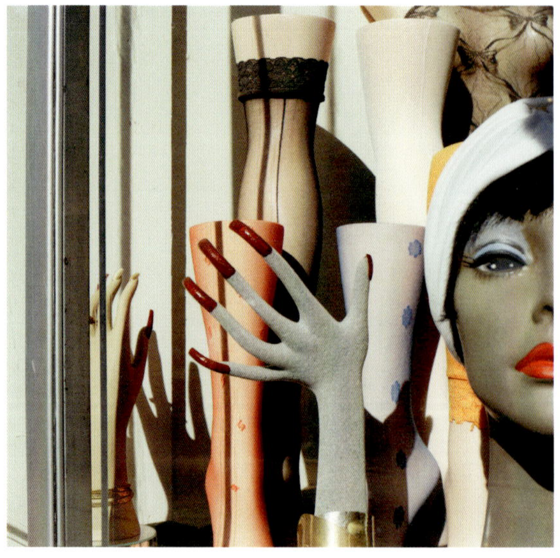

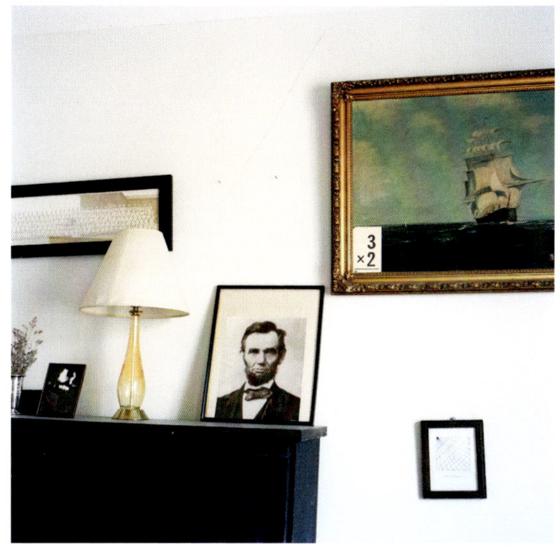
3
×2

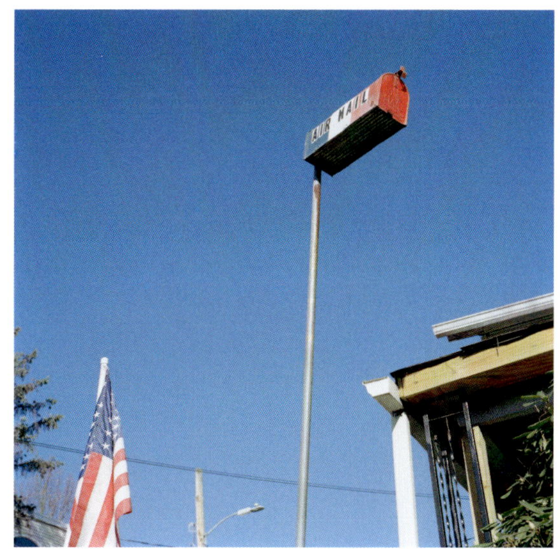
AIR MAIL

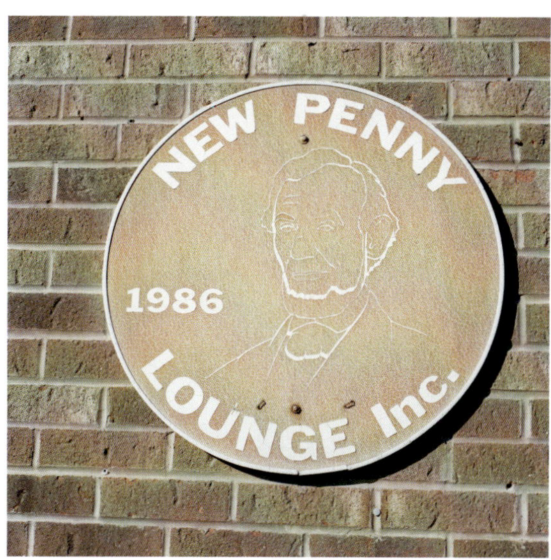
NEW PENNY
1986
LOUNGE Inc.

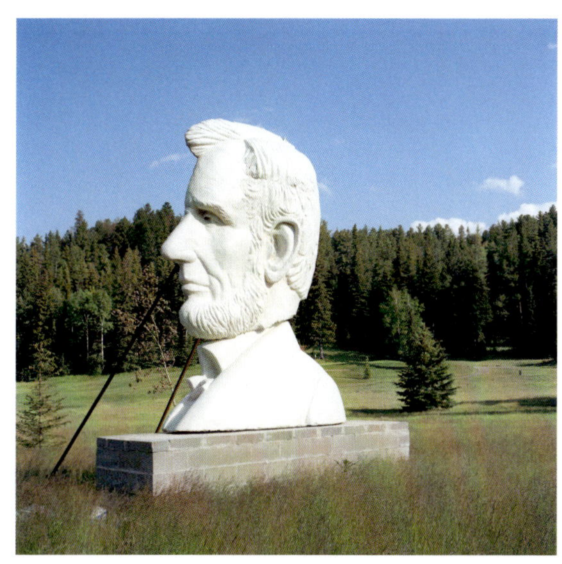

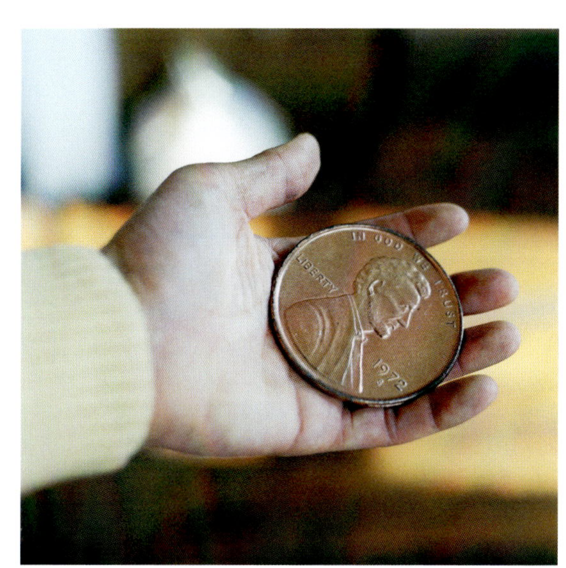
LIBERTY

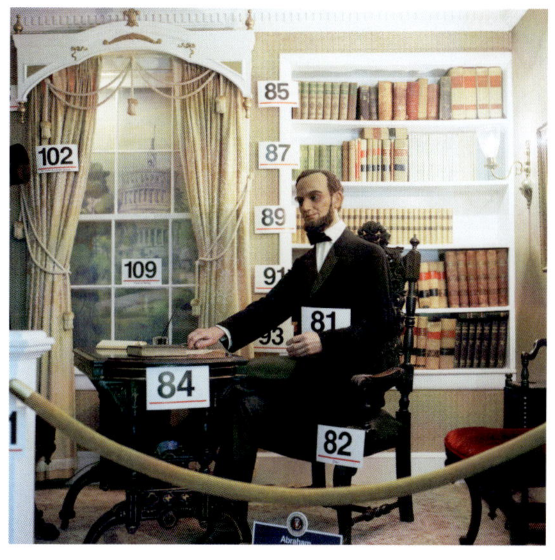
85
102
87
89
109
81
84
82

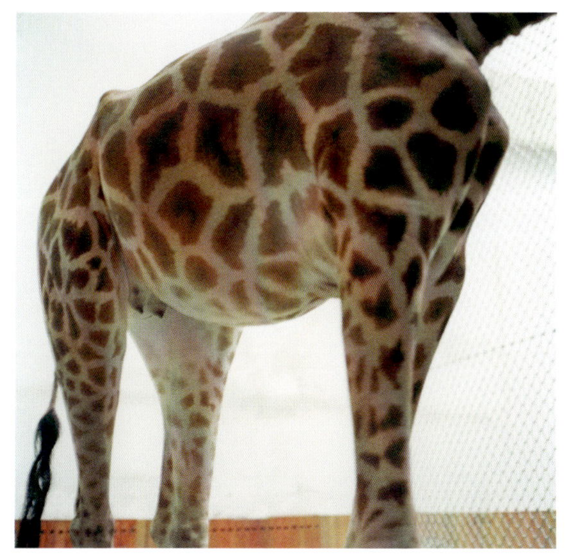

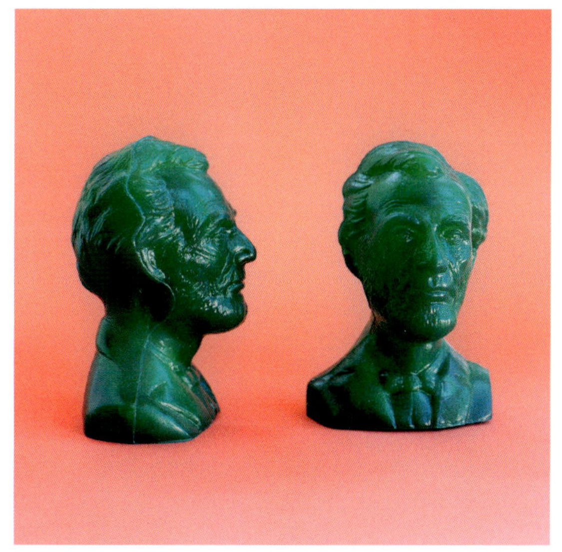

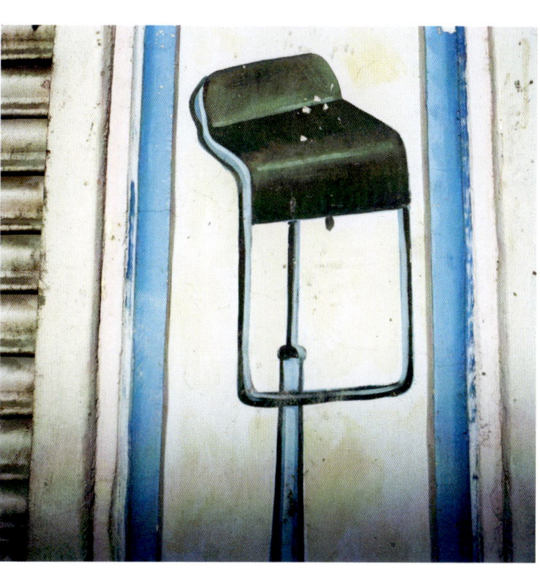

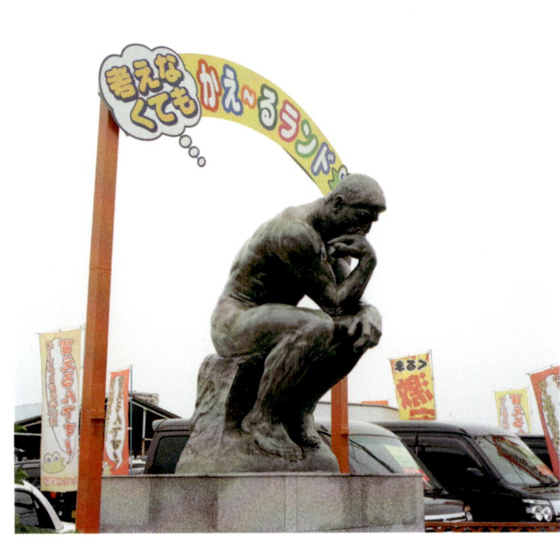
考えなくても
かえ〜るランド

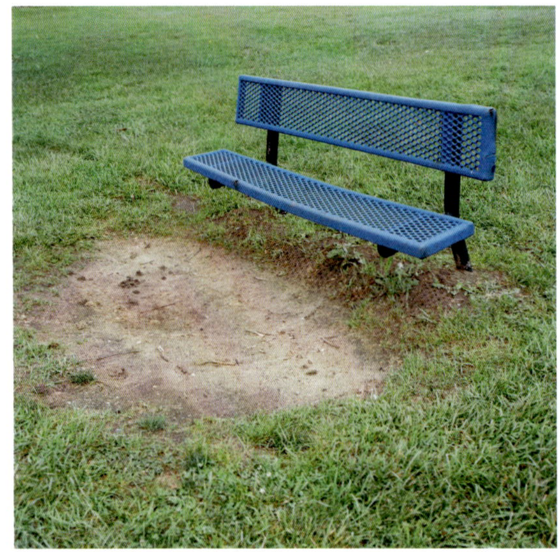

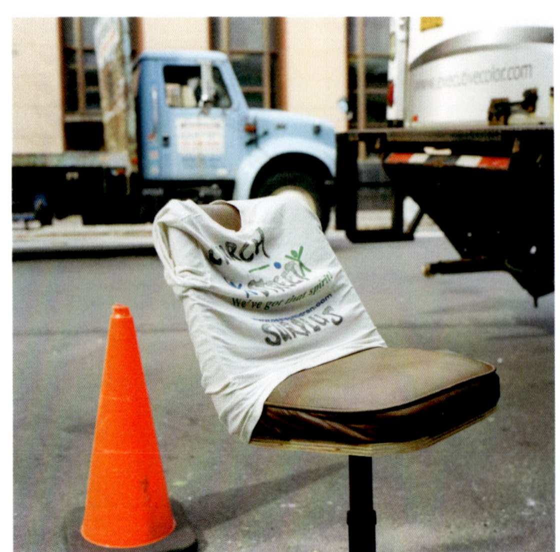

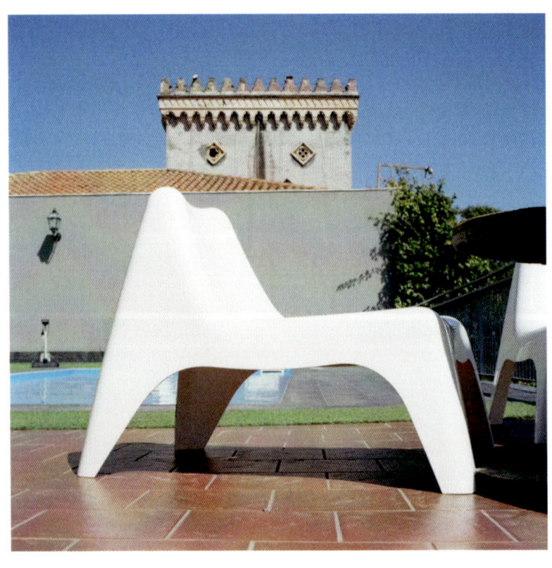

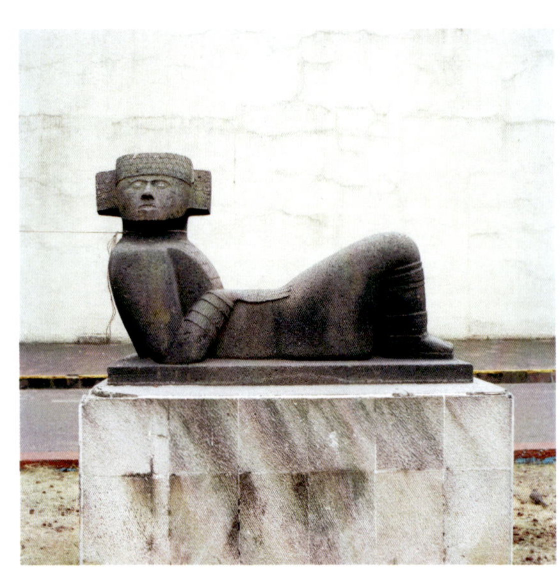

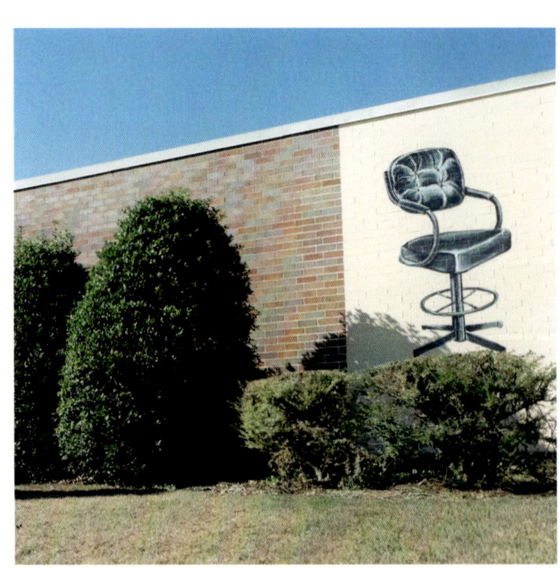

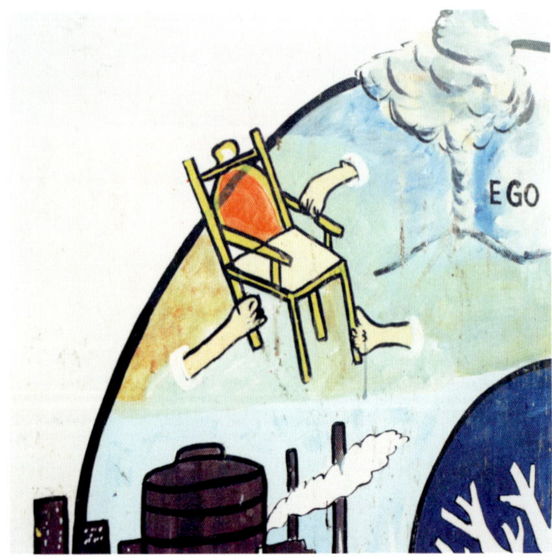
EGO

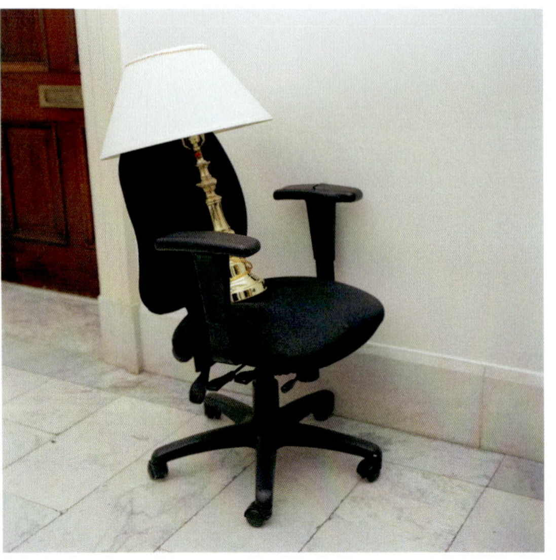

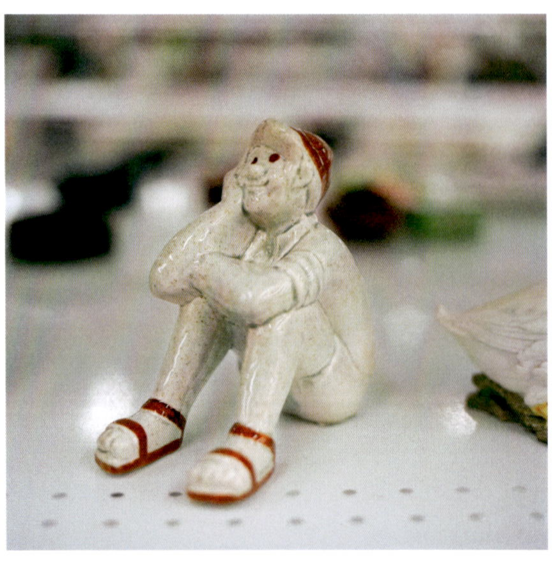

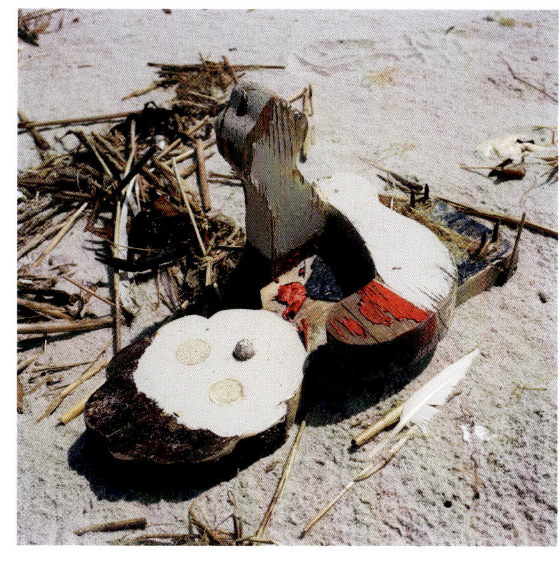
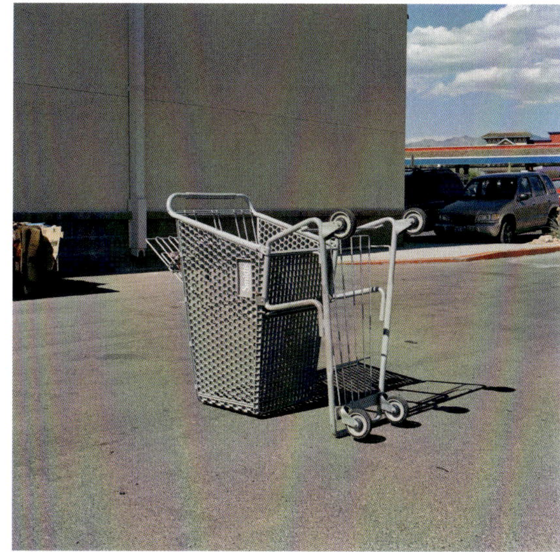
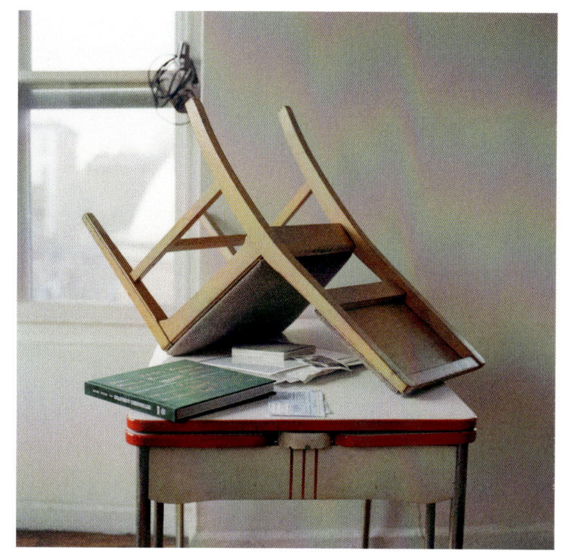
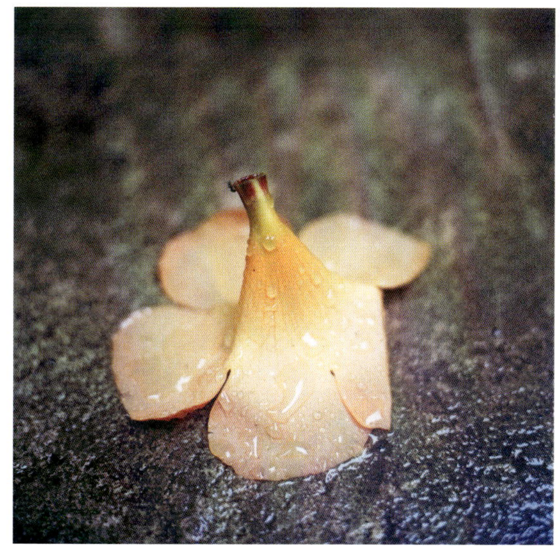
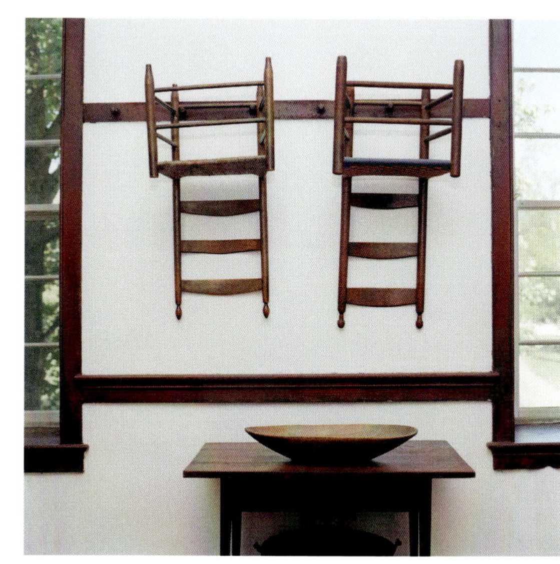
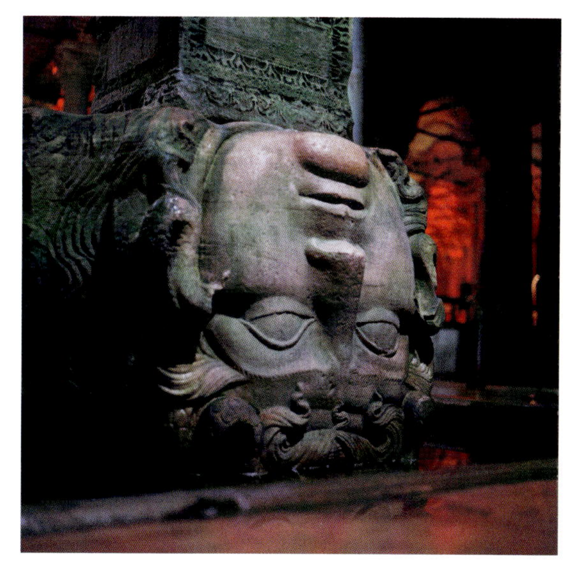
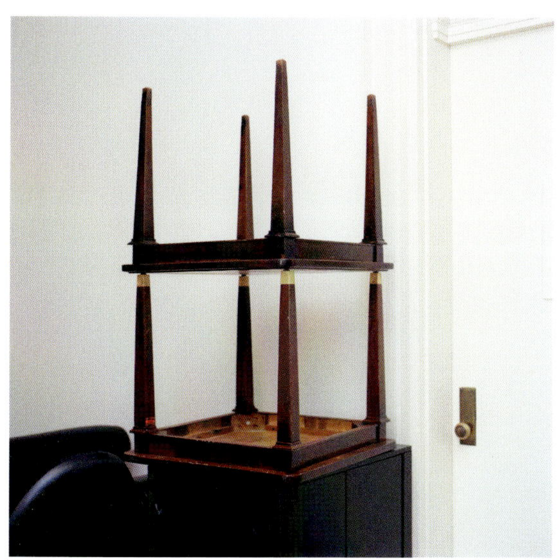
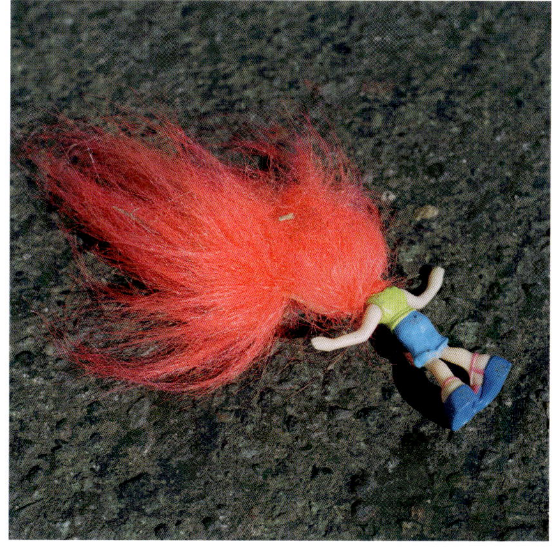
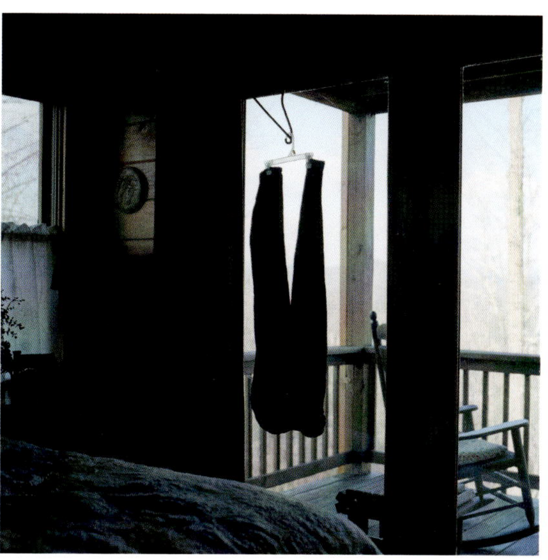

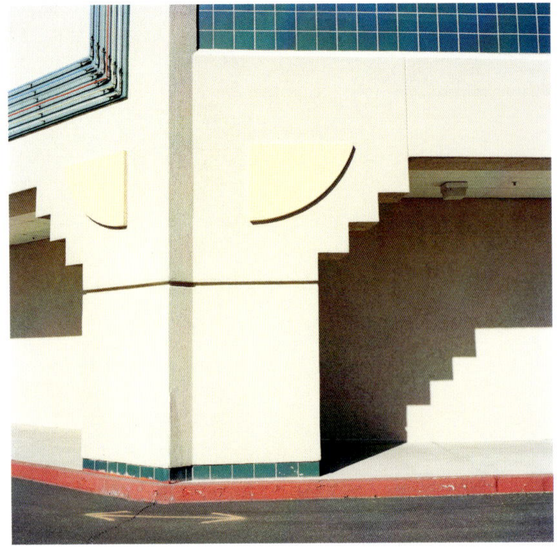
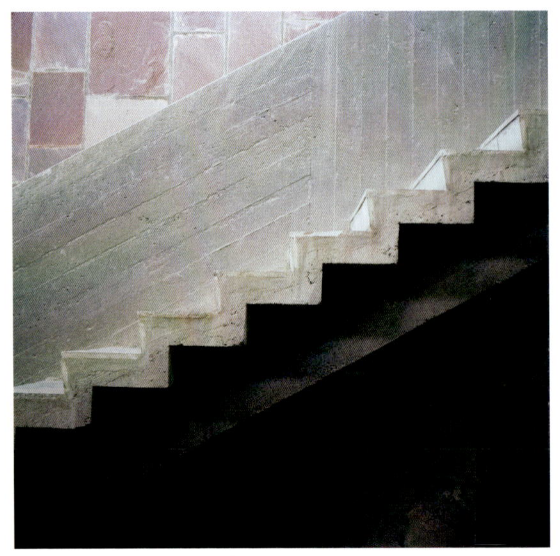
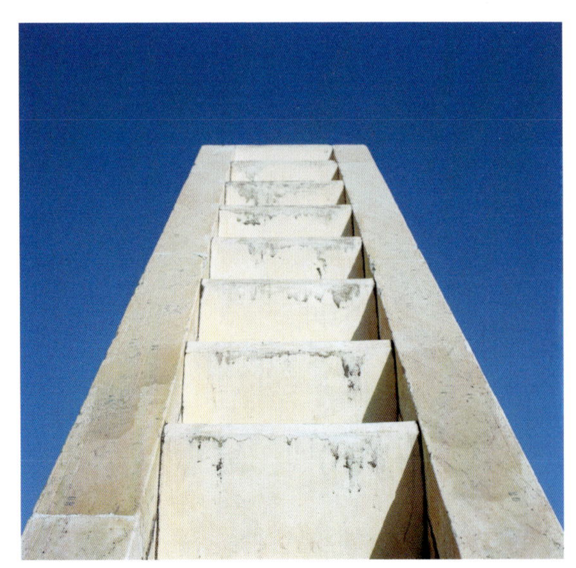
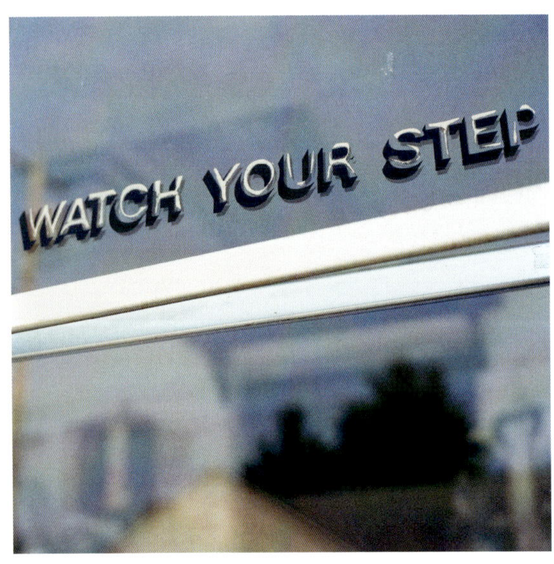
WATCH YOUR STEP
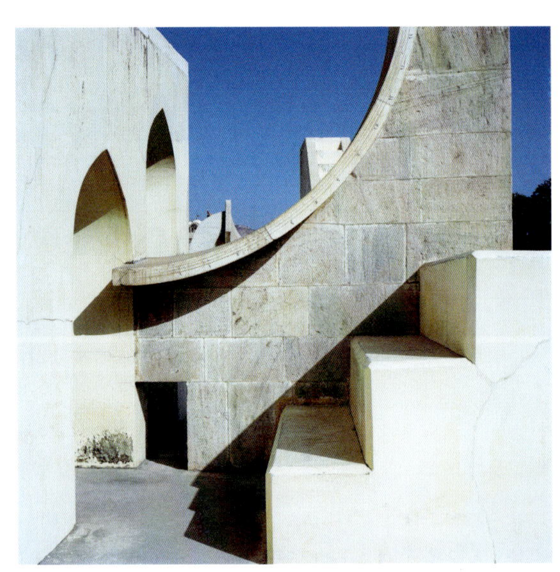
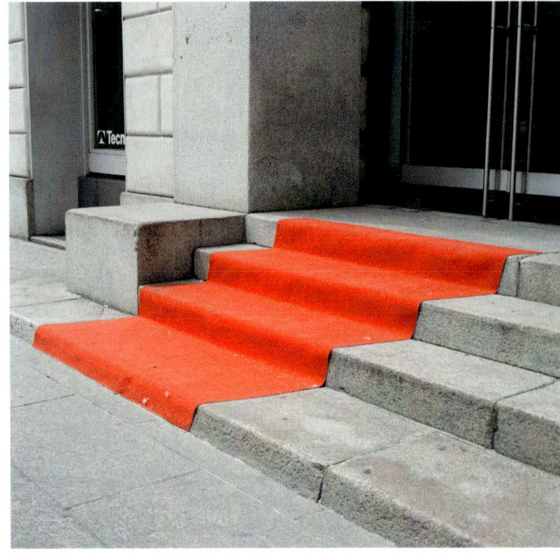
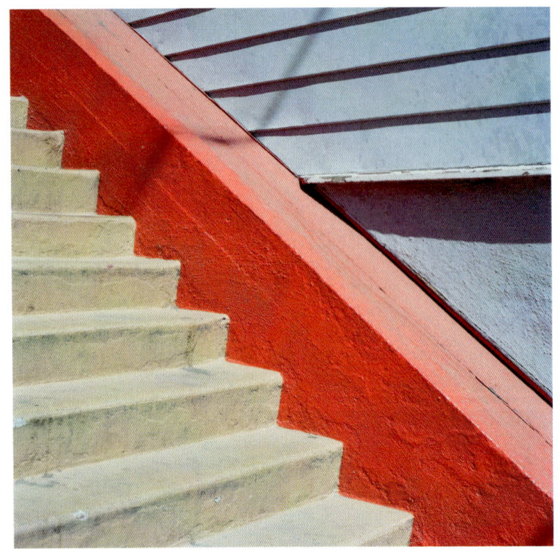
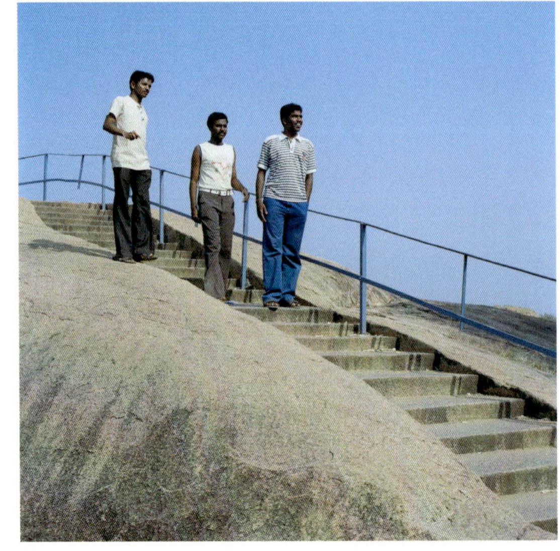
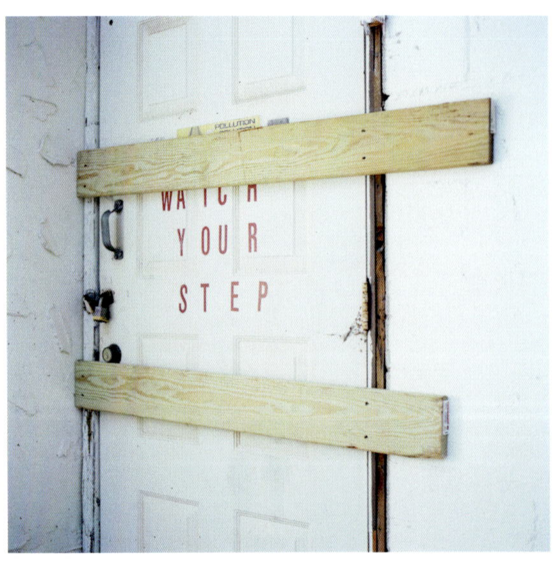
YOUR
STEP

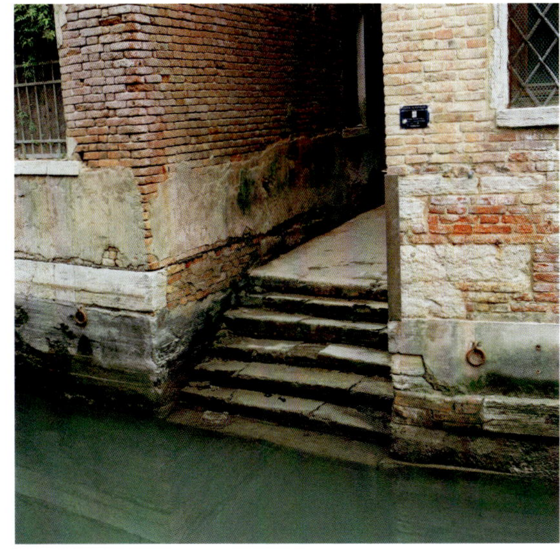

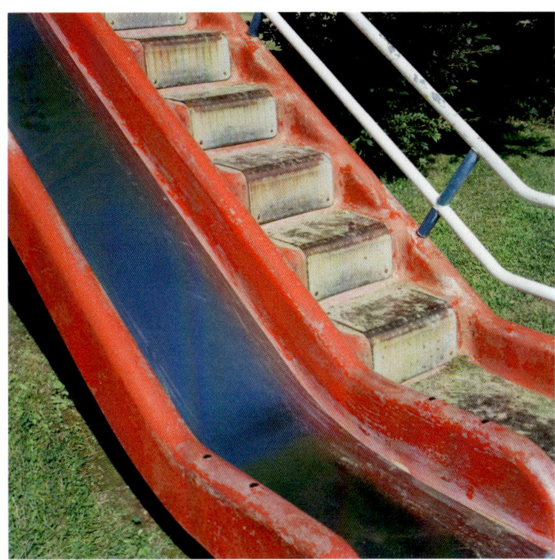

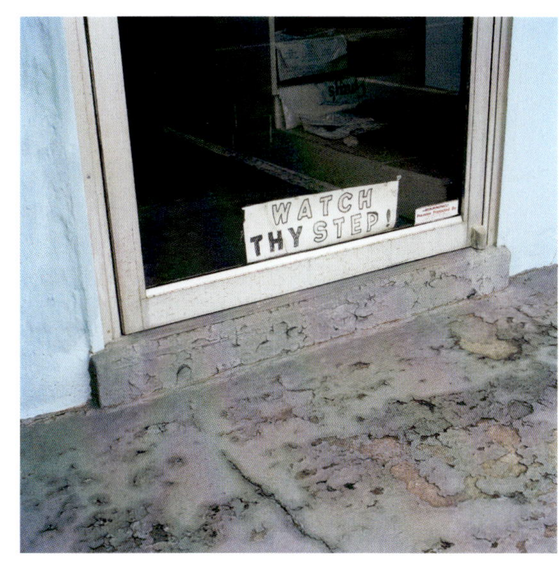

WATCH
THY STEP!

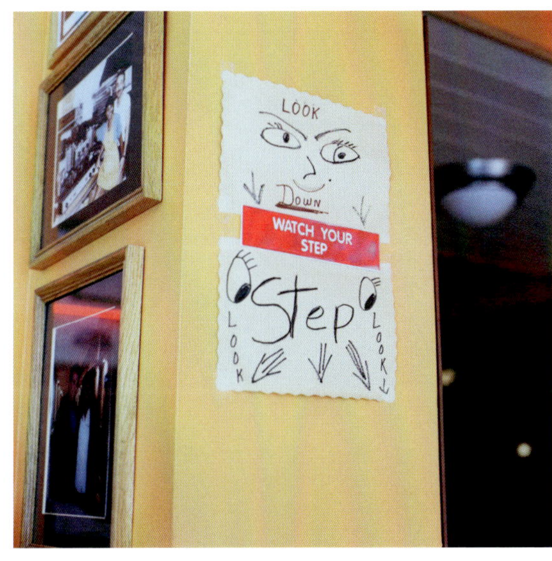

LOOK
DOWN
WATCH YOUR STEP
Step
LOOK
LOOK

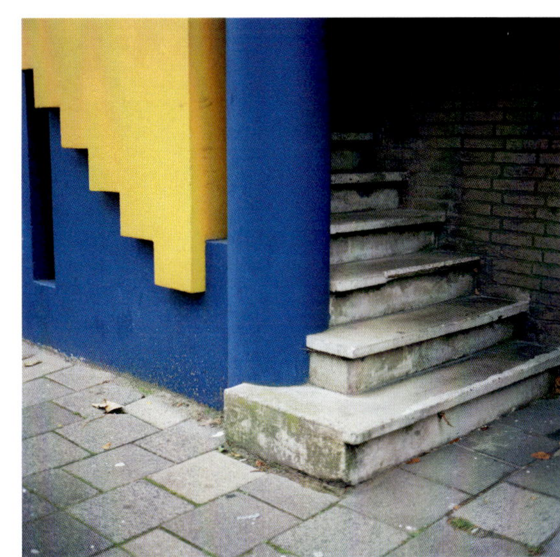

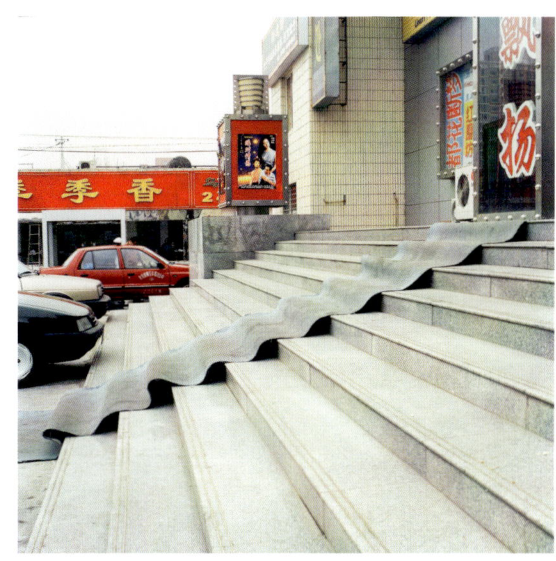

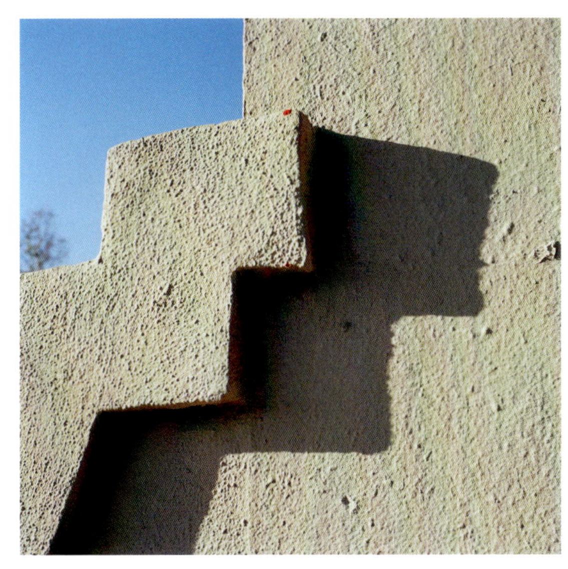

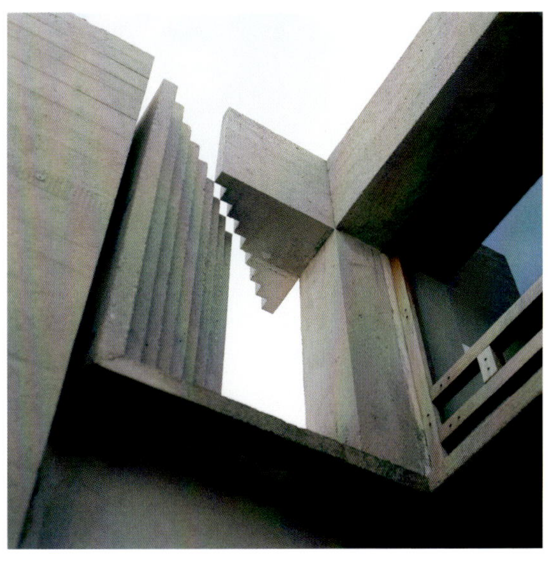

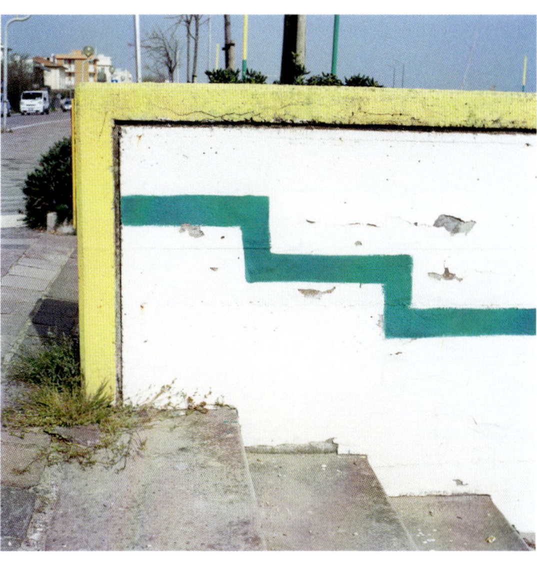

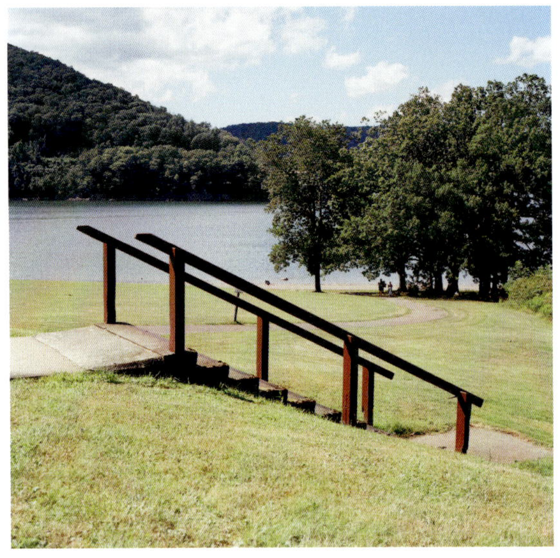

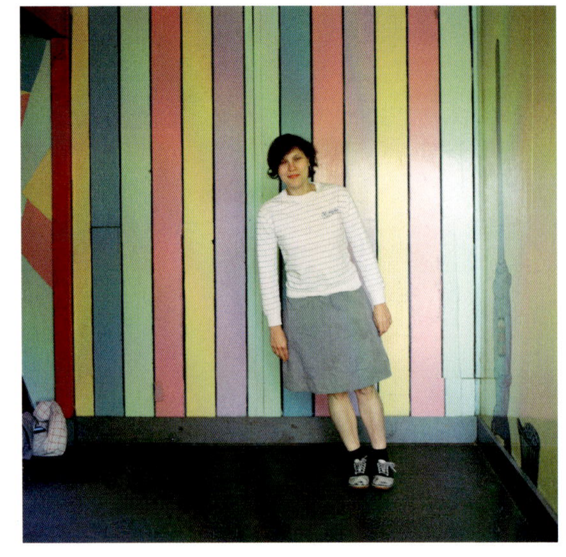

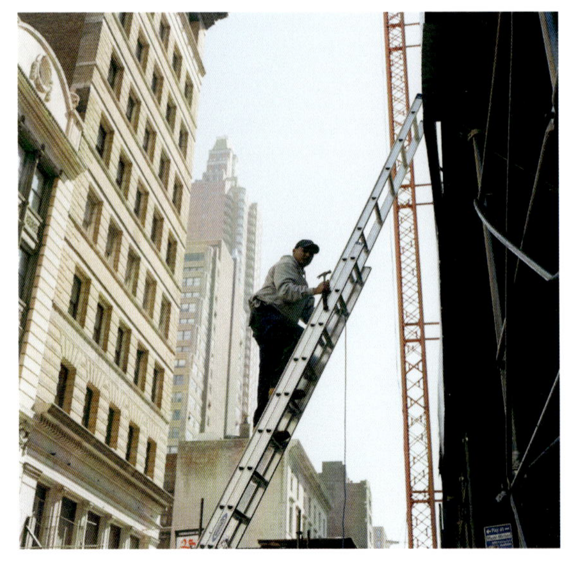

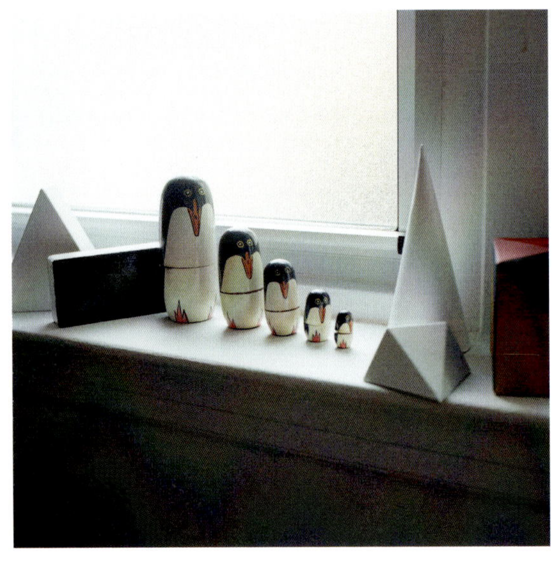

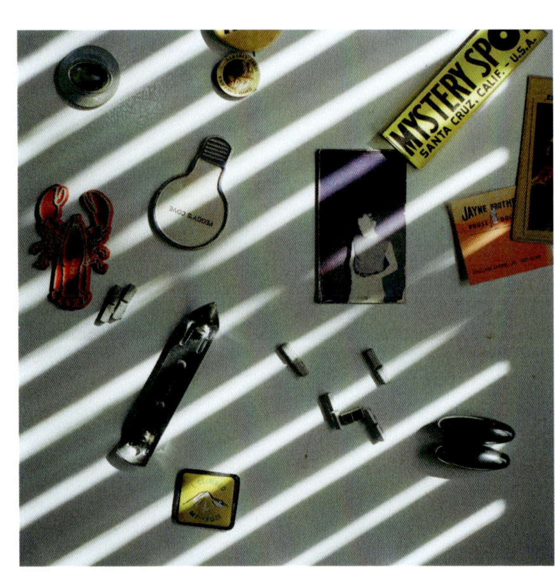

MYSTERY
SANTA CRUZ, CALIF. - U.S.A.

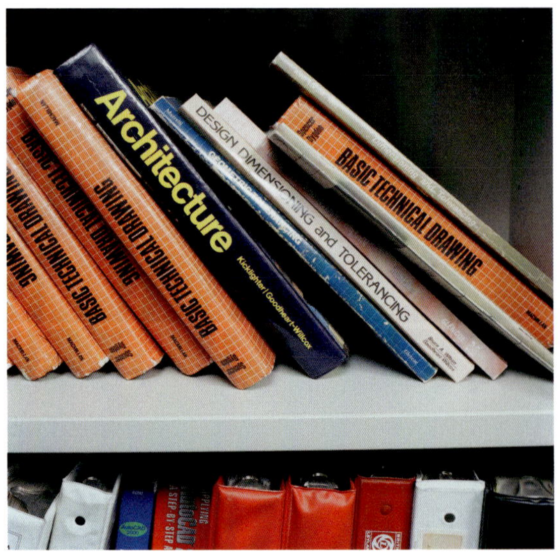

Architecture
BASIC TECHNICAL DRAWING
DESIGN DIMENSIONING and TOLERANCING

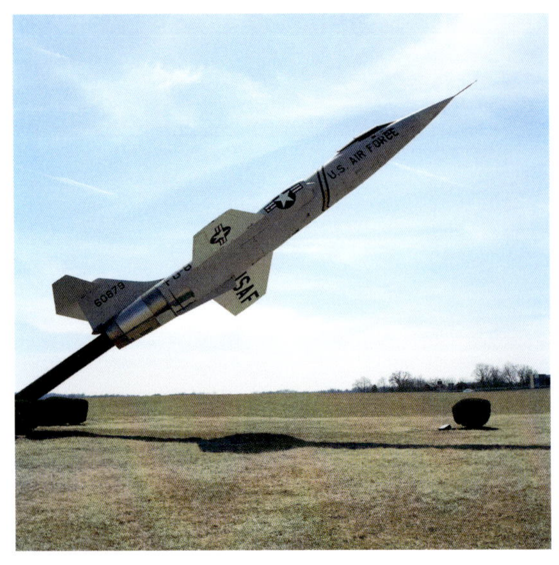

U.S. AIR FORCE
USAF

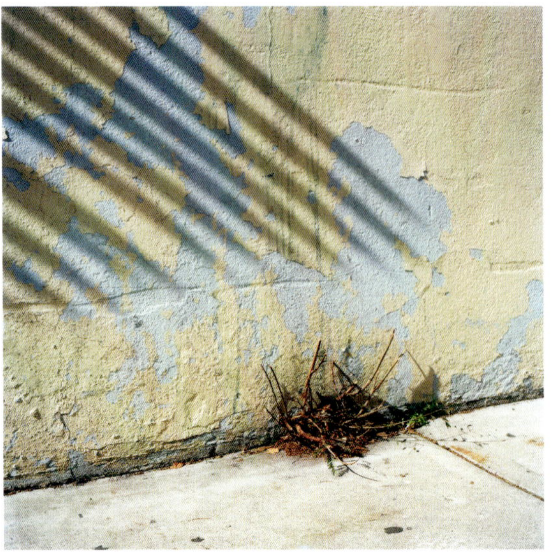

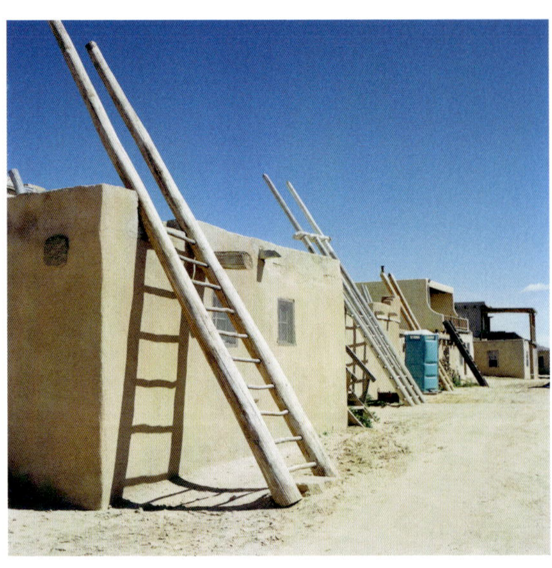

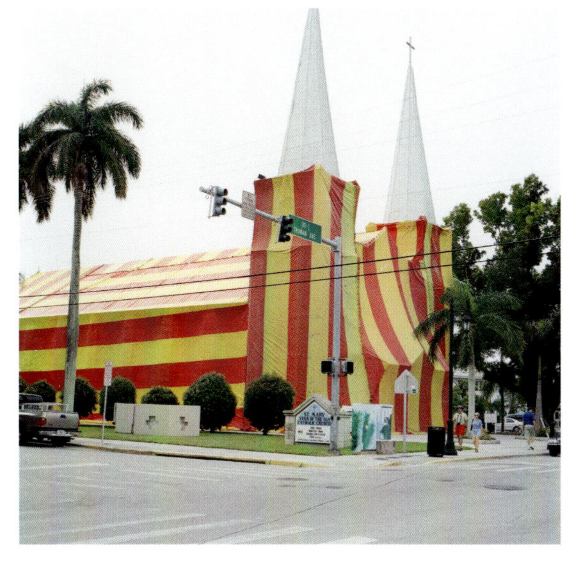
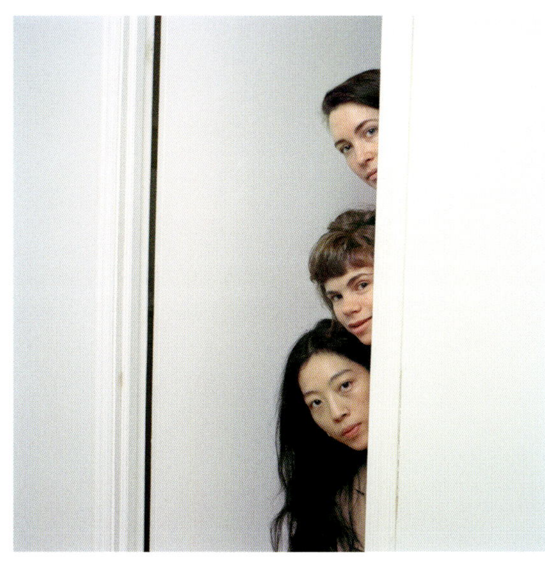
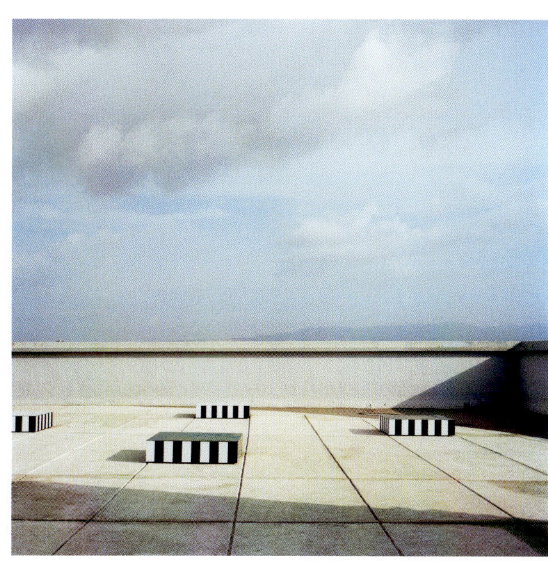
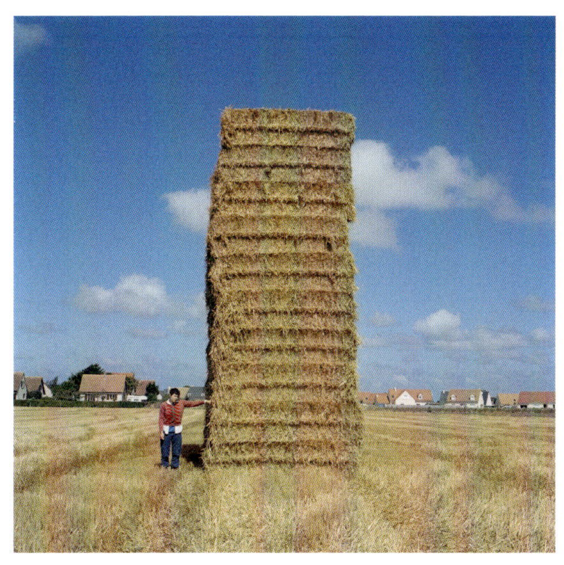
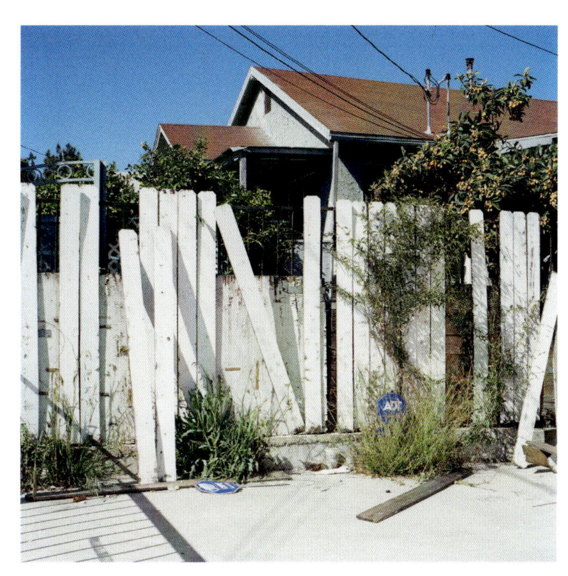
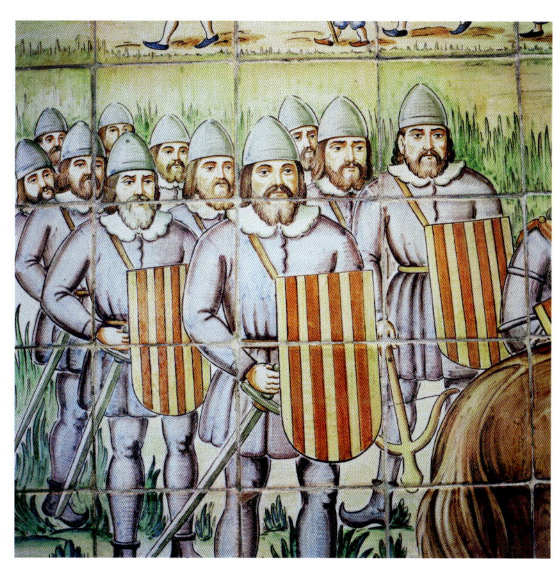
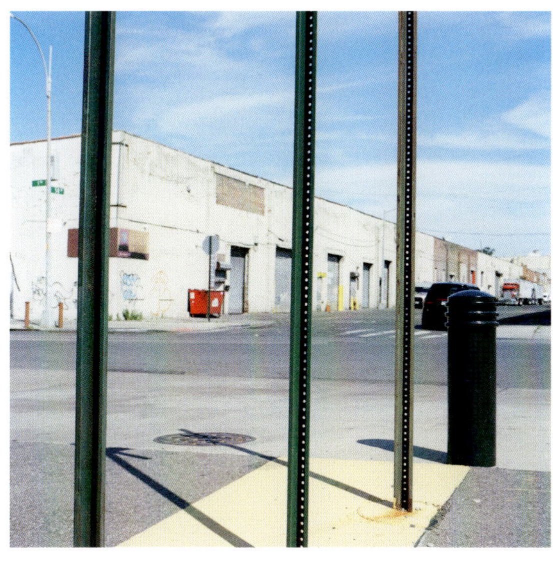
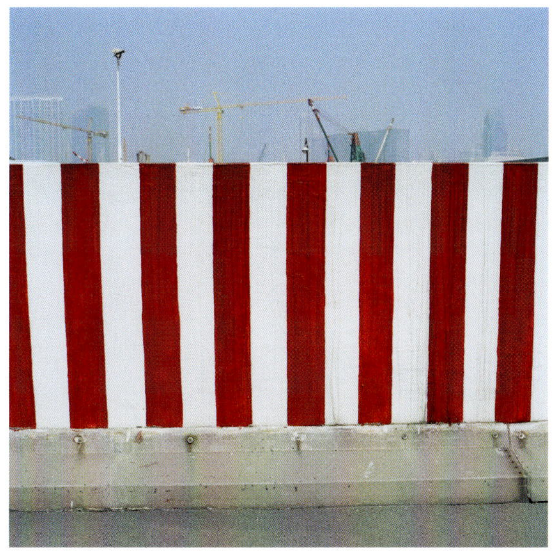
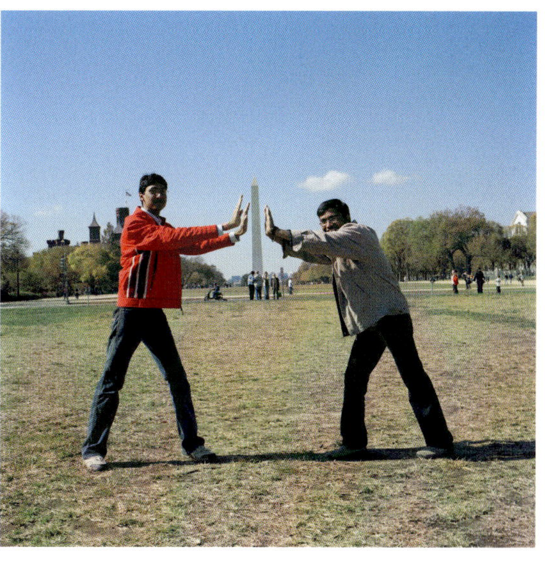

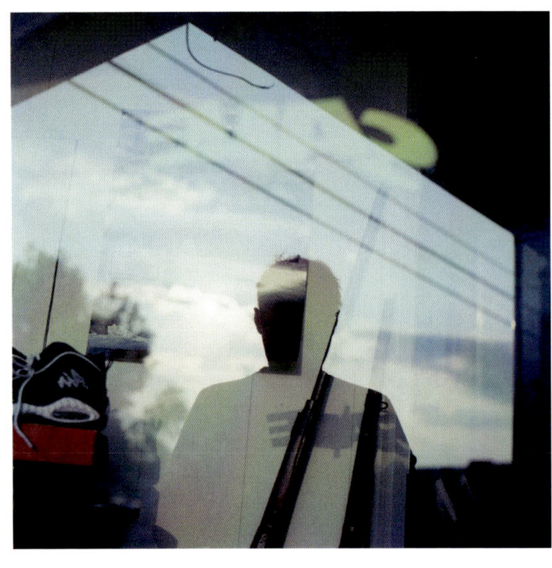
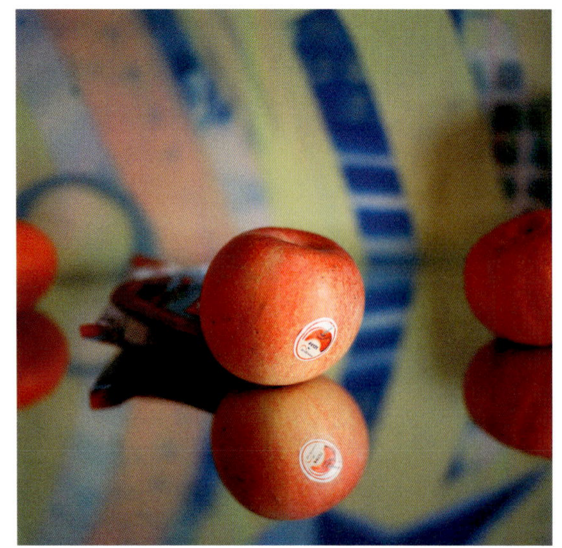
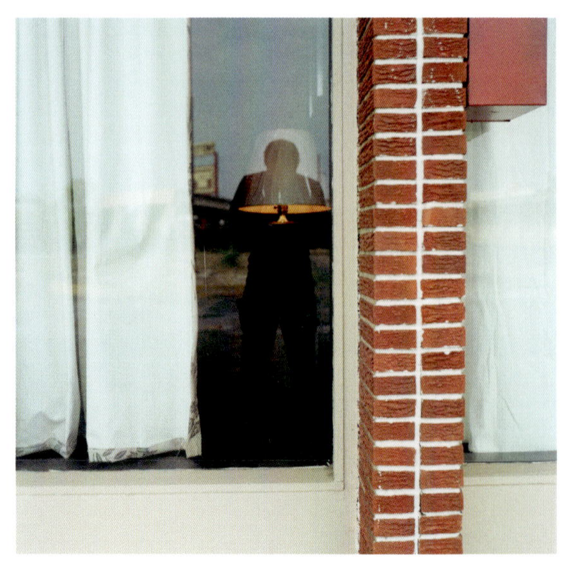
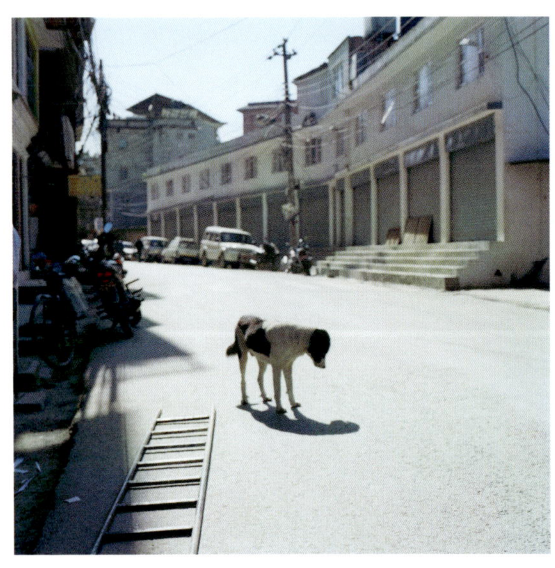
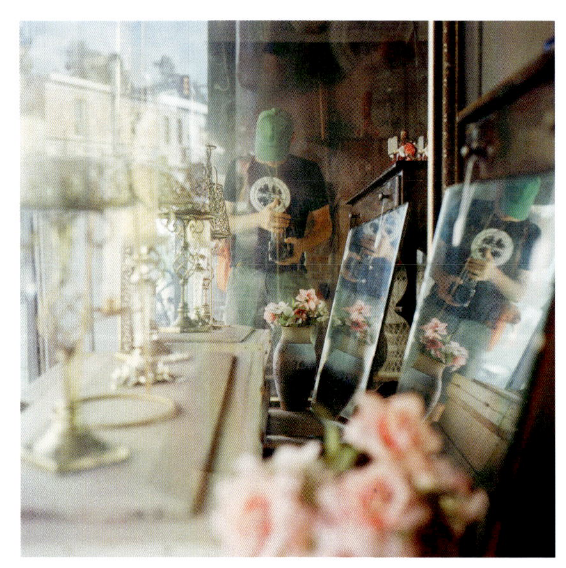
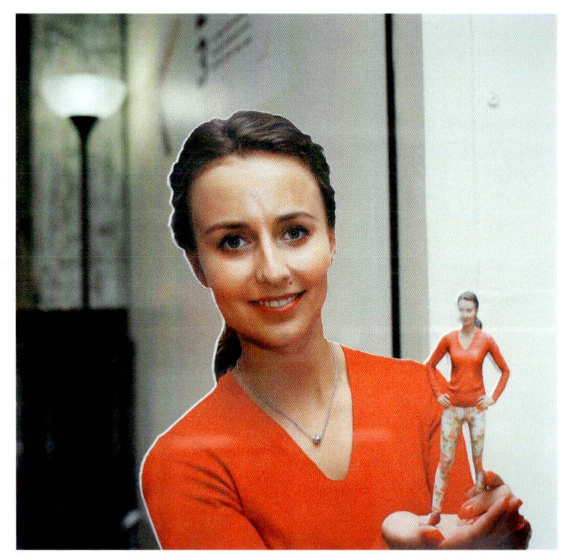
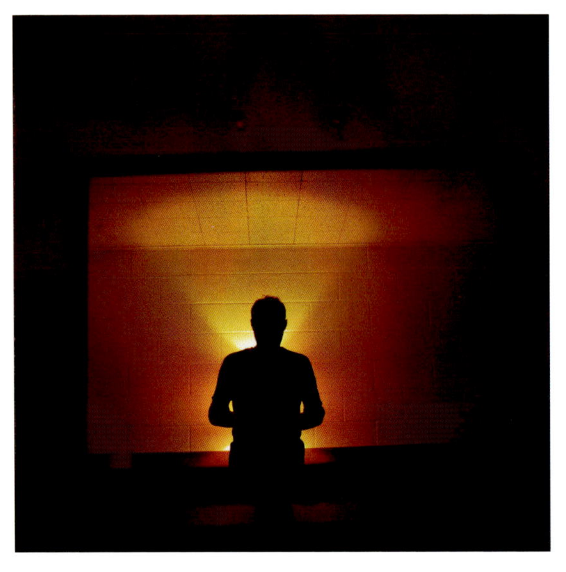
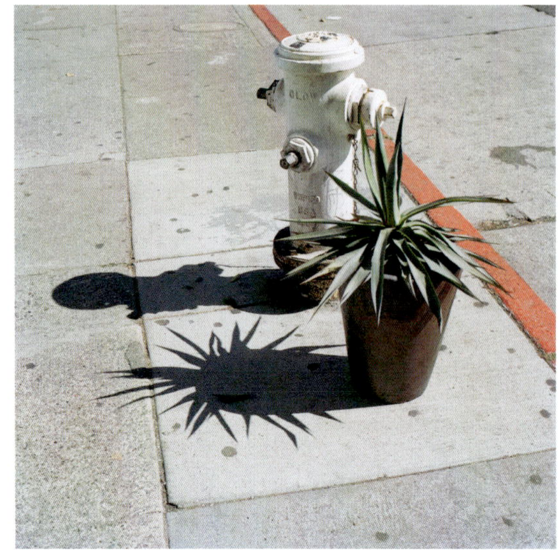
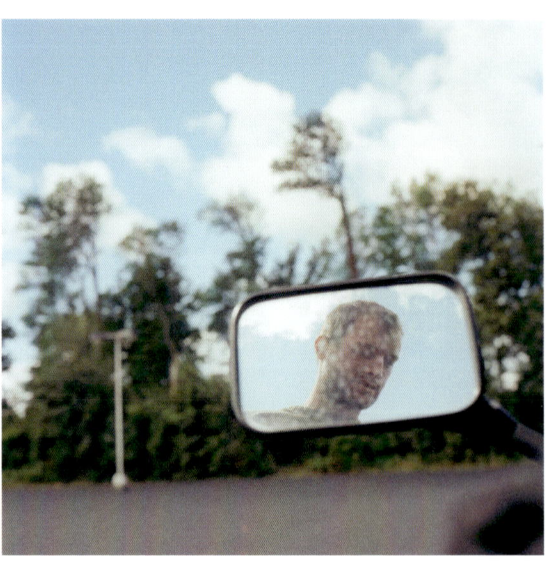

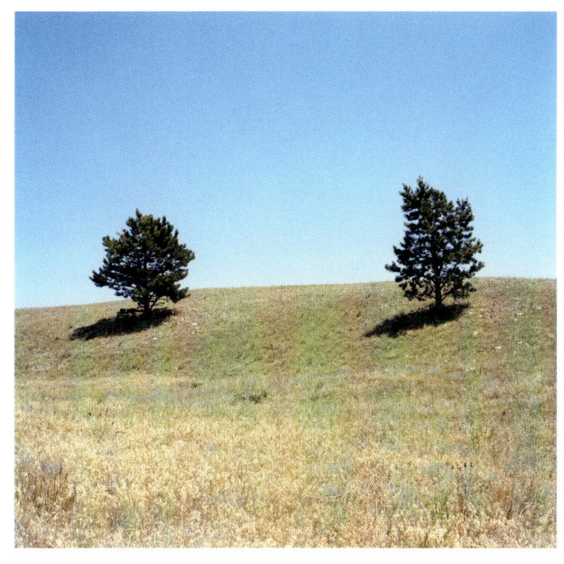
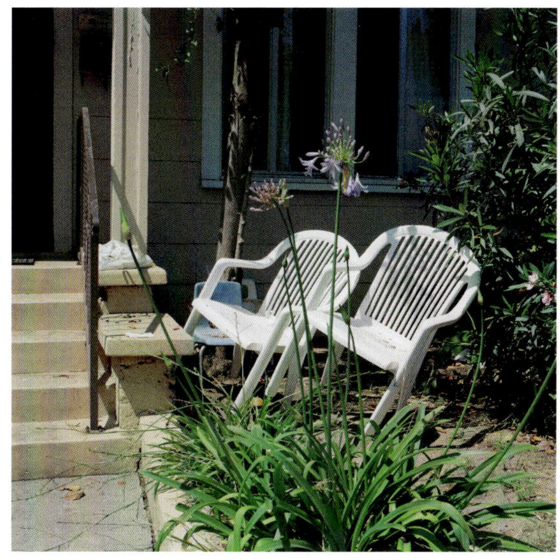
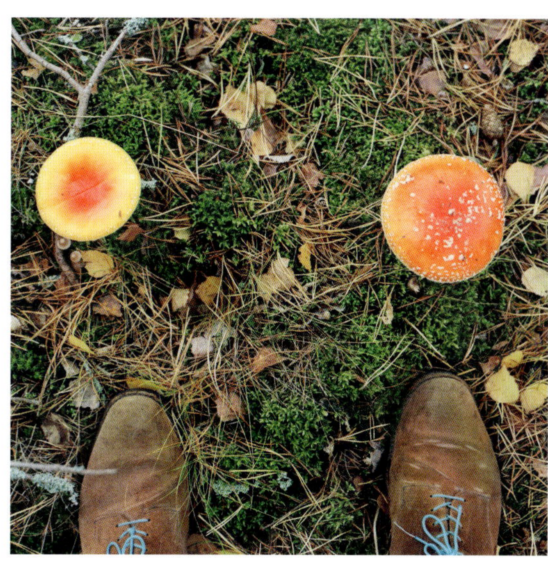
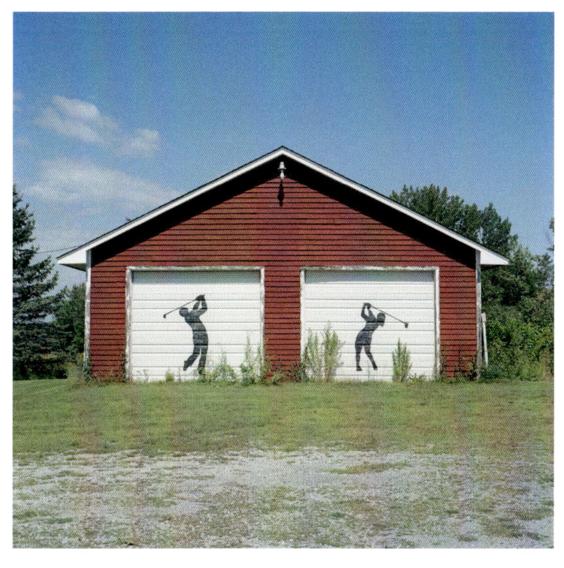
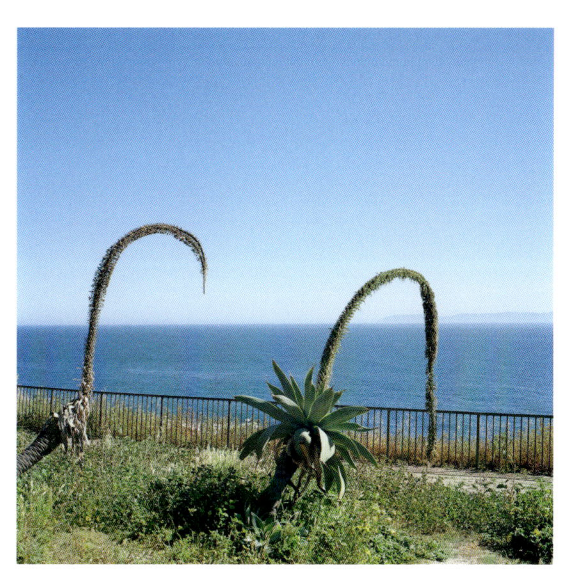
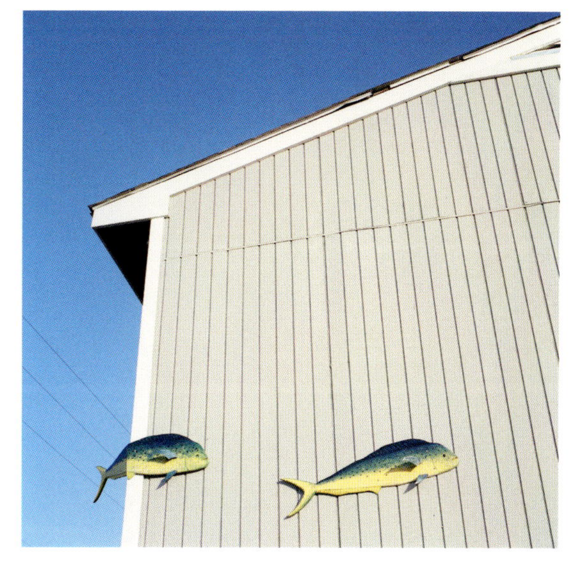
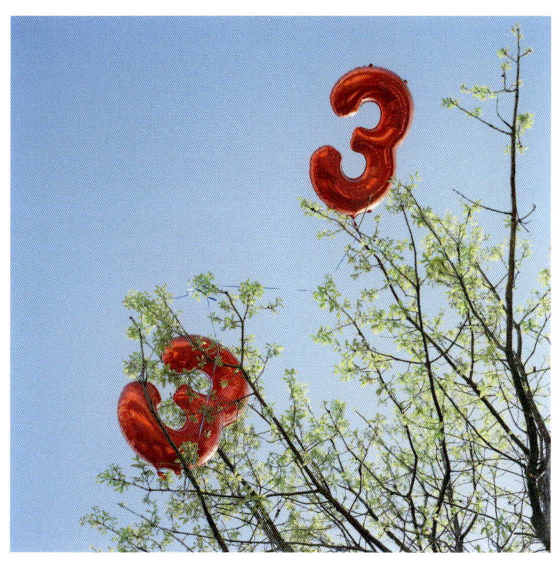
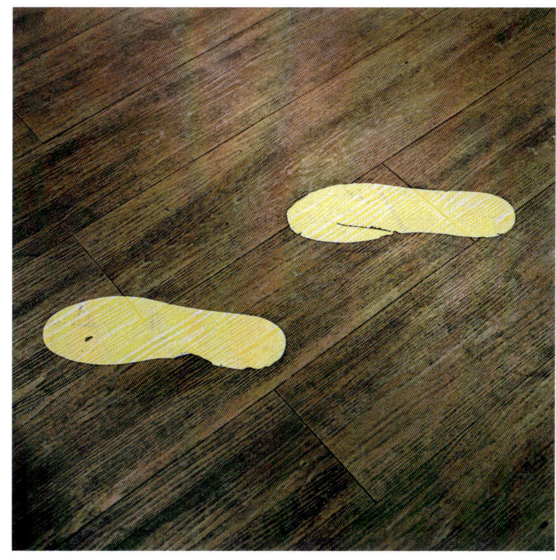
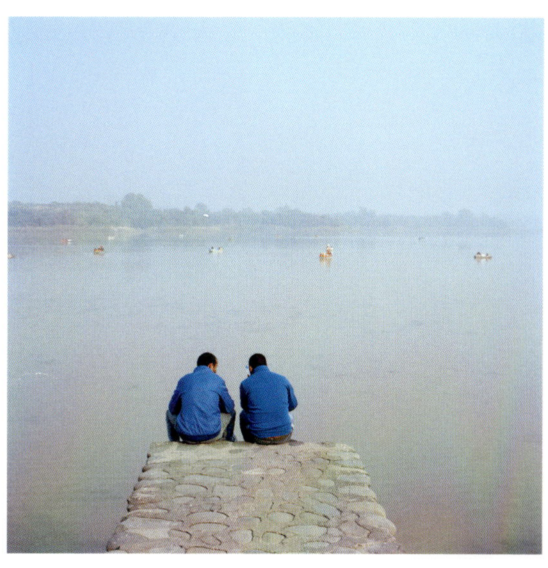

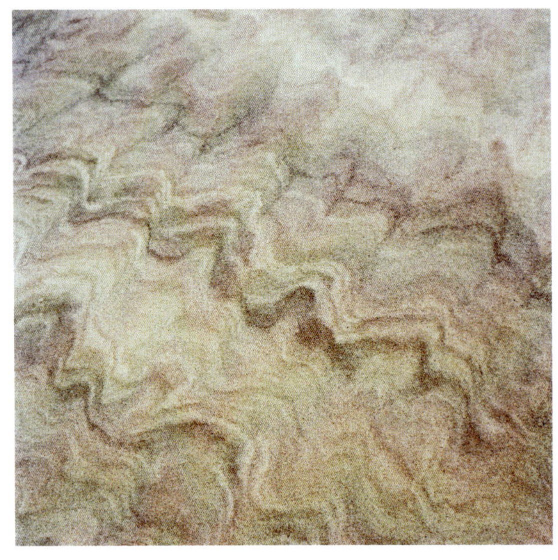
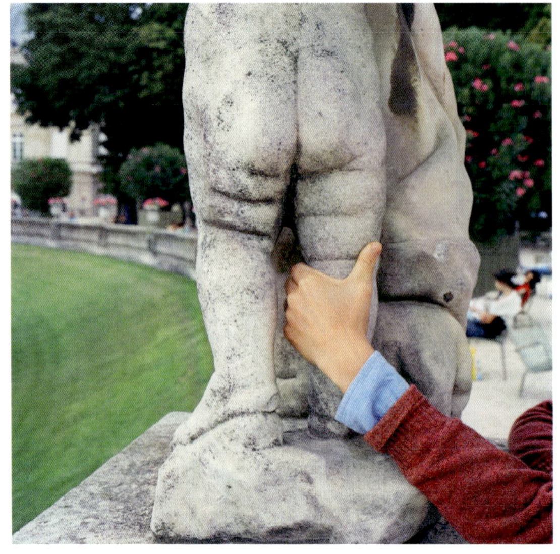
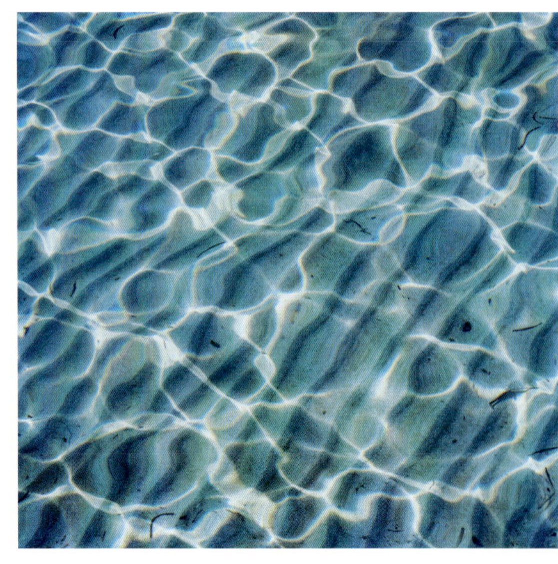
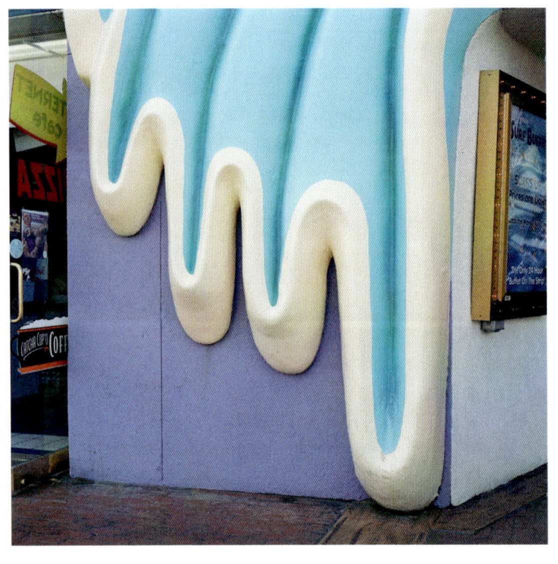
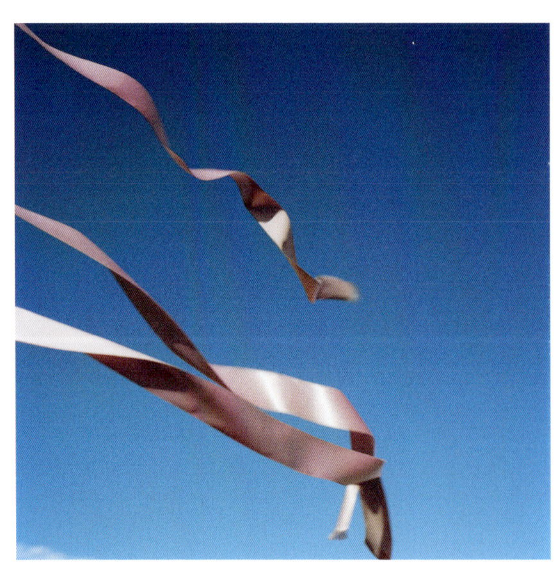
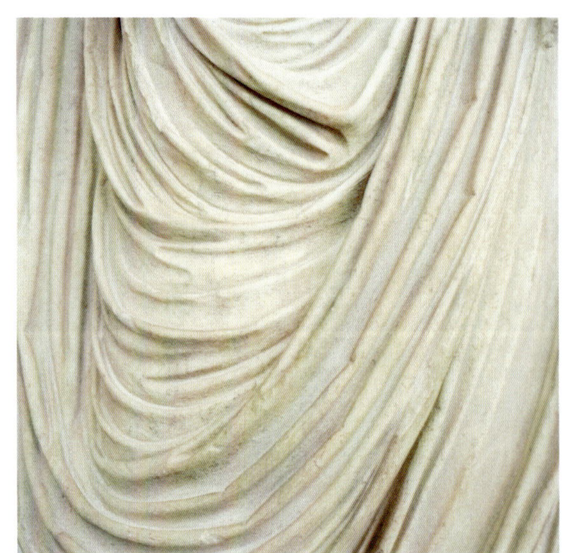
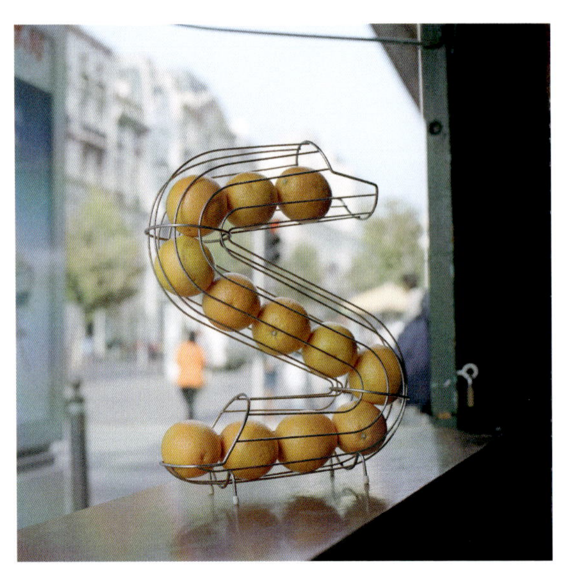
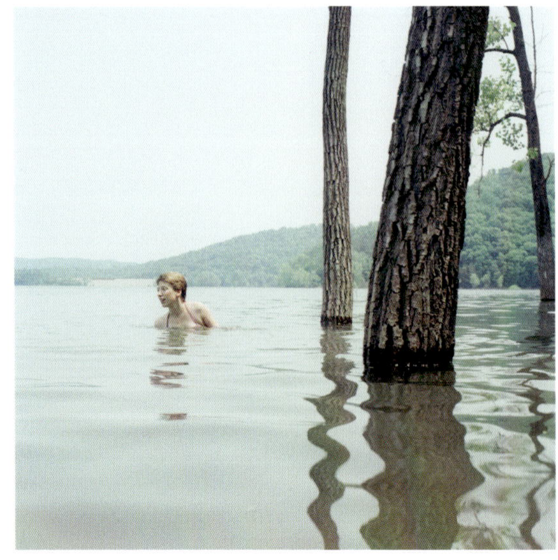
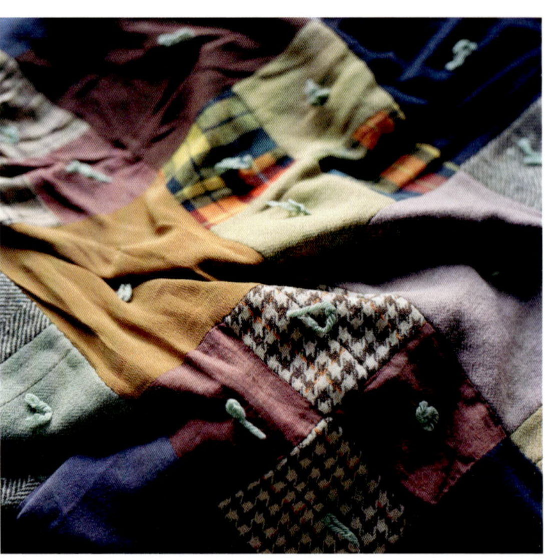

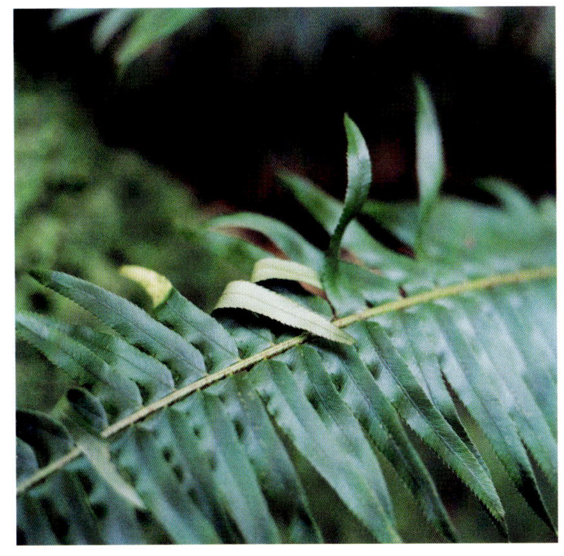
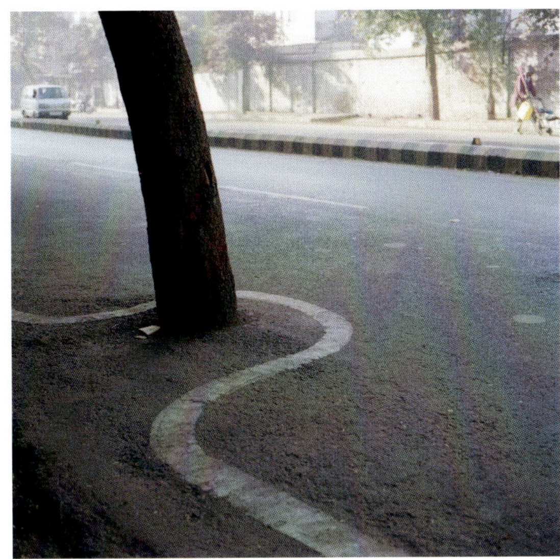
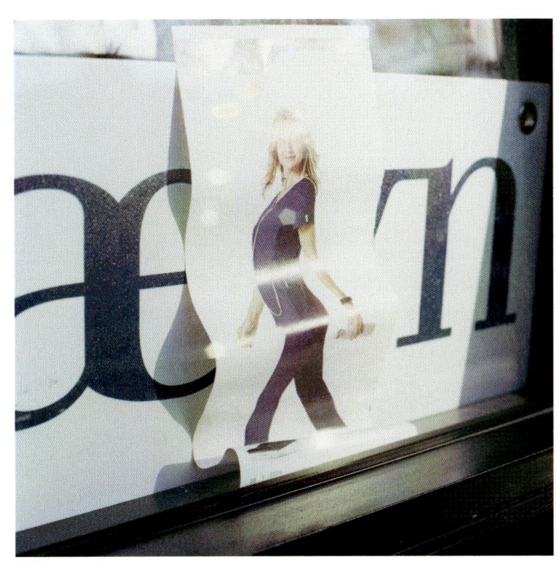
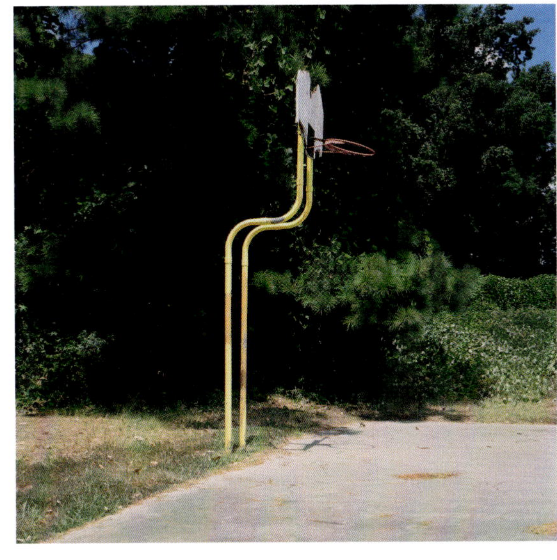
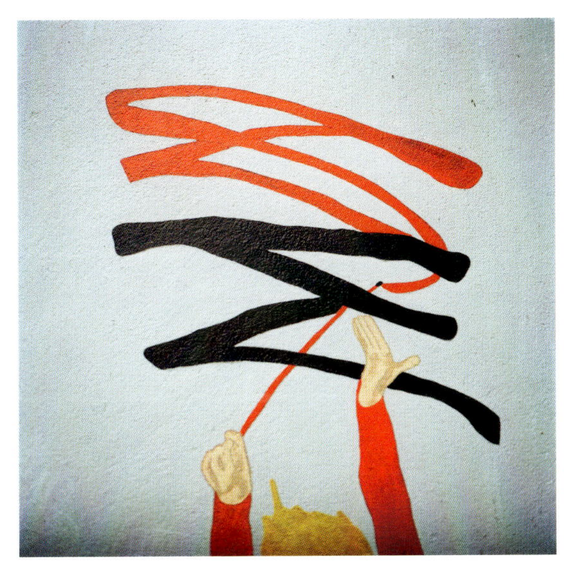
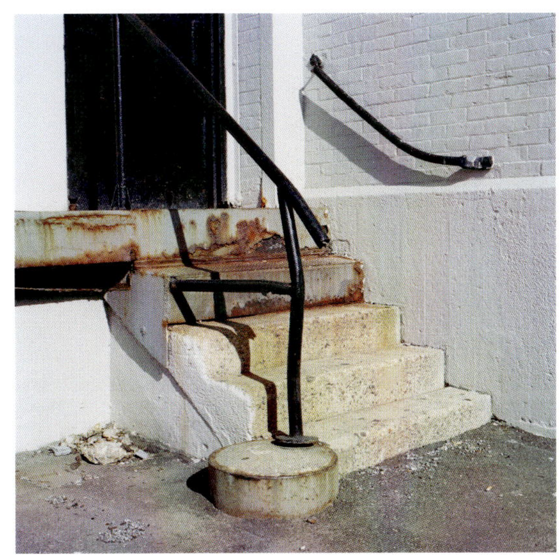
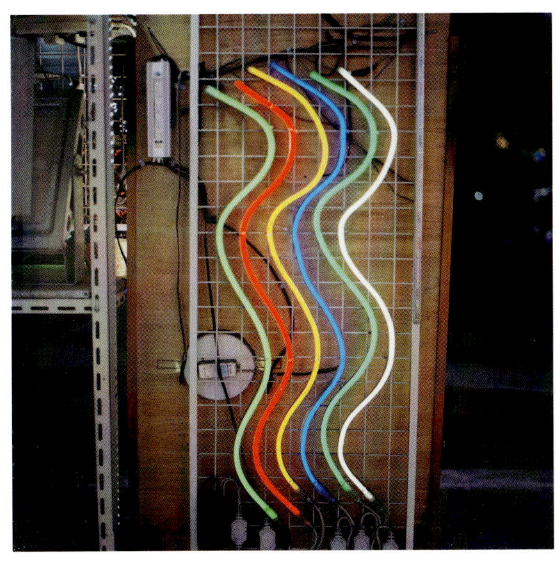
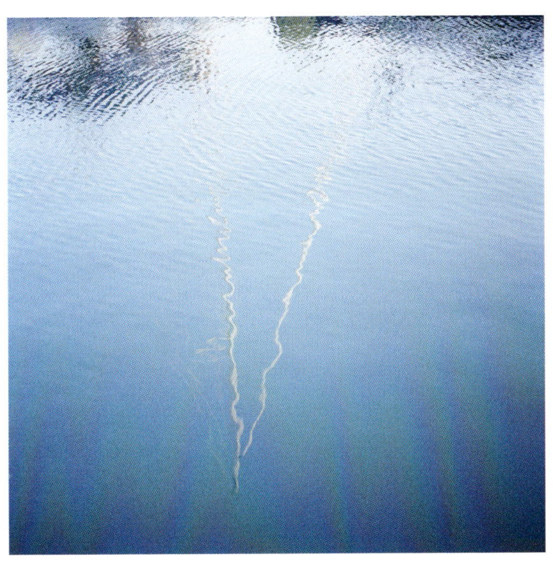
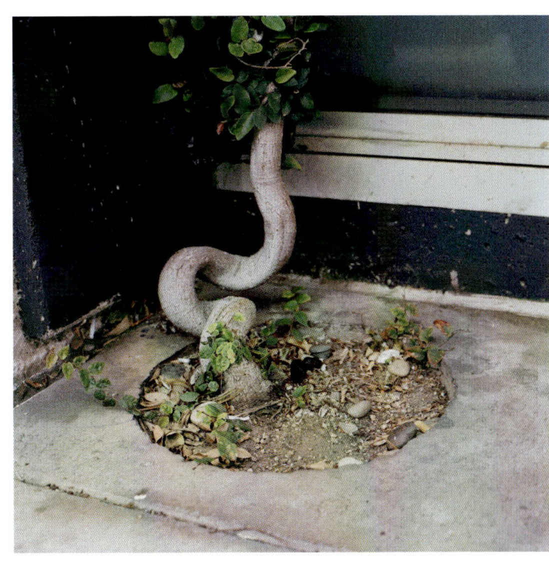

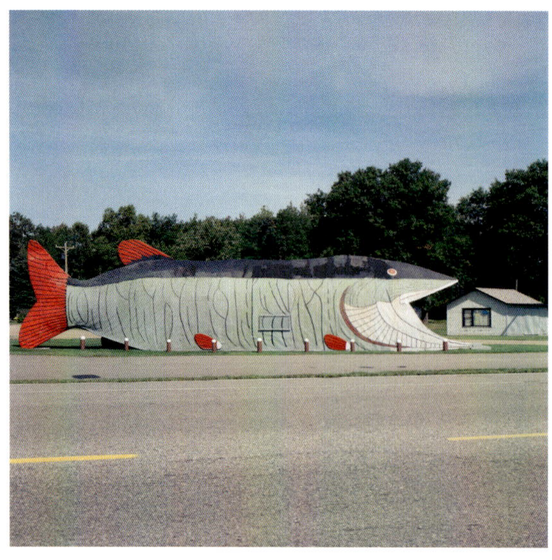

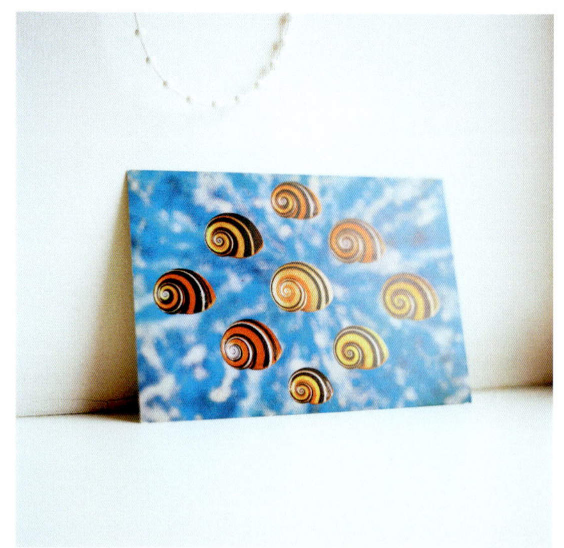

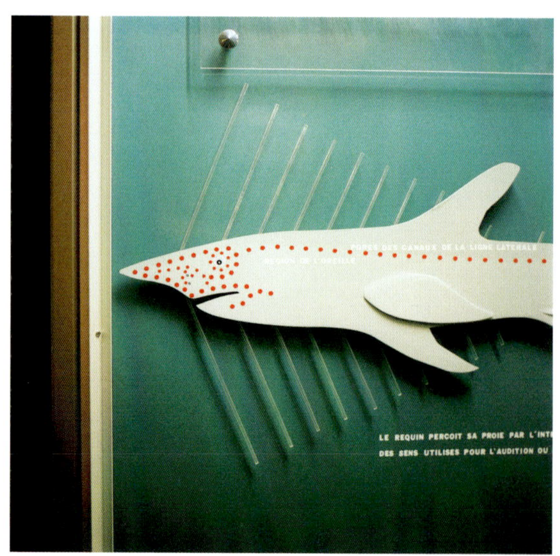

LE REQUIN PERCOIT SA PROIE PAR L'INT
DES SENS UTILISES POUR L'AUDITION OU

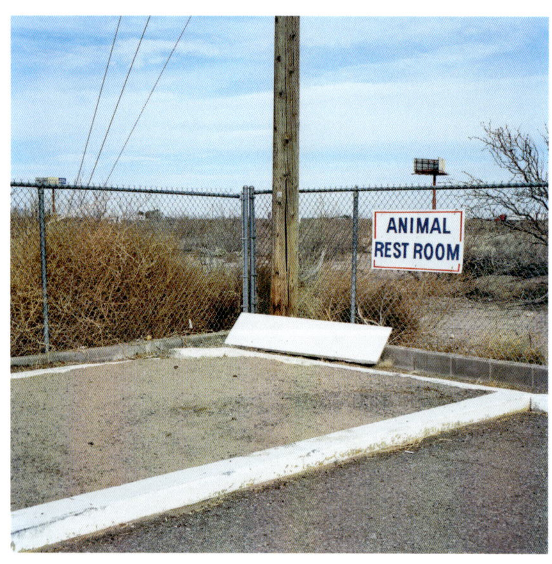

ANIMAL
REST ROOM

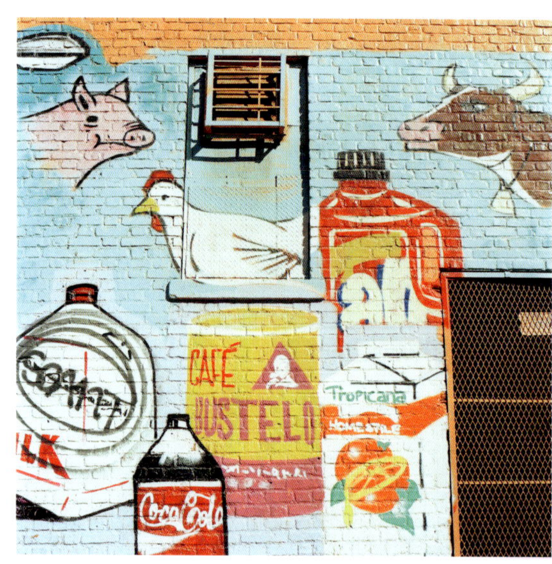

CAFÉ
BUSTELO
Tropicana
Coca-Cola

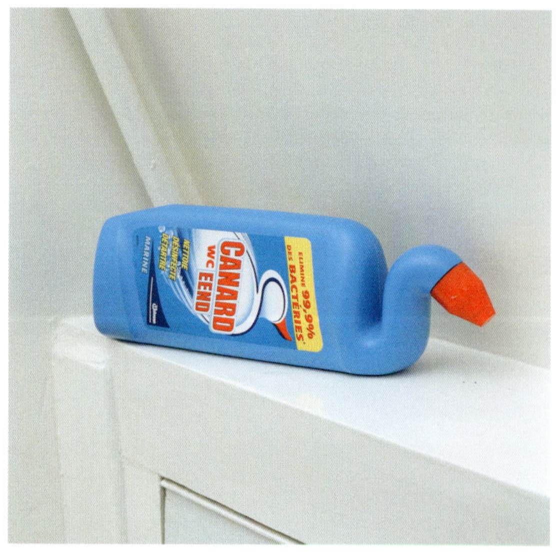

CANARD
WC EEND
ELIMINE 99,9%
DES BACTÉRIES
NETTOIE
DÉSINFECTE
DÉTARTRE
MARINE

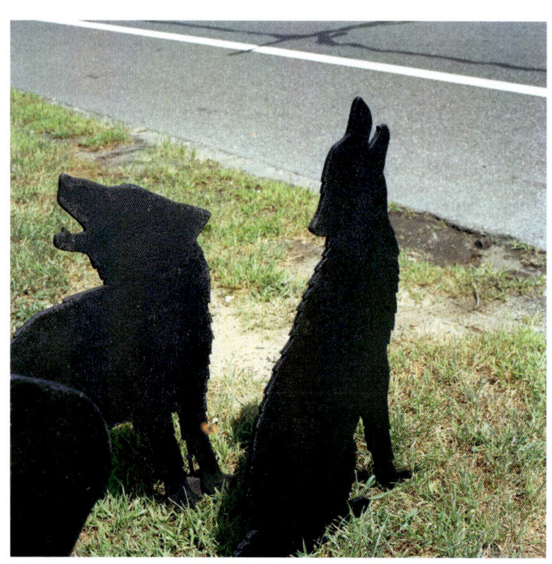

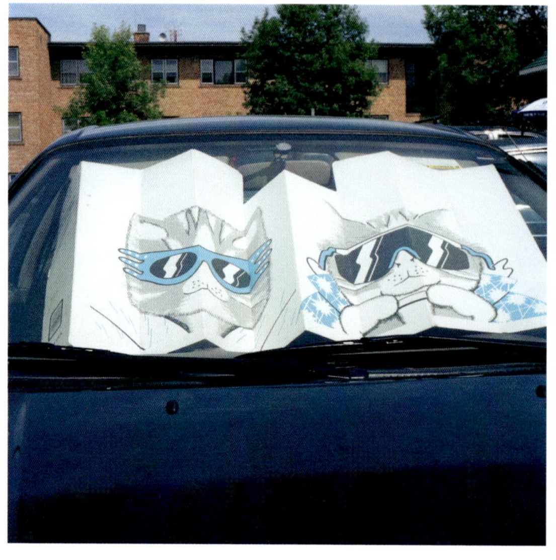

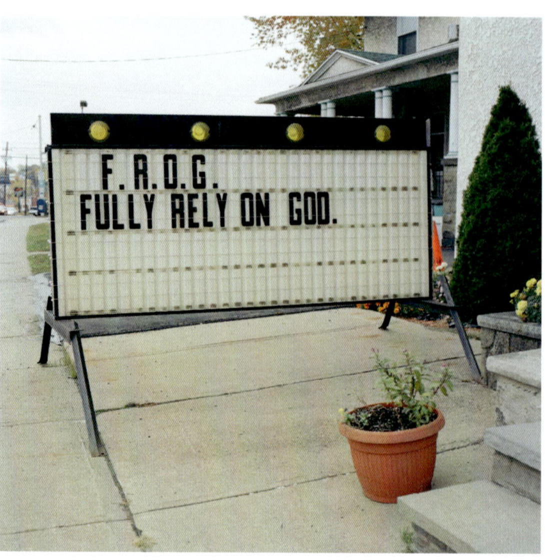

F.R.O.G.
FULLY RELY ON GOD.

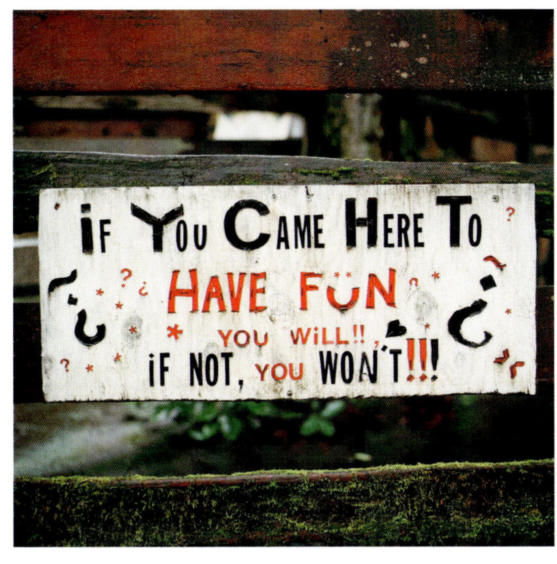
IF YOU CAME HERE TO
HAVE FUN
YOU WILL!!
IF NOT, YOU WON'T!!!
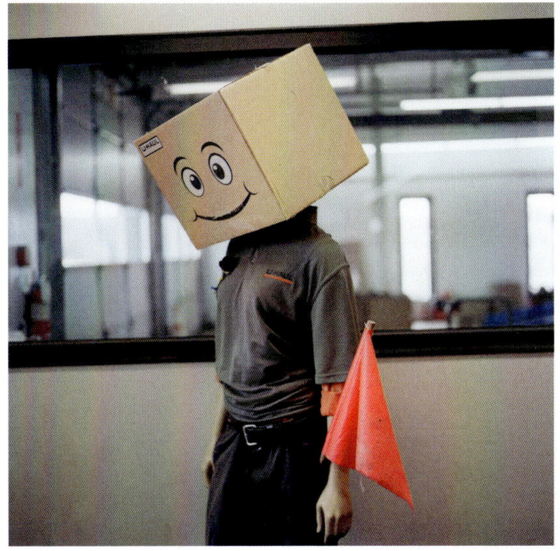
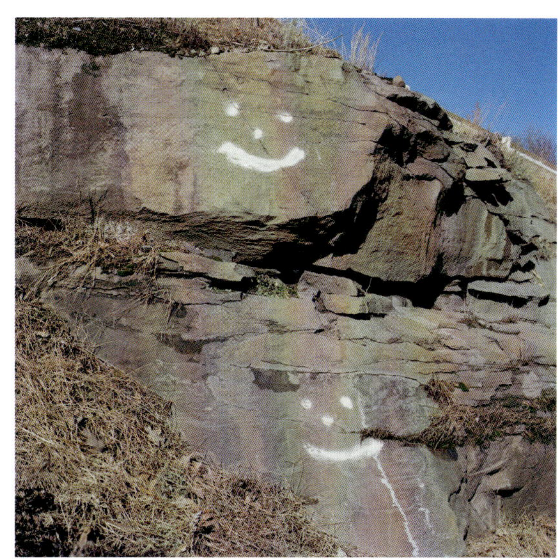
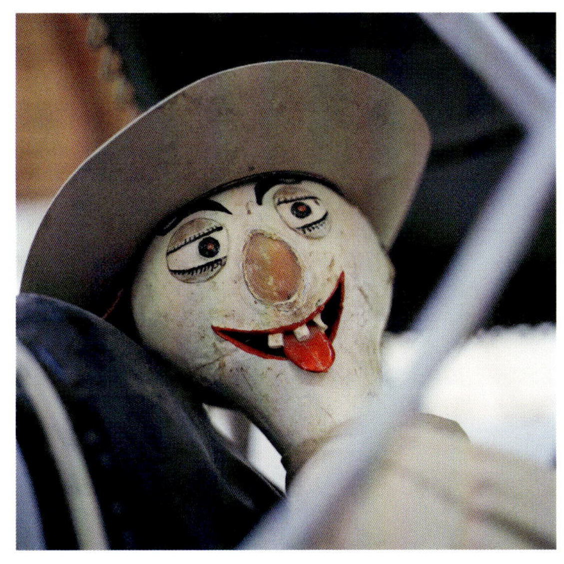
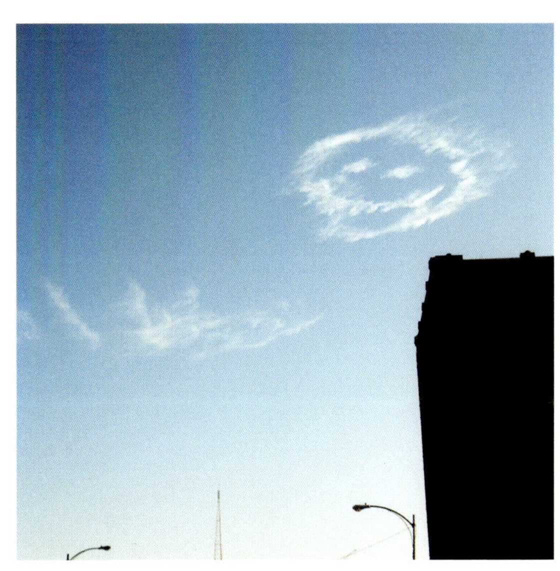
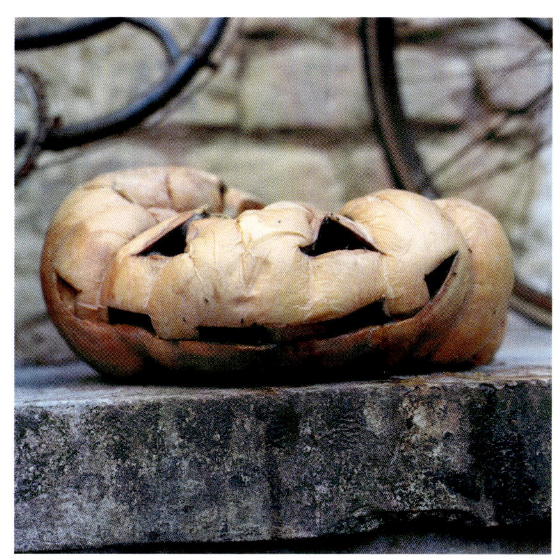
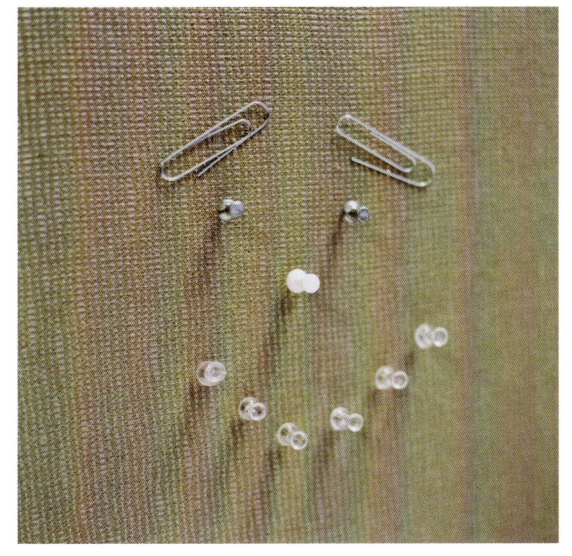
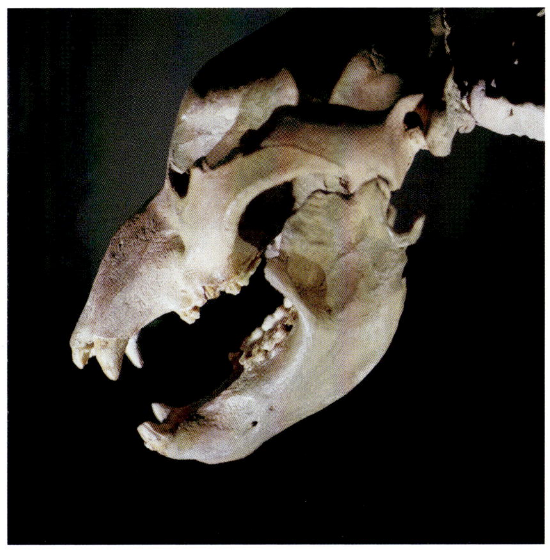
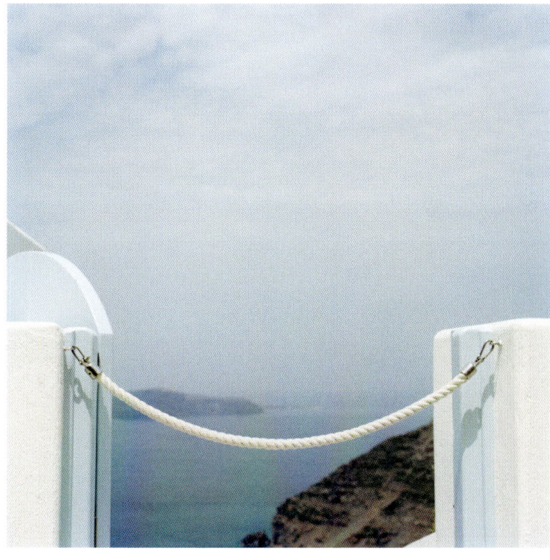

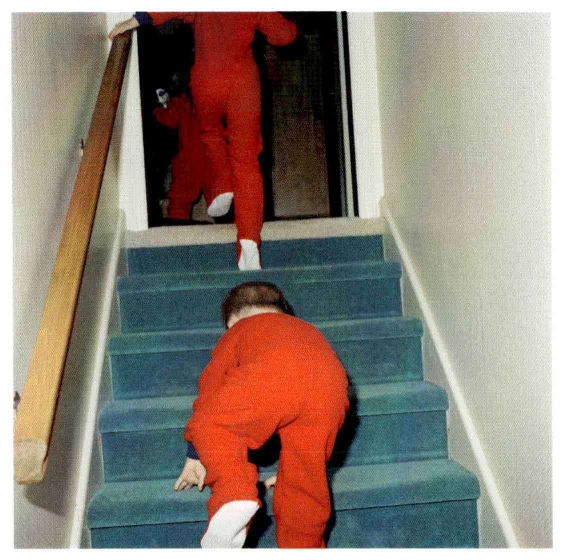

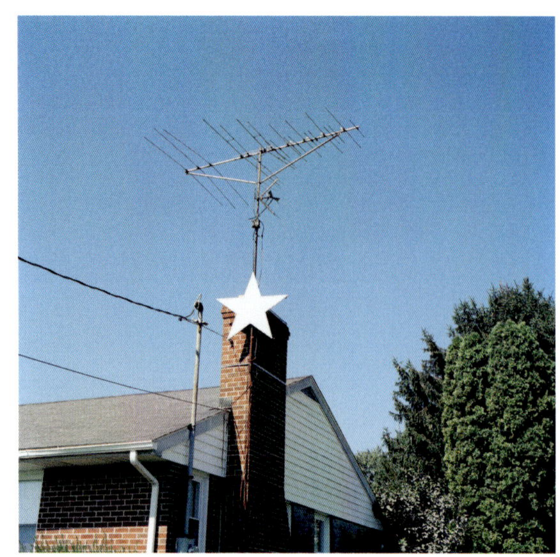

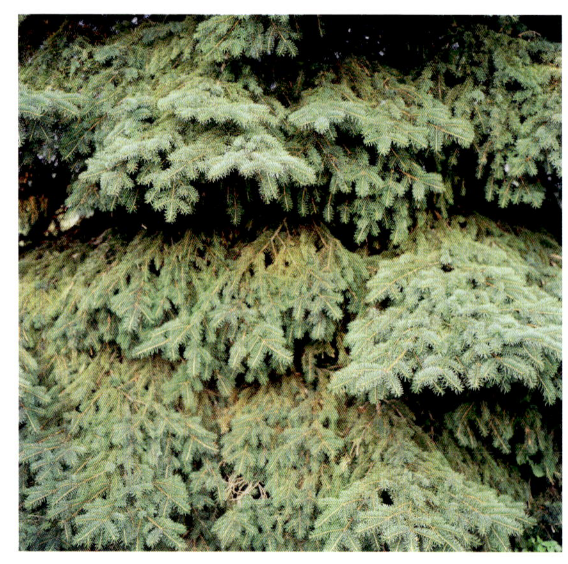

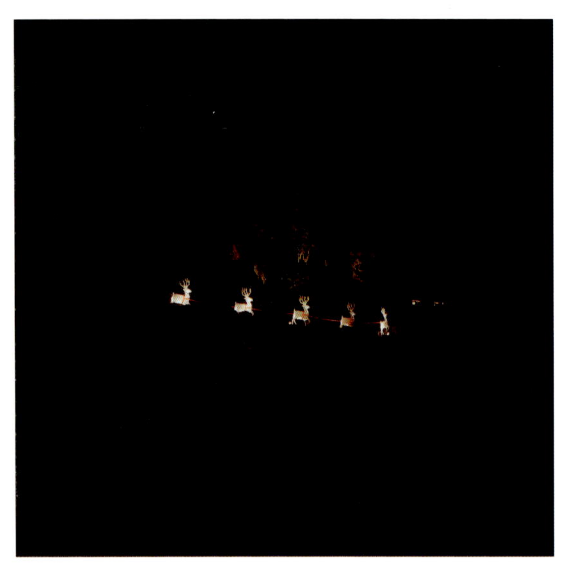

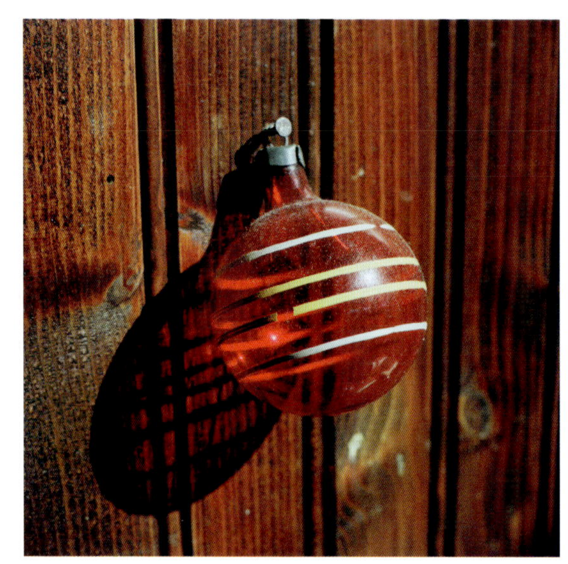

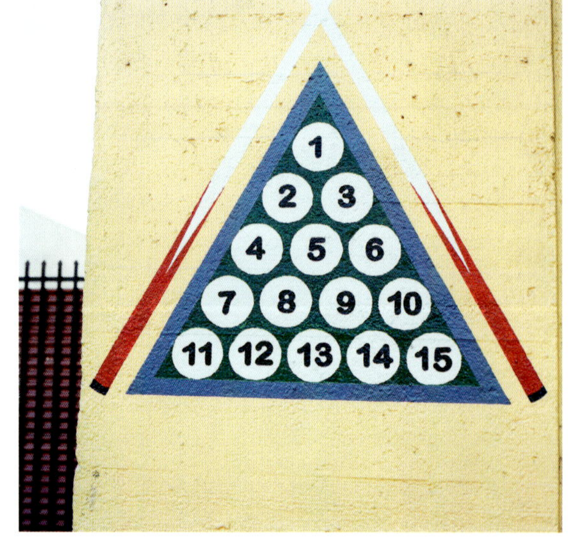

1
2 3
4 5 6
7 8 9 10
11 12 13 14 15

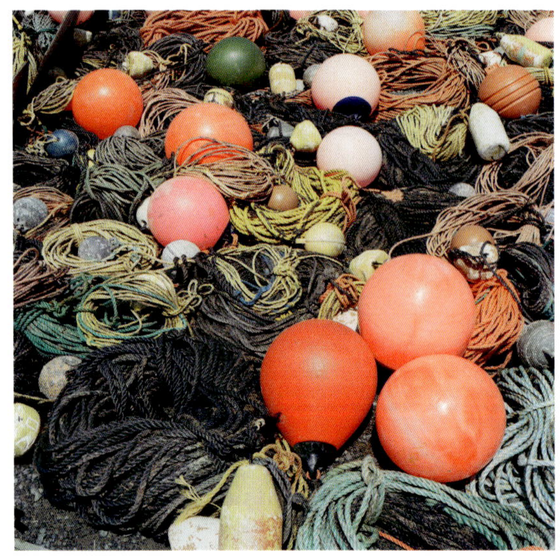

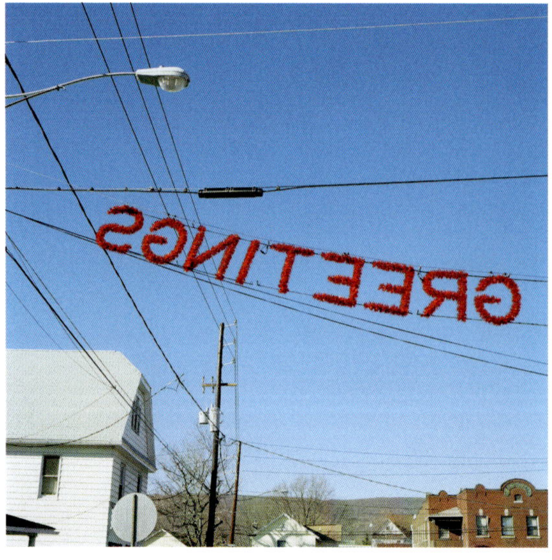

GREETINGS

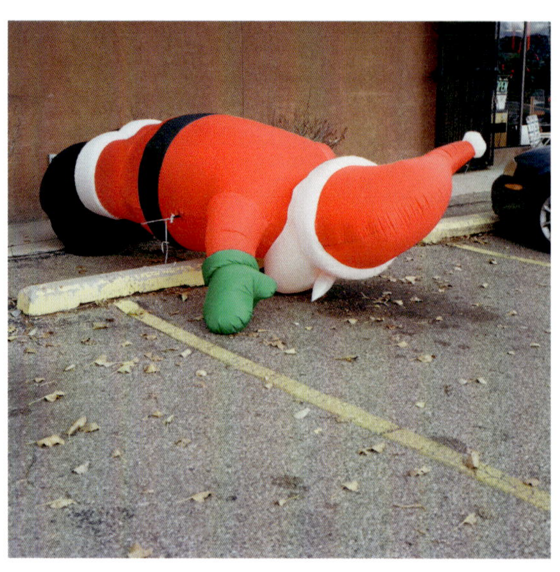

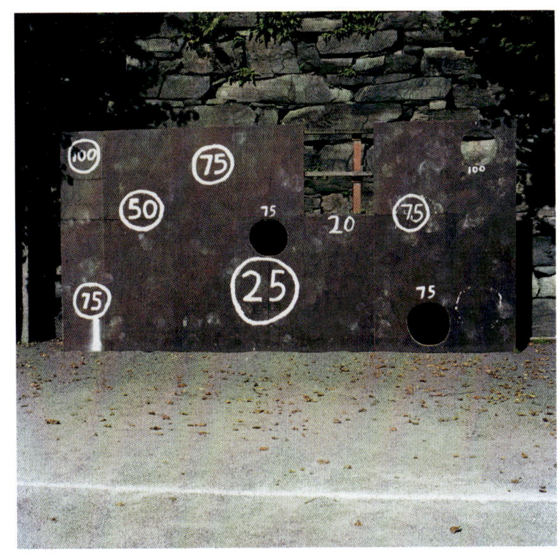
100
75
50
75
20
75
25
75
100
75

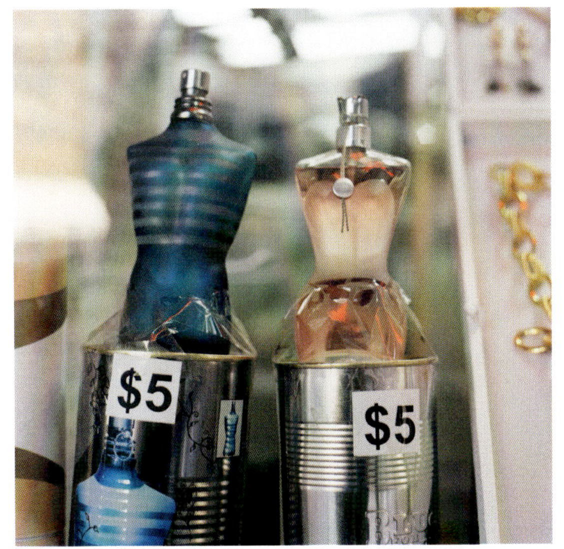
$5
$5

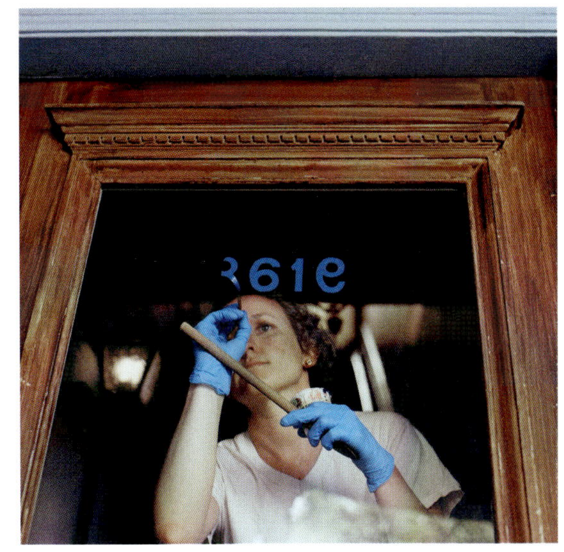

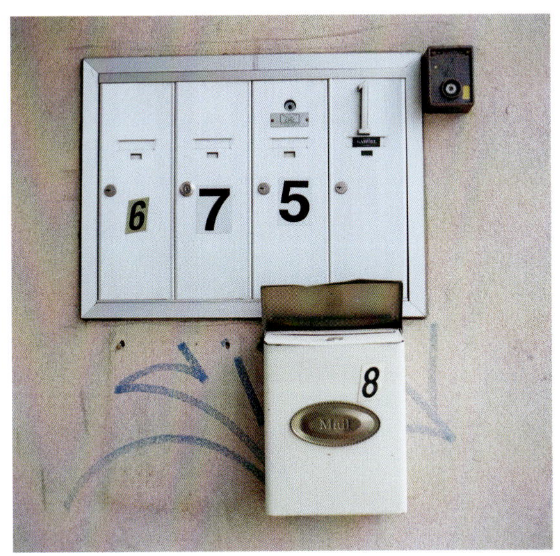
6
7
5
8
Mail

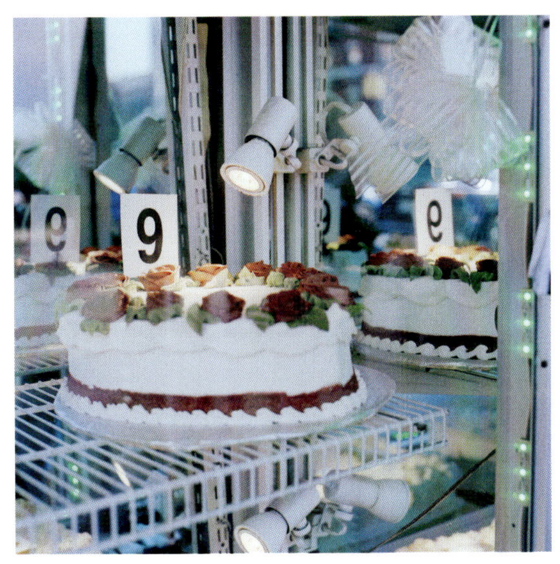
9

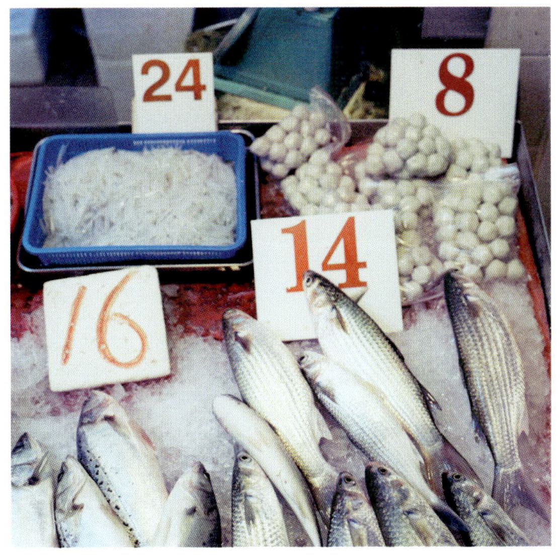
24
8
14
16

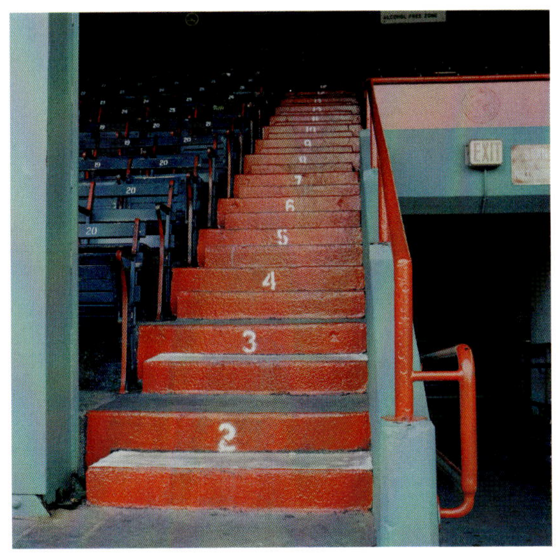
EXIT
6
5
4
3
2

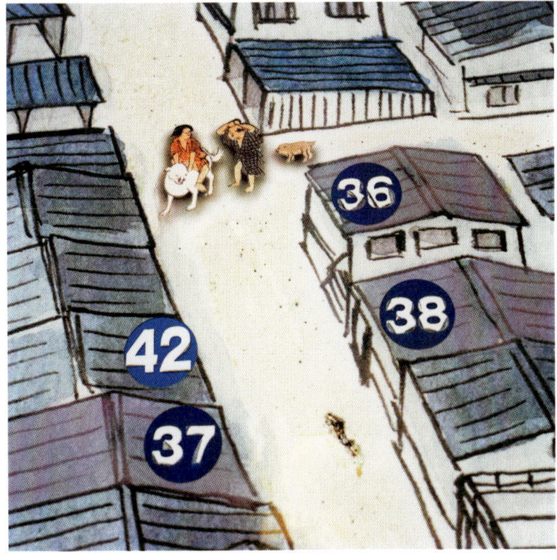
36
38
42
37

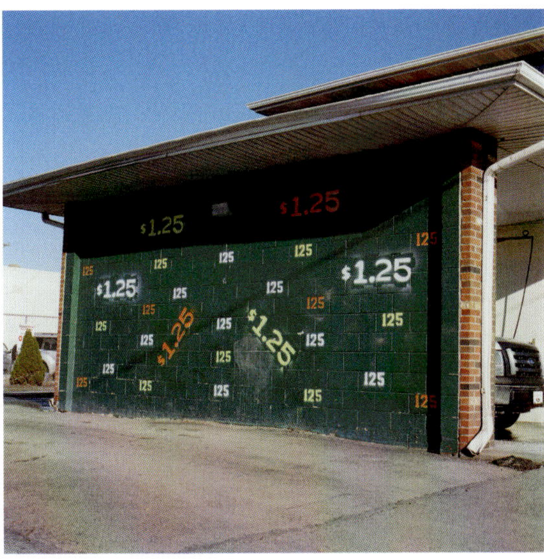
$1.25
$1.25
$1.25
$1.25
$1.25
$1.25
125

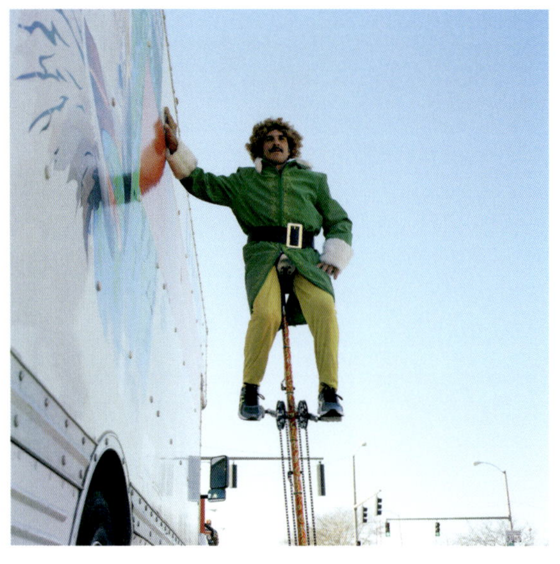

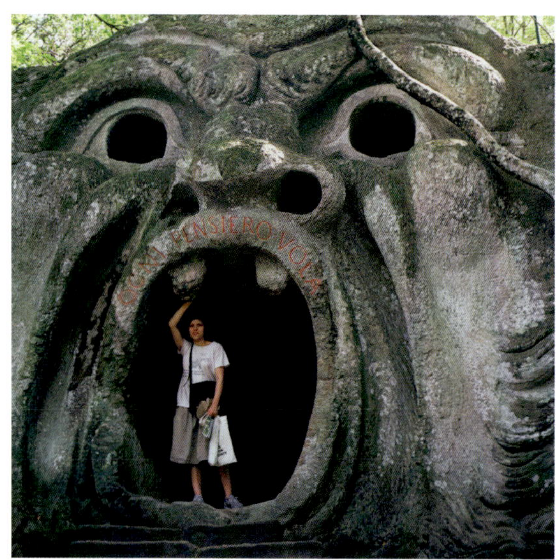

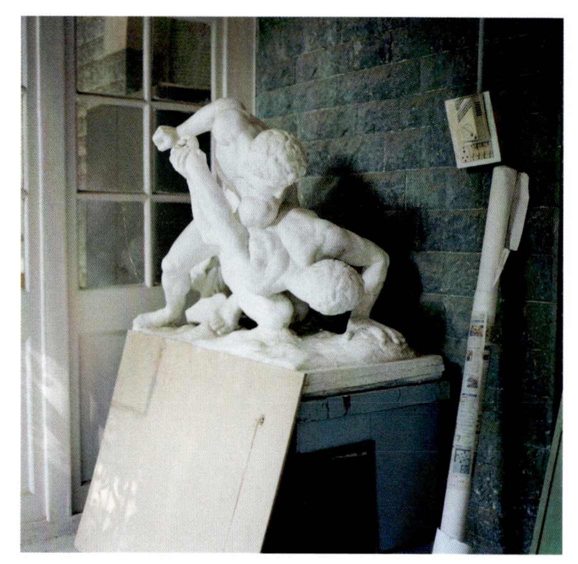

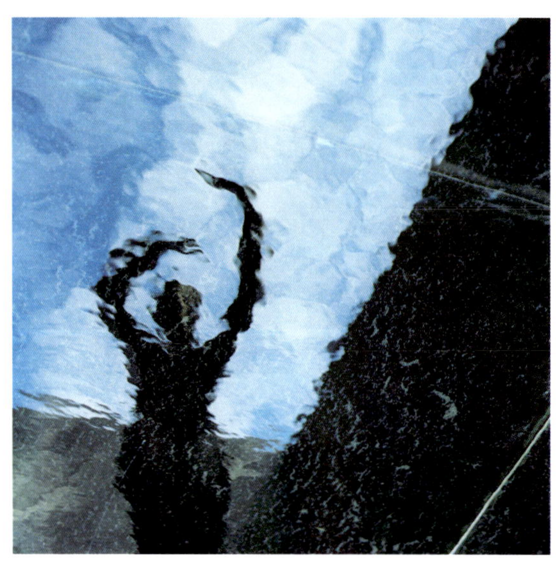

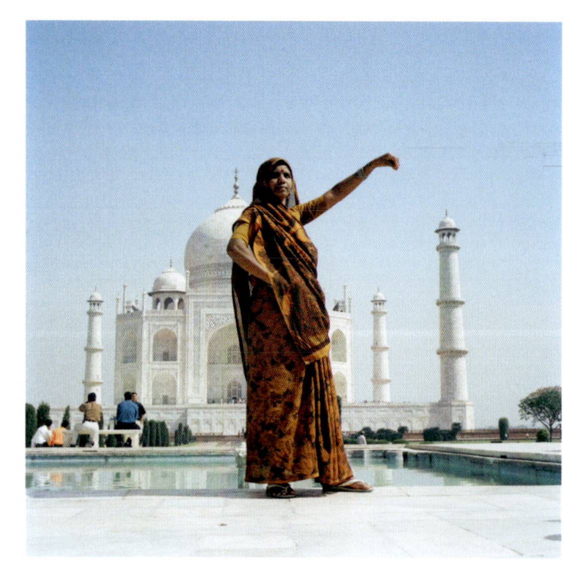

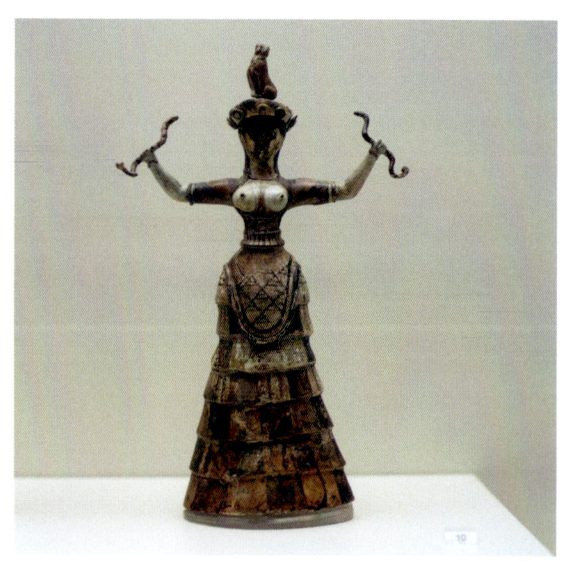

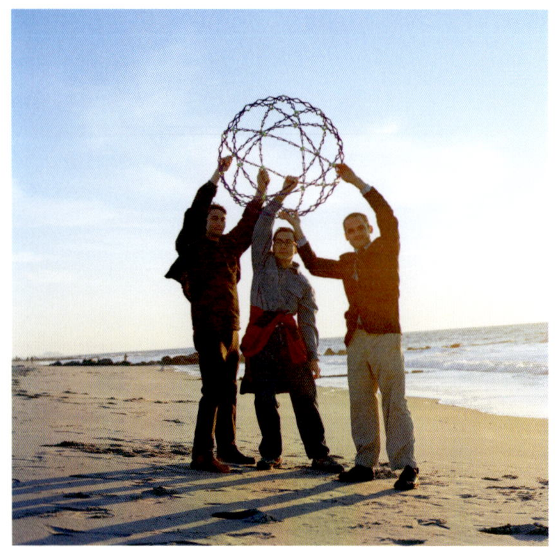

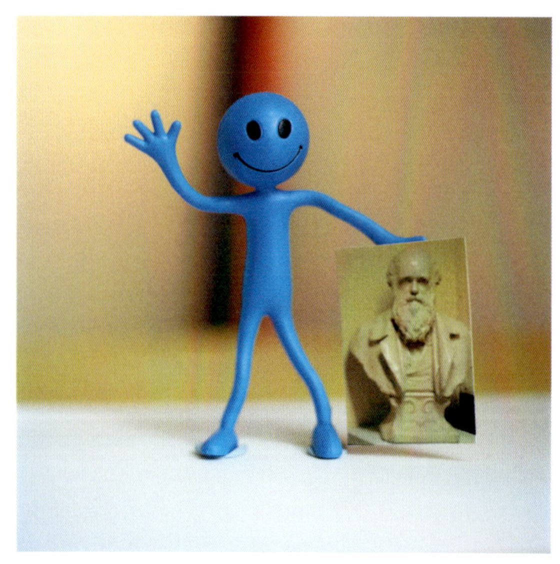

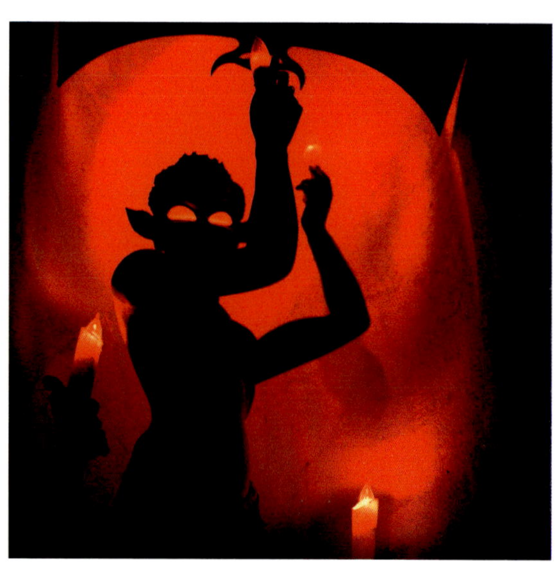

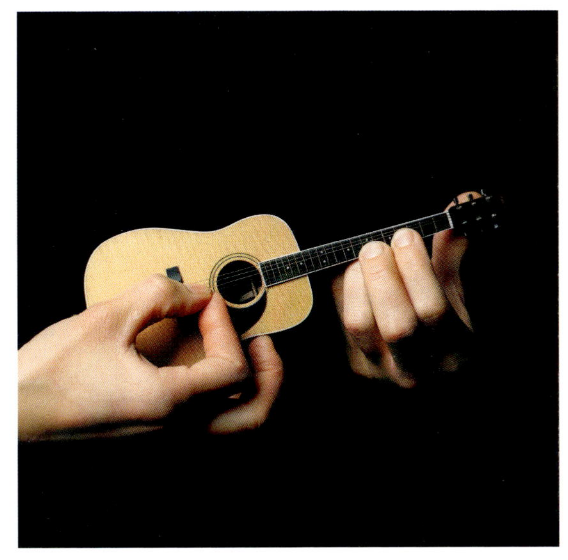

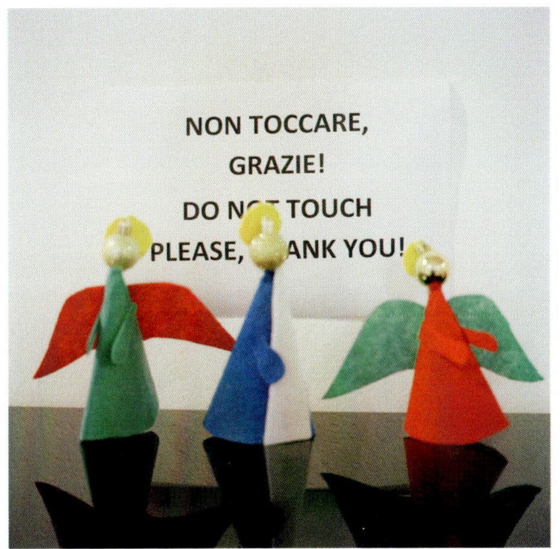
NON TOCCARE,
GRAZIE!

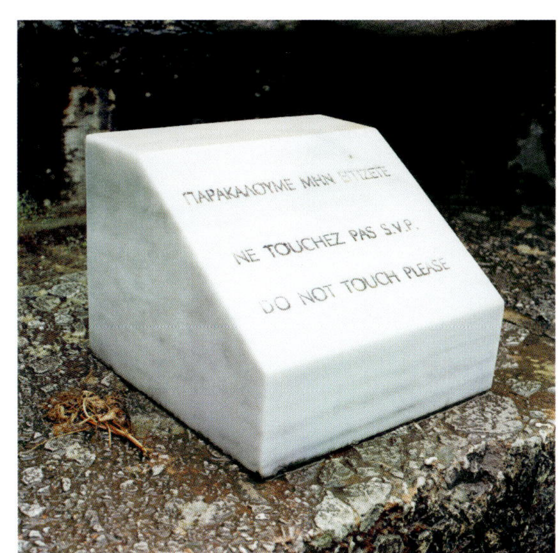
NE TOUCHEZ PAS S.V.P.
DO NOT TOUCH PLEASE

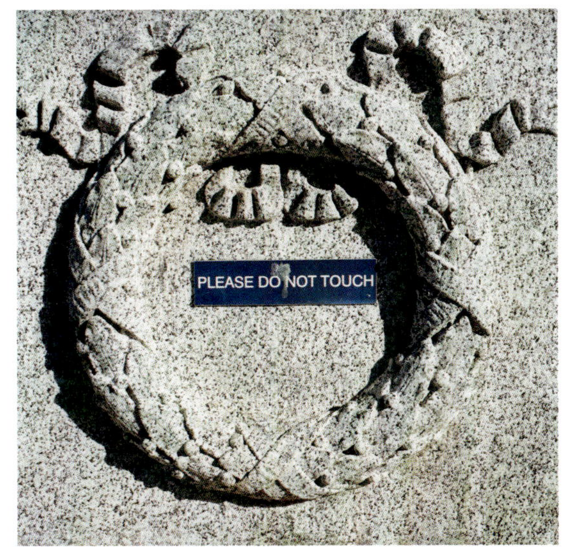
PLEASE DO NOT TOUCH

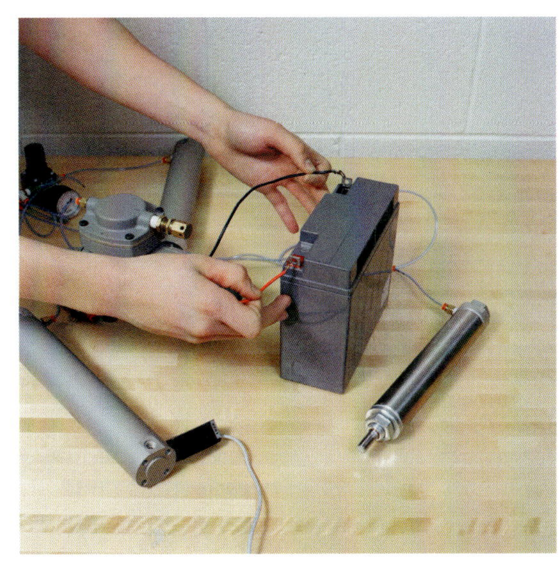

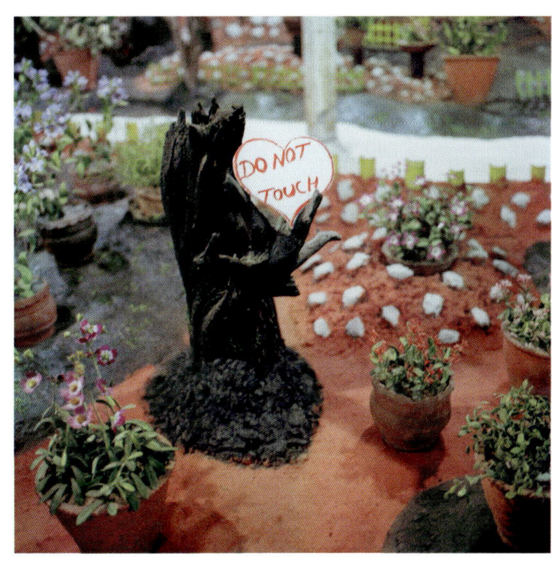
DO NOT TOUCH

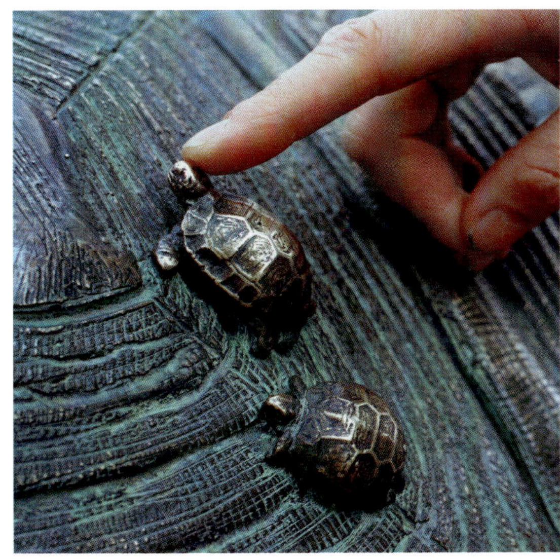

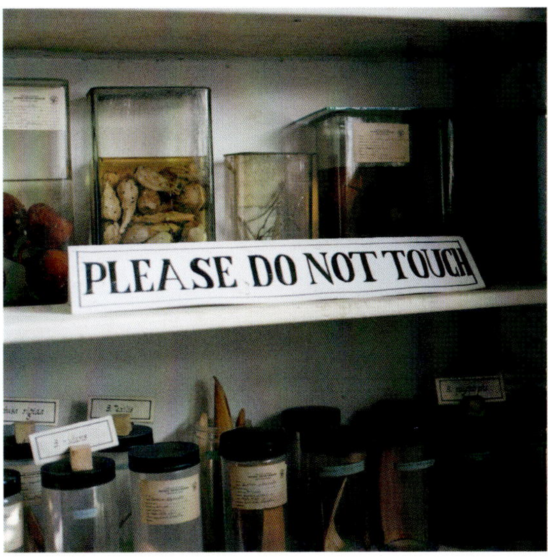
PLEASE DO NOT TOUCH

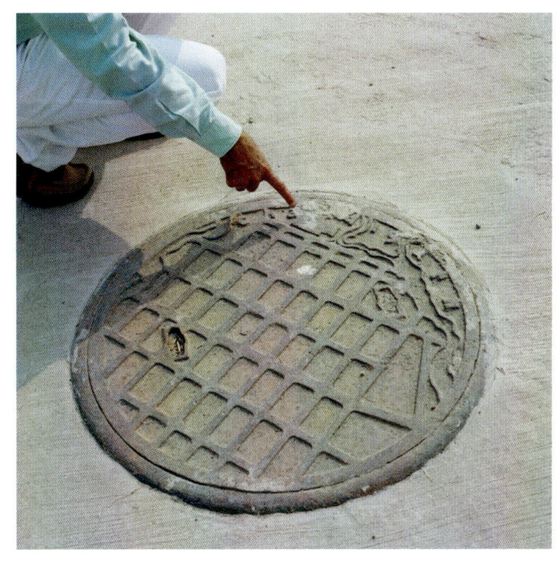

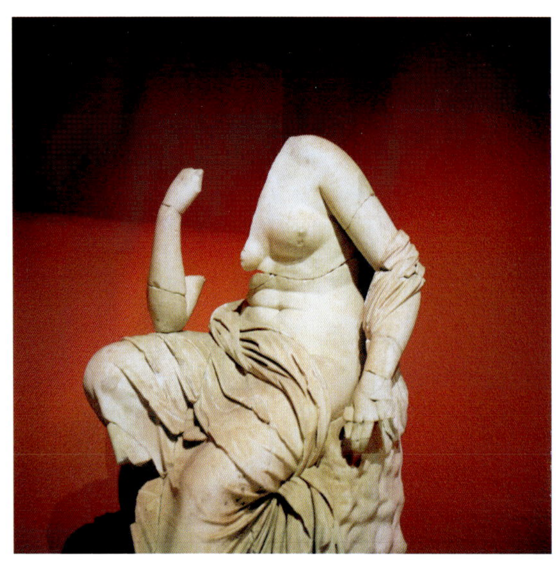

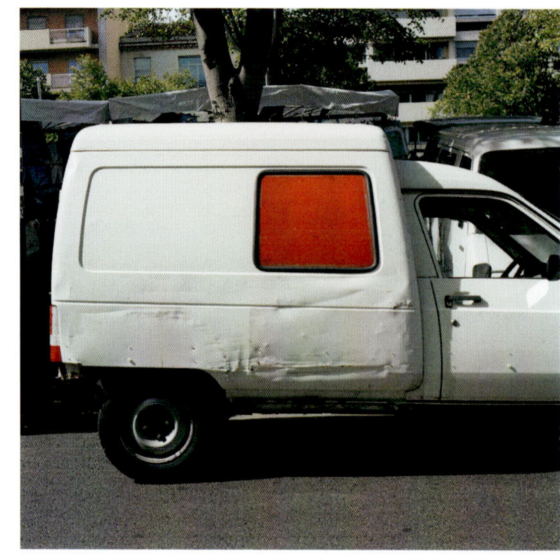

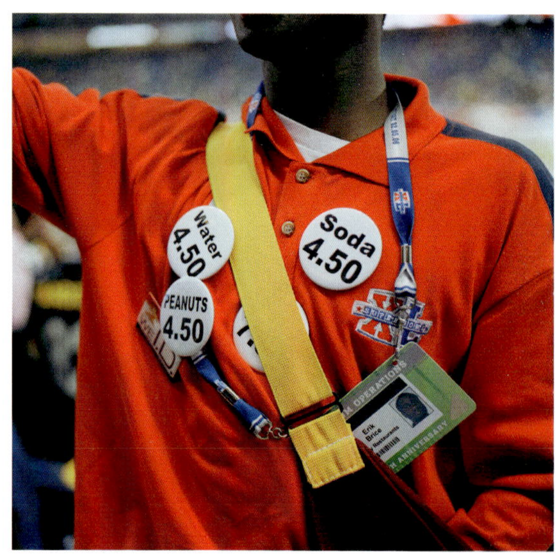
Water
4.50
Soda
4.50
PEANUTS
4.50

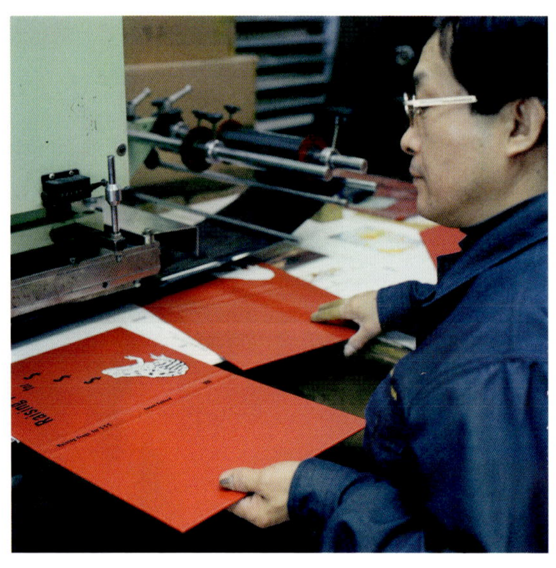

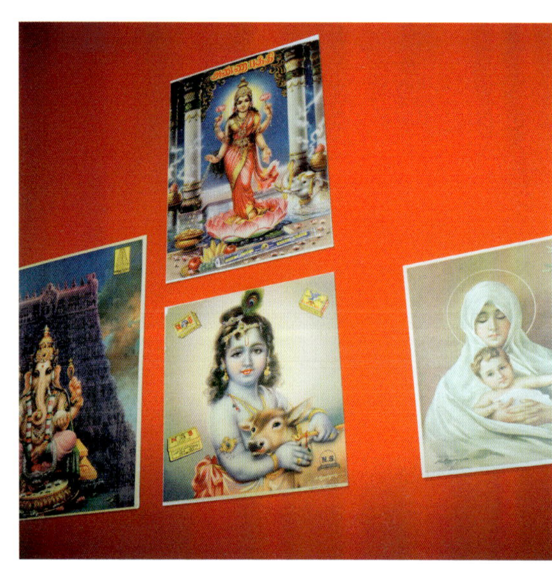

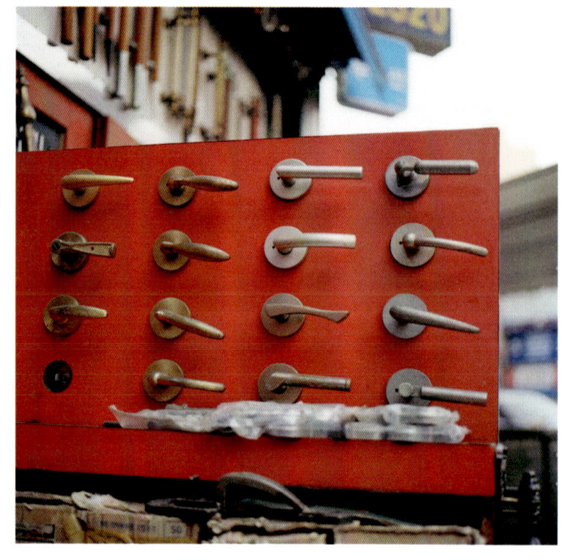

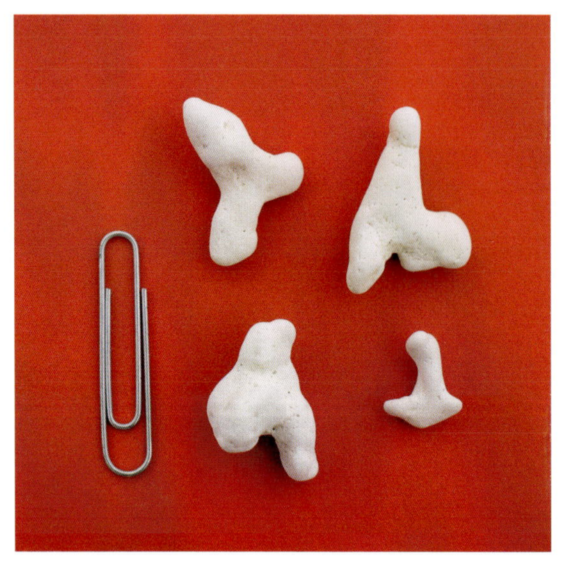

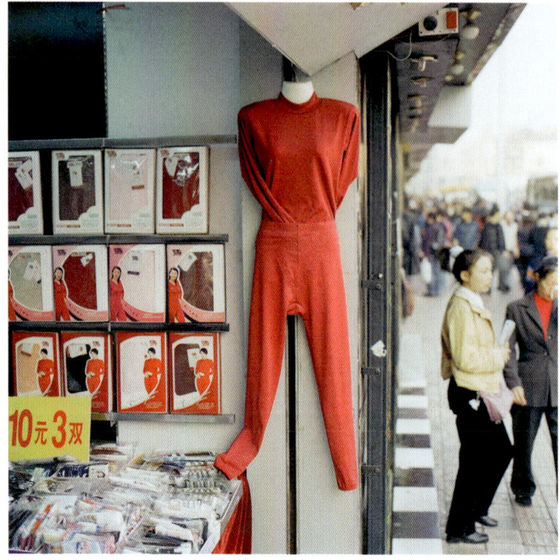
10元3双

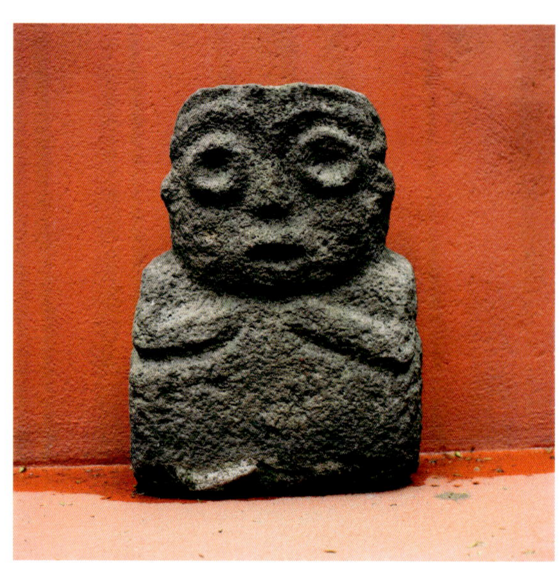

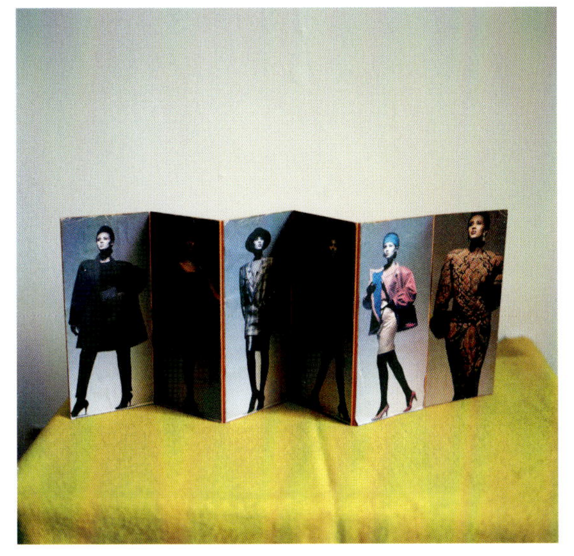

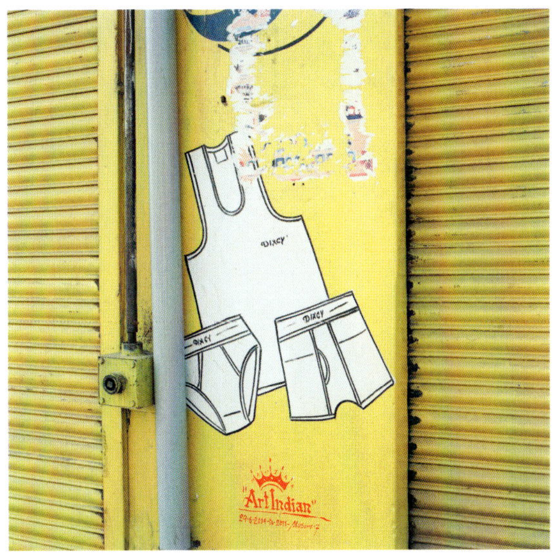

"ArtIndian"

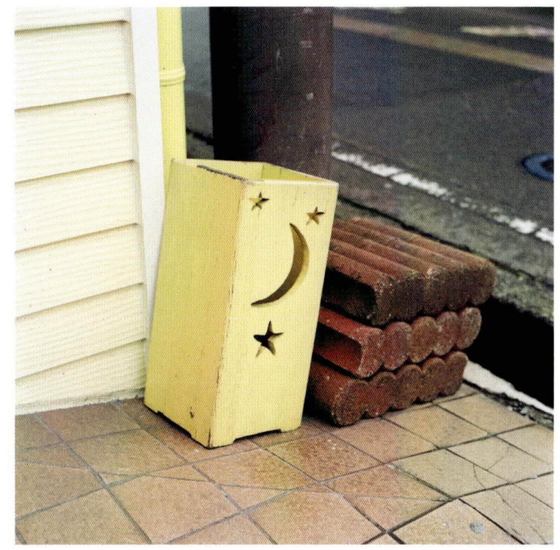

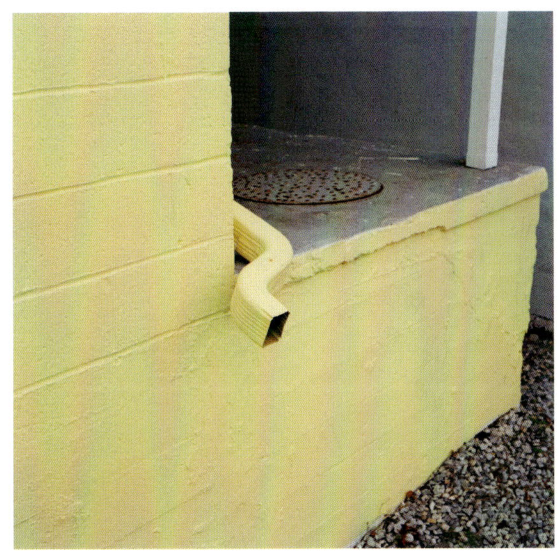

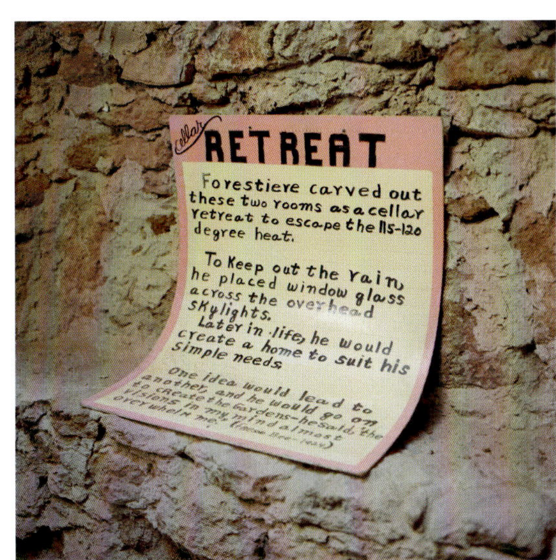

Cellar
RETREAT
Forestiere carved out these two rooms as a cellar retreat to escape the 115-120 degree heat.
To Keep out the rain, he placed window glass across the overhead skylights.
Later in life, he would create a home to suit his simple needs.
One idea would lead to another, and he would go on to create the gardens—he said, the visions in my mind almost overwhelm me.

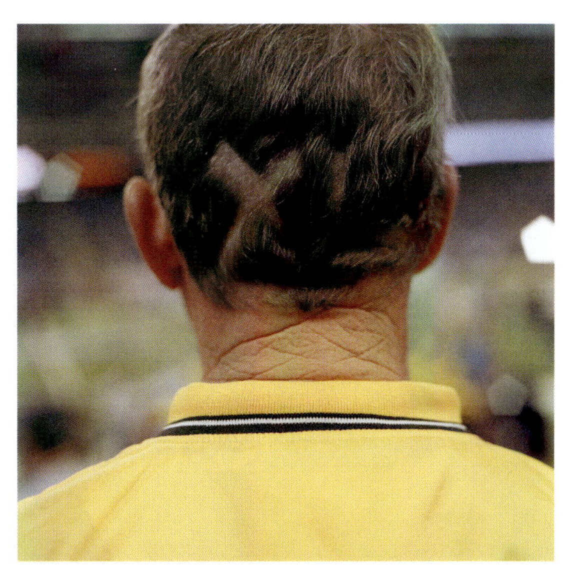

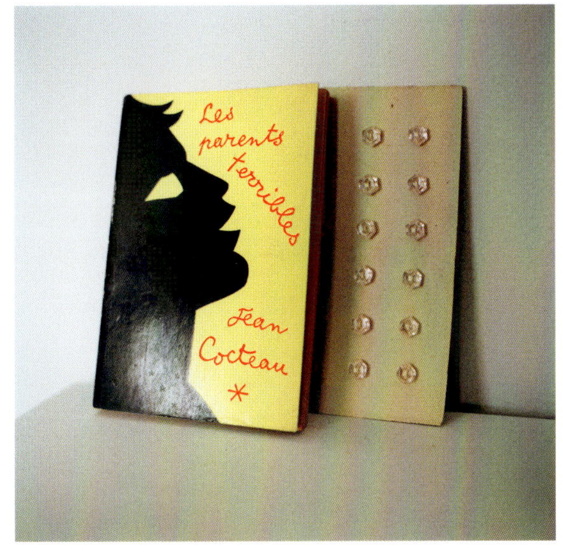

Les parents terribles
Jean Cocteau

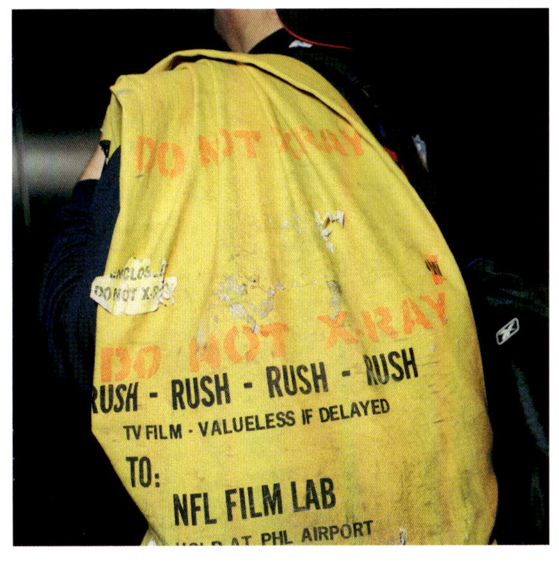

DO NOT X-RAY
RUSH - RUSH - RUSH - RUSH
TV FILM - VALUELESS IF DELAYED
TO:
NFL FILM LAB
PHL AIRPORT

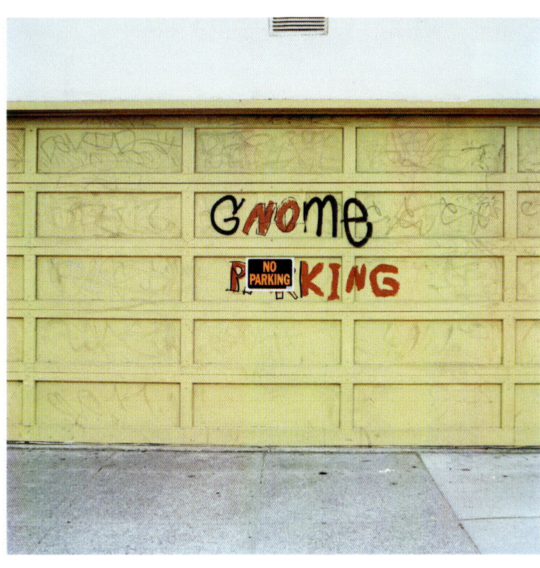

GNOME
NO PARKING
KING

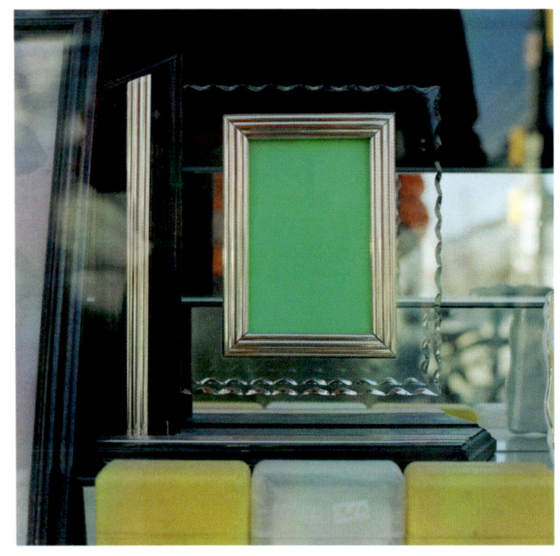

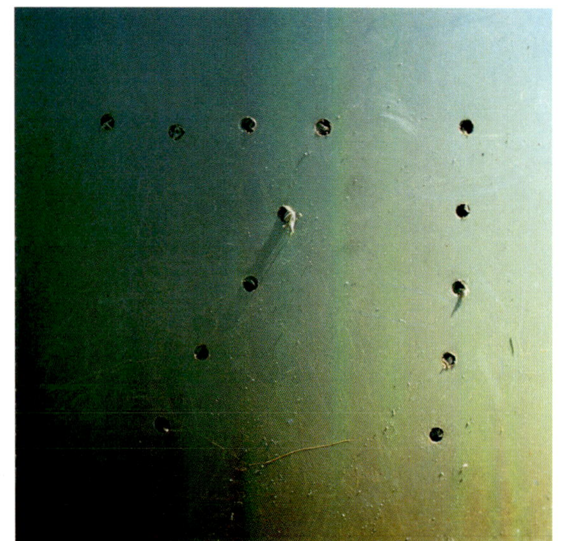

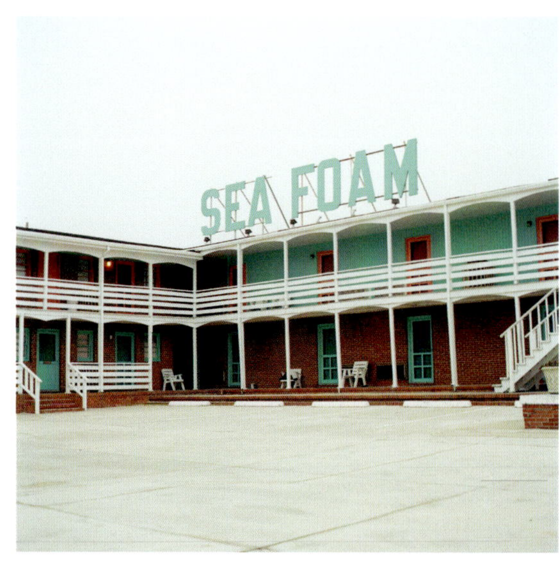
SEA FOAM

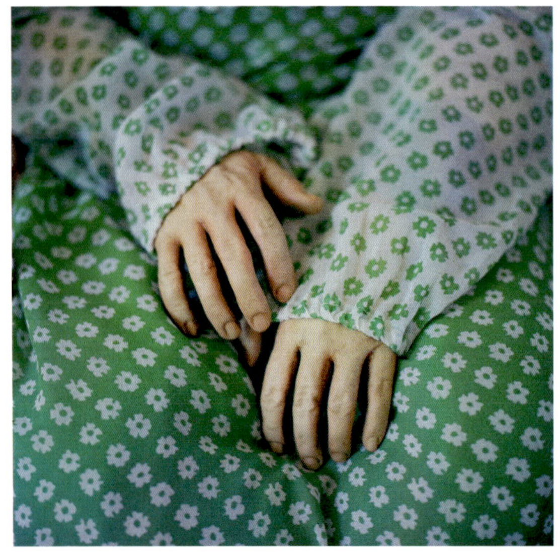

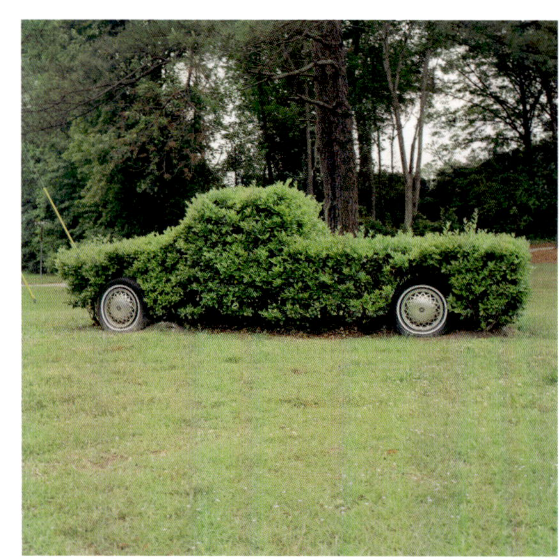

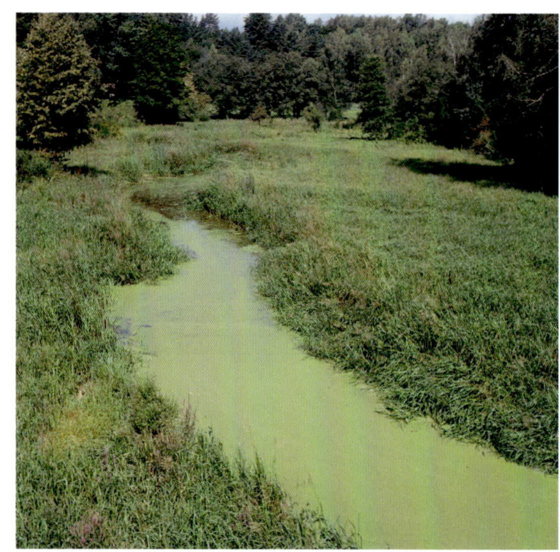

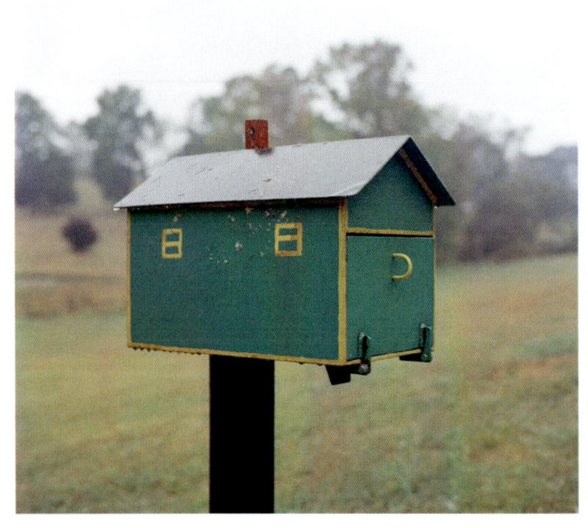

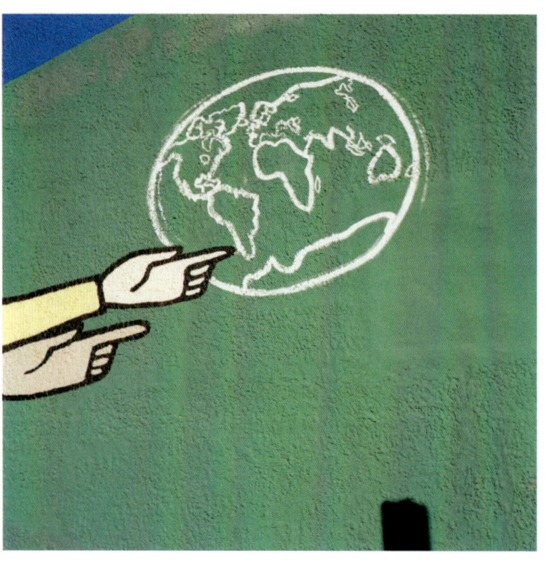

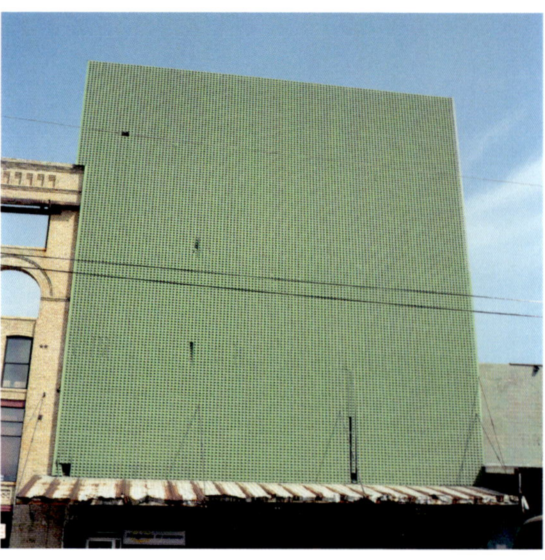

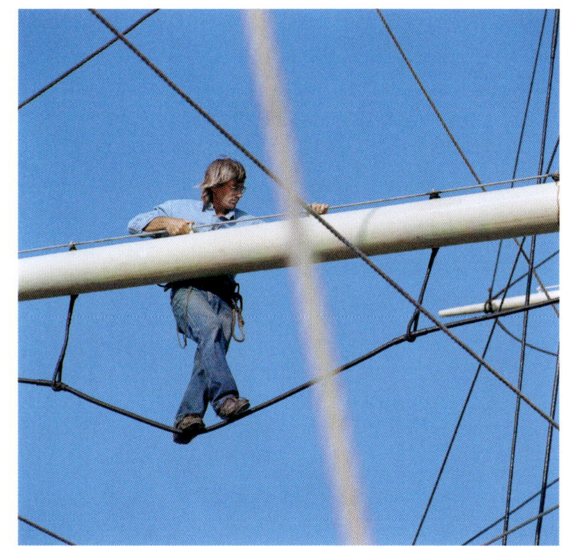

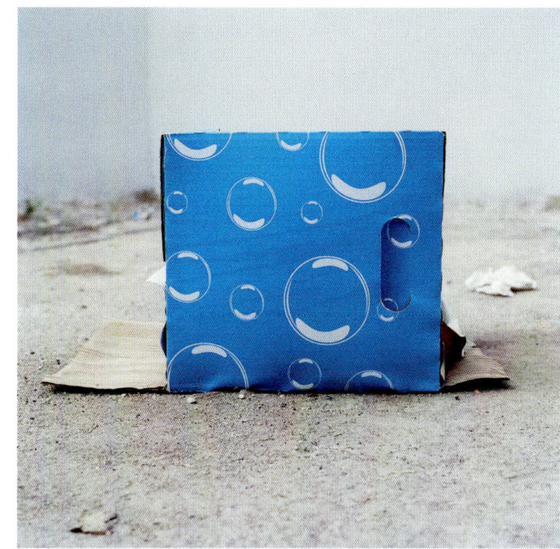

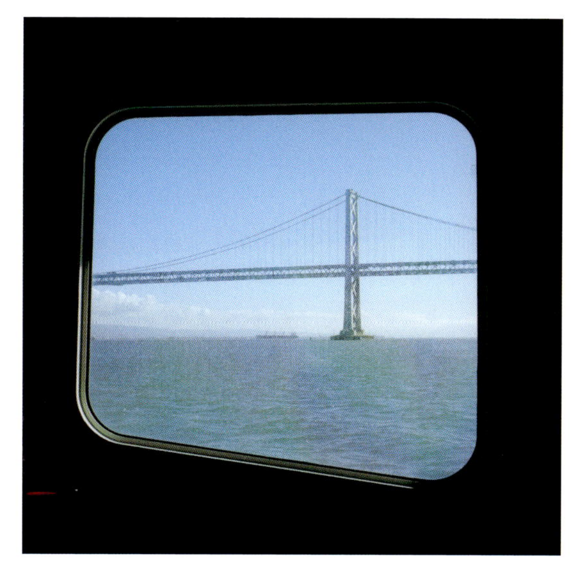

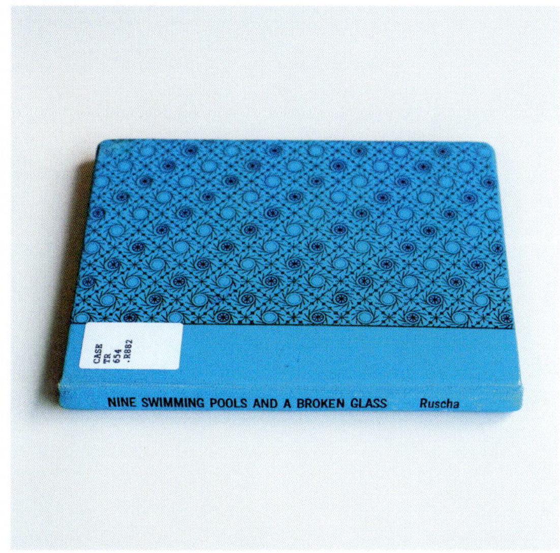
CASE
TR
654
.R882
NINE SWIMMING POOLS AND A BROKEN GLASS
Ruscha

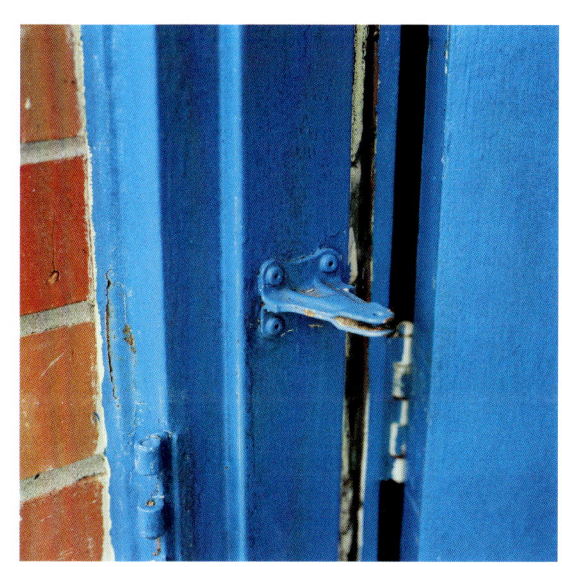

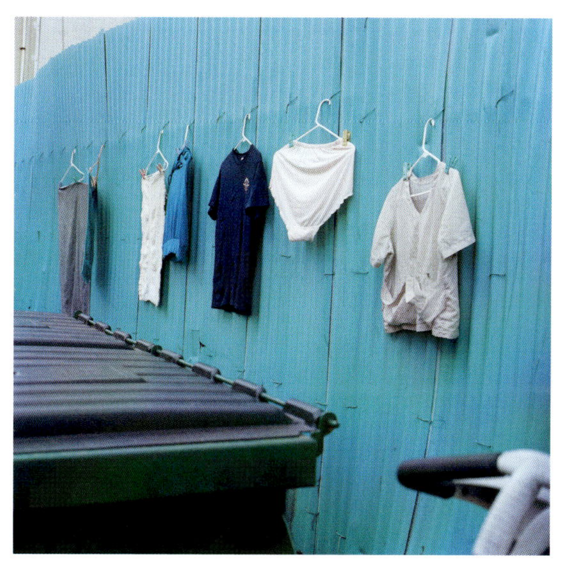

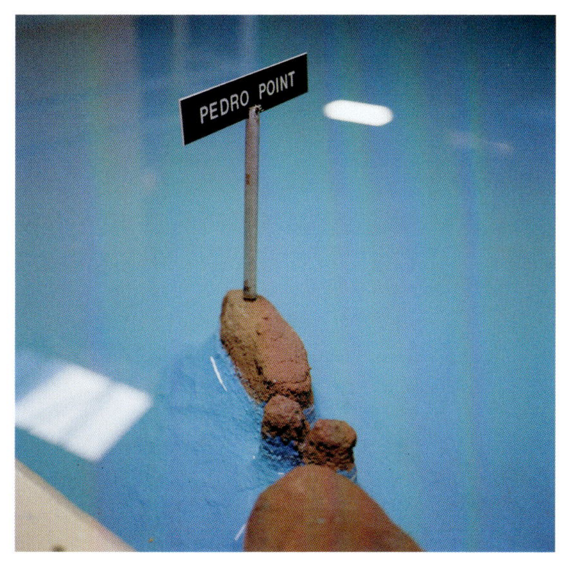
PEDRO POINT

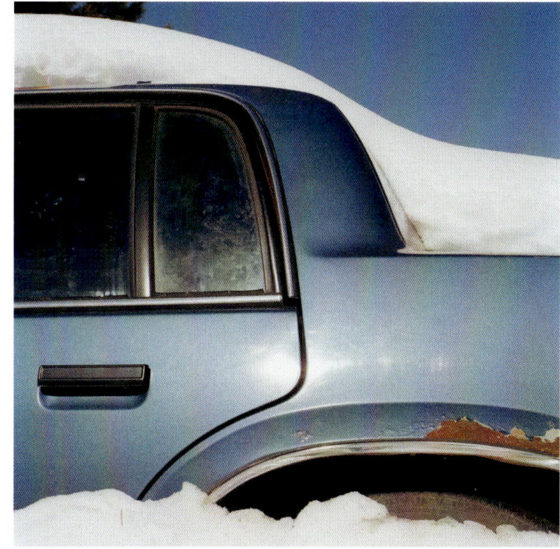

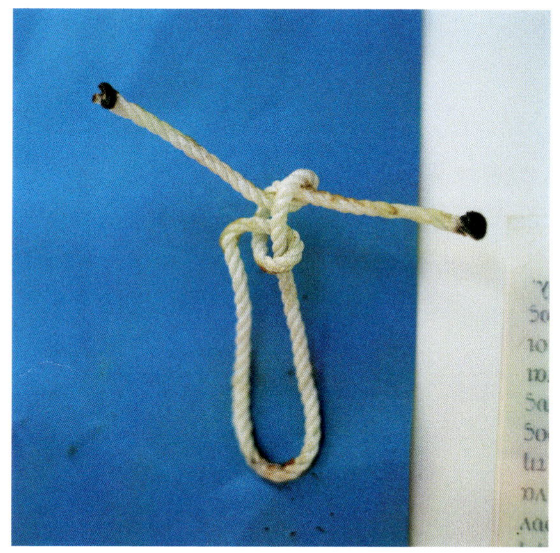

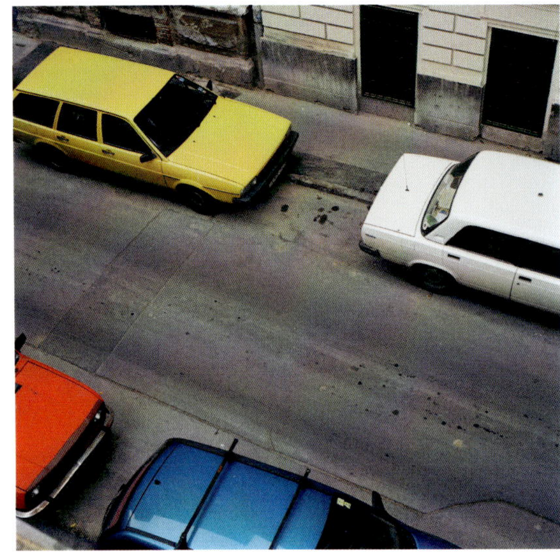

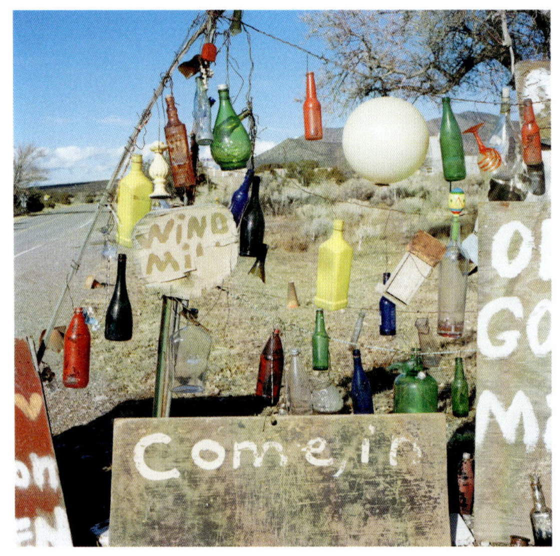
Come, in

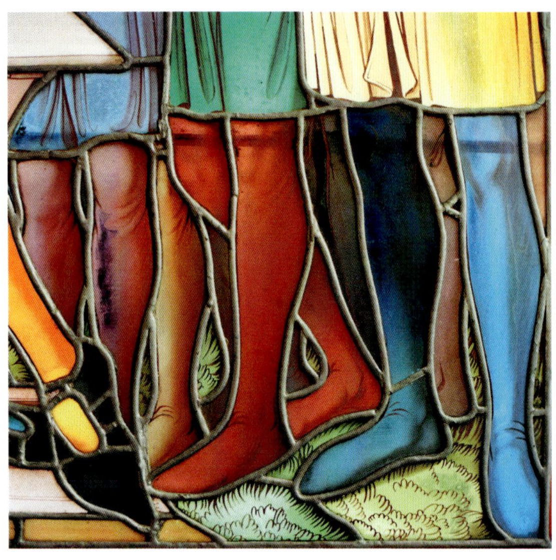

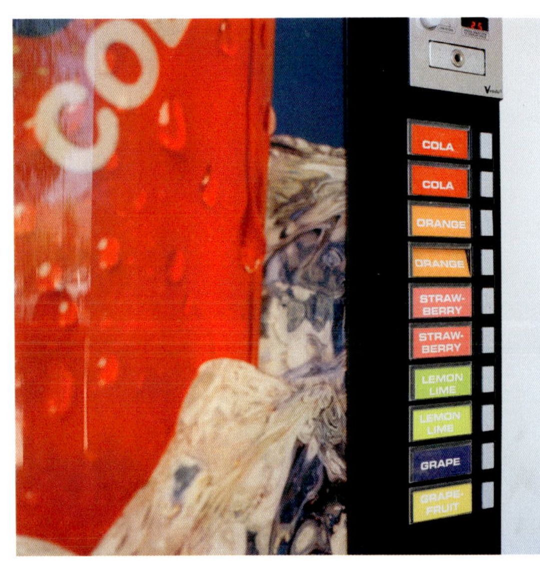
COLA
COLA
ORANGE
ORANGE
STRAW-BERRY
STRAW-BERRY
LEMON LIME
LEMON LIME
GRAPE
GRAPE-FRUIT

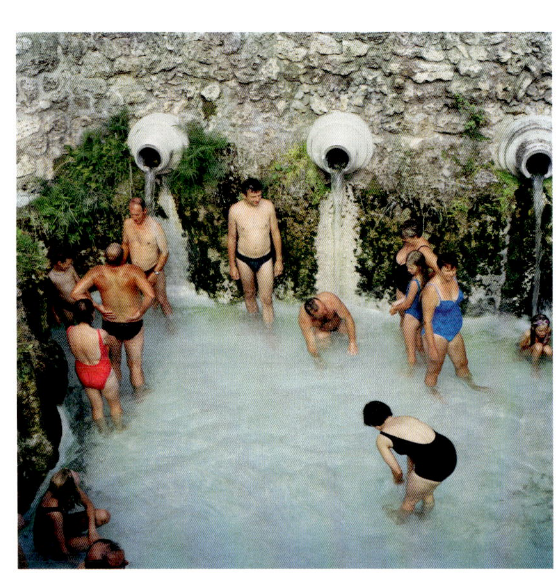

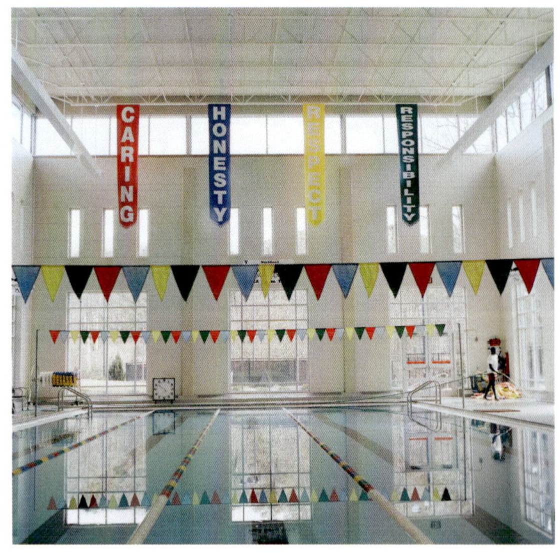
CARING
HONESTY
RESPONSIBILITY

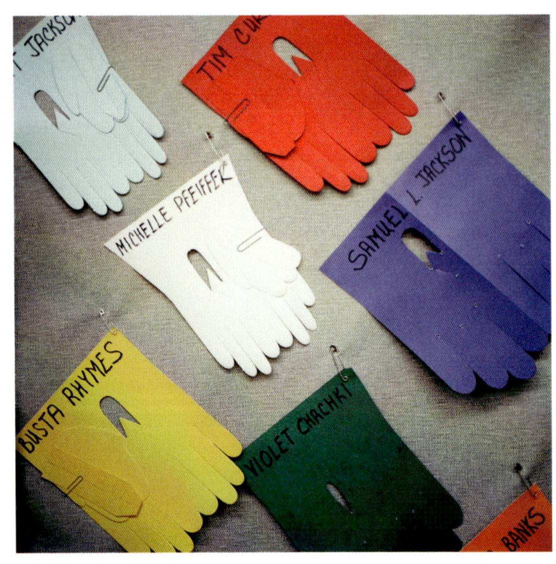
MICHELLE PFEIFFER
SAMUEL L. JACKSON
BUSTA RHYMES
VIOLET CHACHKI

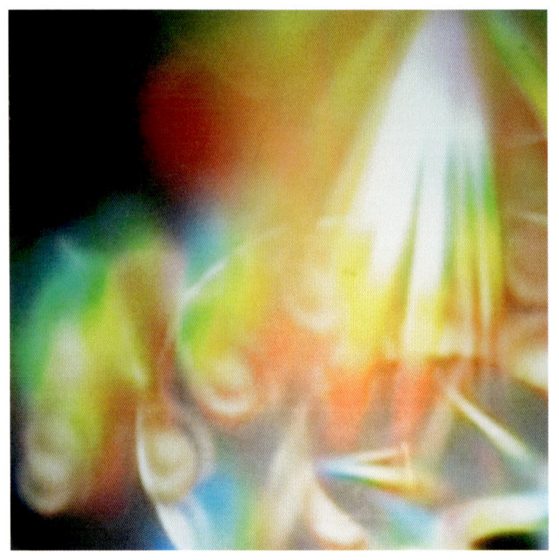

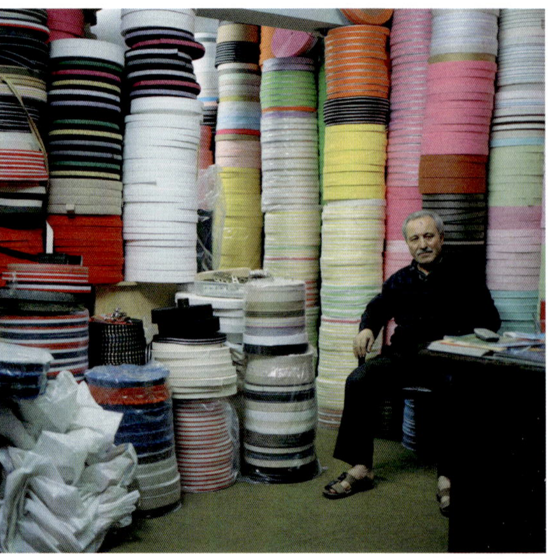

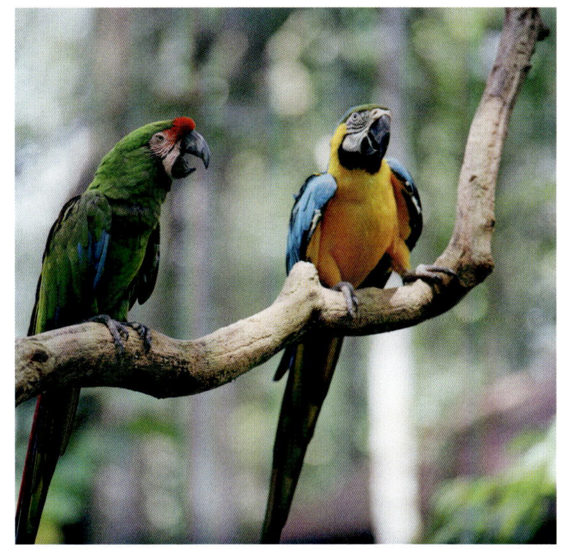
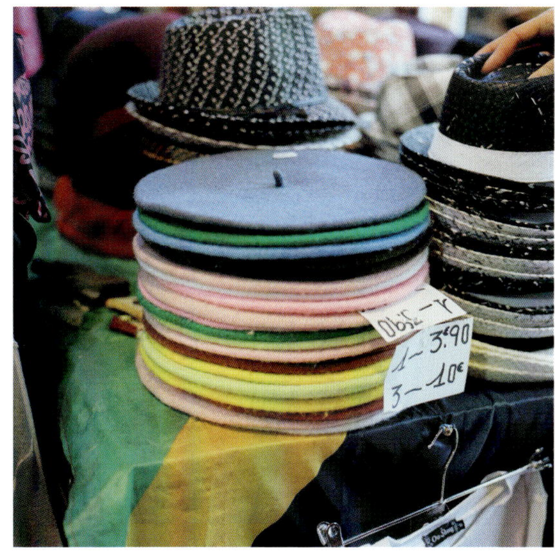
3—10€
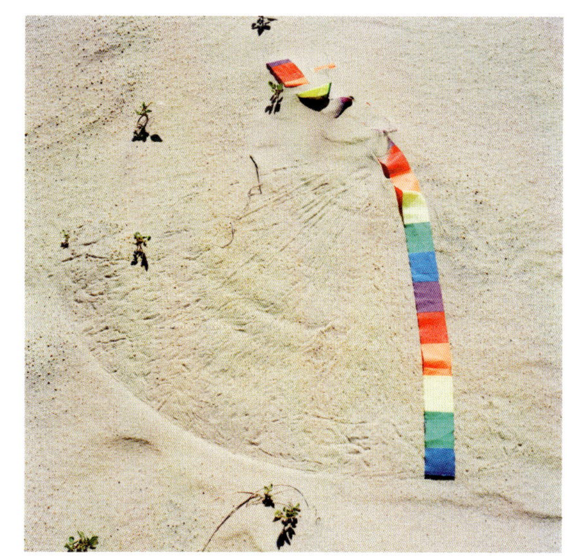
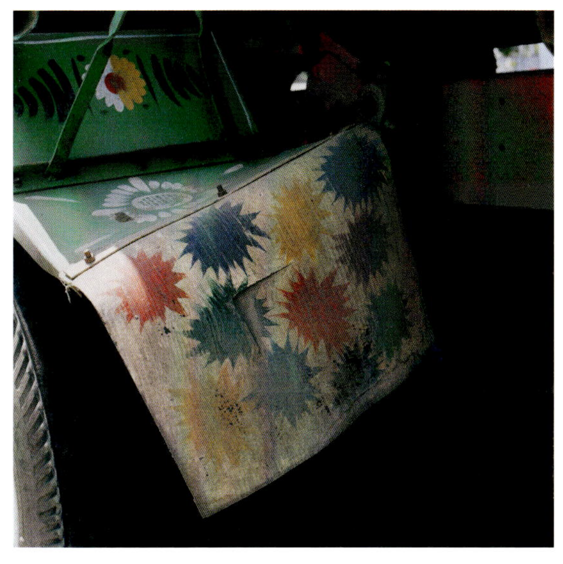
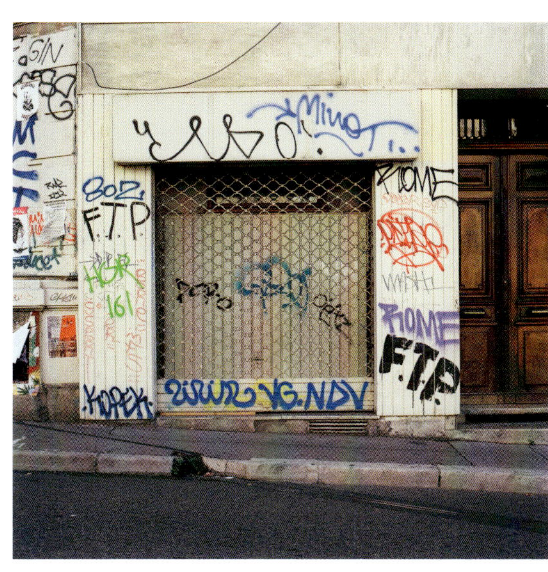
F.T.P
161
ROME
ROME
F.T.P
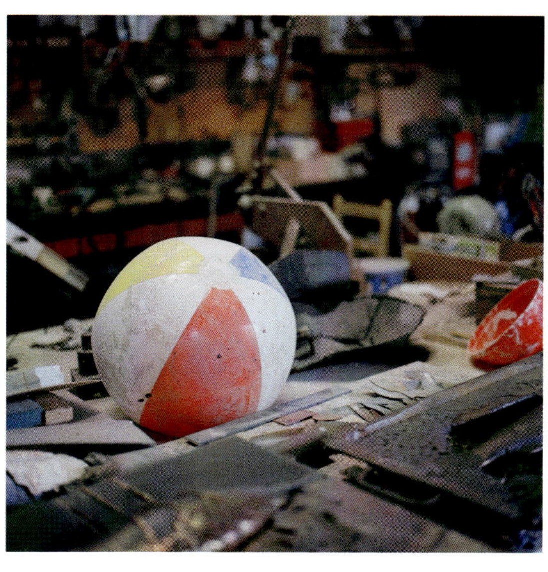
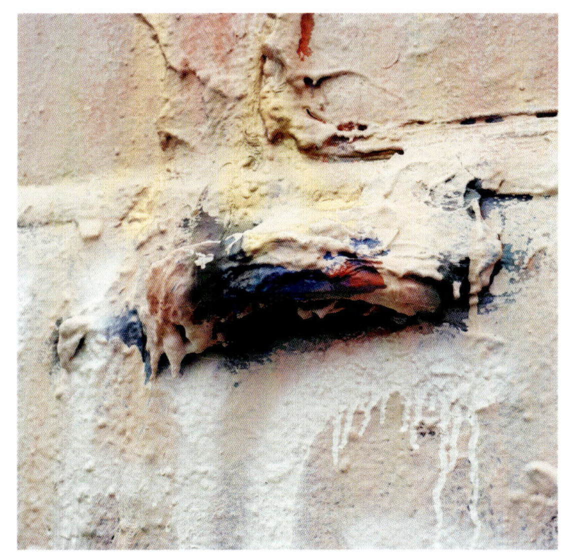
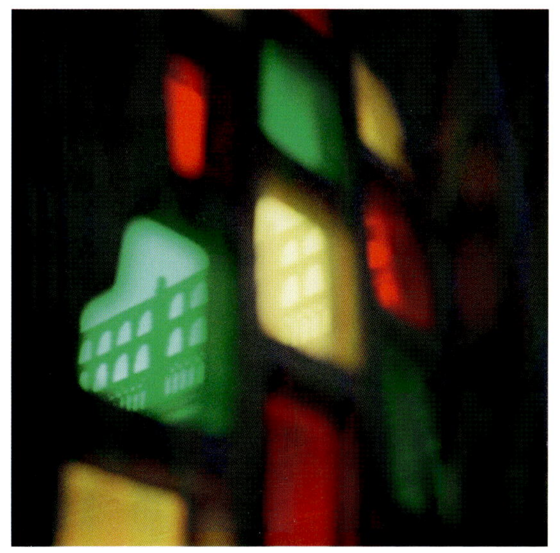
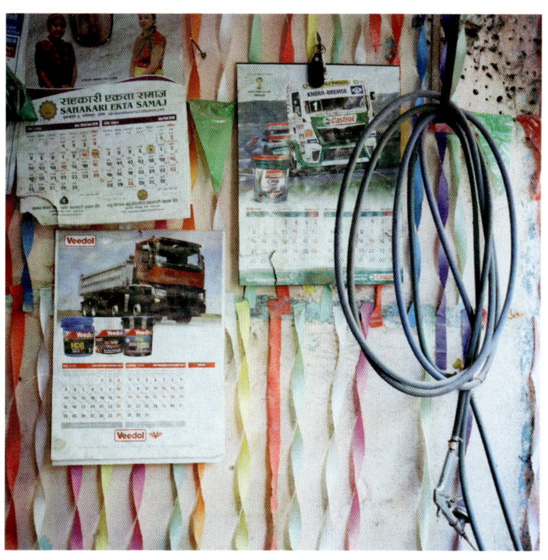
सहकारी एकता समाज
SAHAKARI EKTA SAMAJ
Veedol
Veedol

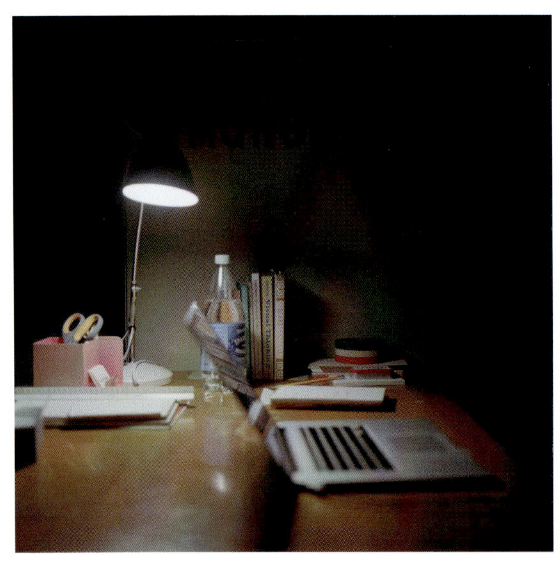
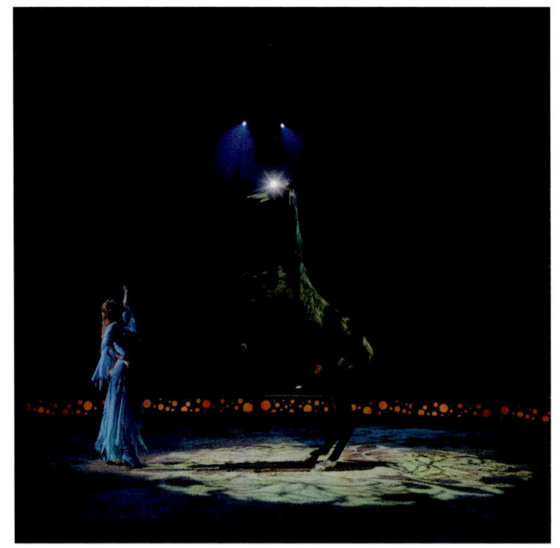
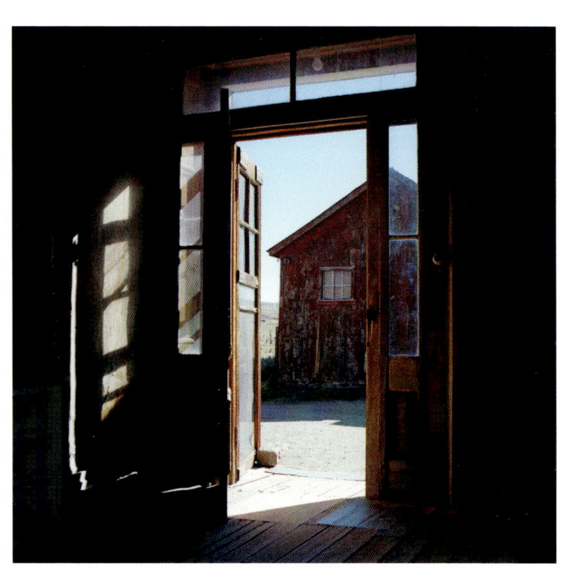
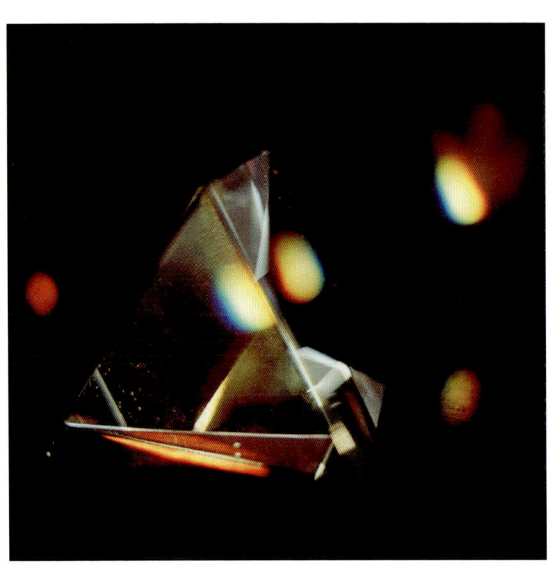
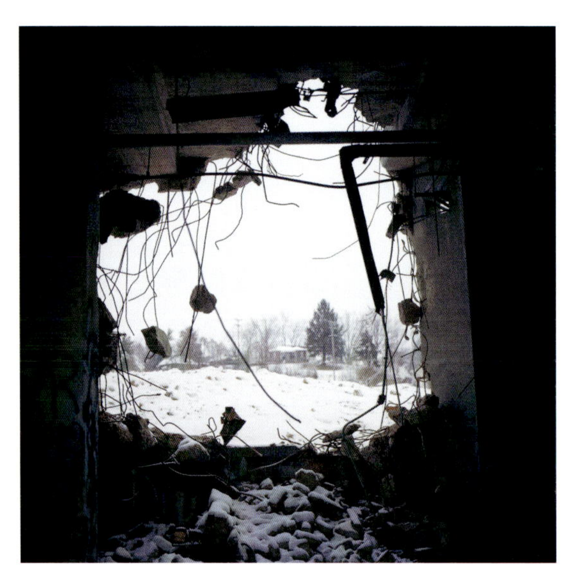
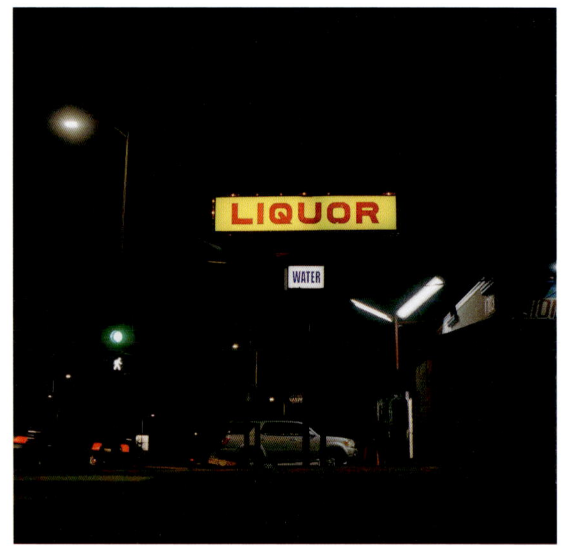
LIQUOR
WATER
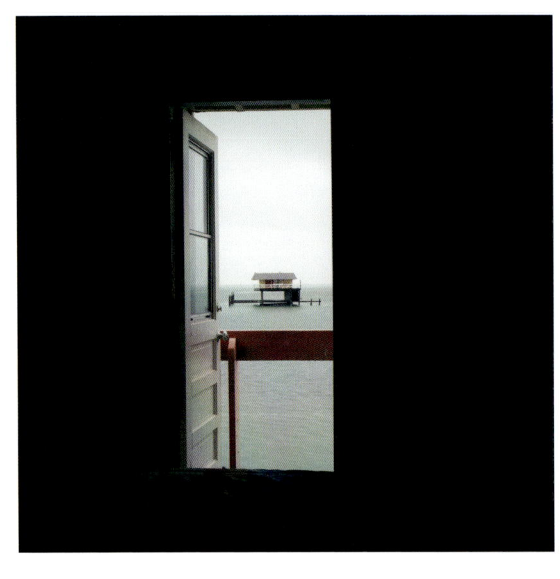
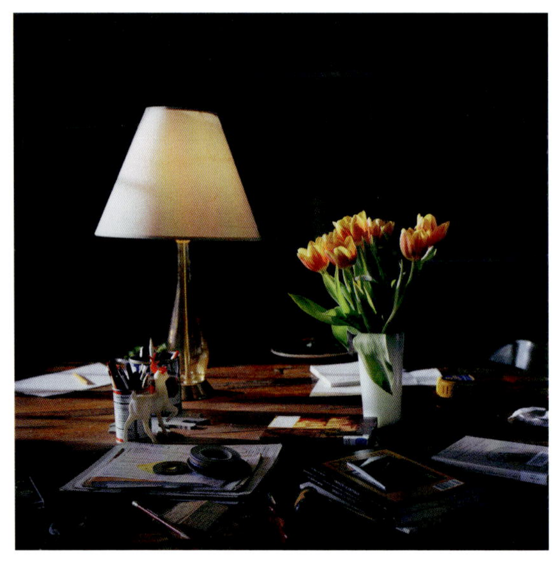
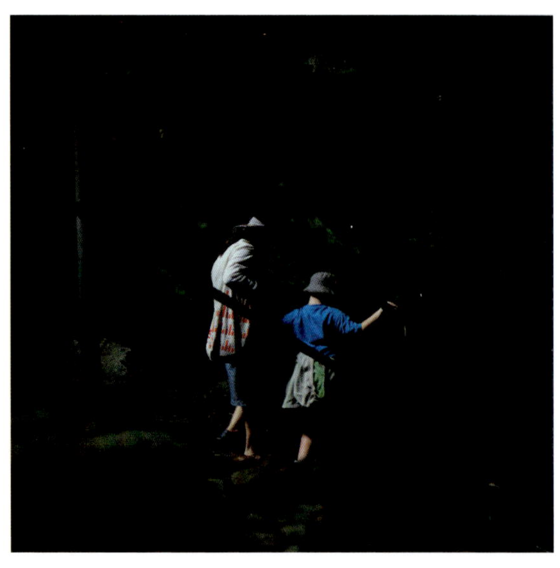

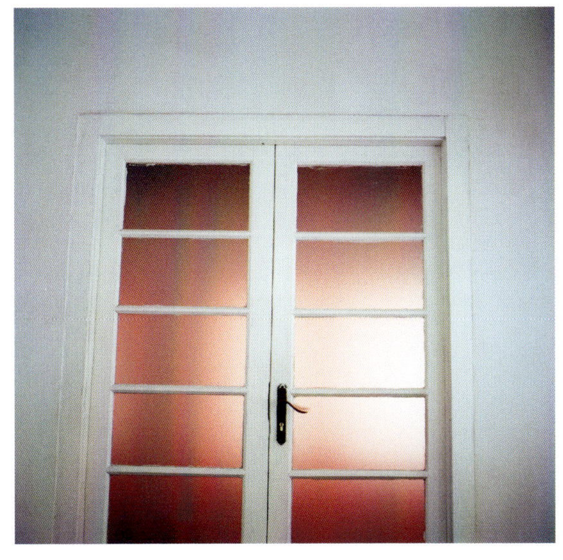
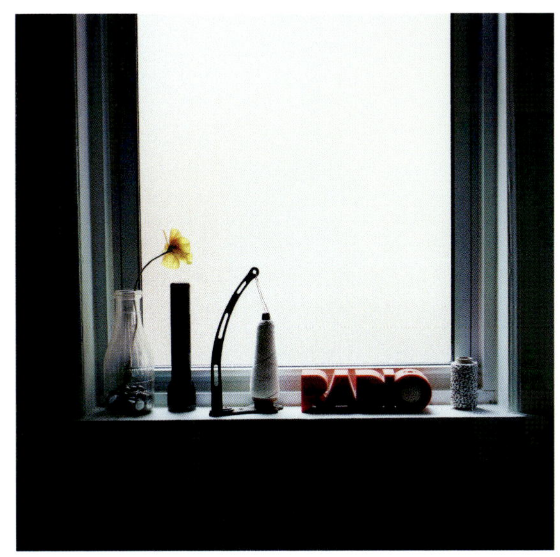
RADIO
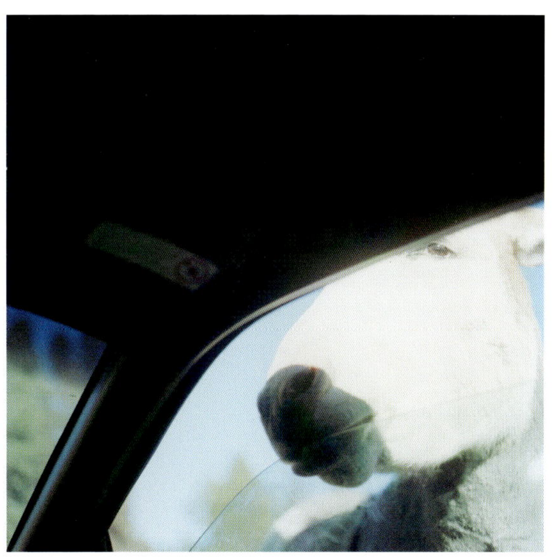
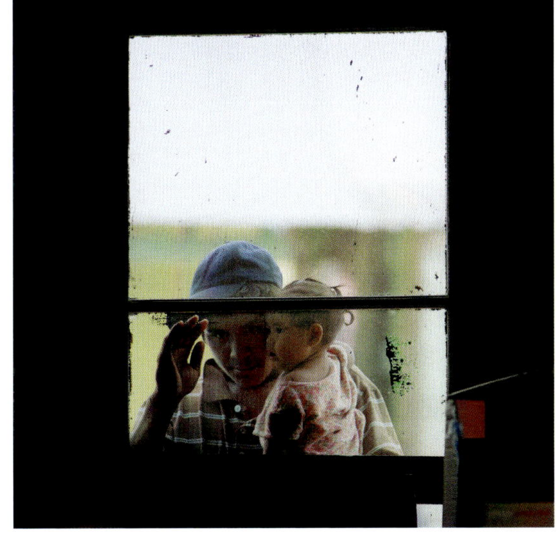
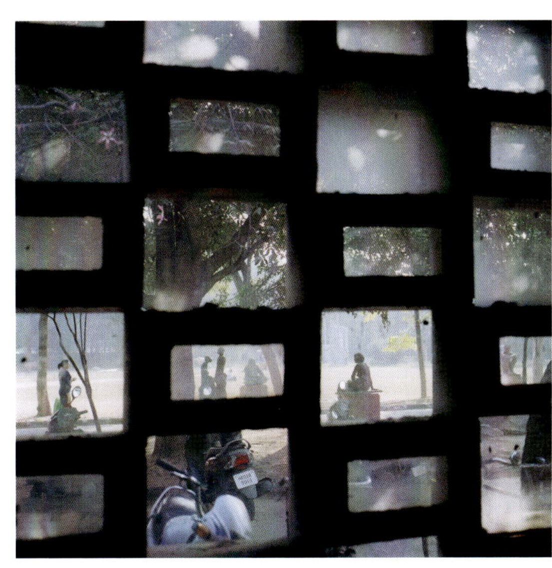
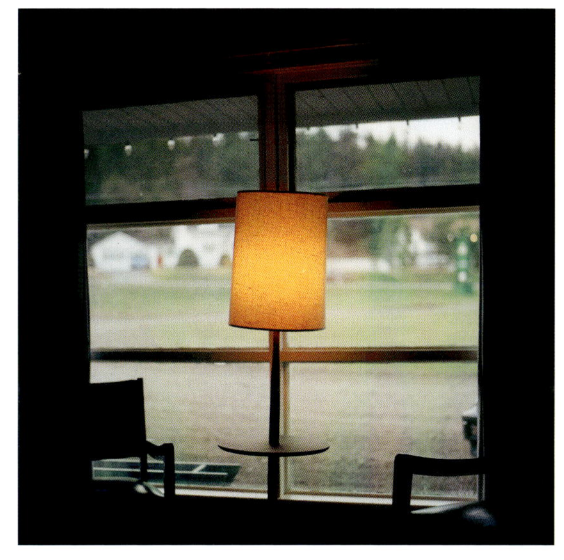
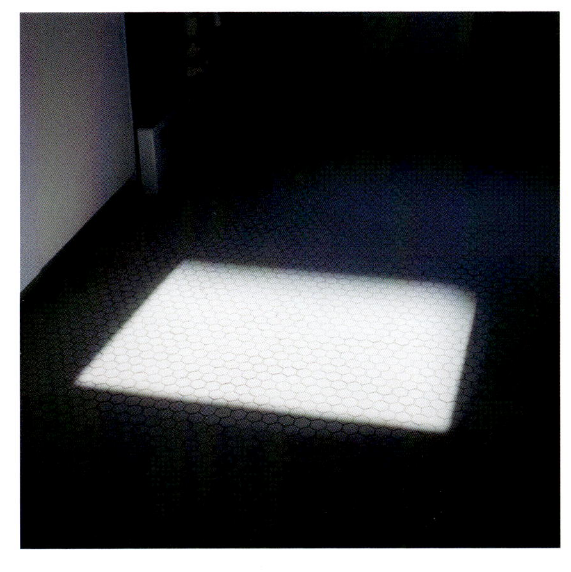
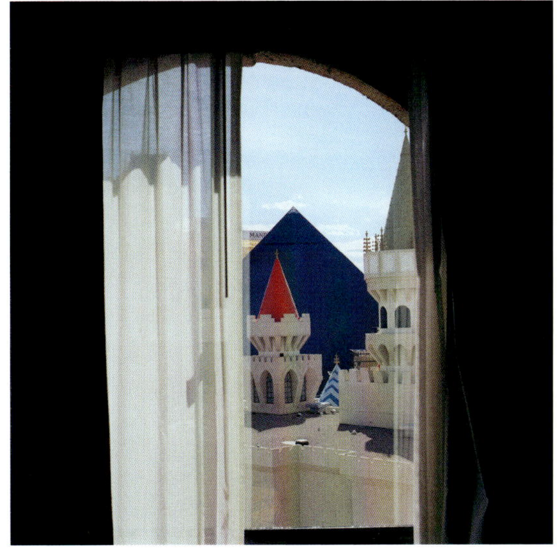
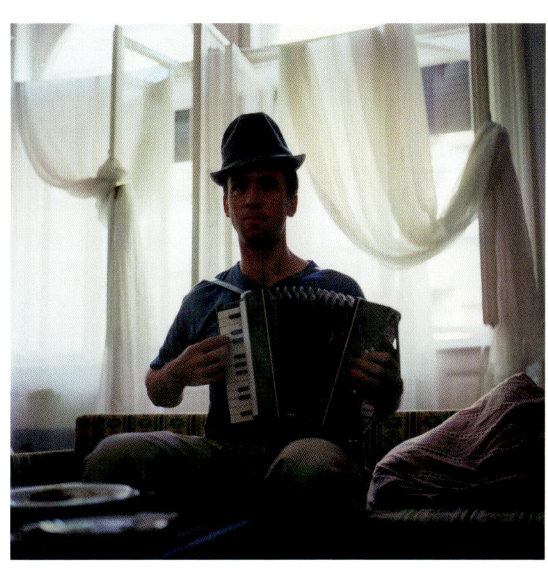

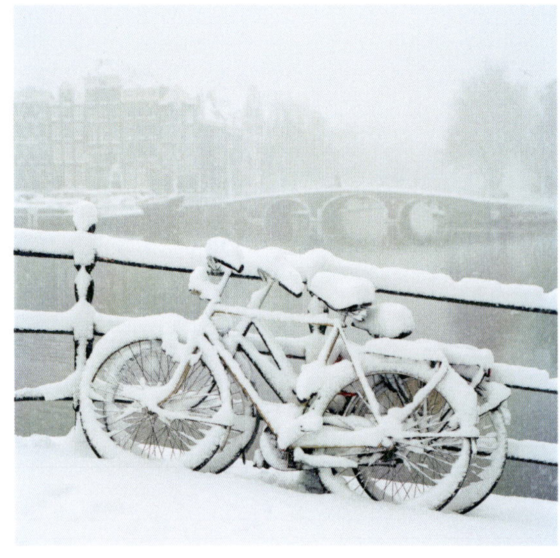
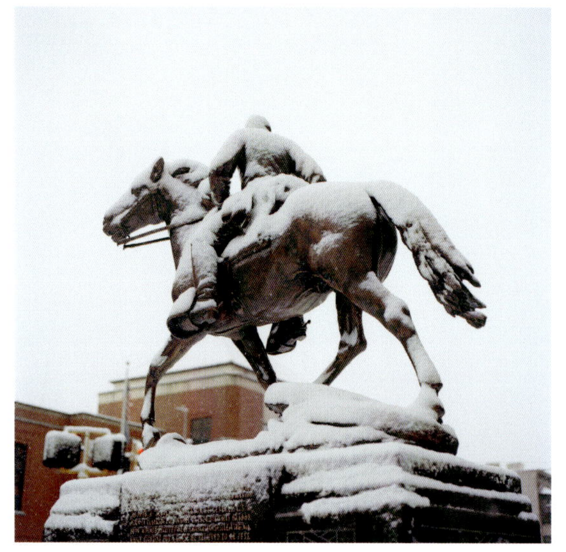
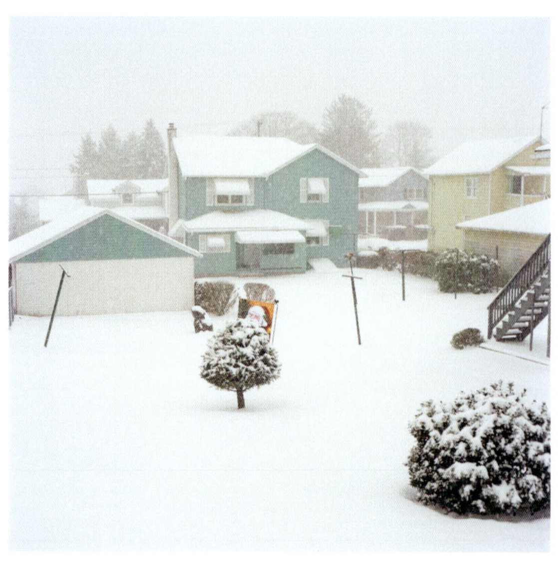
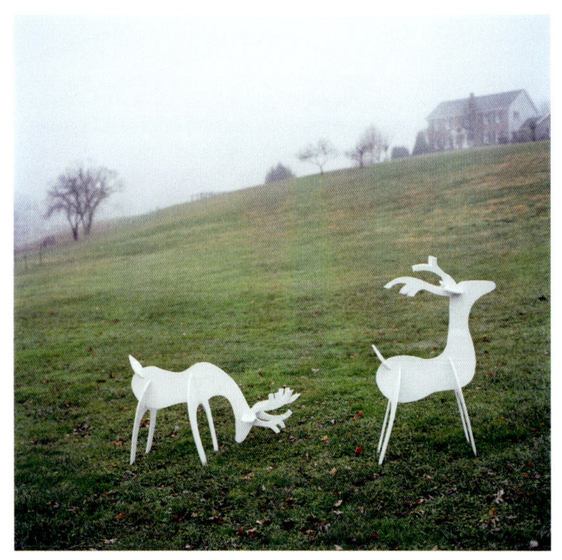
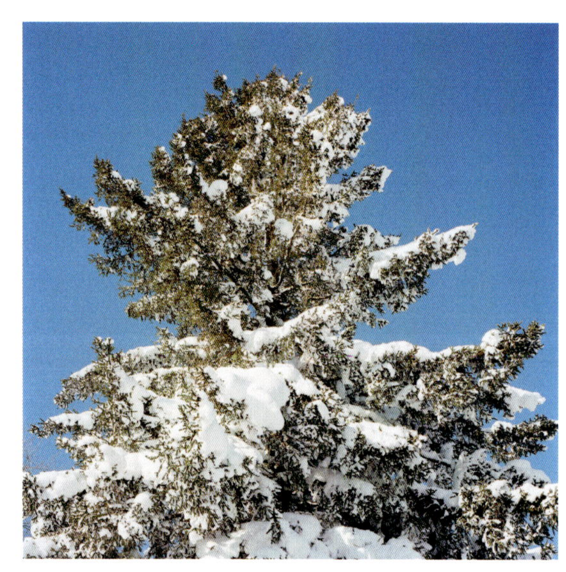
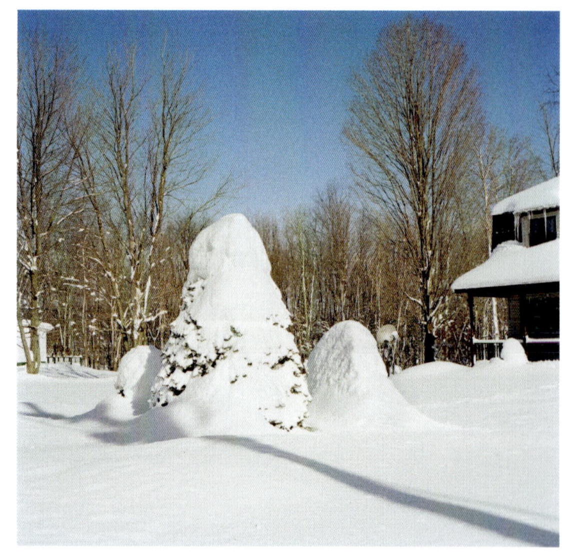
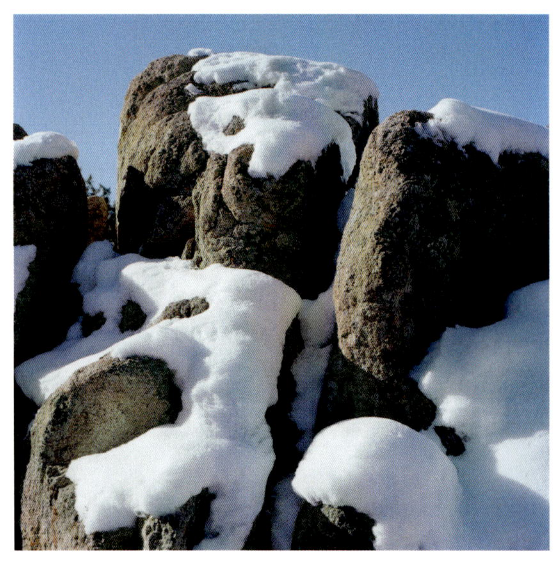
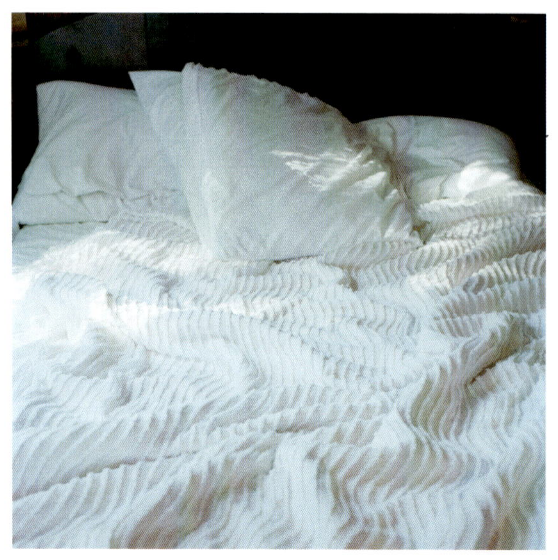
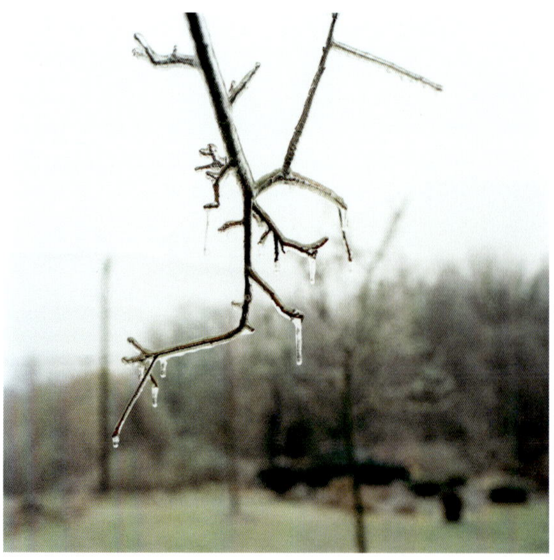

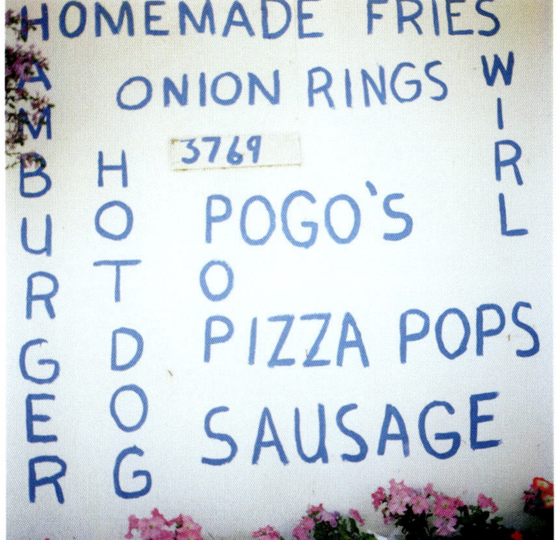
HOMEMADE FRIES
ONION RINGS
3769
AMBURGER
HOTDOG
WIRL
POGO'S
PIZZA POPS
SAUSAGE

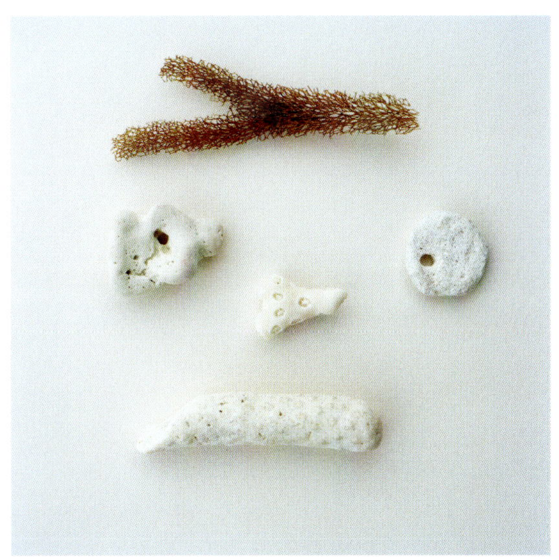

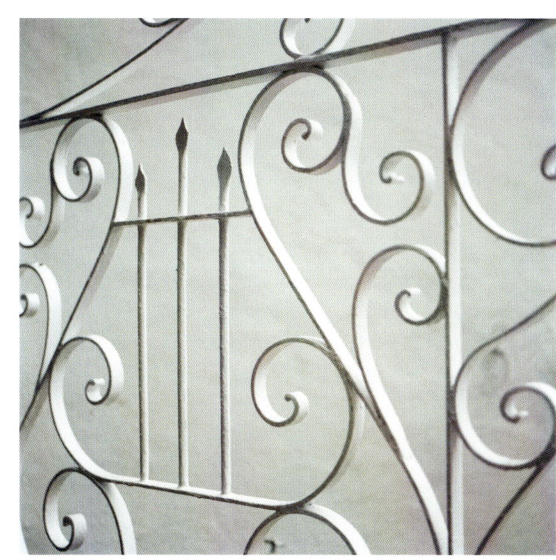

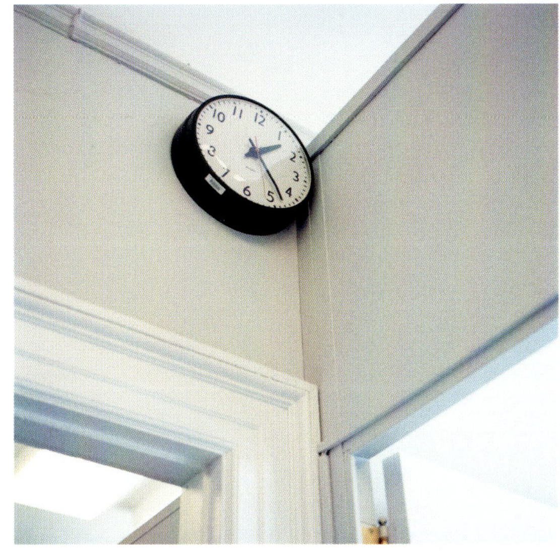

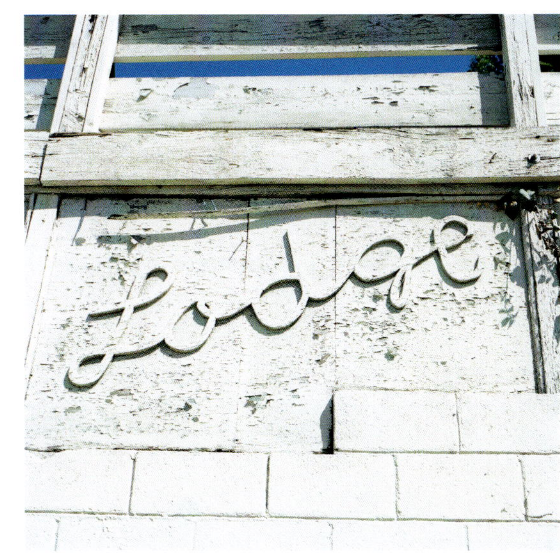
Lodge

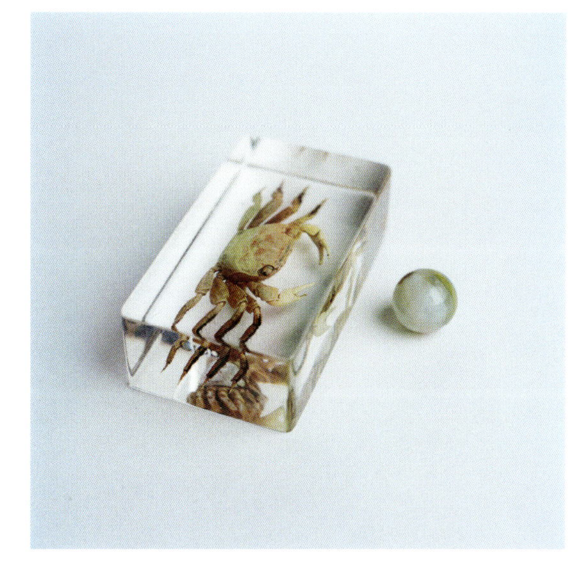

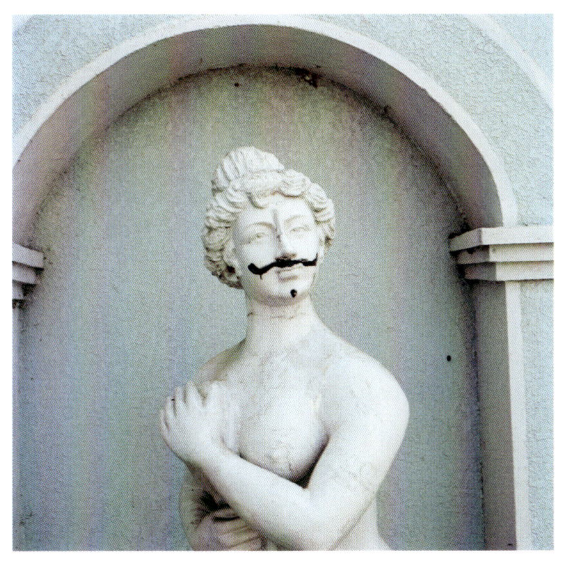

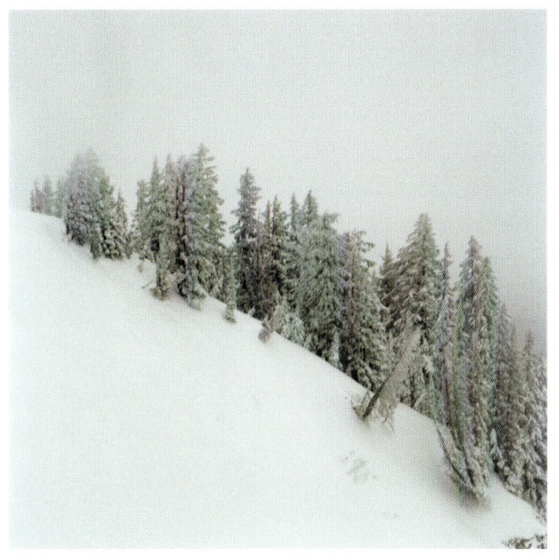

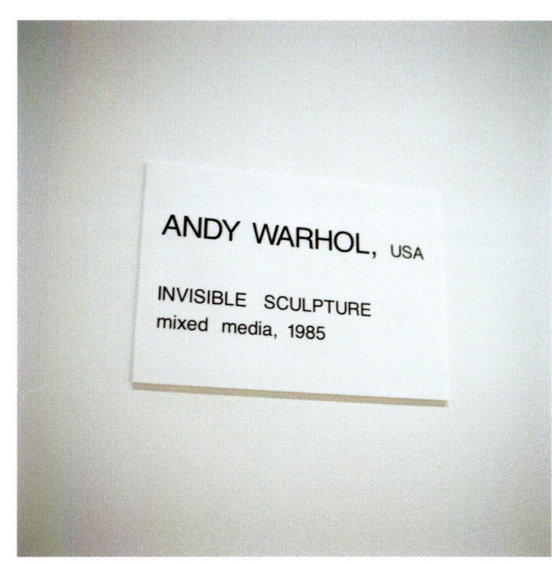
ANDY WARHOL, USA
INVISIBLE SCULPTURE
mixed media, 1985

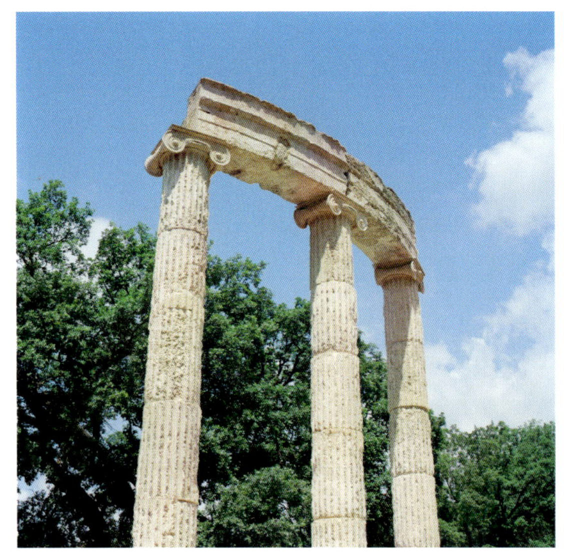

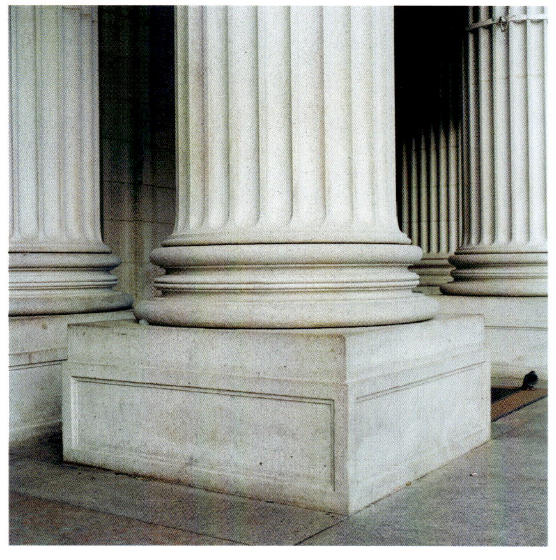

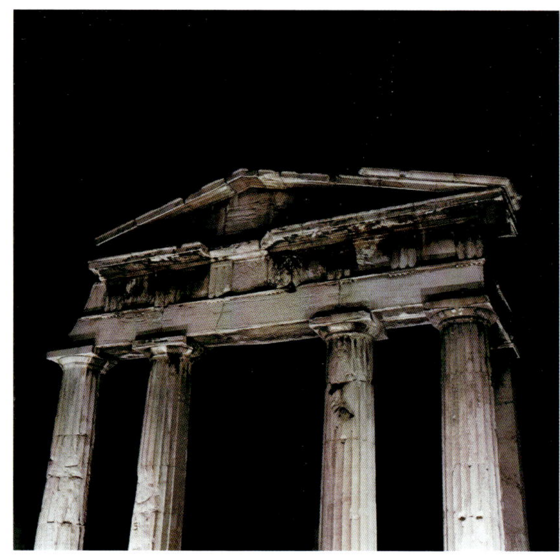

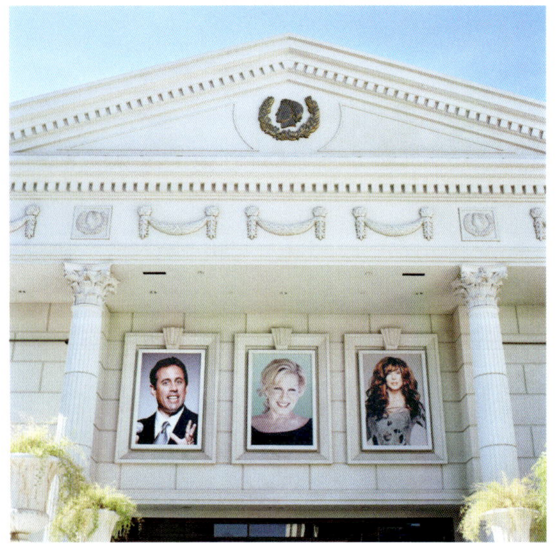

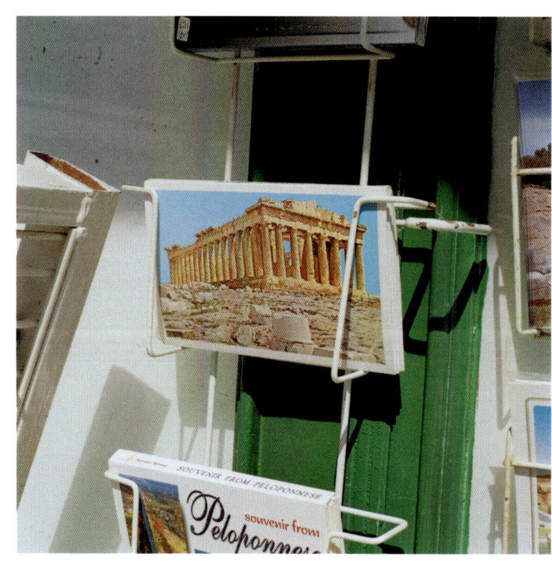

SOUVENIR FROM PELOPONNESE
souvenir from

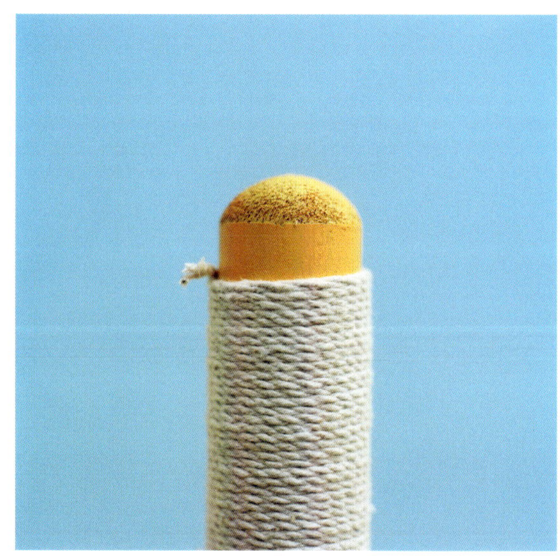

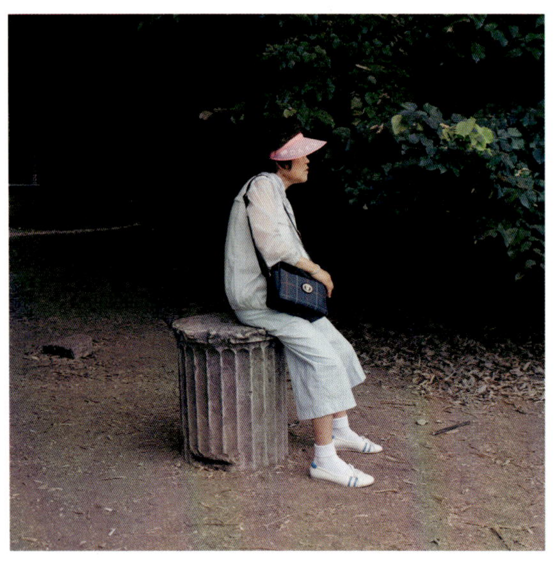

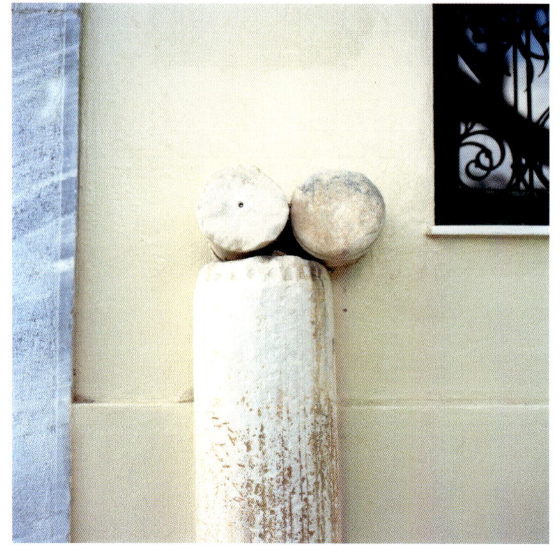

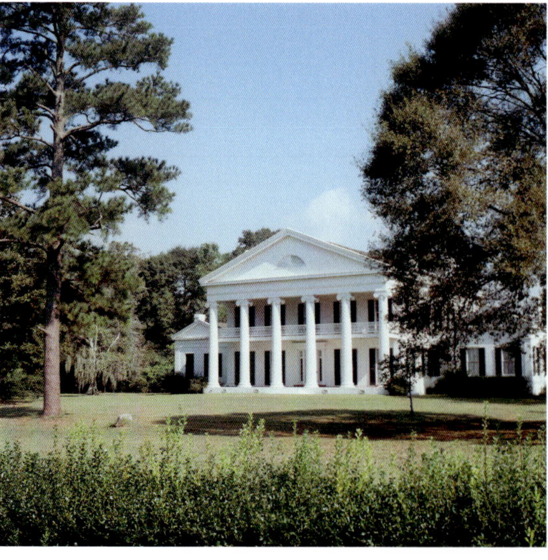

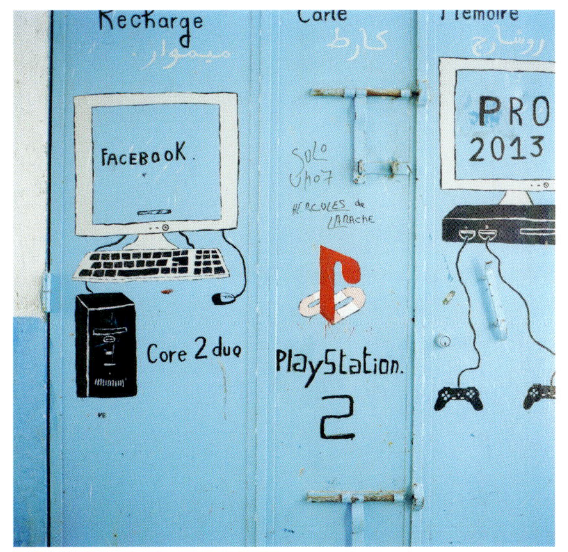
Recharge
Carte
FACEBOOK
PRO
2013
Core 2 duo
PlayStation
2
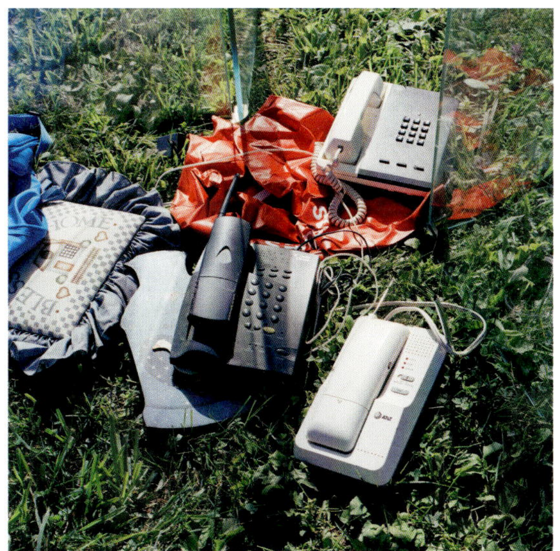
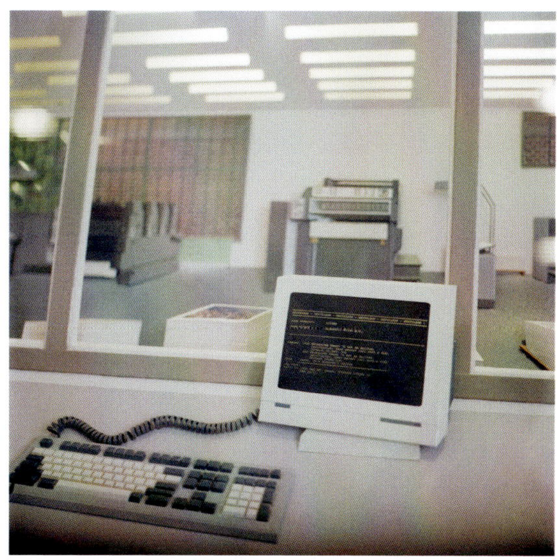
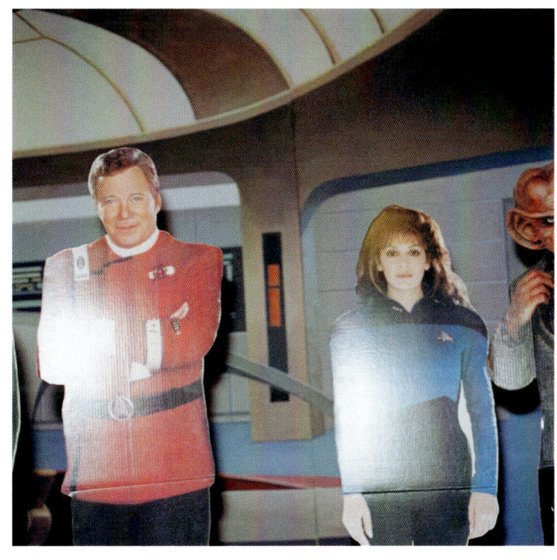
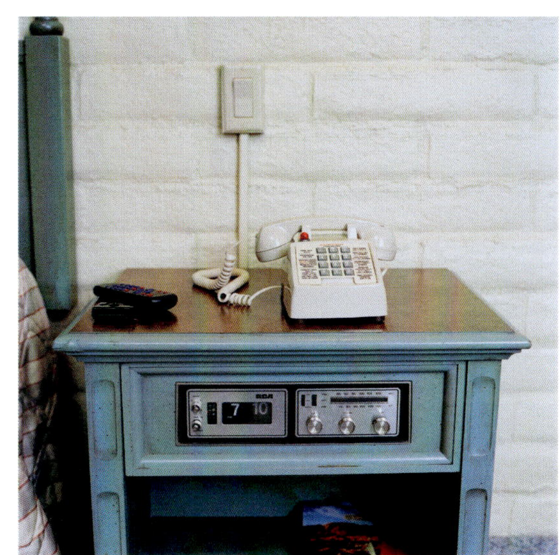
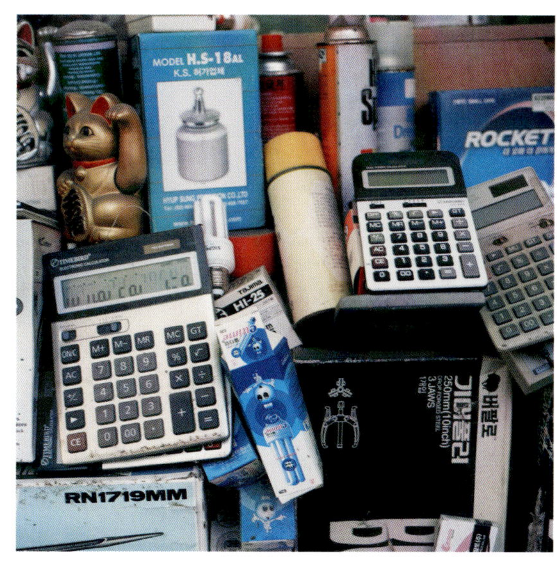
MODEL H.S-18AL
ROCKET
RN1719MM
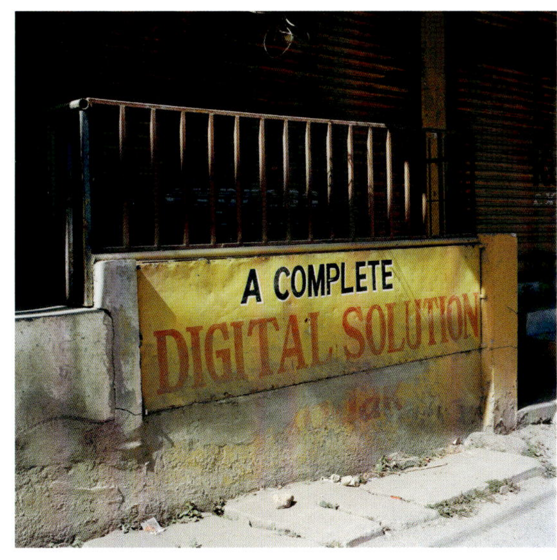
A COMPLETE
DIGITAL SOLUTION
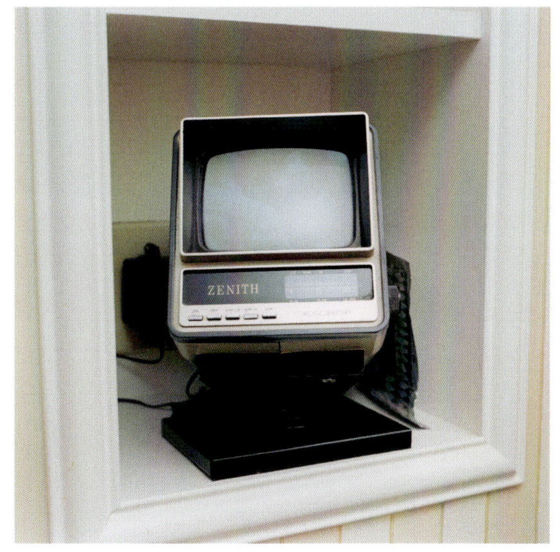
ZENITH
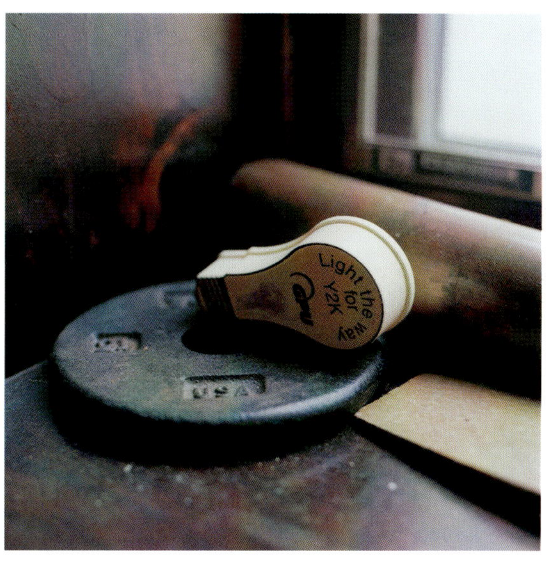
Light the way for Y2K

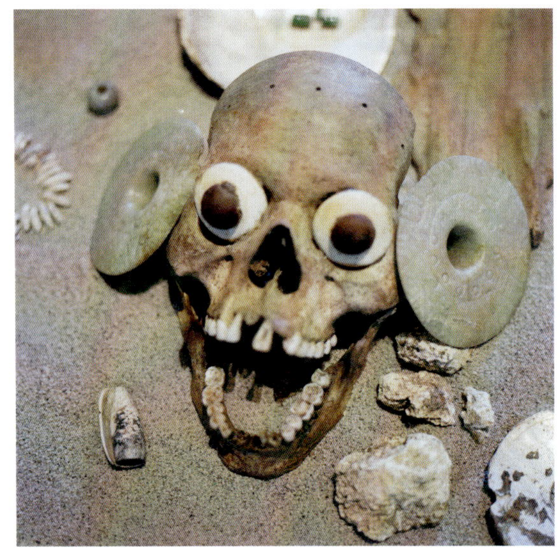

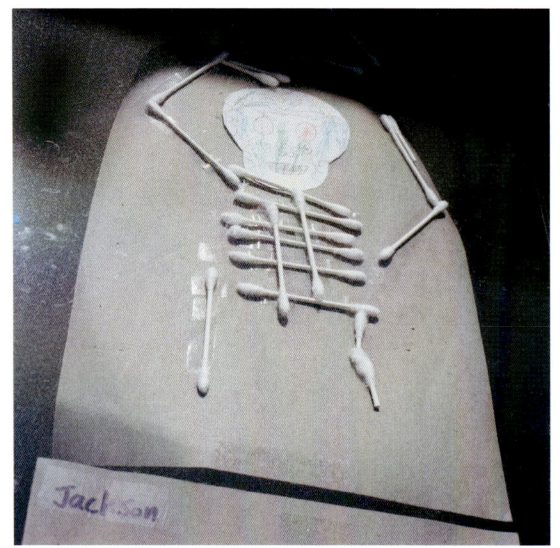
Jackson

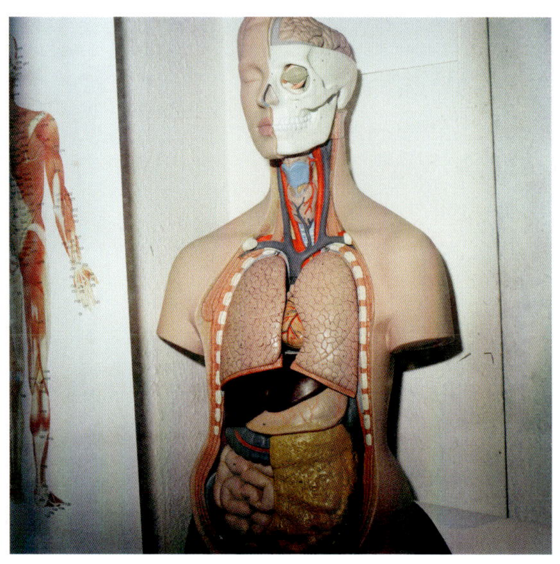

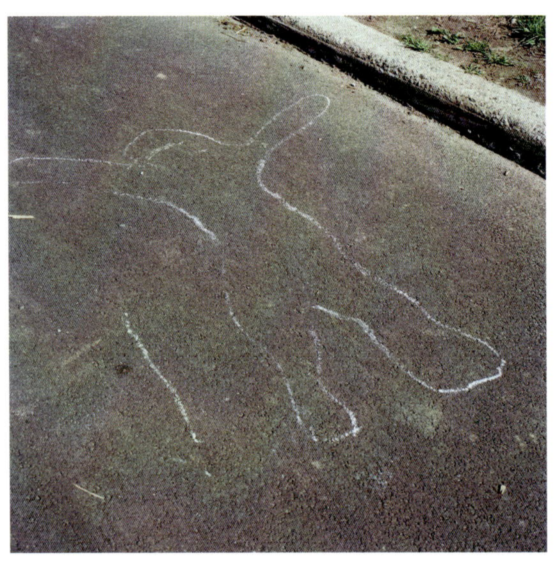

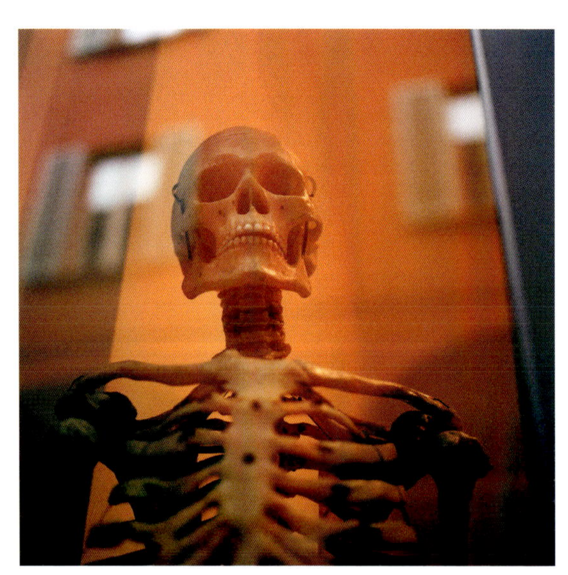

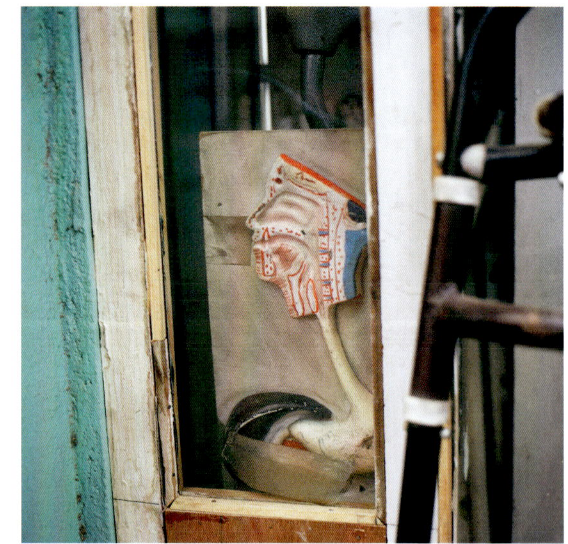

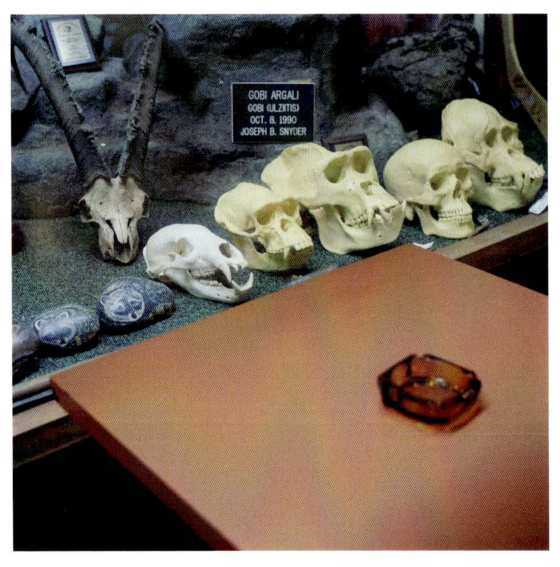
GOBI ARGALI
GOBI (ULZIITIS)
OCT. 8, 1990
JOSEPH B. SNYDER

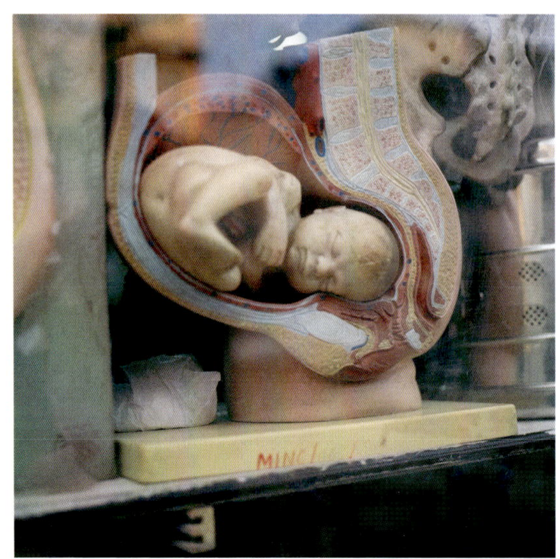

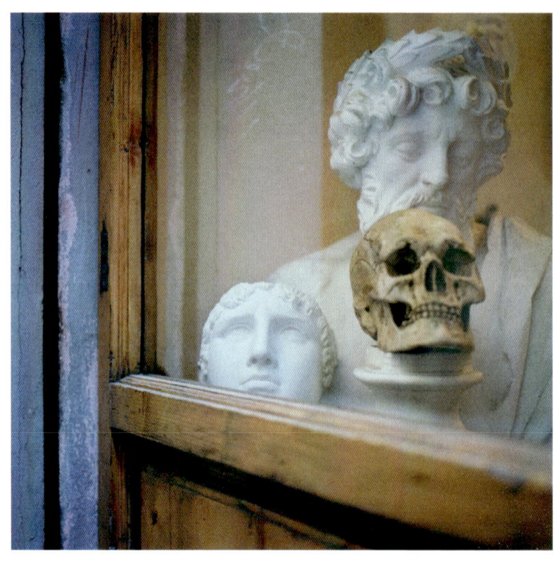

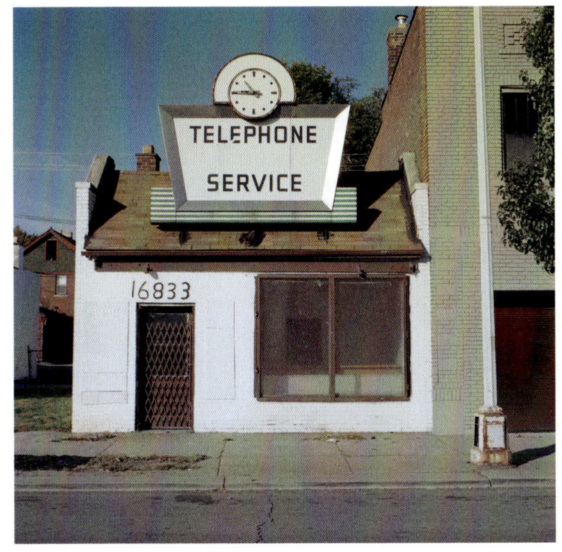
TELEPHONE
SERVICE
16833

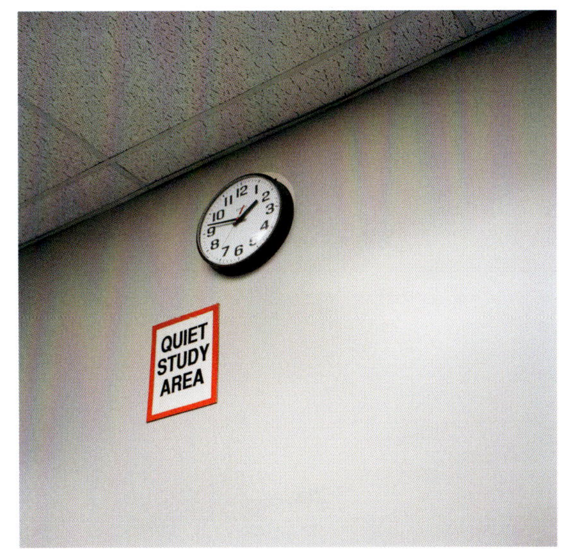
QUIET
STUDY
AREA

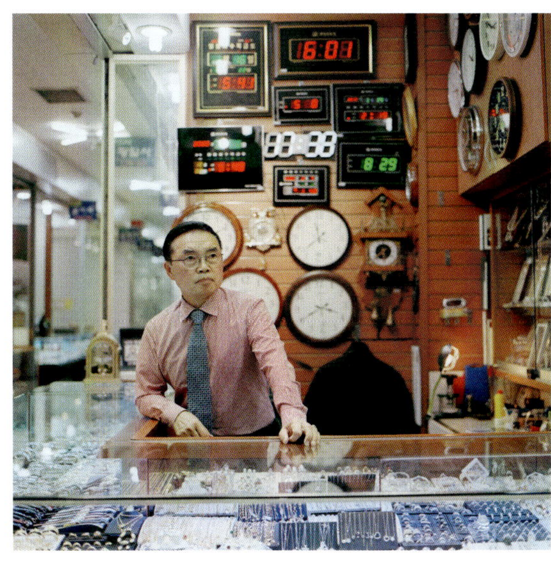

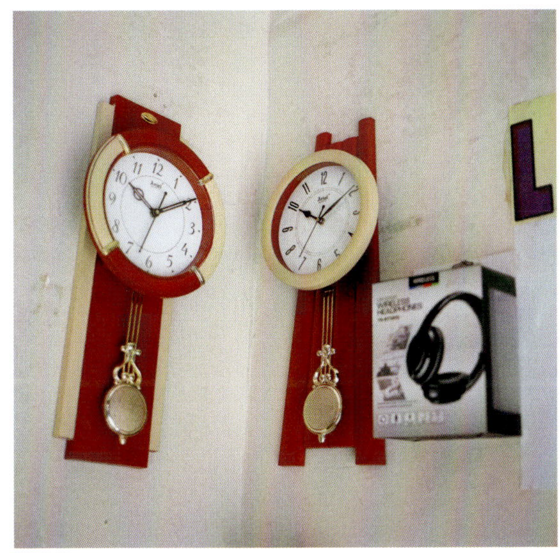

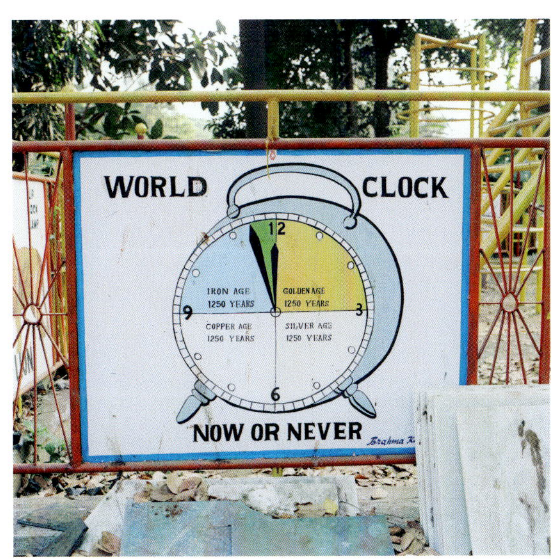
WORLD
CLOCK
IRON AGE
1250 YEARS
GOLDEN AGE
1250 YEARS
COPPER AGE
1250 YEARS
SILVER AGE
1250 YEARS
NOW OR NEVER

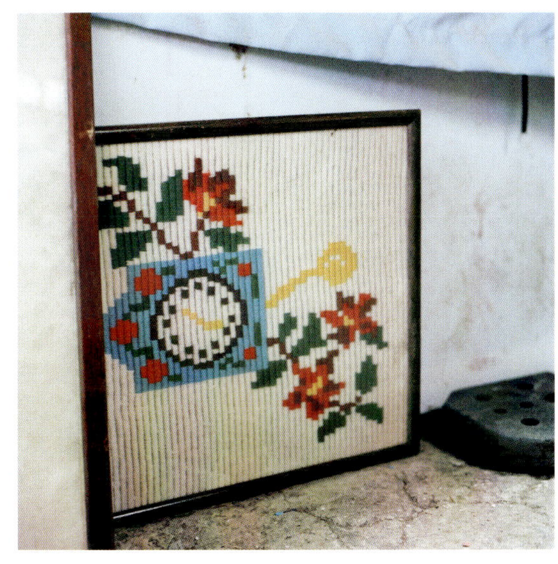

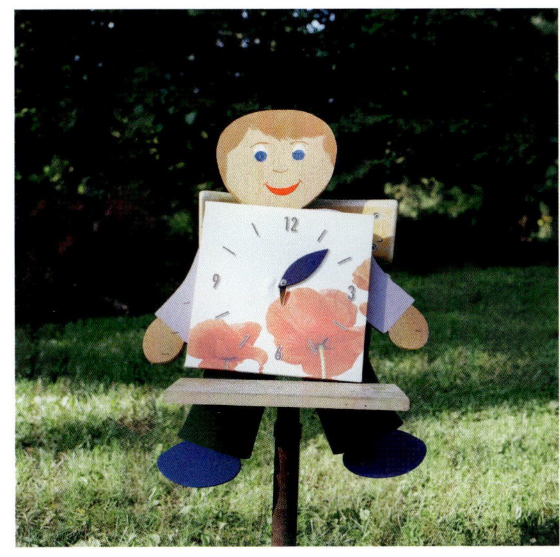

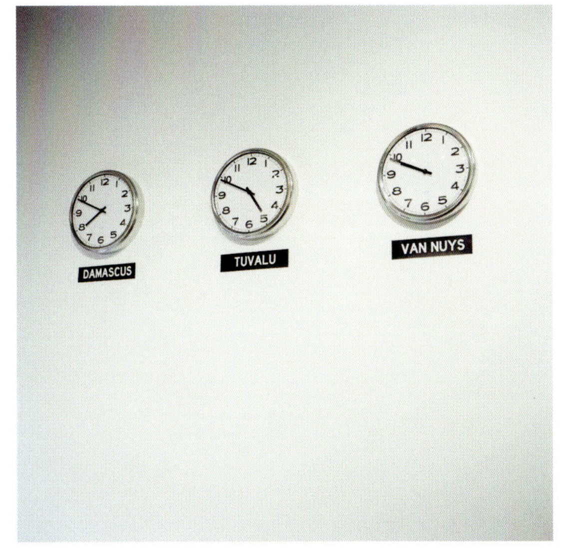
DAMASCUS
TUVALU
VAN NUYS

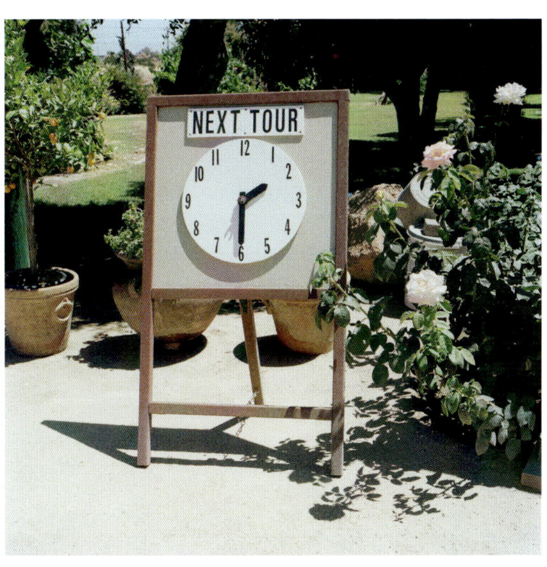
NEXT TOUR

PHOTOGRAPHS: ©2025 JASON FULFORD
THIS EDITION: ©2025 MACK
ISBN: 978-1-915743-46-6
CAMERAS: HASSELBLAD 501CM, 503CX
PAPER: ARCTIC VOLUME WHITE
COVER: INVERCOTE G
PRODUCTION: MORGAN CROWCROFT-BROWN
PRINTING: LONGO, BOLZANO
INSPIRATION: SOL LEWITT *PHOTOGRIDS*
DEDICATION: BEACH BALL